TOWARDS A SOCIETY THAT SERVES ITS PEOPLE

TOWARDS A SOCIETY THAT SERVES ITS PEOPLE

WRITINGS FOR A LIBERATION PSYCHOLOGY
   (forthcoming)

VOLUME EDITORS

ADRIANNE ARON
Committee for Health Rights in Central America

JOHN HASSETT AND HUGH LACEY
Swarthmore College

TOWARDS A SOCIETY THAT SERVES ITS PEOPLE: The Intellectual Contribution of El Salvador's Murdered Jesuits

EDITED BY

JOHN HASSETT AND HUGH LACEY
Swarthmore College

FOREWORD BY

LEO J. O'DONOVAN, S.J.

Georgetown University Press / WASHINGTON, D.C.

CREDITS FOR ART, PHOTOGRAPHS AND SERVICES

Cover art: *One of the commemorative altar panels painted by Fernando Llort for the Chapel of the Central American University in San Salvador.*

Cover photograph: *By Ernesto Canossa.*

Portraits of Ellacuría & Martín-Baró: *By Francisco Campos.*

Portrait of Montes: *By Michael Macquire.*

Information: *From the People of El Salvador who understand.*

Georgetown University Press, Washington, D.C. 20057-1079
PRINTED IN THE UNITED STATES OF AMERICA
10 9 8 7 6 5 4 3 2 1   91
THIS VOLUME IS PRINTED ON ACID-FREE ∞ OFFSET BOOK PAPER.

Library of Congress Cataloging-in-Publication Data

Towards a society that serves its people: the intellectual
    contribution of El Salvador's murdered Jesuits / edited by
    John Hassett and Hugh Lacey.
            p.   cm.
        Includes bibliographical references.
    1. Sociology, Christian (Catholic). 2. Liberation theology.
3. Catholic Church—Doctrines. 4. Church and social problems—
El Salvador. 5. Church and social problems—Latin America.
6. Catholic Church—El Salvador—History—20th century.
7. Catholic Church—Latin America—History—20th century.
8. El Salvador—Economic conditions—1945———. 9. El Salvador—Politics
and government—1979———. 10. Latin America—1948-.
I. Hassett, John J. II. Lacey, Hugh.
BX1753.T673   1991   261.8'097284—dc20   91-37465
ISBN 0-87840-523-2 (paper)

TO THE MEMORY OF

Celina Ramos
Elba Julia Ramos
Ignacio Ellacuría, S.J.
Amando López, S.J.
Joaquín López y López, S.J.
Ignacio Martín-Baró, S.J.
Segundo Montes, S.J.
Juan Ramón Moreno, S.J.

CONTENTS

FOREWORD

Even in our exceedingly dynamic world of complexity and change, contradiction and compromise, there are still voices for the voiceless. Six such voices came from Jesuit priests who lived and died in El Salvador on behalf of human dignity and human rights. They had set themselves to exploring the idea of the university and to making it practical in the light of the theology and psychology of liberation. As priests and scholars, they dedicated themselves to reasoned exposition of the university as a place for the truth that might promote greater justice and peace for their fellow Salvadorans. They joined the universal pursuit of social justice for the marginalized millions whose governments are too often deaf to their struggles, their sufferings, and their human dignity.

Three of the six voices that were silenced in martyrdom on November 16, 1989 are revived in this memorial tribute to their thought. Fathers Ignacio Ellacuría, Ignacio Martín-Baró, and Segundo Montes contributed to a vision of the Catholic university in El Salvador and in Latin America that strengthened its Christ-centered moral and social responsibility for society. Like others who preceded them, they left a legacy of truth and freedom, compassion and justice, faith and love—not only for the living but also in memory of fellow martyrs. Their social outreach grew from a theology of liberation that was grounded, in turn, on hope for the Kingdom of God. Their work and witness were nurtured by a faith in God and by a love of their fellow human beings that transcended the domains and systems of political power, privilege, and material wealth. In their quest for a renewed praxis of the lasting truths of comprehensive social justice, these pastors and academic leaders gave their lives, along with two women co-workers, *ad majorem Dei gloriam inque hominum salutem,* "for the greater glory of God and the welfare of humanity."

These UCA Jesuits made a commitment to viewing the world through the eyes of the poor. Their expertise and social situation led them to criticize capitalism for those ways in which they believed it exploited the poor economically and politically. They did not live to see the collapse of Communism and the renewal of discussions on how market-based economics can function effectively and justly in the present international economic order. Nor did they have an opportunity to study Pope John Paul II's most recent discussion of the social question in his encyclical *Centesimus Annus.* But when they and the UCA, in general, committed themselves to a preferential option for the poor, they surely exercised a prophetic influence on their own university and on many other universities and on their own society and on many others.

By celebrating the lives of these martyrs in this volume, Professors Hassett and Lacey make their vigorous and challenging vision accessible to a wider audience. For us all, this book is an invitation to our own proclamation of the gospel and promotion of justice. Through it, *perduran las voces*, "the voices remain."

Leo J. O'Donovan, S.J.
President

Georgetown University

PREFACE

In the year 1989, Georgetown University was celebrating its two-hundredth anniversary, and, as a body of persons who gather to assimilate and disseminate knowledge, expressing its identity under the theme of "Learning, Faith, and Freedom." The same year, its sister Jesuit institution in El Salvador was under renewed attacks from the establishment for courageously pursuing learning within a climate of faith that seeks justice in freedom and where freedom is a matter of life and death.

Just a few short weeks after Georgetown's bicentennial celebration ended in Washington, El Salvador's witness to an ideal reached a brutal climax. During a fit of military rage, Salvadoran soldiers from an élite, U.S. -trained battalion murdered six Jesuits and two co-workers at the University of Central America José Simeón Cañas. Thus savage violence temporarily silenced the articulation of powerful ideas—ideas considered especially threatening because they explicated and exposed the inhuman living conditions of the oppressed majority both to the oppressed and to the world.

This book attempts to keep alive the ideas of these distinguished men who lost their lives trying to live out their synthesis of learning, faith, and freedom. We are thus privileged to include this volume in the series of publications on that theme which has resulted from Georgetown's Bicentennial.

It is also most fitting that we publish *Towards a Society That Serves Its People* in collaboration with our colleagues from Swarthmore College. Collaboration and the formation of coalitions have characterized the worldwide response to the Salvadoran murders which affect all of us, in and out of universities.

CHARLES L. CURRIE, S.J.
Georgetown University   *Director of the Bicentennial*

This volume is based on the collaborative efforts resulting from the Faculty Seminar on Central America at Swarthmore College and the work of the San Francisco group of the Committee for Health Rights in Central America, and Georgetown University's Bicentennial Office. The book is one of a series of publications resulting from the Georgetown Bicentennial.

This publication has been supported in large part through a gift from Mrs. John R. Gaines. Her assistance and generosity is acknowledged with gratitude and appreciation.

ACKNOWLEDGMENTS

This book and its sequel (in process and tentatively scheduled for publication in 1992) are the products of a collaborative effort of the Faculty Seminar on Central America at Swarthmore College, the San Francisco group of the Committee for Health Rights in Central America (CHRICA), and Georgetown University. They have received the support and encouragement of Rodolfo Cardenal, S.J., Director of UCA Editores of the Universidad Centroamericana José Simeón Cañas in El Salvador. We are grateful to Father Cardenal for granting us permission to translate and publish the articles in this volume and for providing the photographs used in the book.

Numerous people have contributed to this volume's completion. The encouragement of our colleagues has been important—especially of Tom Bradley, Jim Kurth, Hans Oberdiek, Barry Schwartz (Swarthmore College), Adrianne Aron (CHRICA), and Mark Risk. For assistance in locating copies of the works of Ignacio Ellacuría, Ignacio Martín-Baró, and Segundo Montes, we wish to thank Minda Hart (Reference Librarian, Swarthmore College), Laura Lomas, Adrianne Aron, Joe Betz, and Sylvia Rosales-Fike. Our translators, Adrianne Aron, Phillip Berryman, James Brockman, S.J., Maria Ines Lacey, and Anne Wallace all completed their assignments promptly, with work of high quality. Eleanor Liccio provided some fine secretarial support. Susan Johnson (Office of Corporate and Foundation Relations, Swarthmore College) spent hours of her time and expertise in successfully raising funds to cover the costs of the translation, and other projects—including a faculty exchange between Swarthmore College and the UCA, and a conference on the thought of Ellacuría, Martín-Baró, and Montes on November 17, 1990—organized by the Faculty Seminar on Central America. Michael Macguire provided the photograph of Segundo Montes. Arthur Schmidt provided assistance on some points of historical detail. Patrice La Liberté of Georgetown University Press performed editorial work that significantly enhanced the quality of the book.

We also gratefully acknowledge the financial support for this volume which was generously provided by The John D. and Catherine T. MacArthur Foundation, the William J. Cooper Foundation, Bill and Kathy Rieser, and an anonymous donor.

Finally, we make a special acknowledgment to three people. James W. England, Provost of Swarthmore College, supported our work in numerous ways, Charles Beirne, S.J., Vice Rector of the UCA, encouraged us and facilitated our contacts with the Central American University and Georgetown University Press. Both maintained a continual,

heartening interest in the progress of this work; and so has Frances
Cuneo whose contribution has been indispensable. Without her many
hours of work—performing computer searches in the library, getting the
bibliographies into shape, organizing, typing, putting our editorial revisions onto computer disks, transferring from disk to disk—this volume
would not have been completed on time. We are most grateful for her
collaboration, patience, good cheer, and commitment.

Swarthmore College   J.H. and H.L.

...perduran las voces

Ignacio Ellacuría, S.J.

Born
November 9, 1930

Entered the Society
September 14, 1947

Ordained priest
July 26, 1961

Died
November 16, 1989

Ignacio Martín-Baró, S.J.

Born
November 7, 1942

Entered the Society
September 28, 1959

Ordained priest
June 27, 1970

Died
November 16, 1989

Segundo Montes, S.J.

Born
May 15, 1933

Entered the Society
August 21, 1950

Ordained priest
July 25, 1963

Died
November 16, 1989

Comprehending Reality from The Perspective of The Poor

JOHN HASSETT AND HUGH LACEY, EDITORS

In the early morning darkness of November 16, 1989, six Jesuit priests and two women co-workers were murdered at the Central American University (Universidad Centroamericana José Simeón Cañas or UCA) by members of an elite, U.S. trained battalion of the Salvadoran army. This massacre forms part of a much bigger picture. For well over a decade, repression and war have raged in El Salvador, producing more than 75,000 deaths and more than a million refugees. Behind this picture lies an unjust socio-economic system which impedes the access of the poor majority to even the most basic human necessities. What is so striking about El Salvador, however, is that repression has not stopped many poor people from organizing a popular movement in order to work for and claim their rights, and as they do so, display a re-markable vitality, resilience, and courage.

The Jesuits of the UCA were murdered because of the role they played *as intellectuals, researchers, writers, and teachers* in expressing their solidarity with the poor. They constantly affirmed that God is the God of life who cares especially for the poor, they publicly denounced the prevailing political and economic order, they eloquently documented the sufferings of the poor, they systematically taught that the problems of El Salvador demand profound structural transformations that require the participation of the poor majority, they openly challenged the democratic credentials attributed to recent Salvadoran governments, and they insistently advocated a negotiated settlement to the war. Martín-Baró wrote (1987b):

> "Archbishop Romero's assassination was an action informed by the intelligent calculation that its symbolic value would be as significant as the loss that his death represented for the cause of the Salvadoran poor; it was intended not only to put an end to a life and a voice, but to annul, once and for all, the liberating role of religion in El Salvador" (chapter 20, *this volume*).

Perhaps the same thing would be said about his own and his colleagues' murders almost a decade later. The two women, Elba and Celina Ramos, were murdered simply for being there.

The murders at the UCA have been featured quite prominently in the U.S. press, but usually only in relation to their immediate legal and political ramifications. The press focuses on the Jesuits because they are seen as important people; and, indeed, the publicity and revulsion occasioned by their murder did push Congress to halve the military aid it appropriated for El Salvador (though with conditions that later enabled President Bush to restore the full amount), and to keep insisting that the murderers be brought to justice. It is, of course, important to bring the murderers to justice, but that is only a first step towardss eliminating repression and U.S. complicity in it, and then towardss completing the process of liberating the poor who are struggling to claim their lawful rights. We cannot understand the significance of the deaths of the UCA Jesuits unless we understand how their lives were connected with the aspirations of the poor majority.

Despite all the publicity, the UCA Jesuits are in fact not well known. Few know their names, and even fewer know what they did and what they thought. This is not surprising since the categories used by the press, when reporting on those who are in conflict with the interests of the dominant powers, tend for the most part to be those of numbers, positions, and status, not those of human faces, hearts, minds, and relationships. Abstracting as they do from both the bigger picture that frames their deaths and the concrete details of their lives, these categories fail to help us grasp why the Jesuits were killed. Instead the press keeps repeating variations on the theme that they were killed because the Salvadoran military believed that they were the "intellectual leaders" of the Farabundo Marti Nacional Liberación Front (FMLN), the guerrilla organization which, at the time of the murders, was conducting an offensive inside the city of San Salvador. It thus repeats the murderers' own propaganda, perhaps hoping that we will see ignorance as the real failing of the Salvadoran military, or even hinting that there might have been some justification for the murders.

Although they are little known in the United States, three of these six Jesuits were significant scholars and writers: Ignacio Ellacuría, Ignacio Martín-Baró, and Segundo Montes. Behind their individual contributions, there was both profound collaboration, in which the other ·ee Jesuits (Juan Ramon Moreno, Amando López, and Joaquin López y López) also played their special roles, and an original conception of the university in which the pursuit of truth is tied to the service of social justice.

The fundamental aim of this book is to offer a representative sample of the writings of Ellacuría, Martín-Baró, and Montes in order to make their intellectual contribution available to an English-speaking audience, and hopefully to initiate a process in which greater and more significant intellectual interaction develops with our Central American colleagues. This aim is tied to a further number of motivating considerations. We wish to honor these murdered Jesuits and their co-workers; to express solidarity with our colleagues at the UCA and other Central American universities who are experiencing repression, and also with the popular movement in Central America.* We also seek, in a modest way, to resist those who killed the Jesuits in the hope that their ideas would die with them. We also continue the challenges that their work represented to the dominant viewpoints in political discussion and to the policies of oppression and repression that they disguise. Finally, drawing inspiration from the UCA Jesuits' conception of the university, we wish to reaffirm the best values of the university as university: the pursuit and teaching of truth in a collaborative, collegial process that transcends international boundaries; the assumption of public responsibility for the truth; and the articulation of the links between truth and justice.

What must it be like to write of and in a society in which you know that the next word uttered or written may well be your last? Obviously the authors whose words we have here translated and edited were aware of the power of their words, not only among the poor whom they served and learned from, but also and particularly among the power elites of El Salvador who defend their privileged life so tenaciously against all meaningful efforts at social change in their country. As we prepared these translations for publication, we were struck by the prolific output of the three writers (see the Bibliography), the breathless pace of their prose, and its staccato-like rhythms. These qualities of their writing style become more and more pronounced as the November of 1989 approached. Many of their essays seem less and less polished, more in need of revision and structural reorganization. One has the impression that they sensed that time was running out on them, that the most important thing was to get their words down on paper, to make their appeal to rationality and to Christian love as quickly as possible before all further verbalization was silenced.

In editing these essays we have made every effort to be faithful to the ideas of their authors. Such commitment, however, has not deterred us from deleting, from time to time, material that we deemed repetitious or unnecessary to a clear understanding of the text's principal themes.

---

*The tragic irony of the women's brutal deaths should be noted. Because Elba Ramos and her husband, Abdulio, were worried that their fifteen-year old daughter might not be safe, they got permission for the women to sleep in a spare room in UCA's faculty quarters. (Traditionally all Latin American university campuses are off-bounds to police and military personnel.)

For personal portraits of the six Jesuits and their co-workers, Elba and Celina Ramos, see Sobrino *et al.* (1990). For information on the legal proceedings related to the murders, see periodic reports published by the Lawyers Committee for Human Rights (330 Seventh Avenue, New York, NY 10001).

Whenever such deletions were made we have so indicated in the body of the text. We have, in several cases, also inserted subheadings in order to make the structure of a complex text more apparent. (We have not, however, added editorial commentaries in order to explain the complex and abstract concepts sometimes present in their writings. The occasional interpolation of a date or transition phrase is enclosed in brackets [thus].) We are confident that the revisions undertaken by us are consistent with those that might have been initiated by the writers themselves had they not lived under the constant threat of that fateful knock at the door to which the poor majority of their country has become so accustomed.

We have grouped the essays of the three Jesuit scholars into five sections, so that the wide range and integrity of their contributions, as well as the way they interact with one another, become apparent. This structure also helps to highlight the various dimensions in which their thought is linked dialectically with the practices of the poor who continue to struggle towardss a society that serves its people.

Vision of the University

One major intellectual contribution of the UCA Jesuits is their vision of the university. The four articles in Section III of this volume represent important statements of this vision and of the UCA's attempts to realize it concretely. It is derived from a number of sources: firstly, from the responses to the compelling claims for justice that are voiced by the popular movement, including the Christian Base Communities (CBCs) which some of the Jesuits served in a pastoral capacity; secondly, from the sharing of the growing practice in Central American universities (including the national University of El Salvador) of linking the university's mission with service to the needs of the poor majority; and, thirdly, from the decision of the Society of Jesus, in the 1970s, to make the preferential option for the poor central to its spirituality in the contemporary world. However, the most distinctive source of their vision was the theology of liberation. To our knowledge, the UCA represents the only attempt, fully informed by the theology of liberation, to articulate and structure a university. Section I of this volume contains two of Ellacuría's articles developing this theology (see also Ellacuría, 1976a; 1990d). For a brief statement of Ellacuría's contribution, see Berryman (1990). These are difficult and abstract writings, but they are very important contributions to the theology of liberation.

THE CONTRIBUTION OF THE THEOLOGY OF LIBERATION

The specificity of the theology of liberation lies in its stance, location, and perspective. Rooted as it is in the concrete conditions and liberatory struggles of the poor majority of Latin America, it draws not only upon biblical and traditional sources, but also essentially upon dialogue with the popular organizations as well as upon the biblically-based reflections of numerous CBCs. In Ellacuría's theological writings, the notion of "the Kingdom of God" is central, leading to these two fundamental questions: What stance do the values of the Kingdom of God require in the face of the current conditions of the poor? What do the struggles of the poor contribute to the growth of the Kingdom of God?

When such questions are posed, the following six are typical of the positions that emerge. 1) The quest for justice is an integral dimension of Christian faith; indeed love of neighbor only finds its complete meaning in the context of justice, which is understood as present (to a first approximation) wherever there is a robust embodiment of both civil/political and economic/social/cultural rights (Ellacuría, chapter 3; Montes, chapter 7). 2) There is a subtle, dialectical interplay between Christian salvation and historical liberation—the historicity of salvation (Ellacuría, chapters 1 & 2; Martín-Baró, chapter 20). Thus, we cannot identify the *real* with the *actual*; there are genuine *possibilities* that have not yet been realized in actual society. To address the real, one must seek out what is possible in the light of the constraints of the actual. (This principle informs all the writings selected for Sections II, IV, and V.) In particular, it is possible that there be a fuller embodiment of the values of the kingdom of God: love that seeks embodiment in structures of justice, solidarity, cooperation, compassion, humility, truth, and freedom—even if, in the actual world, individualistic and competitive values predominate and are reinforced by the structures of power. 3) Engagement in political action can be an integral component of faith, while one recognizes that there are important distinctions between faith and politics and between the kingdom of God and historical institutions. 4) The current condition of the poor majority in Latin America represents a grave injustice. 5) Fundamental structural transformation is necessary to right this injustice, which is discerned as institutionalized and systemic. However, structural change as such is not sufficient; the principal agents of this fundamental transformation need to be the people themselves. Emphasizing the complex dialectic of the personal and of the social is one of the hallmarks of the theology of liberation. (One of Ellacuría's principal contributions to this theology is his account of the view of the human person that makes this emphasis essential; see chapter 2.) The importance of this dialectic is often reinforced by social analyses that go beyond social scientific accounts by bringing in the categories of "idolatry" and "sin" as explanatory principles of the actual reality of Central America. 6) The value of solidarity with those struggling for liberation has primacy in contemporary Christian life—"the preferential option for the poor," or, in a creative twist introduced by Ellacuría and Sobrino, "solidarity with the poor-with-spirit" (Ellacuría, chapter 2); see also the *Spirituality of Liberation* by Jon Sobrino (1988).

It is deeply rooted in the Christian tradition, even if customarily ignored, that sources of new life and new vision emerge among the poor and the marginalized, for it is especially among them that God is encountered. Despite the dehumanization that one also finds among them, the poor constitute a privileged locus for the growth of the Kingdom of God. Among them one finds the resources to resist the idolatries that shape the lives of those who occupy privileged places in the dominant structures of power. Idolatry is present whenever lives are shaped in their day to day detail by objects other than God: wealth, power, comfort, pleasure, security. The values of idolatry are individualistic and competitive, and they are embodied in structures of domination. They conflict with the values of the kingdom of God that are listed above. The idolatrous are also intolerant of those who pursue the values of the Kingdom—intolerant to the extent of requiring their persecution and sometimes their martyrdom. The theme of idolatry—especially concerning the idol of wealth—and persecution frequently recurred in the writings of the UCA Jesuits (see Ellacuría, 1990e; Martín-Baró, 1985i). Perhaps the horrors that El Salvador has experienced during the past fifteen years have been so enormous that the usual categories of the social sciences simply pale in light of the reality. Only the grip of these idols, demanding the sacrifice of so much human life, could explain the horrors, and the contempt and the hatred of human beings. Jon Sobrino, the UCA theologian who was spared death because he happened to be out of the country, stated simply that his friends were killed because they touched the idols (Sobrino, *et al.*, 1990).

GRASPING REALITY

In the biblical conception, idolatry not only corrupts values, but it also distorts perception and understanding. This leads us to the university. From the preceding section we can extract four principles that have direct significance for the university: **1)** To grasp the real, one must seek out what is possible given the constraints of the actual. **2)** There is a complex dialectic between the personal and the social. **3)** Among the poor sources of novel possibilities can develop. **4)** The perspective of the poor is essential for gaining a thorough grasp of reality. These principles pervade the UCA Jesuits' thinking about the university: simultaneously these frame the vision of the university and become tested as viable principles as the teaching and research practices, informed by them, are developed. In the long run, their credibility does not rest upon their having been derived theologically, but upon whether they can be vindicated in historical practice.

The kingdom of God remains the horizon of all the thought and practice of the UCA Jesuits. Given this horizon, what is the task of the university? Or, rather, how does one contribute—*qua* university or member of the university—to building the kingdom of God? (In addition to

Section III in this volume, see also Part III, Sobrino, *et al.*, 1990.) For the UCA Jesuits the university has its own integrity, its proper task, its defining values: 1) pursuit of truth, in community; and 2) educating professionals to serve the common good. Thus, there can be an identity, in the lives of intellectuals, between commitment to the core values of the university and commitment to build the kingdom of God. These values are not subordinated to the interests of privileged élites, revolutionary political parties, or the institutional Church itself.

These Jesuits had a robust sense of reality, nurtured by the enormous suffering all around them and the persistent threats on their lives. Truth is grasping reality—not only the actual, but also the genuinely possible—which requires exposing the reigning ideology. The objective of the intellectual life is to articulate reality, not to exercise the intellect as such. Gaining truth requires contact with reality—a commonplace, of course, in the experimental sciences, but not in those social sciences for which a survey of the actual replaces that exploration of reality that might discern as yet unactualized possibilities, or not in those humanistic studies that do not recognize reality beyond perspectives.

National reality

Ellacuría (chapter 9, Section III) argued that the primary object for the university in El Salvador is "national reality," that is, to grasp the condition of life of the Salvadoran majority in all its concreteness, with attention to its variations with history, its variability across groups, and its moral significance; to discern its causes, the possibilities latent in it, and the actual obstacles to actualizing more just possibilities. Note that moral categories are necessary for an adequate grasp of reality. When one approaches investigation of national reality in this way, in order to explain important events it is necessary both to look beyond the intentions of the agents involved and to discern the material and social conditions that are presupposed in the agents' behavior. One must also recognize that any form of self-understanding that abstracts from the material and social conditions of that self's life is inherently limited.

Limit-situation

"National reality" became a key notion for Ellacuría in articulating his vision of the university. He also introduced the notion of "limit-situation," borrowed from the German philosopher, Karl Jaspers (Ellacuría, chapter 3). El Salvador, he pointed out, is experiencing a limit-situation: that is, given its entrenched poverty, divisive social groups, and armed conflicts, its actual institutions are incapable of maintaining the normal order, so that, one way or another, novel possibilities have to be actualized. They can be actualized in the form of the power elites unleashing violence and repression (which their institutions and laws expressly do not permit, and which in normal times are contained) in an attempt to maintain the established order. Or they can be actualized by movements, which aim to re-order society, gaining a creative impetus—with new historical agents coming to the fore and new modes of organization showing their viability. Thus a limit-situation is a privileged moment when the illegitimacy of the power structure is exposed with special clarity and the urgency of finding genuinely new possibilities is apparent. Awareness of the limit-situation in which they were living added a dimension of vitality to the intellectual work of the UCA Jesuits, and it helps to explain how they could be so productive despite the conditions in which they were working. Martín-Baró took the notion of "limit-situation" a step further. He clearly identified the poor-with-spirit as the locus for the emergence of those novel possibilities both in human lives and in the inter-relations that could move the quest for justice to a new level (Aron, 1990).

Social outreach and critical consciousness

Working out the implications of the national reality and the limit-situation, it becomes clear that the university cannot be impartial. There is no way to grasp reality that is neutral between the maintaining or the transforming of actual structures and ways of life. In order to grasp national reality in a limit-situation, it is essential to adopt "the preferential option for the poor." The perspective thus offered, rather than imparting a special interest to the university, turns the university back to its fundamental value—the search for truth in all its concreteness. Rather than being opposed to "objectivity," this perspective in fact provides a necessary condition for a comprehensive grasp of reality that can help to uncover the liberating possibilities latent in the actual historical moment. In accordance with this insight, the university—in both its curriculum and its research projects—will be informed by a *"proyección social"*, or a social outreach program in which students, teachers, and researchers engage the national reality directly as it is experienced by the poor majority. They can then shape collaborative projects of social transformation which are reflective of the needs, aspirations, capabilities, and direction of the poor majority (chapters 9 & 10). In order not to reduce the personal to the social but, at the same time, to keep the dialectic of the personal and the social vital, the university will also assume the role of developing "critical consciousness" (*"concientización"*) among its members. Thus social outreach projects and personal consciousness formation mutually enhance each other. Martín-Baró explicates in detail the multiple dimensions of the meaning of this *concientización* (see chapter 11).

The UCA Jesuits were often attacked for "politicizing" the university—and, of course, their kind of university does have political repercussions. Moreover, a stance of social commitment is often held to be contrary to that of "detachment" which is commonly said to be the appropriate stance to adopt for the pursuit of truth. Such detachment, according to Ellacuría and Martín-Baró, is an illusion, an ideological disguise for the perspective of privilege and power. Either the pursuit of truth is a pursuit informed by the values of privilege and power, or it is a pursuit informed by the values of compassion and solidarity with the poor majority—especially in a limit-situation there is no way to avoid making a choice. The Jesuits backed their choices for the latter neither with sentimentality nor as an imperative of political activism, neither with biblical fundamentalism nor as an appeal to the Church's authority, but with rigorous, creative, penetrating, and distinctive scholarship.

The articles we selected for this book exemplify the kind of research and scholarship that derive from the UCA's vision of the university. They also provide both a compelling and distinct portrait of the actual reality of El Salvador and are a continuing exploration of the sources of and obstacles to liberating possibilities. Even where they are not definitive or in need of theoretical refinement, they provide a point of reference for further investigation and analysis. Indeed, despite the methodological weaknesses of some of them and the programmatic nature of others, we suggest that any adequate interpretation of events in El Salvador needs to be in dialogical contact with the body of work from which we have drawn these articles.

Characteristic themes from the writing of Ellacuría, Martín-Baró, and Montes

This is not the place to attempt an overview or a critical assessment of the intellectual contributions of Ellacuría, Martín-Baró, and Montes. We leave their writings to speak for themselves, and offer the bibliographies of their work as aids to further study. However, we will highlight themes of each of the three writers in order to provide some initial guidelines.

IGNACIO ELLACURÍA

Ellacuría, the UCA's rector, was the principal author of the vision of the university that the UCA aimed to become. He also edited *ECA, Proceso,* and *Revista Latinoamericana de Teologia,* and wrote widely as a philosopher, theologian, and socio-political analyst.

Ellacuría's writings on ethical and political theory display an interesting methodology, a subtle mixture of theory and practice. (In addition to chapters 2 & 3, see also other works available in English: Ellacuría, 1977b; 1982b; 1982c; 1988b.) These articles typically have a concrete point of departure which may be a significant event (e.g., the 1969 war between El Salvador and Honduras—chapter 3), a piece of legislation and a range of commentaries on it (e.g., regarding the 1976 legislation on land reform—chapter 4), a socially significant actual phenomenon (e.g., unemployment—see 1982b), or a new combination of circumstances (e.g., changes that suggest novel possibilities for a negotiated settlement to the war in El Salvador—see 1989e). Then the theoretical moral principles that illuminate the issue and inform possible liberating projects or policies are brought into play. In these articles, Ellacuría takes the various parties involved in the issues very seriously. He scrutinizes their words and their actions, drawing out their presuppositions and implications—with a keen eye to discerning the ideological uses of moral discourse which legitimate oppressive structures and the repressive institutions which support them.

Central to Ellacuría's methodology is the view that the meanings of such key terms of moral theory as "property," "democracy," "human rights," and "violence" cannot be comprehended abstractly or dissociated from their uses in concrete historical circumstances and what they apply to within different socio-economic structures. Their meanings are variable, and they are shaped and refined (sometimes with particular acuteness, as when one is in a limit-situation) in response to actual events—in discussions, manifestoes, negotiating documents, legislation, constitutions, treaties, international agreements, etc. Similar methodology is present in the articles by Montes and Martín-Baró in Section II and in parts of other articles by them (chapters 14 & 16 in Section IV and chapter 19 in Section V). Because this is a mode of moral thinking that is explicitly sensitive to the dialectic between the personal and the structural, it does not project a detailed model of the desired social structures for a liberated society. It grounds moral critique not upon how closely actual society may reflect such a model, but upon how adequately it serves human life and how it provides space for the growth of liberating possibilities.

Sometimes Ellacuría uses this methodology within a more inclusive theological analysis. This is particularly the case in his criticism of capitalism (e.g., chapter 2 in Section I, chapter 8 in Section III), a theme that frequently gained his attention, even more urgently with the demise of state socialism in Eastern Europe. His critique begins with an assessment of the actual condition and tendencies of societies now under capitalism, what possibilities can be projected, and what alternative possibilities there might be. Among others, he discerns the following four tendencies: 1) the widening gap between the rich minority and the poor majority; 2) the process of exploitation and oppression becoming harsher (e.g., as manifest in the international debt and how the mechanisms for servicing it put the greatest burden on the poor); 3) continuing ecological destruction; and 4) "the conspicuous dehumanization of those who, pressured by the nervous and harassed productivism of having, of amassing wealth, power, honor, and the ever-changing gamut of consumer goods, opt to give up the difficult task of achieving their own being" (chapter 8).

Tendencies like these, Ellacuría maintains, cannot be reversed (except perhaps in certain select locales). Rather they are symptoms of the fact that the capitalist order cannot be *universalized*. The values embodied in the lives of the privileged of the capitalist order *cannot* be embodied in all lives; and, in order for these to be embodied in the lives of the privileged, the requisite conditions limit the human possibilities of most others. The concrete reality of Latin America speaks to this truth.

> "That truth demonstrates the impossibility of reproducing and, especially, of enlarging significantly the present historical order. It demonstrates, even more radically, its undesirability, since it cannot be universalized and it brings with it the perpetuation of an unjust and predatory distribution of the world's resources, and even of each nation's resources, for the benefit of a few nations.... So [the liberation movements]...seek an order which will provide a human life not only for a few but for the greater part of humanity. The developed world is not at all the desired utopia, even as a way to overcome poverty, much less to overcome injustice. Indeed, it is a sign of what should not be and of what should not be done *(from* chapter 2).

This is the prophet speaking, denouncing the actual order: since capitalism cannot be universalized, it cannot eliminate oppressive and dominating relations that lead to dehumanization and destruction. Prophets also announce; they point to the hidden possibilities; they ask: Are there alternative possibilities? Ellacuría knew that those actually in power use violence (repressive as well as oppressive) to nip in the bud any alternative possibilities. That is why the resilience of the popular movements of El Salvador was so important to him. New possibilities, with a hope of being universalized, depend upon the option for the poor, upon solidarity, and upon "putting work before capital." Only the outcome of practice will determine if these are genuine possibilities; but if they are not, the prospects for the future are dim—adding a further urgency to the research tasks that he had laid out for the university.

IGNACIO MARTÍN-BARÓ

Martín-Baró was the vice-rector of the UCA, the director of its public opinion institute (IUDOP), and the editor of *Revista de Psicología de El Salvador*. Most of his writings are in social psychology.

It is well known that, in order to mediate between theologically-derived principles and practical norms for action, the theology of liberation adopts analyses from the social sciences, especially the dependency analysis and other neo-Marxist analyses. The theology of liberation, however, insists that structural change alone cannot usher in a liberated society, one in which everyone has an opportunity to live a full life, in which the various dimensions of the human person (material, intellectual, spiritual, and social) can be reasonably fulfilled. There is a dialectic, not a unilinear determination, between the social and the personal, something profoundly recognized in Paulo Freire's educational methods based on the awakening of critical consciousness. Building on Freire, Martín-Baró recognized the need for psychological as well as social theoretic mediations, and he began to chart a program for "*the psychology of liberation*" (Section V; see also the sequel to this book *(forthcoming.)*

One fundamental idea of the program is that the focus of clinical psychology should become the needs and pathologies of the poor majority, and that the practice of psychology, together with its theoretical and empirical investigations, should assume the perspective of the poor. In light of the actual reality of El Salvador, this has led in the first place to the psychological study of violence. What are the pathologies (both for the violated and the violators) resulting from the various forms of violence (of war, repression, crime, the family)? And how can they be treated? (See Martín-Baró, 1990k.) What are the psychological roots of violence? What input can social psychology provide for developing effective alternatives to violence? Secondly, it encourages the study of the pathologies of marginality, those derived from homelessness, being deprived of land, forced migrations, unemployment and underemployment, the inability to "define" one's own life, and being in the grip of the dominant ideology. (Montes also takes up some of these issues in chapter 13.) Thirdly, "the psychology of work" gains prominence both in addressing the mental health of work, including the pathologies of alienation, but more positively in how to develop "alternative values" of work: "solidarity and cooperation, sobriety and persistence, sensitivity and capacity to sacrifice." These values are closely linked with Ellacuría's philosophical argument that work is more central than property to meaningful lives that all can have the opportunity to live (chapters 2 & 8). Fourthly, programs are sought that will enable members of the poor majority to claim greater control over their own lives. What are the psychological factors that favor becoming involved in popular organizations and developing critical consciousness? What are those that lead to "liberatory" rather than to "illusory" religion? (See chapter 20.) How can psychology contribute to undermining religion's role in maintaining ideology? What programs can support the peoples' recovery of their historical and cultural identity? We have mentioned already the resilience of the people in the face of the repression. This, Martín-Baró affirms, derives from the "virtues" of the people. How can psychological programs reinforce the conviction that these virtues must play an essential role in creating a more just society and strengthen them in the face of persistent attempts to inculcate individualistic values in the people?

Another fundamental idea of the psychology of liberation is that the practice of psychology cannot be separated from social and political action. This is especially apparent in dealing with the pathologies derived from violence. It is not enough to treat the psychological effects of torture, the murder and disappearance of family members, and the bombings—as if people can be psychologically well within an environment of terror. Here we are dealing with pathologies that manifestly have social, economic, and political causes. Prevention requires that we address these causes. Thus the dialectic of the personal and the social must be at the center of attention. To adjust people to a given social structure is not treatment. Rather, genuine treatment serves their participation, and their wanting to participate, in the communities and organizations of the liberation movement.

SEGUNDO MONTES

Montes, a sociologist, was director of the UCA's human rights institute (IDHUCA). His research ranged widely over the actual social structures and movements of El Salvador, while paying close attention to the possible sources of innovation. In many ways his is conventional, neo-Marxist social analysis of the type commonly associated with the theology of liberation, an analysis of class conflict, class struggle, and class consciousness. But he has an attentive eye on the fine grain, the distinctiveness of El Salvador, and to phenomena and opportunities usually not noted from conventional Marxist viewpoints. He published extensive studies of the complex system of patronage in El Salvador, of the migration caused by the war (especially to the United States), of the relationships between the emigrants and their family members in El Salvador, of the effects of these relationships on the Salvadoran economy and class struggle, and of human rights abuses.

The possibility of democracy was a repeated theme in his writings. He exposed the "democracy" of the ruling elites and their U.S. patrons, emphasizing that a deep embodiment of the full range of human rights—economic/social/cultural as well as civil/political rights—not elections as such, is what defines democracy. These rights include that of participation. A decade ago he saw little hope, in the short run, for the conditions needed for the exercise of this right coming into being (chapter 6). But shortly before his death, Montes came to see the foundation of real democracy in the communities of refugees who had organized themselves in exile and returned home (Montes, 1989k; see also Compher, Jackson, and Morgan, 1991). Like his colleagues, he held that liberation could only be achieved through the movements of the people themselves—not ushered in by elites, whether local or foreign, whether elected or militarily installed.

Besides those of the refugees, he detected other achievements among the poor that pointed towardss their possible role in building democracy. In a controversial article, after pointing to the vast gap between the rich minority and the poor majority, he offered the analysis that the monetary economy, the productive system, and the control of work are all under capitalist control and reflect El Salvador's dependent place in the international capitalist economy (chapter 12). Then he argued that the bulk of the people do not gain their livelihood from this economy or even participate regularly in it. These people survive in virtue of relations that are established outside the main capitalist economy. The existence of these relations explains their ability to survive and organize during times of extreme crisis, such as the limit-situation they have been enduring for more than a dozen years. There are two economies, according to Montes, but they are intertwined. Clearly the non-capitalist one needs the capitalist system, for even the gains from meager employment are necessary for survival; equally, without the non-capitalist system in place, the work force, which is necessary for capitalist production, would not survive. He goes on to compare capitalism in El Salvador to a cancer:

> "The Salvadoran economy was non-capitalist but the capitalist mode of production was brought in from outside and implanted on this economy and grew at its expense. Little by little it [the cancer] has invaded and penetrated the original organism and gradually weakened it. The capitalist mode continued to develop and gain strength while suffocating the host, almost to the point of strangling it. However, it needs the host in order to live; if it kills the non-capitalist mode of production, it will commit suicide and disappear as Salvadoran capitalism, since it is not autonomous" (chapter 12).

The actual "democracy" in El Salvador places the state at the service of the capitalist economy, whereas a real democracy would need to draw from the human resources of the majority who have demonstrated their capability to sustain life.

Concluding remarks

Montes' image of capitalism as a cancer complements Ellacuría's argument that capitalism cannot be universalized and Martín-Baró's psychological studies of the pathologies generated by this system. And the pointing by Montes to a surviving alternative mode of economic and social organization, combined with Martín-Baró's discernment of the "virtues" displayed in this alternative mode, adds a material base to Ellacuría's theologically grounded identification of the poor-with-spirit as the locus from which transforming possibilities might emerge.

Whether or not these conclusions can be sustained in the final analysis, it is clear that a university that adopts the preferential option for the poor is able to generate novel and significant research and scholarship, whose import is recognized way beyond the university.

The Jesuits drew strength from the lives of people within the popular movement. Some of them acted as parish priests in poor communities and established close contacts with refugee communities. It was this link with the people that enabled them to discern possibilities that are not readily apparent to mainstream social analysis. Now the peasants draw strength from the murdered Jesuits. Three communities of refugees who have returned to El Salvador from Honduras have named themselves respectively after Montes, Martín-Baró, and Ellacuría—witness to a remarkable interaction between intellectuals and the poor-with-spirit.

Shortly before he was murdered, Archbishop Romero said: "If they kill me, I will rise in the Salvadoran people" (Ellacuría, 1990e). It seems that the same may be true of the three intellectuals whose writings appear in this book.

Concepts of Liberation, Faith, Justice

Ignacio Ellacuría

1. Liberation Theology and Socio-historical Change in Latin America*

TRANSLATION BY JAMES R. BROCKMAN, S.J.

Liberation theology aims at a change not only in Latin America's persons and society, but also in its socio-historical structures and, by extension, in those of other parts of the world, according to the particular circumstances in each case. The change is denominated and interpreted in liberation terms. The liberation that can be stated in theological terms as a liberation by degrees from sin, from the law, and from death also can be stated in historical terms as liberation from everything that oppresses people and prevents them from enjoying their call to be God's free children.

This theology has its point of departure in an experience, which accompanies it in all of its theoretical development and consists of the physical proof that the greater part of the population of Latin America lives under conditions of dehumanizing poverty and of social and political oppression. These conditions have resulted from historical structural injustice, for which different social subjects (classes, nations, empires) and different economic and political dynamisms are responsible, whether by commission or omission. In light of this situation, liberation theology, first as a more or less reflexive movement of faith, and then as explicit rational reflection, asks itself what Christian faith has to say, both about causes and about solutions. And it likewise asks itself what action should come from that faith in order to make sure that oppressed peoples succeed through liberation processes in becoming free peoples, who as such can realize and enjoy the presence of God's reign among humans to the extent historically possible.

This is posed in different ways according to whether one stresses the *liberation of theology* (Segundo, 1976) or the *theology of liberation* (Gutiérrez, 1973). In the first case, what is proposed directly is that faith and theology be liberated, insofar as they themselves have made ideological

---

*Ellacuría (1987h; see the Bibliography in the back of this book.

19

and social contributions to making religion and/or Christian faith part of the oppression. Thus faith and theology can ready themselves to fulfill their proper function of duly accompanying personal and social liberation processes. In the second case, what is proposed is to use the social power of faith and of the church directly in the socio-historical liberation of peoples. What is most important in liberation theology, we are told, is liberation; but in the first case the immediate objective is the liberation of theology, while in the second case it is liberation from structural injustice, which will necessarily force a liberation of theology. But in each case, what is intended is to develop a genuine and total theology; that is, one based on a genuine and total Christian process, one embracing all the demands of the kingdom of God.

It is important to emphasize that even in the second case, and with greater justice in the first case, liberation theology intends to be (a) something strictly theological, and (b) something that can be considered a total theology.

Statement (a) means that liberation theology intends to situate itself in the theological tradition and in the mode of rationality that theology intends to be, without ignoring the fact that theology has understood itself as knowledge under different forms of rationality. Therefore, liberation theology is not a sociology or a political science, but a specific mode of knowledge whose sources or principles are revelation, tradition, and the magisterium—at whose service certain mediations are placed. If among these mediations that of the socio-economic-historical-political sciences has a certain importance, that does not necessarily imply that it is transformed into being one of these sciences with theological language, any more than the [previous] classical preference for the mediation of philosophy necessarily made the earlier theology a form of philosophy. In intention, in methodology, in the facts, liberation theology shows itself more and more to be a theology.

Statement (b) must be emphasized in harmony with statement (a) for it says that liberation theology is not a regional theology, but a total theology. It is not a theology of the political, but a theology of the kingdom of God. Certainly, it does have a clear political vocation, for it is political to seek the liberation not only of persons but of peoples, and not only from psychological oppressions but from socio-historical oppressions. This aim must be carefully kept in mind, for it does make the theology, at least in part, a political theology, yet not in such fashion that all that matters is the theology's political significance and effectiveness, because liberation theology has its strict theological consistency. And this consistency obliges it to take as object (distinguish object treated *from* object intended) what is judged to be the object of a total theology. Understanding this object as the kingdom or reign of God keeps it, on the one hand, from leaving out any part of the actual revealed message and, on the other hand, lets it approach the things of this world connaturally. For ultimately the kingdom of God, the central point of

Jesus' message, alludes to the reigning presence of God in this world, to the God who becomes history so that history can rise up to God, to God's humanization and mundanization so that human beings and the world can be divinized. All this, in liberation theology, is the conviction that human beings will be able to become human only when by God's gift they are more than human, according to the traditional thought that finds such happy expression in Saint Augustine. And what is true of human beings is also true of the world and of history.

But insisting on the total theological character of liberation theology ought not hinder its political effectiveness, since faith and theology have, or should have, a clear vocation to liberate from sin in all its forms, not excluding its objectifications, from the law in all of its modes through which power prevails over those who have less of it, both inside and outside the religious domain, from death in all those processes that nullify life or even snatch it away prematurely.

While liberation theology is a complete form of understanding the Christian faith and putting it into practice, it is still not in itself sufficient to bring integral liberation to persons and to peoples. Furthermore, it exists alongside other forces which have also become aware of the state of oppression in which the mass of the people live. These others also have been stirred by the oppression and, as socio-historical forces have resolved to struggle for this liberation according to their own specific character. This raises the question of what the relationship of liberation theology should be to these other forces, since without them it is not possible to achieve the liberation that this theology claims to seek in order for God to reign in the world and to be all in all. The question especially arises, both in practice and in theory, not only in regard to the so-called revolutionary movements that have raised the banner of the people's liberation, but also in regard to any other historical movement that in fact has the same aim. On the one hand, it can be hypothesized that liberation theology is not sufficient by itself to lead people to an effective liberation, and that liberation movements are not sufficient by themselves to give people an integral liberation. Such a hypothesis arises from the conviction that there is no salvation (or liberation) without God as he is given and revealed to us in Jesus. But on the other hand, it is a hypothesis that depends upon the verification that Jesus' salvation, which far from divorcing itself from historical liberation processes, instead mandates those very processes on account of the transcendental unity of the history of salvation. There are not two histories, but one single history in which the presence of the liberator God and the presence of the liberated and liberator human being are joined together. The old formulations of how to unite faith with reason in the interpretative, and then grace with nature in the realizable, are presented in a new form in liberation theology. It is a way of asking how to interpret the world unitarily from the standpoint of theology, it is a faith in search of understanding, asking how in history to bring about the kingdom of

God which leaves outside itself nothing that is, nothing that has been created.

Typology of Certain Attitudes towards the Political Challenge of Liberation Theology.

Liberation theology has to do with the political, and this makes it have to do with politics. It has a clear purpose of liberation and of effective liberation, especially in its *theology of liberation* model. It is this model or plan that presents additional difficulties, for the *liberation of theology* model, rather than entering into relationship with strictly political and revolutionary processes, enters primarily into relationship with problems of de-ideologizing, which permit a certain separation from political praxis. The difficulties arise from the type of attitude with which we face the problems. By "attitude" we understand both the position and the fundamental disposition that are adopted in wanting to realize liberation theology in history. The liberation that this theology proposes must be allied in some way with those forces that also struggle for the liberation of the mass of the people. This is the integral liberation that begins with the liberation of the poor.

NAIVE MORALISM

Naive moralism is not a common attitude among those who move in the ambit of liberation theology, but insofar as it does exist it occurs in different forms. In one form naive moralism assumes that the Christian faith ought to stick to the sphere of morals, both personal as well as social and political, and also that the Christian faith in its pursuit of liberation must not soil its hands with the not very moral practices of politics or with the more or less necessary evils of political movements. Moreover, it tends to become a general and universal moralism that forms abstractions, that avoids facing up to concrete actions under the pretext that these always contain something of politics (which is evil or ambiguous), and that especially avoids setting its sights on historically determined political objectives, since none of them is suitable to the demands of the kingdom. In its most extreme form, naive moralism desires to reduce the function of Christian liberation strictly to changing hearts and proclaiming abstract ideals. It seeks not to be called partisan, as if all social and political forces were equally good or equally bad and, as if one could not discern from one's faith which is the one that contributes more to liberation illumined by the light of the gospel. This attitude highlights the differences between the manner of seeking liberation on the part of faith and on the part of political action, corresponding to the specificity of faith and that of political action, but it does not succeed in joining them together properly. They are treated as two different things, two related things, but things whose relationship is established more in terms of parallelism than in terms of mutual determination and, as needed, in terms of interaction.

FUNDAMENTALIST FANATICISM

Those who expect every liberation to come only from faith maintain attitudes of fundamentalist fanaticism and messianic simplism. They suppose that there is a specifically Christian solution to political, economic, and social problems, although perhaps not to technological problems. Other theoretical mediations are considered not necessary for discerning causes and proposing solutions, and neither are practical mediations needed to put them into practice. In order to find connaturally what will really liberate the poor, they say it is enough to live an unadorned Christianity. This is not a form of spiritualism but rather, on the contrary, it is an effort to extend the liberating message of the gospel connaturally to whatever human problem is presented. In effect, there is no real problem for which a solution cannot be found through faith. This leads frequently to an undifferentiated radicalism in denunciations and to a utopian idealism in proposals for solutions. It is the gospel without commentary, not only for one's personal life, but for the life of society. Will and commitment are enough to do away with oppression. This mind-set shows perfect fluency for negation, but always finds it a little harder to sketch out the content of what is affirmative. Whatever is not the gospel ideal of seating the poor on their thrones and casting down the powerful from their seats is compromise and is unacceptable. At most, a minimum of interpretative schemes and of organization is believed enough to achieve power and transform reality. [For persons with these attitudes] liberating praxis will dictate along the way what must be torn down and what must be built up. This radicality, or rather radicalism, easily leads to measuring good or bad, efficacy or inefficacy, by its grade of radicalism without measuring sufficiently the consequences or reckoning its historical timeliness. For such people there is blind faith in the goodness of one's own attitude and position and a messianic assurance of triumph. The important thing is that the flame not go out, that hope and passion not be extinguished. Delay in the triumph or the leaving of corpses by the wayside does not matter. God will finally triumph with his people. The appropriate cry here is "revolution or death," everything or nothing.

This attitude highlights the force of faith and its historicity, its ability to itself alone make history and to realize liberation in some way. But it pays no attention to the stubbornness and opacity of oppressive reality, to the possible slowness of historical events, to the totality of historical complexity which cannot be denominated either theoretically or practically by the contents of faith or even by the light of faith in search of new contents.

REDUCTIONISM

Reductionism has two faces. The one looks at and interests itself only in those aspects of Christian faith that have immediate political relevance, leaving in the shadows or in suspense other aspects and even the transcendent dimension of historical actions. The other sees faith, at least in its relationship to the political, purely as a prior instance or, at best, a present instance but one subordinate to the demands of political action. Faith thus becomes a propaedeutic of political action, and at most it is preserved as an accessory activator of commitment, but not as an agent of enlightenment and a critic of the historical actions themselves. That task is entrusted to the social sciences and, in particular, to Marxist analysis. Scientific analyses and the aims derived from them are assumed to be sufficient for undertaking correct actions and even for forming the persons who will carry them out. For reductionism, it may be faith that awakens consciousness and prepares for the leap to political action, but faith involves the danger of interfering with political logic, so it is better to leave it in suspense, if not eliminate it altogether. Faith commitment and faith experience are left abandoned in the implicit supposition that it is enough to love other people in order to love God, that it is enough to promote justice in order to perform the service that faith demands, that it is enough to incarnate oneself politically among the poor in order to serve the Jesus of the kingdom who is hidden in them. Under the pressure of political action, either there is no time to develop faith or it is thought that action itself will lead to a deepening of faith within commitment. In any case, faith development will be allowed and even encouraged only insofar as it furthers revolutionary political action, even though it puts certain limits on it both in the order of sentiments (changing hatred into love) and in the order of actions (reducing violence to the minimum necessary). In sum, for reductionism what is essential in the confluence of the liberating message of faith and revolutionary political commitment is thought to be found in the struggle for the liberation of the poor, but in such fashion that the message must be subordinated to waging the struggle effectively and achieving the triumph. If this is accomplished, faith will have performed its task, and that is the way it should be, because hope and faith are transitory, whereas love is what is final and most important.

REALISM

Realism supposes and represents a balanced attitude that takes into account both what is positive in the gospel's contribution to political action itself and the limits of that contribution, precisely because of the specific relativity and the autonomy of both areas. Realism also takes into account both what political action can really do towardss actualizing the kingdom of God and the limits that are characteristic of it. Hence it looks equally at political action with its political results (open or closed to transcendence) and at the realization of the kingdom of God. Then it considers what these possess that is relatively specific, in spite of their reference to determined historical situations, and which can or cannot be in conformity with the kingdom of God. This attitude of believing realism substantiates that the gospel message is indispensable for a total liberation of human beings, peoples, and structures. So, if this salt evaporates, so too do the real possibilities that this total liberation may gradually come about in history. But it also substantiates that the gospel message is not enough, because it does not have tools of its own, either for discerning the causes of oppression and the proposals of liberation or, still less, for carrying them out. Realism also leads to the conviction that no political form is perfectly adequate to the demands of the kingdom, but it does not therefore regard them all as equal or dispense with them all for the sake of a purism that has no meaning in a historical world.

In the first place, this keeps realism from being indifferent and makes it able to reject for Latin America the different forms of capitalism that have been principally responsible for the plight in which the majority of the population lives; in the second place, realism makes it favor those political movements that not only work on behalf of the poor and of the mass of the people, but realism also provides that this vast majority go on to become more active social and political subjects.

All of this supposes, first of all, that the liberating power of the faith is to be promoted to the maximum. Negatively, this requires eradicating everything that in its preaching, its rules, and its lived experience limits faith's liberating potential; positively, it requires developing among believers, both of the rank-and-file and of the hierarchy, whatever in faith itself is intrinsic to a commitment to justice. Next, it supposes that naive attitudes can be overcome by demanding a continually more objective and better-founded knowledge of the theoretical and practical mediations through which the world is interpreted and transformed in one or other direction. Along with that, realism also looks for a permanent discernment of the signs of the times, which to be a correct discernment will have to include the corresponding analysis in the contribution coming from faith. Finally, realism supposes that forms of collaboration will be worked out in the liberation processes themselves. These forms can be different for the church as an institution and for believers, especially for lay people who may desire to commit themselves directly to determined political courses and even to particular parties and organizations. The preferential option for the poor, understood in a realistic way, is what must rule in these options, but with care taken to find those processes that better lead to total liberation. This must be done without letting oneself be deceived by the thousand and one forms of cover-up that the existing systems of domination and even one's own personal, or group, or institutional weaknesses can take.

This brief typology of attitudes does not pretend to be exhaustive either as a general classification or as a description of each of the types. Its particular objective is to demonstrate that the fourth type [i.e., realism] is best suited to finding the most effective way to reconcile the autonomy of faith with the unavoidable demand that this same faith effectively promote justice and liberation. Realism is the most appropriate because it best fulfills a series of principles that must be judged essential in this matter. These are: a) salvation (or liberation) from its beginning in creation is to be understood as an action of God, which should be known and accepted consciously and even thematically; b) the ensuing conscientization and acceptance supposes the maximum possible exercise of faith, which, the more it is cultivated, will be better positioned to further that process of salvation (or liberation); c) that same faith must be operative and must be so in terms of liberation, which cannot be reduced to a liberation from sin as guilt, but must be a liberation from sin and from evil as dominant objectifications, and it must be a liberation in search of a freedom that is reflected in personal expansion and in setting up a new world where the existence of the new human being will be favored; d) the efficacious faith requires entering into a relationship [properly] articulated with the processes and even with the social and political groups that most favor liberation, supposing that liberation is always a process willed by God; e) faith, in that articulation, ought to contribute what is most specific to it as a force of liberation and of hope, and also as a practical criterion of what ought not to be as well as an illuminative utopian criterion of what ought to be; f) the consequent work with persons and communities takes on a special meaning as long as it revitalizes a faith coming from God, a faith that is personal but which must open itself to action in the world—all with the intention of fulfilling in persons and in the world the gospel's vision and values as the leaven in the world's transformation; g) and finally, the preferential option for the poor implies a concrete criterion of discernment, inasmuch as the greater good of the poor mass of the people becomes the touchstone of any political process or group.

Models of relationship with social and political movements

The predominance of one or other of the attitudes developed in the foregoing leads to the adoption of one or other practical model relevant to the political and social movements that really do struggle for the liberation of the mass of the people and of the poor. Many models of relationship are possible. Taking into account what has been presented up to now, we can stylize and schematize the facts and convert them into type-models. It is evident that it is not a matter of all of them being exemplars or of all of them having the same Christian value. Rather, they are models in the sense that they schematize a whole series of behaviors.

THE SUBSTITUTION MODEL

The substitution or cancellation model holds that what is really important in what liberation theology proposes is liberation and, fundamentally, socio-economic-political liberation. Preaching and bringing about the kingdom of God are directed towardss such liberation, since, once achieved, liberation will be able to open itself to other values. What is now most necessary, and consequently most important, is to achieve the revolutionary triumph. When it is a question of survival, all else, even matters of faith, can go on hold. If it makes sense in any case to become anathema for one's brothers and sisters, it is precisely in working for their liberation, to which one must subordinate everything else. To add a theological defense of this position, it can be said that no one has greater love than those who give their life for others. So one can be serving Jesus even without knowing that he is in the hungry, in the imprisoned, in the persecuted and, ultimately, in the poor. From this perspective, the moment can arrive when it becomes necessary not only to break with the institutional church and, with much greater reason, to disobey its prescriptions when necessary, but even to give up cultivating faith practices, insofar as this cultivation can impede or curb the revolutionary struggle. In this model's extreme version, if being a revolutionary and being a Christian are exclusive of each other, one must opt for being a revolutionary, since this is the more fundamental ethical demand and the more imperative mandate in a world where injustice, exploitation, and domination prevail. Liberation theology has already done much in introducing us to the political struggle. What the pastoral attention ought to do [derived from the substitution model] is prepare the best practitioners to leave the ministry of the word and become promoters of liberation. Such persons would be effective doers of those actions that really liberate peoples, which is the ultimate objective both of religious activity and of political action. This presumes, of course, a complete subordination to the political organization of the church organization—both of the grass-roots communities and of other ecclesiastical structures. It also converts subordination of faithfulness to the institutional church to faithfulness to the revolutionary movement. Such a pastoral program thus favors the substitution of political experience and values for Christian experience and values.

This extreme can be reached by one of two ways: either by partisan pressure, which in the long run sees Christian faith as a brake on the revolution; or by the practical pressure of the revolutionary class struggle which Leninism claims to be the best theoretical and practical antidote to the absurdities of religion. At the bottom of this whole process there is a revolutionary secularization of the gospel's subversive principles and values. Faith can be the initial pedagogue to awaken the people from dogmatic sleep and immobility, but that is at best a transitory state which, ideally, must disappear and which is to be tolerated only so long as it does not conflict with the dictates of the party. In the most positive interpretation [by the substitution model], the revolutionary struggle is the dialectical transcending of faith which is subsumed in the higher study of the revolutionary process, once its limitations have been negated and its dynamisms used. What comes after the antithesis in the synthesis is what comes after faith in the revolutionary process.

THE SUPPORT MODEL

The support and contribution model maintains the autonomy of faith and provides that this faith be energized and developed, but it does everything possible to put this energized and developed faith at the effective service of revolutionary movements or, more generally, at the service of the socialist process. This model does not urge explicitly that liberating faith be engaged on behalf of the historical revolutionary process in such a way that this engagement exhaust its reason for being. But this support model does consider that one of faith's important missions is to promote the struggle for justice and that this cannot be done effectively except by opting for some one of the political movements. Such movements are to be helped religiously and politically, and limits are set accordingly by whatever criticisms faith might offer.

In this model, it is not enough to place oneself autonomously at the service of the poor and oppressed, or even to place oneself at the service of the revolutionary process from an independent position. Instead, one would have to seek to place oneself at the service of that concrete organization which in each case proves to be the vanguard of the revolutionary process. What faith and even the institutional church might do autonomously for the poor and for the revolution is not much valued. The preference in this support model is for development of the forces that can really take power or keep themselves in it, overlooking the failings that the struggle for political power necessarily brings with it. Ideally, this is not considered to be a manipulation of the faith, at least in principle. The promotion of justice through a political option need not be separated from faith, nor even less need it entail a diminishment of faith. Rather, both in principle and in ideal, the more vigorous and incarnated that faith is, the greater will be its contribution to the cause of justice. Besides, the partisan choice is made from faith.

Indeed, initially faith does stimulate the concerned to political commitment; secondly it stimulates to revolutionary political commitment wherever structural injustice is the defining characteristic of the situation; finally it stimulates to effective actions and, therefore, support of those undertakings that can combat injustice and institute a new social order. It is faith that keeps one from belonging to parties that justify the status quo, in one form or other, and it is faith that gives one the stimulus to put oneself at the service of the parties that combat the status quo and that try to substitute for it whatever will support the causes and rights of the people. This can be a personal option, by choosing to integrate oneself fully into a political party or into a revolutionary movement where one can then try to arouse its transforming effort without giving priority to seeing that gospel values are present in the means and immediate objectives. It can also be a group option. For example, when a base community or an aggregate of them chooses as a group to place itself at the service of a determined political organization, but without abdicating its Christian vocation. Such a group option involves dedicating all its temporal actions to supporting its chosen priorities. Political commitment can also be an institutional option, done when a part or all of the institutional church confronts established political power by aligning itself with some other social or political option. This was the case with the Polish hierarchy who more or less openly confronted the communist régime by supporting the Solidarity union. . . . In all these cases, the efforts are not to create a dissident critical Christian element within a party or revolutionary movement. Instead these groups would favor what is held in common rather than what is different, and what they would add to them rather than what they would subtract from them.

THE SOCIAL COLLABORATION MODEL

The social collaboration model is based on the conviction of what is specific to faith and to the institutional church and what their limitations are. What is specific to faith and to the church is not the promotion of those political and technical aspects that, while necessary to establish the kingdom of God in history, do not exhaust the constitution of the kingdom and are not an immediate concern for the believer as believer or for the church as church.

The political and technical aspects of the kingdom of God [in history]—as well as those that pertain to science, culture, play, and such—are objects of faith, not formally, but only as they favor or disfavor the proclamation of the kingdom of God. To put it in a way that is inexact in its exclusiveness but correct in its aim, one could say that in the unity of the kingdom of God "that God be the king" (that is, that the kingdom should be God's), is the objective of salvation (or liberation). But how the kingdom is to be fashioned, as a socio-historical reality, is the objective of history. In the history of salvation the dynamisms of history and the dynamisms of salvation are united for good and for ill. Between them there is a structural mid-point so that they are mutually co-determined to the degree that the unity, rather than the elements that constitute it, is the kingdom of God and the history of salvation. But this does not prevent those elements from being distinct and from needing to remain distinct so that this unity may have the richness and the authenticity integral to it. Attending only to the political element—but the same would be valid in a different degree for other elements, such as the scientific area, the technological, the cultural, and so on—it can be said that it determines and is determined by the Christian element, whatever way that determination may be realized. But the political element does not therefore mix with or sustain the Christian element. Still less is the political element realized by the characteristics and the dynamisms of the Christian element. What is political, while being political, determines and is determined by what is Christian, while being Christian. The determination between the political and the Christian elements is not in the form of parallelism or necessarily in the form of causality, although to simplify the question it could be accepted that there is a certain interaction.

Accepting this explanatory scheme based on structural unity and on the co-determination of various elements, which are not simply "elements" but "elements of" the structural unity—although they are not the pure unity of the "of" but rather something that has its own proper characteristics because it is such an element—we can understand why the social collaboration model, without interrupting its unity with what is political, still is not blended with it and is not situated on the same plane.

This is more obvious inasmuch as salvation (or liberation) refers to persons, and in that there is no special problem. Persons must be liberated from sin, from concupiscence in its many forms (of the flesh, of money, of power). That is, persons, in their interiority and in their personal communication with others, must become each a new creature, each a new human being, each concretely another Christ, in such fashion that in the new life it is no longer the old self but Christ who is the principle of life, of modes of being and of modes of acting. From this point of view, the difference between the contribution of what is Christian and the contribution of what is political becomes measurable. But this is also verifiable in the collective dimension of faith beyond the personal or interpersonal dimension. Human beings who have been liberated as Christians can do much for the revolution or for social change; but the social mission of faith and of the institutional church is not reduced to that. Let us examine this.

It cannot be denied that the institutional church is a social force. Leaving aside entirely for the moment the question of faith, it is an institution formed of millions of people linked together in a hierarchical order and with its own doctrine and multiple channels of action vis-à-vis other social forces. This social power has frequently led it into the temptation to become a political force. To be better understood, if we make a division between what is proper to society and what is proper to the state (never mind whether this way of putting it is quite precise or is relevant to the present times; also, we could speak, instead, of civil society and political society), we must say that the institutional church should be situated formally in the area of the social, in the area of civil society. On the other hand, if we also make a division between what is political power and what is social power, that is, between the power that comes from, goes to, and is in the complex state structure and the power that comes from, goes to, and is in the complex social structure, then we must say that the institutional church must be situated formally in the area of social power. So, the social collaboration model, through which faith and the institutional church want to contribute to the realization of the kingdom of God and, concretely, to the social change demanded by structural injustices, holds that the institutional church is and must be a force that moves directly and formally in the area of the social and not in that of the state. And it holds that the church must resort to social power and not to political power to realize its mission.

The church and faith can have their own distinct efficacy in shaping the social. It is not just that the church is in itself a social force which, when wielded evangelically, is simply the carrying out of its mission; it is that if the church proposes also to be a political force, it is like the salt that loses its flavor—whether dominating other political forces or putting itself at their service. Without expanding on the reasons why this happens—and that it has always happened ought by now to be a forewarning—one can appeal to that essential statement in the gospel [when Christ] asserts that the Son of Man has not come to be served but to serve and that therefore the Son of Man and his disciples ought not to act like the lords of this world who try to dominate. These words indicate the profound difference between political power and social force, between the dynamic of domination and the dynamic of liberation, between the ambition of wielding authority and the submission of service. Efficacy need not be renounced for this reason, but efficacy in this case comes from social pressure, through the word and the gesture, and not from managing political power. Conflict will doubtless come about when this social pressure is exerted wholly and entirely on behalf of the mass of the people and the people's movements with their consequent clashes with the dominant classes and structures. But it will not be a conflict resulting from acting against anyone; rather it will be a conflict resulting from acting on behalf of the oppressed mass of the people. This is a labor of partiality that does not exhaust all that should be done in other undertakings, but it is a labor proper to the church as a social force and a labor in which the power of faith contributes something that cannot be replaced. Examples like that of Archbishop Oscar Romero, with his church of San Salvador, show that this model has its unique distinctiveness and effectiveness.

With this approach, the specificity and autonomy of faith and of the institutional church are saved. Neither the church nor any part of it, not even a Christian as a Christian, is to be subordinated to any political enterprise and, of course, not to any government. This is especially valid of the church as an institution and of its distinct parts, not excluding the base communities. Social commitment in support of justice is one thing, but subordination to other organizations, especially those of a political kind, from whom orders or assignments to action are received, is something else. It may be that an act or a line of action determined independently by the church or by parts of it favor one organization more than another, but this should be a consequence, not a principle. It is not acceptable to identify the option in favor of the poor as coincident with an option in favor of the revolution, nor the option for the revolution as coincident with the option for a particular revolutionary organization, nor the choice of a particular revolutionary option as coincident with the option for a particular vanguard. To presume these options to be equivalent is a mistake that bears enormous consequences.

There is a strict gradation, and the church's formal commitment, on the basis of the gospel, must be to the mass of the people, while its commitment to other steps is conditioned by its continuing discernment. Only in exceptional cases does the occasion arise for the institutional commitment to go beyond favoring the structural changes demanded by the mass of the people for realizing their own liberation. Archbishop Romero used to warn about the possibility and danger of making absolutes of popular organizations, and of the danger of subordination to any popular organization as if it were an absolute.

Only distrust in the historical efficacy of faith can lead one to abandon its growth in order to be dedicated to the growth of other enterprises. Those other political enterprises are necessary, as are also those that are scientific, technological, and so forth. Faith has something to say about them, sometimes a word of reproach and at other times a word of encouragement. Faith can launch one onto strictly political work inasmuch as politics can be understood as a more universal way of living out charity. But it is difficult to find a case in which it is more beneficial for the people, the mass of the people, that the church abandon its preaching and the fulfillment of the faith for a political commitment. There is so much to do in the social dimension, and so much pressure can be exerted on the political from the social dimension, that one should not easily fall into the temptation to transform the social dimension of faith into a political one. Politics, after all, moves on the suprastructural level, while social action moves on the level of human subjects as well as on the structural level. Life expresses itself more in the social than in the political, and the social presents both a more natural place for the church and a lesser temptation as well. However, resorting to social action is not done by way of separating oneself from the world or by shunning commitment. Social action is not a way to fortify the church or avoid dangers for it; rather it is a way to contribute to the historicizing of the kingdom of God, that is, a way to realize historically what concerns are proper to the church and what human beings most need. Strict separations cannot be made. It is rather a question of accents. But accents are important.

This attention to what is social instead of to what is political is rooted in the social, nonpolitical character of the institutional church as

well as in the "more real" character of the social, that is, in the fact that
the participative character of human beings is expressed more in and
through the social rather than the political. For example, there is the
whole area of labor unions and of the educational scene, where faith can
promote and inspire styles of action in an effective way. Although there
is a nominal possibility of Christian-inspired parties and governments,
in reality this does not happen and it entails a great danger of manipulating Christianity. There can be Christian-inspired politicians, but it is
unlikely that Christian-inspired parties and governments, still less con-
fessionally Christian ones, can be authentically Christian. Rather, it is
more feasible, although not easy, to develop relationships with social
forces so as to stimulate and guide them by means of Christian inspiration. All this will ultimately have effects in the political sphere, where
pressure should be exerted by acting as a social force and through social
forces.

Liberation theology and Marxist movements.

The purpose here is not to discuss the relation of liberation theology
to Marxism in a general way. This has already been done on repeated
occasions, and furthermore, it exceeds the scope of this discussion. What
I am doing here, by way of example, is to place the liberation theology
movement in relation to the various Marxist-oriented social and political
forms that propose socio-historical change in Latin America.

Liberation theology has arisen in good measure among those experiencing the human disaster that the prevailing different forms of capitalism have created in Latin America. This experience is in its immediacy
an experience of the unjust poverty and even destitution that afflict the
greater part of the population. It is primarily an ethico-religious experience, such as Moses had when he realized how his people lived in
Egypt. He imputed their plight to the oppression by the Pharaoh and,
more generally, to the oppression by the dominant class of Egypt. Liberation theology in Latin America also imputes the plight of the oppressed
to the rich and powerful. It is a plight that makes the poor cry out with a
cry that reaches to heaven.

It is an ethico-religious imputation, referring more perhaps to persons than to structures, more to personal wills than to social laws. The
"rich" are seen as the ones responsible for the condition of the "poor,"
not only because they do not help them as they should—a traditional
point in the usual historical preaching of the church—but because they
are seen in one way or another as directly responsible for the poverty
and as actually causing it. Hence the spontaneous ethico-religious reaction of aligning oneself with and for the poor and, only as a consequence, against the rich.

This fundamental and founding experience [of human disaster] is accompanied by a theory that proposes to explain the phenomenon scientifically and that offers not only an alternative to it, but one way to overcome it. This is what Marxism does propose; but it is the part of Marxism that explains capitalism's mechanisms of exploitation, that proposes a different economic system with its corresponding political system, and that contrives a revolutionary praxis able to overthrow the capitalist system and introduce the Marxist system. In addition, say these theorists, experience shows that only the Marxist movements are doing anything effective to end the stage of capitalist exploitation. From this comes the conclusion that those who desire to do something effective towardss overcoming injustice and liberating the mass of the people must take advantage of what Marxism is doing both in the theoretical and in the practical areas. Thus, at first the advantages of Marxism's contributions were appreciated more than the difficulties, both immediate and mediate, that could issue from it.

At first, liberation theology advocates, in their eagerness to be of service to the liberation of the mass of the people, became radically anticapitalist, and in this their positions coincided with Marxist positions. Meanwhile, the universal church in its social teaching had also gradually been convinced that a capitalism unmodified by moral principles was a veritable plague on humanity. Both Vatican II's *Gaudium et Spes* (Vatican Council II, 1975) and later papal encyclicals have pointed out capitalism's excesses with growing insight and severity. But, far from thinking of capitalism as intrinsically bad, these document writers tried to see in it the appropriate model for the democratic development of peoples. Thus, it must be corrected, it must be reformed according to the teachings of Christian morality, but capitalism does not have to be abolished. All the more so [they said], since real socialism, the other alternative, has seemed to the church much worse, especially for the church itself, but also for peoples. The condition of the North Atlantic capitalist countries has been compared with that of the countries where socialist régimes have been imposed. From this, the conclusion drawn was that in every respect what went on in the former was incomparably better than what went on in the latter, the socialist countries. Little attention was paid to what went on in the rest of the world, where disastrous economic, social, and political conditions resulted from other forms of capitalism. From all this it was thought that a reformed capitalism would be the appropriate system to resolve the problems and that such a system would provide the best context in which the church's being and its mission could be consolidated. So it can be said that the church's social doctrine thus stated is an attempt to reform and humanize capitalism.

But the liberation experience in Latin America was different. Capitalism in its historical realizations appeared in Latin America not only as intrinsically bad, but also as contrary substantially to the gospel. This capitalism was irreformable. It could be made to produce lesser evils, but it could not be conceived as the ideal model in which human beings would be really human and in which the mass of the people would hold the position they deserve in God's eyes. The idea that capitalism is good for the strong and so the weak, as the strong get richer and distribute some of their wealth, can take advantage of it—this is not according to the gospel. The gospel way, what the kingdom of God demands, is to develop a system in which the mass of the people, the poor, are the true subjects of history, if not because they are poor, at least because they represent the majority of peoples and the majority of humanity. [Thus in Latin America] there was real experience of capitalism and its evils and not real experience of socialism and its evils. The result is that liberation theology, instead of seeking and favoring a reform of capitalism, strove to achieve a reform of socialism. Socialism was thought of as a system more advantageous for the cause of the poor and, consequently, in virtue of its preferential option for the poor, as more in keeping with the historical realization of the kingdom that Christian faith must promote.

Thus the anticapitalist position becomes a prosocialist one. First comes the anticapitalist position, the perception not only by experience but by reason that the ills of Latin America come not from the hardness of heart of the wealthy but from the very structure of the system, both in its internal, local configuration and in its connection with world capitalism, especially with that of the United States, which sets itself up as the political and military guardian of that arrangement. Thus, anticapitalism leads to anti-imperialism directed against United States imperialism. The liberation of Latin America must be not only a liberation from the capitalist system but also a liberation from United States domination. Supporting anticapitalist and anti-imperialist processes thus becomes one of liberation theology's modes of historical action. It thus arrives at an obvious collaboration with Marxist revolutionary movements that are entirely devoted to that same task, even though defects both in Marxist theory and practice are noted in liberation theology. However, and in consequence of the foregoing, the liberation advocate is one who *is* anticapitalist but one who *is* not anticapitalist in the same way the pro-Marxist is, still less like one who *is* a Marxist. Liberation theology and the movements that are under its inspiration *is* and *are* Christian, although their different attitudes and the various models vis-à-vis social change can lead them to certain practical deviations that in the long run can transmute their reality. But in such case they will have abandoned what liberation theology is. Hence it is not right to impute to liberation theology what no longer belongs to it.

THE BIBLICAL POOR AND THE OPPRESSED CLASSES

One of the points on which there tends to be convergence is the question of the poor in the case of liberation theology and of the oppressed classes in the case of Marxism. Here class struggle becomes an item of coincidence. It is thought that liberation theology's concern for the poor, when it is a matter of looking for a way to be really effective, ought to incline naturally towardss interpreting the biblical category of the poor as a class and, to be consistent, it should also incline towardss favoring a political practice that involves class struggle. That latter is essential to Marxism, at least in its more orthodox form. However, certain clarifications need to be made so as to avoid simplisms. Perhaps care has not always been exercised in this matter and, although liberation theologians have not usually been guilty of confusion, there may have been confusions and also exaggerations in some practical actions and in some grass-roots movements.

First of all, it is not out of place to recall the famous text of Karl Marx that refers to class struggle:

> As for me, I do not deserve credit for having discovered the existence of classes in society or the struggle between them. Long before me, bourgeois historians had already explained the historical development of this struggle, and bourgeois economists had explained its economic anatomy. What I have contributed that is new has been to demonstrate: 1) that the existence of classes is only joined to determined historical phases of the development of production; 2) that class struggle leads necessarily to the dictatorship of the proletariat; 3) that this same dictatorship is of itself merely a transition to the dissolution of all classes and to a classless society. (Marx, Letter to Joseph Weydemeyer, 1852).

The text implies that classes and class struggle come about historically in a certain spontaneous manner that pre-Marxist authors had already discovered as a certain law of history. This point is important because liberation theology would agree with this understanding, neutral up to a point, which says that indeed there are classes and class struggle. To which liberation theology adds that the situation in Latin America shows that it is the dominant classes who have initiated the struggle and the violence, not only by forming the dominated classes but by keeping them under domination. Thus the incipient historical responses of the dominated classes are simply that—responses to a preceding, ongoing violence, responses provoked not only by the objective condition of the dominated classes, a condition defined by destitution and injustice, but provoked also by the perception that their condition is due to the violence being committed against them.

From Marxism, then, liberation theology has appropriated the idea that this phenomenon first of classes and then of class struggle is found specifically in a definite historical phase of the development of production. In the case of Latin America this historical phase is still the present phase, something that perhaps is not true in the more developed countries, where production has followed other courses. From Marxism also liberation theology has appropriated the idea—and this is very much in consonance with Christian inspiration—that it is necessary to arrive at the abolition of classes, leading to a classless society, such as the one that the biblical message forcefully proclaims in metaphorical language.

All these points of convergence may incline us to conclude that the poor whom the Bible speaks about are the proletariat that Marx speaks about and that, consequently, the way of liberation for the poor is *per se* through a dictatorship of the proletariat. However, more mature and critical liberation theology does not accept these propositions. Between saying that the biblical poor are the dominated classes (understood as a socio-historical category, whether by bourgeois or Marxist thinkers) and asserting that the biblical poor have nothing in common with those classes, there is another position. Liberation theology holds that much more differentiated position.

The biblical poor have many material similarities with the oppressed classes, but they are not identified with them *per se* for the following reasons: **1)** although the majority of the biblical poor and the reason for their poverty have much in common with the oppressed classes, the biblical concept of the poor is wider and, concretely, cannot be identified with the proletariat strictly understood; **2)** God's special preference for the poor is not reduced to their purely socio-economic liberation, but attends to their personal condition and to their historico-transcendent liberation; **3)** the poor of Yahweh, even having as they do a strict socio-historical reality, are not reduced to being a socio-historical category; **4)** the poor, in order to contribute fully as agents to their own integral liberation and that of others, without abandoning their historical condition, must incorporate the spirit of the Christian message so that they will be genuinely poor-with-spirit [that is, *not* dispirited and *not* degraded]; **5)** although there can be stages coincident with the oppressed social classes in the historical struggle, what the oppressed classes alone can accomplish through their revolutionary struggles is not sufficient either for integral liberation or even for exclusively historical liberation; **6)** that such coincidence can hardly be sufficient, even though the dictatorship of the proletariat as it has historically occurred is through the actions of those in the vanguards of the political parties.

DIFFERENCES BETWEEN LIBERATION THEOLOGY AND MARXIST POLITICS

This differentiated position leads to practical conclusions. Liberation theology can do no less than approve and in many cases support those Marxist movements that are genuinely revolutionary and not purely bureaucratic, especially in the concern they show and the work they do for the poor, both when it comes to denouncing the oppressions of the capitalist system and when it is a matter of effectively managing to overcome the various forms of destitution, injustice, and oppression. This is true especially in the case of popular organizations, for which Marxism and power taking are not essential elements but rather instrumental aspects of the struggle to make the mass of the people the agents of their own historical destiny. But, at the same time, liberation theology cannot help differentiating itself from Marxist policies, and this in various ways. Liberation theology will aim, first of all, at strengthening the mass of the people in their faith. This does not imply weakening their social commitment, but it does imply that they are to become responsible as a distinctive people preferred and chosen by God to realize history an integral liberation that goes beyond an exclusively political approach. In this way there is an autonomy that must be respected. Liberation theology will also try to strengthen the contribution of Christian faith to social change, because, even without being subordinated to any political enterprise, faith, those who live that faith, and the church of the faithful have their own power, which must be independently placed at the service of the historical realization of the kingdom. Finally, liberation theology will urge political and/or social movements that say they are serving the oppressed classes, to do so in fact and as a first priority and not to subordinate their service to their own institutional consolidation. And liberation theology will urge them to adjust their choice of means and their hierarchy of values to what Christian faith sets forth as the spirit of every possible liberation.

With these differentiated principles, liberation theology removes the political and ideological anathema that weighs on Marxism and on any of the other progressive positions in many circles in Latin America, including many broad popular sectors. It also strives to work with Marxism in a positive way. This cooperation does not extend to accepting Marxism's more philosophical doctrines insofar as they may relate to a closed materialistic system. Rather, it is limited in the theoretical area to the heuristic use of the scientific analysis of socio-historical and specifically economic questions contributed by Marxism. Thus, in practical matters liberation theology is dedicated to promoting everything positive that may be found in popular movements and liberation movements, without forgetting to criticize whatever may be bad in them or to encourage those elements that can be bettered. Thus a clear distinction is made from other positions within the church, and this constitutes one of the points of debate vis-à-vis liberation theology. But for that debate to be useful, it cannot be carried out by caricaturing liberation theology's global position, as happens in the first of the instructions from the Sacred Congregation for the Doctrine of the Faith on liberation theology (1984). Marxism has not disfigured the interpretation that liberation theology makes of the essential points of the Christian message, and liberation theology does not maintain a naive position before the political practice of the various Marxist movements. Rather, it moves with distinct nuances and different tendencies in the setting here described.

Liberation theology and violence

Critics associate liberation theology not only with class struggle, but also more specifically with revolutionary violence. Incitement to hatred extends and radicalizes class struggle they say, and hence revolutionary violence becomes the characteristic weapon for the masses seizing power. Hatred, class struggle, and revolutionary violence are seen not only as tolerated in liberation theology but also as provoked by it. However, if this is not quite so simple in regard to Marxism, it is much less so in regard to liberation theology.

DEIDEOLOGIZATION OF VIOLENCE

Contrary to this portrayal by its critics, liberation theology arises from a profound experience of both the general condition of and the acts of violence as they make up the social framework of Latin America; and it proposes with all its power to transcend that state of affairs and get rid of this violence. From this standpoint, liberation theology strives to be an undertaking that de-ideologizes violence; it refuses to accept the principle that violence is bad, however generated. One can certainly accept that every act of violence, every act that does some evil through force, is not good; but one can immediately add that violence is preached and asserted in many ways and that by no means are all these ways univocal or, still less, uniform. Some instances of violence are worse than others. Classical moral teaching, which takes such pleasure in distinguishing species and nuances among sins from many viewpoints, ought to use the same precision when speaking about the distinct gravity of the different forms of violence. Liberation theology proposes formally and, in the last analysis, that every form of violence be transcended, that violence in all its forms be eliminated—disappear. But it does not therefore allow the most serious forms of violence to be reinforced under the pretext that all violence is bad. Instead, it asks questions about the distinct forms of violence and their effects, according to the criterion and the perspective from which it focuses on problems, which is the preferential option for the poor, the plight of the mass of the people.

From this perspective, which is completely consonant with the message of the Bible, liberation theology concentrates first on the kind of violence that weighs upon the mass of the people in the form of structural injustice. This is the injustice that affects the whole of political, social, economic, cultural, and other structures in which people necessarily have to live and which by their very structuring keep them from living humanly. It is not just that these structures do not make it easier for them to live a humane life, but also that they hinder it by depriving people by force, which is often legalized and institutionalized force, of the means that are indispensable for living as human beings.

Oppression in all its forms and, speaking more generally, every kind of structural injustice, is the worst form of violence, because it affects the majority of the population and does so in what is most sacred and profound: the preservation and improvement of life itself. And it is the worst form of violence even though it presents itself in modes and manners that lack the dramatic effect apparent in other forms of violence. Liberation theology sees as violence and as a source of violence everything that it calls social sin which, in the Latin American context, is in great part the result of the prevailing capitalism—both in the center-periphery, North-South relationship as well as in the corresponding reflection within each country. The principal reflection of this violence, but not the only one, is the condition of poverty and destitution that fundamentally affects, not only the quality of life, but the very fact of living.

Repression is also part of this structural violence. When it is not just an ideological fakery staged for the sake of image and propaganda and becomes police repression or repression carried out by death squads, it tends to show up in extreme forms that often destroy its victims subjectively and objectively. The state of violence that prevails by reason of structural injustice cannot be maintained except by the unjust force of added violence. This repression tries to hinder the struggle against injustice by taking preventive measures. It unleashes state or class terrorism when revolutionary movements have arisen or even before that, when popular protest has begun against conditions that are becoming unbearable. Popular protests arise from the galling inequality between the few who have everything and the many who have almost nothing, but it also comes about because of the mechanisms of accumulation and exploitation that have generated these inequities. To describe it this way is not an academic fantasy; it comes from observation of the forms in which violence is found among many of the peoples of Latin America.

Liberation theology makes this situation its primary datum. It not only perceives that it is a reality that profoundly affects the greater part of the population, especially in the poorer countries, but it stigmatizes it as a most grave sin. What Exodus portrays as the great cry of a people reaching to the presence of Yahweh, as a growing demand for liberation, liberation theology portrays likewise, seeing the situation of Latin America in the same terms. The reading of Exodus as one studies this analysis leads one, first of all, to understand as primary justice the longing for liberation of this people which is so very oppressed and repressed. In the second place, it leads one to search as Moses did for those effective means that can bring liberation. But at the present time there is a historical separation of Moses' two dimensions, the political and the religious. Liberation theology places itself rather in the religious dimension, but it seeks a relationship with the other, the political dimension, which in its radicality is now maintained only by the revolutionary movements.

VIOLENCE THAT OPPRESSES AND VIOLENCE THAT LIBERATES

Liberation theology, then, accepts in principle the morality and even the Christian congruity of the violence that liberates from the other, more radical, forms of violence, provided that it take place in the proper context and with the proper conditions. In this it follows classical morality, only in a more rigorous and restricted form, in that it permits certain forms of violence only in the face of structural, repressive, and oppressive violence. The violence of structural injustice, especially when it goes to the extremes of preventing the achievement of human life and closing off all less violent means of seeking redress, is a supreme evil that can and even must be combated with effective means, including armed struggle. In its characterization of evil, liberation theology puts into relief the social character of structural injustice more than its political character (tyranny), to which classical moral teaching usually referred, considering that the social is more defining than the political. But, in spite of armed struggle's limited licitness, it is always an evil, and it can only be used in proportion to the greater evil that is willed to be overcome. Its evil is to be measured above all in relation to the short and long term harm that most will suffer. And when the good of the mass of the people is subordinated to the taking or the keeping of political power by a revolutionary movement, the right to armed struggle is invalidated.

On the other hand, not just any violent means can be employed. There are means that are so intrinsically and totally wrong that their use is forbidden. Hence revolutionary violence must never take the form of terrorism. By terrorism is understood the category of actions performed against helpless persons in a violent way, placing their life or physical integrity in danger. Something is not terrorism because it emanates from groups previously described as terrorists; terrorism and terrorists are to be measured by the actions actually committed. From this standpoint, even legally established governments can be in the strict sense terrorists in a distinct degree. Revolutionary movements also fall frequently into the temptation to commit terrorist actions.

It is likewise not acceptable to propagate hatred in any of its forms as a subjective condition favorable to revolutionary violence. The enemy do not cease to be human persons because one wants to liberate them from their role as oppressors or violent repressors. The hard task of loving the enemy, including the social enemy, remains a challenge for the Christian. Of course, a class as such is not a person that can be loved or hated, but there is a danger of introducing into the rejection of a class the rejection of the persons that belong to it. Revolutionary struggle must not make one forget that the gospel is more in favor of peace than of war, more in favor of service than of domination, more in favor of love than of confrontation.

It is possible that liberation theology has at some times and in some places been somewhat naive about revolutionary violence's real possibilities and about its mixture of good and evil. It can be accepted that the revolutionary changes needed in Latin America cannot be attained without traumatic movements. The whole body social and politic is now organized towardss the welfare and the dominance of the dominant elite and towardss the service of the imperial powers. If urgent, drastic changes are desired, this involves transformations that will encounter very strong resistance. In these cases it is not easy to pass from ethical necessity to political possibility. The revolutionary triumphs in Cuba and Nicaragua made a global revolutionary change seem imminent in all of Latin America, or at least in some countries. The failures in Argentina, Uruguay, Chile, Bolivia, and Brazil, the ferocious bloodshed in Colombia and Guatemala, the harshness of the struggle in El Salvador, have shown that one must not be politically naive. Religious fundamentalism can lead to social suicide.

On the other hand, the use of force to remain in power, as well as poor economic performances, are making liberation theology more cautious. Certainly, régimes that are only slightly reformist are not bringing even minimal liberation to the mass of the people. Neither are the political democracies generating social democracies or even a break in the circle of destitution and structural injustice. For all these reasons, although liberation theology tends to sympathize more with popular organizations and revolutionary movements, it does not because of this degenerate into the simplism of identifying its utopian aim with the concrete forms that these both take. Perhaps liberation theology can accept certain revolutionary processes as a lesser evil and maintain a position of critical vigilance and balanced support before them, but it cannot descend into facile simplifications that ignore the relativity and the peccability inherent in the persons who direct these processes, as well as the complexity of the set of social processes that a national project implies.

By way of conclusion

Liberation theology, in point of fact, has had and continues to have a momentous political significance. That is how it is seen in the Rockefeller Report (1969), in the Santa Fe propositions (Council for Inter-American Security, 1980), and in the constant attacks that we see it endure from conservative forces outside and inside the church. Such forces reckon that, although it may not be by itself a force capable of transforming the condition of Latin America through revolution, it can still become an important factor in the combination of forces that make up the revolutionary movement. And some of the Marxist movements have even removed the "sanbenito" label of the opium of the people from the faith that liberation theology defends. These even ascribe a positive role to faith in the liberation struggles.

Such recognition is not unfounded. Faith, religion, and the church continue to be especially significant and influential elements in the social fabric of Latin America, especially among the poorest. If faith and the church take an outright stand on the side of the people's cause, if intra-ecclesially and extra-ecclesially they implement the preferential option for the poor and stop conservatively supporting the established order, something important will have been achieved. Medellín and Puebla alerted the reactionary forces who calculated correctly what a change so substantial in the church and in its preaching could signify for the continent. The partisans of national security have called this a Marxistizing of faith and Marxistizing of the church, because everything that conflicts with the dictates of their theory of national security and with the demands of capitalism is branded as Marxist. These accusations are not only verbal. In the last ten years many people have been murdered in an effort to force the church and its more avant-garde bishops, priests, and lay people to abandon their new stance of denouncing injustice and of encouraging movements that advocate justice or revolution. But that has not stopped the movement. Liberation theology continues to expand and consolidate as a strictly theological movement, but also as pastoral praxis. In both, it continues to contribute to social change in Latin America.

This advance and consolidation continues in two areas. The first is within the church—not without enormous resistance. This area is decisive. If the Latin American church as such could really be gotten to take the same course as Medellín and Puebla, not only would it be profoundly transformed, becoming much more evangelical and more evangelizing, but it would become a very important force for the advance of liberation and for liberation in conformity with gospel values. The other area calls for synchronizing this force with the people's liberation needs. The way to do it has not always been found, a way that joins short- and long-term efficacy to respect for characteristic Christian selfhood and for the relative autonomy of that selfhood. It is a hard problem, for which a once-and-for-all answer has not yet been given. There are still hesitations and discussions. Much already written about the points we are treating in this exposition as well as previous and various practical attempts does not coincide with what we have detailed here. But this is not the time to analyze other positions. What has been written is sufficient to outline the problem and to put some fundamental questions into proper perspective. What is finally important is to save the fullness of the revealing and liberating message of God in Jesus Christ and to achieve its full efficacy in history, in the conviction that the better the first undertaking is developed, the more effective will be the second; but also in the conviction that praxis is necessary—that is, the realization in history of the kingdom of God so as to achieve the fullness of that message theoretically, experientially, and efficaciously. Things have begun to move. What is important now is that the new spirit not be stifled. For the moment, there is still hope that this will not happen.

Ignacio Ellacuría

2. *Utopia and Prophecy in Latin America**

TRANSLATION BY JAMES R. BROCKMAN, S.J.

Utopia and prophecy, if presented separately, tend to lose their historical effectiveness and become idealistic escapism; and so, instead of becoming forces for renewal and for liberation, they are at best reduced to functioning as a subjective solace for individual persons or for whole peoples.

That is not the case in the classic manifestations of prophecy and of the great utopian concerns. It is not so in the Bible of course, but neither is it so in other significant events of the history of salvation. However, a real danger must be acknowledged. It repeatedly happens that utopia and prophecy are separated and both prophecy and utopia are disincarnated, whether by subjectivist reductionism or transcendentalist reductionism. They are read in a timeless cipher of eternity. However, Christian eternity is inexorably linked to temporality ever since the Word became history.

To achieve an adequate conjunction of utopia and prophecy, however, it is necessary to situate oneself in the proper historical place. Every conjunction of these two human and historical dimensions, if it is to be realistic and fruitful, must be situated in precise geo-socio-temporal coordinates. Otherwise the unavoidable thrust of the principle of reality disappears, and without it both utopia and prophecy are a mental game, more formal than real. But some historical places are more favorable to the emergence of prophetic utopians and of utopian prophets. It is said that in cultures that have grown old there is no longer a place for prophecy and utopia, but only for pragmatism and selfishness, for the countable verification of results, for the scientific calculation of input and output—or, at best, for institutionalizing, legalizing, and ritualizing the spirit that renews all things. Whether this situation is inevitable or not, there are nonetheless still places where hope is not simply the cynical

---

*Ellacuría (1989b); see the Bibliography in the back of this book.

44

adding up of infinitesimal calculations; they are places to hope and to give hope against all the dogmatic verdicts that shut the door on the future of utopia and prophecy and the struggle.

One of these places is Latin America. At least, this is a preliminary supposition that I shall return to. For the moment, I can point to facts such as revolutionary movements and liberation theology. In the case of Latin America not only can the theoretical relationship between utopia and prophecy be better historicized, but the general outlines of a utopian future of universal extent can also be marked out through a concrete exercise of historical prophecy.

To think that utopia in its own intrinsic formality is something outside of every historical place and time supposes an emphasis on a single characteristic of utopia to the neglect of its real nature as it is found in the thought of those who have been true utopians in one form or another. There is no escape from the historicity of place and time, although neither is it inevitable to remain locked into the limits of a certain place and a certain time. Neither can it be said that the best way to universalize prophecy and utopianism is to try and abolish or escape every limiting conditioning. In themselves, prophecy and utopia are dialectic. Prophecy is past, present, and future, although above all it is the present facing the future and the future facing the present. Utopia is history and metahistory, but above all it is metahistory, although springing from history and inexorably referring to history, whether it be by way of escape or by way of realization. Hence our need to place our feet firmly on a fixed earth in order not to lose strength as Antaeus did when he was lifted off the ground.

That is what I propose to do here, by setting forth prophecy as method and utopia as horizon in the historical context of Latin America, from an explicitly Christian perspective in regard both to prophecy and to utopia.

Christian utopia can only be constructed from prophecy, and Christian prophecy must take into account the necessity and the characteristics of Christian utopia.

The historical concretion of Christian utopia is not settled in advance and even less *a priori*, and only a concrete Christian utopia is operative for historicizing the kingdom of God. This global affirmation includes a whole set of affirmations, which I am not going to anticipate here, since my development will explain their meaning and justification. Such affirmations are: (a) that there is a general and undefined Christian utopia; (b) that this general utopia must be concretized in historicosocial terms; (c) that this utopia is in relationship with the kingdom of God; (d) that the kingdom of God must be historicized; (e) that the kingdom of God is made operative by actually working towards a concrete utopia.

THE KINGDOM OF GOD AS UTOPIA

Certainly, Christian utopia, arising from Christian revelation, from tradition, and even from the magisterium, has certain characteristics without which it cannot be called Christian. For example, a utopia that means to be Christian cannot set aside the prophecy of the Old Testament (prophets and nonprophets), the Sermon on the Mount, the Last Supper discourse, the book of Revelation, the primitive community, the fathers of the church, the great saints, or certain conciliar and papal documents. But the importance of these or other characteristics, their joining together to form a whole, their historical realization in each time and place, is not only an evolving problem but an open-ended one. Solutions to the problem must be attained by means of an option which, when all is said and done, is an option by God's people, whose organic character has priority over the hierarchical (Rom. 12:4-8; 1 Cor. 12:4-31), and in whom there is room for many charisms, functions, and activities, some more pertinent than others in defining the observable historical characteristics of Christian utopia.

This utopia can be called general and universal, because it possesses certain minimums that cannot be absent, at least in the intention, and because it points towards a universal future with an eschatological outcome. This utopia must be concretized precisely to bring the kingdom of God closer. Up to a certain point, Christian utopia and the kingdom of God can be considered the same, although when one speaks of Christian utopia one accents the utopian character of the kingdom of God and not its other characteristics. But the concretion of utopia is what historicizes the kingdom of God, both in the hearts of human beings and in the structures without which that heart cannot live. This is not the time or place to develop the idea, much treated by liberation theology, that a historicizing of the kingdom of God must be achieved in the personal, in the societal, and in the political. Although liberation theology has historicized the kingdom in its own way, all of the church's tradition has always tried to do this. If one reads, for example, *Gaudium et Spes* (Vatican Council II, 1975) or the various papal encyclicals on the church's social teaching, one sees there the need to historicize, if not the kingdom, at least the faith and the Christian message. Whether this be done with greater or lesser prophetic and utopian vigor, the need to do it is still recognized.

The question, then, is how better to achieve that concretion, accepting the fundamental proposition that the general and universal utopia is already proclaimed and promised, so that its concretion not only cannot negate it or supersede it but must live by it, although creatively, because the same Spirit that animated it in its earlier and foundational dynamisms keeps on making new dynamisms possible. The reply points towards Christian prophecy. Prophecy, rightly understood in its complexity, is at the origin of the universal and general utopia. That same prophecy is needed for the concretion of utopia, a prophecy that will need the help of other instances—for example, that of the magisterium—but cannot be replaced by them. Without prophecy there is no possibility of making a Christian concretion of utopia and, consequently, a historical realization of the kingdom of God. Without an intense and genuine exercise of Christian prophecy, the concretion of Christian utopia cannot be arrived at theoretically, much less practically. Here too the law cannot replace grace, the institution cannot replace life, established tradition cannot replace radical newness of the Spirit.

PROPHECY: CONTRASTING THE KINGDOM OF GOD WITH A PARTICULAR HISTORICAL REALITY

Prophecy is understood here to be the critical contrasting of the proclamation of the fullness of the kingdom of God with a definite historical situation. Is this contrasting possible? Are not the kingdom of God and historical realities with their worldly projects two radically distinct things moving on different planes? The reply to this objection or question, although complex, is still clear. The fullness of the kingdom is not identified with any personal or structural project or any determined process, but it is in necessary relationship with them. One need only see how the Old and New Testaments approach the matter. There can be, according to the case, greater importance given to the transcendent than to the incidental, to the inner than to the outer, to the intentional than to realizations. But one of the two aspects must always be there. The kingdom of God is, after all, a transcendent history or a historical transcendence in strict parallel with what the life and person of Jesus is, but in such manner that it is the history that leads to the transcendence, because indeed God's transcendence has become history ever since the beginning of creation.

The fullness of the kingdom of God, which implies that all of the kingdom of God and all of the projection of the kingdom of God be taken into account, must be placed in contrast with a definite historical situation. For example, if the kingdom proclaims the fullness of life and the rejection of death, and if the historical situation of human beings and of structures is the kingdom of death and the negation of life, the contrast is evident. The contrasting of a historicized kingdom makes manifest the limitations (lack of divinization or of grace) and above all the evils (personal, social, and structural sins) of a definite historical situation. Thus, prophecy, which initiates this contrasting, is able to predict the future and to go towardss it—assuming indeed that there is the general vision of the kingdom previously alluded to, which God's revelation has been making known to humanity in various ways. In this manner, which could be called dialectical, the desired future is sketched as a way of reaching beyond the present, reaching beyond the limits and the evils of the present, which are historical limits—as a future more and more in accord with the demands and dynamisms of the kingdom. In turn, the present, reaching beyond the announced and hoped-for future, helps to surpass those limits and those evils.

HISTORICAL COMMITMENT

When prophecy is conceived thus, it is seen how necessary it is so that utopia not become an abstract evasion of historical commitment. "*Religious* misery is, on the one hand, the *expression* of real misery and, on the other, the *protest* against real misery. Religion is the sigh of the oppressed creature, the heart of a heartless world, just as it is the spirit of a situation without spirit" (Marx, 1844). But, if this is so, it does not have to become the opium of the people, as the same text of Marx goes on to call it. If it is more a protest than a mere expression, if it is more a struggle than a mere comfort, if it does not remain a mere sigh, if the protest and contrast become historical utopia which negates the present and impels into the future; if, in short, prophetic action is initiated, then history is made by way of repudiating and surpassing and not by way of evading. Thanks to prophecy, utopia does not fail to be efficacious in history, even though it is not fully realizable in history, as is the case with Christian utopia. If it were not realizable at all, it would run the almost insuperable risk of becoming an evasive opium; but if it must achieve a high degree of realization and is put into close relation to prophetic contradiction, it can be what animates correct action. A utopia that is not in some way what animates and even effects historical realizations is not a Christian utopia. It is not even an ideal vision of the kingdom; instead, it is an idealistic and ideologized vision of itself. For example, if nothing is done towardss turning swords into plowshares but it is only dreamed about evasively, utopia fades away. Instead of fighting against the arms race, it becomes a bucolic expenditure of leisure time. This is not the intention or the reality of utopia and of Christian prophecy.

But if utopia cannot really be Christian utopia without prophecy to inspire it, neither will prophecy be really Christian without the animation of utopia. Christian prophecy lives by Christian utopia, which, as utopia, lives more and is nourished by the intercession that the Spirit makes throughout history. But, as Christian, utopia lives more by the proclamation and the promise that are explicitly and implicitly expressed in the revelation already given. A prophecy that did not take into account the proclamation and the promise already given would be ill-prepared to contradict evil. And especially such prophecy would be wholly unprepared to put together a historical design of something that would try to respond to the concrete demands of the kingdom of God, such as it has been proclaimed from of old, but especially by the historical Jesus.

Priority in the fullness of Christian action is to be attributed to the revelation and the promise of Jesus, even in the destructive phase of prophecy. This is still more valid when what is sought is to realize God's will or designs, for whose discernment both the Spirit of Christ and the historical outlines of Jesus of Nazareth's march through history are indispensable. It almost seems tautological and unnecessary to say that the Christian character of utopia cannot be given in fullness except from Christian faith explicitly accepted and lived, although without ignoring either that the Spirit can make use of Christians who are not formally such and even of anti-Christians, like Caiaphas, to announce and realize some fundamental features of Christian utopia.

It happens, however, that what is given must be actualized, in Zubiri's meaning of the term.* (For him, *actualizar* does not primarily mean to update or make conform to current style, as it generally means in Spanish.) To actualize means to give present reality to what is formally a historical possibility and, as such, what can be taken or left, what can be read in one way or another. What must be actualized, then, is what is given; but the reading and interpretation of what is given, the option for one part or other of what is given, depend on a historical present and on historical subjects. The historical actualization of the already given utopia arises especially from the intercession (signs of the times) that is being given through the Spirit in history. But these signs of intercession are historical, even though what is signified by them transcends the merely historical. The Spirit once again has priority for that transcendence, but in inseparable relationship with historical concretions. This is valid for the interpretation and even more so for the realization.

Indeed, utopia has a certain idealistic character that is ultimately unrealizable, but at the same time it has the character of something asymptotically realizable in a permanent process of approximation and, therefore, it implies theoretical and practical mediations taken more from the *categorial*** dimension of history. It is, of course, a Christian utopia that is under discussion, and thus it maintains very explicitly the transcendent dimension of the kingdom. But even this dimension cannot be formulated apart from what is categorial, even in the most strictly evangelical formulations. It is not only or primarily a language problem—the kingdom as a banquet, as a field of labor, and so forth—but of something deeper, of the unavoidable need to make the kingdom's transcendence historical. This is easy to see in the moral recommendations related to daily life, but it also refers to political and social objectifications—cases about soldiers, about authorities, about laws,

---

*Note: Xavier Zubiri (1898–1983), a Spanish philosopher, was Ellacuría's teacher. His influence on Ellacuría's thought is significant. For a brief overview and bibliography of his work, see *The Encyclopedia of Philosophy* (1967), vol. 8, pp. 282–83.

**Ellacuria's Spanish reads *categorial* (*de la historia*) throughout this article, not the more familiar "*categórico*." J.B.

about social customs, and so on. Such cases occur not only in all of the Old Testament but also in the New.

And so, it must be unitarily sustained that the Spirit's intercession in history is needed in order to hit upon the transcendent character of the categorial and to categorize the transcendent interpretively and practically. It is by means of the true and the false, the good and the bad, the just and the unjust, and so forth, unitarily valued from what is faith as gift received and as daily practice, that the transcendence of the historical is grasped and, in turn, something that is unitarily historical and suprahistorical is projected and realized transcendently. What prophecy gathers and expresses is the historico-transcendent intercession of the Spirit, which makes present the utopia already offered and contrasts it with the signs of the times. Thus prophecy and utopia, history and transcendence, nourish each other. Both are historical and both are transcendent, but neither becomes what it is meant to become except in relation to the other.

Latin America today is a privileged place for prophecy and utopia, although so far the actualization of its prophetic and utopian potentiality is far from being satisfactory.

It is not a willful or arbitrary affirmation to designate Latin America at the present time as a privileged place of utopia and prophecy. Its own reality and some of its achievements prove it.

As a reality, it is a continent with particular characteristics like those attributed to the Servant of Yahweh. This condition makes it like other regions of the world, almost the greater part of the world's regions. It is a region ill-treated ever since the armed conquest made [four centuries ago] by Spanish Christendom. Without losing its human heart, it nonetheless has its face disfigured, almost unrecognizable as human except in its pain and tragedy (Is. 52:2-12); it has, besides, almost lost its own identity as a people (Hos. 1:6-9; 1 Pet. 2:10). But that identity, which in great part shapes it as an objective reality, contains a very active protest awareness and, more specifically, a very live, Christian liberation awareness. All this places it in an excellent position to exercise a strong theoretical and practical prophecy. This is confirmed by its great and significant achievement in this regard with its recent martyrs and prophets, who have arisen everywhere in every stratum of the people and of the church. Latin America is a region whose great potentiality and wealth of resources contrast with the state of destitution, injustice, oppression, and exploitation imposed upon a great part of the people. This provides an objective basis for the contrast of utopia, found in its rich potentiality, with prophecy, already present in the negation of utopia by the everyday reality. The ceaseless revolutionary movements in the political area and the Christian movements in the religious area are distinct ways that a powerful collective utopian and prophetic awareness has reflected and apprehended the objective reality.

Consequently, Latin America struggles both outside and inside the church in a powerful attempt to break its chains and build a different sort of future, not only for itself but for all humanity. The conditions suffered in its own flesh, along with its effective protest, constitute trustworthy evidence that convicts the historical world order, and not only the international economic-political order. By negation these are a proclamation of a different order. The actual truth of the present-day historical arrangement is cruelly reflected, not only or principally in the fringes of destitution and, especially, of degradation in the wealthy countries, but in the reality of the third world, consciously expressed in Latin America's many-sided protest.

That truth demonstrates the impossibility of reproducing and, especially, of enlarging the present historical order significantly. It demonstrates, even more radically, its undesirability, since this present order cannot be universalized. It brings with it the perpetuation of an unjust and predatory distribution of the world's resources, and even of each nation's resources, for the benefit of a few nations. The result is that prophetic and utopian Latin America does not seek to imitate those who today are in the forefront and position themselves on top. Rather, it seeks a different order in the objective and in the subjective, an order that will allow a humane life not only for a few but for the greater part of humanity. The developed world is not at all the desired utopia, even as a way to overcome poverty, much less to overcome injustice. Instead, it is the sign of what should not be and of what should not be done.

This historical movement is reflected inside the church as something qualitatively new. The preferential option for the poor, understood in a radical and effective way in which the poor are those who take the initiative dynamically, can, first of all, transform the church radically, and it can thus become the key to and the energizer for what a Christian utopia must be as a historical liberation project. Such a movement is reflected already in the different theoretical and practical forms of liberation theology, which in itself is an effective kind of prophecy for animating a new historical Christian utopia. That is why it is feared both inside and outside the church.

But the privileged place that Latin America is for prophecy and utopia must not lead to the illusion that all of it or all of the Latin American church is presently exercising the prophetic-utopian mission. Latin America in its entirety is shaped by the same "sin of the world" that affects the rest of humanity. The "structures of sin" prevail there, and Latin America is not only the passive subject that endures them but the active subject that produces them. The modes of realizing the capitalist pseudo utopia and, in far lesser degree, the socialist pseudo utopia prevail in the makeup of the society and peoples of Latin America. The

economic as well as the social, political, and cultural modes of capitalism are reproduced and aggravated in Latin America because it consists
of dependent societies, the kind that have to leave the waste products
from their operations within their own boundaries instead of sending
them elsewhere, as more powerful nations try to do. There are no reforms of capitalism in Latin America, although some attempts at reforms of socialism have begun. Nowhere is the preferential option for
the poor in force, or anything beyond the dynamism of capital and the
demands of the international order. A way has not even been found for
the primary subject of the processes to be the dominated and oppressed
people. But it is not right to lay all the blame for all the ills of Latin
America on others, because such an exoneration either legitimates or
covers up behaviors and actions that are totally blameworthy. The systems, the processes, the leaders, even though dependent, still assume
and even take advantage of the wrongs of their dependence.

Neither is the whole church in Latin America, nor even a large part
of it, fulfilling its vocation of utopian prophecy. Scandalous as this is in a
situation like Latin America's, a continent where injustice and faith live
side by side, a great many Christians, including religious, priests, bishops, cardinals, and nuncios, not only lack the prophetic charism but contradict it and even set themselves up as adversaries and persecutors of
prophecy and as favorers of the structures and forces of domination, so
long as these structures and forces do not put their institutional advantages and privileges in jeopardy. Although the part of the church that
performs an anti-prophetic and anti-utopian task is not a majority in the
institutional church, nonprophecy and even distrust of any form of
prophecy do prevail. Prophecy tends to be confused with the misnamed
parallel magisterium. If the preferential option for the poor is taken as
the touchstone, a certain nominal respect for it can be seen after long
struggles, but the hierarchy has done little to put it into practice. If the
criterion is the stance taken towards the liberation theology movement,
there has been some formal improvement, but distrust continues, if not
more subtle forms of attack.

However, even though there are these negative aspects, it cannot be
ignored that, as was said earlier, there has been a flowering of utopia
and of prophecy in Latin America, situating its people and in some way
its church in a vanguard position for defining what is to be its mission in
the present-day world. This cannot be seen from an abstract place, still
less from a place incarnated in the structures of the dominant world.

*Latin America's utopian prophecy points towards a new form of
freedom and humanity through a historical liberation process.*

The very reality of Latin America, especially when seen from the
vantage point of Christian faith, constitutes a radical prophetic protest

against the international order, both in its North-South confrontation and in its East-West confrontation. It is also a protest against the attitude, behavior, and expectations promoted by those in the cultural vanguards and the models previously proposed as ideals of freedom and humanity.

DEPENDENCY

The clash of interests in the North-South and East-West conflicts makes most countries in the world more and more dependent and systematically impoverished. In particular, it gets them into a loss-of-identity process through the pull towardss imitation, which reinforces their dependency and even slavery. This is not to deny that there are in the advanced capitalist and socialist countries valuable theoretical and practical principles that can and should be assumed critically and creatively by other countries. Simply going back to a supposed primitive state is impossible and can lead to multiple forms of dependency. Furthermore, it is impossible to escape the only real history, that of interdependence, in which all peoples must necessarily play a part. But the imperialistic form in which North-South, East-West relations exist must be rejected for the good of the countries that suffer it and for the good of the countries that impose it.

This is an indictment made very clearly by dependency theory and then by liberation theology. It has been understood and expressed prophetically by John Paul II in *Sollicitudo Rei Socialis*, following Paul VI's *Populorum Progressio* (Paul VI, 1967) and Vatican II's *Gaudium et Spes* (Vatican Council II, 1975): "Each of the two blocs harbors in its own way a tendency towards imperialism, as it is usually called, or towards forms of neocolonialism: an easy temptation to which they frequently succumb, as history, including recent history, teaches" (John Paul II, 1987, #22).

A phenomenon as dramatic as Latin America's external debt is one of the clearest symptoms, both in its origin and in the way its payment is demanded, of how unjust is the relationship and how deadly is the harm done to peoples, when supposedly the desire is to help them (De Sebastián, 1987). In general, it can be said that the present type of relationship between the powerful and those who are not as strong is making a few countries or social groups richer, while the majority are made poorer and the breach between them widens and becomes more serious. In the case of the foreign debt, it can be seen concretely how the originating loans were often made one-sidedly and with the complicity of governments and the upper social classes yet without any benefit whatever for the mass of the people. But the demand for payment of these debts weighs especially heavily on the common people whom it deprives of the possibility of escape from their poverty through harmonious development. It favors the interests of capital much more than the demands of labor, thus contradicting a basic principle of humanity, the priority of work over capital, and a basic principle of the Christian faith, the priority of the many poor over the few rich. The world thus comes to be ruled by the lack of solidarity, mercy, and concern for others, and hence shaped and formed by injustice and opposition to the gospel. It shows itself as the patent and verifiable negation of the kingdom of God proclaimed by Jesus.

CRITIQUE OF CAPITALISM

In particular, Latin America's actual situation points out prophetically the capitalist system's intrinsic malice and the ideological falsehood of the semblance of democracy that accompanies, legitimates, and cloaks it.

It is customary to ask why the voices of Latin American prophecy do not denounce the socialist politico-economic forms of the socialists and tend instead to design utopias of an anticapitalist type. The factual reason is that prophecy currently devotes itself to present evils and these, for the most part, are due to capitalist forms of domination. The evils of the socialist systems, both in the economic and the political arenas, appear in situations like those in Cuba, Nicaragua, and some revolutionary movements. But, excluding extreme cases like that of Shining Path in Peru, the evils of the socialist systems cannot begin to compare with the dimensions and degrees of the evils of the capitalist system in Latin America. Hence, historical prophecy is directed mainly to rejecting capitalism rather than socialism.

The church, previously more inclined to condemn socialism than capitalism and readier to see in the latter correctable defects and in the former intrinsic evils springing from its very historical essence, today tends to place both systems on an equal footing at least. "As we know, the tension between East and West is not in itself an opposition between two different levels of development but rather between two concepts of the development of individuals and peoples, both concepts being imperfect and in need of radical correction. . . . The church's social doctrine adopts a critical attitude towards both liberal capitalism and Marxist collectivism" (John Paul II, 1987, #21). But local prophecy should be centered, by its very nature, on the negation of what is in fact the cause of the evils that affect a determined reality.

In regard to capitalism especially, once it passed through its stage of pitiless exploitation in the Western countries, permitting the first accumulation of wealth, its intrinsic malice has been observed in all its magnitude only beyond the boundaries of the rich countries, which in numerous ways export the evils of capitalism to the exploited periphery. The problem is not just that of the foreign debt or the exploitation of raw materials or the search for third world sites to dispose of the wastes of all sorts that the more developed countries produce. More than that, it is an almost irresistible pull towardss a profound dehumanization as an intrinsic part of the real dynamics of the capitalist system: abusive and/or superficial and alienating ways of seeking one's own security and happiness by means of private accumulation, of consumption, and of entertainment; submission to the laws of the consumer market promoted by advertising in every kind of activity, including the cultural; and a manifest lack of solidarity in the individual, the family, and the state with other individuals, families, or states.

The fundamental dynamic of selling one's own goods to another at the highest price possible and buying the other's at the lowest price possible, along with the dynamic of imposing one's own cultural norms so as to make others dependent, clearly shows the inhumanity of the system, constructed more on the principle of *homo homini lupus* than on the principle of a possible and desirable universal solidarity. Predatory ferocity becomes the fundamental dynamic, and generous solidarity remains reduced to curing incidentally and superficially the wounds of the poor caused by the depredation.

The fact is that 170 million now live in poverty of the approximately 400 million inhabitants of Latin America. Poverty levels in the third world are not the same as those in the first world; those in the latter would be levels of affluence in the former. (A family of four with an annual income below $10,000 is classified at the poverty level in the United States.) Of the 170 million in poverty, 61 million live in extreme poverty. To overcome this situation, $280 billion would be needed, equivalent to 40 percent of the gross domestic product of Latin America. But this is so difficult as to be almost impossible, because debt service produces a net export of capital, without counting capital flight, which is estimated to be much greater than all the investment and foreign aid received by the whole region. This reality, fomented both by international capitalism and by the capitalism of each nation and due not to the will of persons but to the structure and dynamics of the system, is an overwhelming historical proof of the evils that capitalism has brought about or has been unable to avoid in Latin America.

On the other hand, the ideologized propaganda about capitalist democracy, as the only and absolute form of political organization, becomes an instrument of cover-up and, at times an instrument of oppression. Certainly, in the democratic package come values and rights that are very much worth taking into account, especially if they are carried out to their final consequences and real conditions are created for enjoying them. But the ideologized operation of the democratic model seeks, not to let the people determine their own political and economic model, but to cover up the imposition of the capitalist system and, especially in the case of Central America, the imposition of United States interests. Democracy is supported only insofar as those interests are presumed to be furthered.

Hence, more regard is paid to national security by the United States than to the self-determination of peoples, or to international law, or even to respect for fundamental human rights which are defended derivatively so long as they do not endanger the military and police structures. It is in these military and police structures that confidence is placed for the defense of United States interests rather than in any democratic structure. Thus it becomes a point of honor to have elections involving awful decisions affecting millions of people and to assure the enjoyment of certain civil rights that can only be actively exercised by the economically privileged who have sufficient resources, while much less vigor is shown in demanding an end to murders, disappearances, tortures, and such. Undercover actions by the CIA are even undertaken, involving not only illegal actions but outright terrorist practices.

CAPITALISM CANNOT BE UNIVERSALIZED

But what is most serious is that the offer of humanization and freedom that the rich countries make to the poor countries is not universalizable and consequently is not human, even for those who make it. Kant's keen way of putting it could be applied to this problem: *Handle so, dass die Maxime deines Willens jederzeit zugleich als Prinzip einer allgemeinen Gesetzgebung gelten koenne* (*Grundlegung zur Metaphysik der Sitten*, 421). If the behavior and even the ideal of a few cannot become the behavior and the reality of the greater part of humanity, that behavior and that ideal cannot be said to be moral or even human, all the more so if the enjoyment of a few is at the cost of depriving the rest. In our world, the practical ideal of Western civilization is not universalizable, not even materially, since there are not enough material resources on earth today to let all countries achieve the same level of production and consumption as that of the countries called wealthy, whose total population is less than 25 percent of humanity.

That universalization is not possible, and neither is it desirable. The life style proposed in and by the mechanics of development does not humanize, it does not fulfill or make happy, as is shown, among other indices, by the growing drug consumption which has become one of the principal problems of the developed world. That life style is motivated by fear and insecurity, by inner emptiness, by the need to dominate so as not to be dominated, by the urge to exhibit what one has since one cannot communicate what one is. It all supposes only a minimum degree of freedom and it supports that minimum freedom more in externals than internals. It likewise implies a maximum degree of unsolidarity with the greater part of human beings and of peoples of the world, especially with the neediest.

And if this type of historical law, which proposes to go on shaping our times, has scarcely anything of what is human and is fundamentally inhuman, it must even more clearly be said to be anti-Christian. The Christian ideal of finding happiness more in giving than in receiving— and still more than in seizing (Acts 20:35)—more in solidarity and community than in confrontation and individualism, more in personal development than in accumulating things, more in the viewpoint of the poor than in that of the rich and powerful, is contradicted and hindered by what is in practice, beyond the enunciated ideal that commits to nothing, the real dynamism of the present-day models.

CRITIQUE OF THE INSTITUTIONAL CHURCH

From the reality of Latin America there also comes a prophetic protest against the way the institutional church is structured and behaves. The Latin American church has been too tolerant of the conditions of structural injustice and institutionalized violence that prevail in the region. Above all, until recently, the universal church itself has been blind and mute before the responsibility of the developed countries relating to that injustice.

Certainly since the time of the conquest, examples can be found of prophecy both in the church's rank-and-file and in its hierarchy. But at the same time those willing to overlook wrongdoing have been preponderant, showing greater concern for personal and institutional interests than for the oppressed mass of the people and for the kingdom of God. In our own days, Medellín and Puebla, despite their great merit and value, have had little real effect on church structures and behavior. The behavior of martyrs like the bishops Romero, Valencia, Angelelli, and others, although it is not completely rare and exceptional and has been accompanied by that of dozens and even hundreds of men and women—lay people, religious, and priests—is very significant and encouraging. But it is far from being the norm, and it is still seen as "dangerous" and not quite normal.

The universal church, always prompt to condemn Marxism, has been more tolerant of the evils of capitalism, even in its most damaging imperialist forms. There are clear advances by Vatican II and by the recent popes in this respect; very estimable also are some positions taken by the bishops of the United States in regard to their government's stance towardss the Latin American peoples. But it was practically necessary for *Sollicitudo Rei Socialis* (John Paul II, 1987) to appear in order to make things finally clear after the grand impulse given in this respect by the promulgation of *Gaudium et Spes* (Vatican Council II, 1975). However, what has been achieved on the doctrinal plane has scarcely progressed to that of pastoral orientation and to producing a more decidedly prophetic attitude. The church that lives in the wealthy countries does not denounce with sufficient vigor the exploitative conduct of these countries towards the rest of the world. It preaches mercy rather than justice, thus leaving aside one of the central themes of historical prophecy. The fear is still of the evils of Soviet imperialism rather than of the evils of U.S. imperialism, and so the present evils generated by the latter are preferred and tolerated over the potential evils that might come from the former.

Neither has the church made a minimally sufficient effort in Latin America to inculturate itself in a situation very different from that of the North Atlantic countries. It is still thought that there is a historical continuum between the rich countries and the poor countries, and more attention is paid to the unity of language or learning than to the profound gap between the state of economic development and to the position occupied in the international economic order. There is a question here of two distinct inculturations, or two sources of profound diversification which inculturation ought to take into account. On one side is the tremendous difference of cultures, of fundamental modes of being, originated by a complex series of factors (racial, psychosocial, linguistic, educational, and of every sort). On the other side is the likewise fundamental difference in the gross national product and in per capita income, which makes impossible [for Latin America] many of the cultural modes of the wealthy countries. It is not just a question of the indigenous or colored populations but of something that affects the whole continent, if we interpret the continent by looking at the mass of the people. Institutionally, the mentality is still that when it comes to theological thought, forms of religious practice, the world of rituals, and so forth. Latin America is still considered an appendage to Europe and a prolongation of Rome's Catholicism, whereas it is a new reality and, what is more, the majority reality of the Catholic Church.

This very reality is one that itself becomes a prophetic denunciation. It summons to a profound transformation of the way the church sees itself and understands its mission. To ignore this summons, having recourse to the presumed unalterability and universality of the faith and of Christian institutions, is to ignore the Spirit's voice of renewal, which always appears along with some degree of prophecy. This prophecy points out the limitations and evils that the institutional church has picked up as dead weight on its way through history. History has been fundamentally the history of the rich, dominant, and conquering peoples, not the history of the poor peoples, which should have been the fundamental matrix of the church but was lost from the times of Constantine. Although an important remnant of the gospel did not fall into the trap of riches or power and always remained alive, and in the most vivid forms, it has always been poorly tolerated.

The prophecy of denunciation, on the horizon of the kingdom of God, marks out the ways that lead to utopia. Prophecy's *no*, prophecy's negation pointing beyond, in itself generates utopia's *yes* by virtue of the promise that is the kingdom of God already present among human beings, especially ever since the life, death, and resurrection of Jesus, who has sent his Spirit across death to renew all people and all things.

THE PRINCIPLE OF UNIVERSALIZATION

The negation of reductive particularism leads to the affirmation that only a new global project that is universalizable can be acceptable for humanity. Independently of all ethical or theological consideration, the basic principle remains valid that any world order or conception that generates a constantly greater number of people in poverty, that can only be maintained by force and by the threat of humanity's total destruction through increasing ecological destruction and nuclear annihilation, that generates no ideals of qualitative growth, and that gets entangled with constraints of every kind is not acceptable. Out of purely selfish considerations, where the self is all of humanity and likewise the self of each individual, such a world order is nonviable in the long run without the viability of humanity's self. Substantial changes in the conception and in the dynamism of such so-called progress are necessary.

But beyond all selfish realism and realistic selfishness, it is clear that a world order favorable for a few and unfavorable for most is something that dehumanizes and dechristianizes each person and humanity. From a human viewpoint, actions and projects must be measured by the classic "I am human and nothing that is human is foreign to me," meaning that whatever alienation, action, or omission makes another human being a "foreigner" breaks down the humanity of the one who so behaves. From a Christian viewpoint, one is not to pass by the wounded person on the roadside, for then one refuses one's neighbor—the opposite of the "foreigner"—and that is the denial of both the second and the first of the commandments that the Father has renewed in the Son.

The principle of universalization certainly is not a principle of uniformization and, still less, of uniformization imposed from a powerful center on an amorphous and subordinated periphery. That, however, is the way to universalization proposed by those who wish to impose the model of existence that at the moment is more favorable to them. This uniformization is today ruled above all by the laws of the economic marketplace and is a most forceful statement that materialism, not historical but economic materialism, is what determines all else in the last analysis. Contrary to this a universalism must be generated that does not reduce but enriches, so that the entire wealth of peoples may be respected and developed, and their differences seen as the completion of the whole and not as the clashing of the parts. In this way, all the members will complement one another, and in this complementing the whole will be enriched and the parts strengthened.

Universalization must result from the preferential option for the poor, for the universalization resulting so far from the preferential option for the rich and powerful has brought more ill than good to humanity. Until now, the historical world order and the church's institutions have been universalized from a preferential option for the rich and the powerful. In the secular order it has been made by the strong for the strong, and this has brought some advantages in scientific, technological, and cultural advances. But these rest upon great evils for the majority, who are sometimes forgotten and at other times exploited. Also, the church has become worldly. That is, it has followed this fundamental behavior of the "world" and has shaped its message and even its institutions more from the standpoint of a power that dominates and controls than from that of a ministry that serves. Both the secular order and the church have lived by the principle so contrary to the gospel, that devoting oneself to the rich and behaving so as to favor the more powerful is how the mass of the people, how humanity, is better served and how the gospel is better spread. Ecclesiastical pomp in imitation of royal pomp, the establishment of a state political power, submission to the laws of the marketplace, and so forth on the church's part show how it has submitted to the worldly principle that the option for power and for the powerful is what best secures institutions.

Now, this is not the Christian viewpoint. From the Christian viewpoint it has to be affirmed that the poor are to be not only the preferential passive subject of those who have power, but the preferential active subject of history, especially of the church's history. The Christian faith affirms—and this is a dogma of faith that cannot be contradicted under penalty of gravely mutilating that faith—that it is in the poor that the greatest real presence of the historical Jesus is found and therefore the greatest capacity for salvation (or liberation). The fundamental texts of the Beatitudes and of the Last Judgment, among others, leave this point settled with total clarity; many other things are affirmed as dogma with much less biblical support. How this historical subjectuality should be concretized and how it should be exercised is a question open to theoretical discussion and historical experimentation. But it does not for that reason cease to be an operative principle of discernment to ask oneself always what is most needed by the mass of the people so that they can really achieve what is due to them as human beings and as members of God's people.

THE POOR-WITH-SPIRIT

In Latin America prophecy puts more emphasis on the active and organized poor, on the poor-with-spirit, than on the passive poor—that is, the poor who suffer their destitution with resignation and hardly notice the injustice they suffer. It does not deny the importance, even the prophetic importance, that belongs to the poor by the simple fact of their being the poor, for there is no doubt that as such they enjoy Jesus' special predilection and his very particular presence. But when those poor spiritually incorporate their poverty, when they become aware of the injustice of their condition and of the possibilities and even of the real obligation they have in the face of destitution and structural injustice, they are changed from passive to active subjects and with that they multiply and strengthen the salvific-historical value that is theirs.

There is a further argument for searching for the new universal ideal of human being and of Christian, for the new ideal of world and of humanity coming out of the mass of the people (secular version) and out of the poor (Christian version). In reality, they represent the greater part of humanity. This means, again, from the negative-prophetical view-point that many of the various past civilizations have not been really human but rather class and/or nationalist civilizations. From the pro-phetic-utopian viewpoint it means that the goal unavoidably must be the development-liberation of every human and of all humans—but un-derstanding that "all" humans are those who in some way condition the "all" of each human and that those "all" humans are mostly the poor. Until now, development-liberation has not been that of all of the human being nor is it going in that direction, as is shown in the fact that, far from leading to the development-liberation of all humans, it has led to the underdevelopment-oppression of most of them. This is a long histor-ical process, certainly, but the question is whether we are going in the right direction or instead are going towardss man's dehumanization and dechristianization.

In Latin America this prophetic march towardss utopia is driven by a great hope. Beyond all rhetoric and in spite of all the difficulties, there are rivers of hope on the continent. Christian hope thus becomes one of the most efficacious dynamisms for going out of the land of oppression and towards the land of promise.

HOPE

This march from oppression to promise is sustained on hope. It is re-ceived as grace (there would not seem to be many motives for hope, in view of the enormous problems and difficulties in taking hope as some-thing natural), but it goes on being nourished historically and growing in the praxis of liberation. It is a verifiable fact that hope, which ani-mates the poor-with-spirit, inspires them in long and hard processes that to others seem useless and futureless. It is a hope that appears, therefore, with the characteristics of hope against all hope—a very Christian characteristic—although once it appears it is nourished by the results already achieved. It is not the secure reckoning that leads to making an investment with the calculated expectation of desirable fixed-term results; it is not an idealistic dream that removes from reality. Rather, it is the accepting of God's promise of liberation, a fundamental promise that propels to an exodus in which historical goals and objec-tives unite with transhistorical certainties.

In contrast to the emptiness of nonmeaning found in a life that tries to fill itself with activities and purposes without deep meaning, Latin America's poor-with-spirit are a real and effective sign that in the pre-sent-day world there are tasks full of meaning. Thus, in a real criti-cism—that is, criticism from hope-filled reality—of hopeless reality, of the confusion between being entertained or amused and being happy, between being occupied and being fulfilled, space opens for another form of life completely different from the one imposed today as ideal in a consumer society, a society for which improvements are proposed without consistency and without greater meaning. That space is traveled by the poor-with-spirit in a new Christian disposition, which leads to giving their life for others, so that in giving it they find it and they find themselves. It leads to being able to despise all the world, whose conquest means nothing if it means the loss of oneself, of the spirit of oneself (Mk. 8:34-38 and parallels). It leads to emptying oneself to find oneself again after the emptying in the fullness of what one is and of what one can be (Phil. 2:1-11).

The hope of the poor-with-spirit in Latin America—probably in other places also—is something qualitatively new. It is not a question of absolute despair that leads to a type of active desperation in persons who can go ahead and lose everything because they have nothing to lose but the all-nothing of their own lives—which have become unlivable. It is not despair, but hope. Hence, the attitude and the actions are not desperate actions, but attitudes and actions that arise from life and that seek a greater life. This is a verifiable fact in thousands of men and women in refugee camps, in marginal communities, among the thousands of displaced persons, people for whom often it is not "political spirit" moving them but "Christian spirit" animating them. That spirit will have to be historicized and politicized in order for it not to evaporate in fruitless subjectivisms, but politicization is not what is first nor is it what is fundamental.

This hope that arises from life, that arises together with the promise and with the negation of death, is celebrated festively. The sense of fiesta, as it exists in these poor-with-hope, indicates for now that they have not fallen into the fanaticism of desperation and of struggle for the sake of struggle. But neither do they fall therefore into the error of the fiesta purely for amusement that characterizes the Western world—fiesta lacking in meaning and lacking in hope. Fiesta is not a substitute for missing hope; it is the jubilant celebration of a hope on the march. The more or less explicit search for happiness is done in other ways, which do not simply mistake for it the forgetfulness drugged by consumerism or the mere consumption of entertainment. It is not simply in leisure where fulfillment is sought but in the gratuitous and gratifying labor of distinct liberating tasks.

In the search for a historically universalizable utopia, in which the poor, or the mass of the people, will have a determining role, and from the hope that urges them towards utopia, one glimpses a new revolution with the prophetic motto "begin anew." To begin anew a historic order that will transform radically the present one, based on the promotion and liberation of human life, is the prophetic call that can open the way to a new utopia of Christian inspiration.

"To begin anew" does not mean the rejection of all of the past, which is neither possible nor desirable, but it does mean something more than just setting out to make things new in linear development with the previous. It means a real "beginning anew," since the old, as a totality, is not acceptable, nor is the principial dynamism that drives it acceptable (Zubiri).

Even in the most radical of revolutions, total rejection of the past is not possible and is not desirable, because it deprives humanity of possibilities without which it would find itself obliged to begin from zero—which is impossible. In addition, not all that has been achieved is bad nor is it intrinsically infected with evil. There are elements of every type, scientific, cultural, technological, and so forth, whose malignity comes not from their essence but from the totality in which they are enlisted and from the finality to which they are subordinated. There are certainly unacceptable elements, but this is not sufficient to advocate an impossible and sterile nihilism. In this sense, "begin anew" supposes neither previous annihilation nor creation of a new world from nothing.

But neither is it just a matter of making new things; rather, it is a matter of making all things new, given that the old is not acceptable. This belongs to the essence of utopian prophecy. The "if you are not born anew" (Jn. 3:3), the incorporation in the death that gives life (Rom. 6:3-5), the seed that needs to die to bear fruit (Jn. 12:24), the disappearance and destruction of the old city so that the new one can arise in a different world (Rev. 18:1 ff.; 21:1 ff.), and so many other Old and New Testament proclamations offer and demand a radical transformation. For in the Christian interpretation of the new life, death always intercedes as mediation. Certainly, the good news is a message of life, but a message of life that assumes not only the reality of death but the positive validity of the negation of death. To die to the old man, to the world that is past, to the former age, and so on, is a fundamental part of the biblical message. Christian prophecy can go against one or other concrete fact, but in addition and above all it goes against the totality of any historical order where sin prevails over grace. As negation and as affirmation, Christian utopian prophecy proposes to make a radically new human being and a radically different world.

ABUNDANT LIFE

The fundamental principle on which to base the new order remains "that all might have life and have it more abundantly" (Jn. 10:10). This is the utopian cry coming from historical prophecy. The historical experience of death, and not merely of pain, of death by hunger and destitution or death by repression and by various forms of violence, which is so living and massive in Latin America, reveals the enormous necessity and the irreplaceable value, first of all, of material life—as the primary and fundamental gift in which must be rooted all other aspects of life, which in the final analysis constitute development of that primary gift. That life must be expanded and completed by internal growth and in relation to the life of others, always in search of more life and better life.

Not that it is evident what the fullness of life consists of, still less how fullness of life is to be achieved. But it is not so hard to see what it does not consist of and how it will not be achieved. And this not only by logical deductions from universal principles, but by historical verification from the experience of the mass of the people. To seek life by taking it away from others or without concern for how others are losing it, is certainly the negation of the Spirit as giver of life. From this perspective, the basic Christian message of loving others as oneself, and not just that of not wanting for oneself what is wanted for others (pragmatically formulated by the Declaration of the Rights of Man and of the Citizen of 1793 in its sixth article), of preferring to give rather than receive, and of resolving to give all one's property to those who are poorer, are utopian ideals. The prophetic historicizing of these ideals can begin to generate that radical newness in persons and in institutions. With it, not only is there a drive to seek something radically new, but some lines are drawn for the attempts to begin anew, since what has been realized up to now is not on the right way to benefit the greater part of humanity which is made up of masses with scarcely even access to life.

Latin American historical prophecy presents itself in our day as liberation. The utopia of freedom is to be attained by means of liberation prophecy. The utopian ideal of a complete freedom for all human beings is not possible except through a liberation process; hence it is not primarily freedom that engenders liberation but liberation that engenders freedom, even though between the two there be a process of mutual reinforcement and enrichment.

Thus it has been historically. The well-known English liberties of the Magna Carta or of the Bill of Rights are concrete achievements—fewer taxes, just judgments, protection against the arbitrary domination of kings, and so on—obtained by a process of liberating struggle through which definite rights are acknowledged and then formalized in agreements, laws, or constitutions. Basically, it is a process of liberation from injustice, from domination, from institutionalized and falsely justified abuse. Only later on the process of liberalism was turned into the model of freedom and the way to preserve rather than obtain this freedom. But real freedom is obtained fundamentally through a liberation process. This is so in the personal realm, in the communitarian, in the social, and in the political as well. On the other hand, liberalism, as it is contradicted by historical prophecy in Latin America, is today the juridical and formal cover-up for those who have already been liberated from certain oppressions and dominations and who in turn see to it that others do not achieve the same through succeeding and more complex liberation processes.

Both personal freedom and social and political freedom are effectively such only when one "can" be and do what one desires to be and do. . . . Freedom without those very real conditions that make it really possible can be an ideal, but it is not a reality since without due and sufficient conditions one cannot be or do what one wants. But, if besides the absence of real conditions for exercising freedom, liberties, and formal rights, there is positive oppression and domination that hinder that exercise even more, it is not only unreal but positively ideological and hypocritical to talk of freedom. There is no personal freedom when, for example, there is internal domination by very powerful internal preconditioning or external advertising and propaganda that is not duly counteracted. For example, there is no personal freedom in a child, who does not have the intellectual development and the minimum knowledge to be able to discern and counterbalance the weight of internal and external motivations. If parents or educators impose in all sorts of ways their own ideas, attitudes, or patterns of conduct, besides, it is practically a mockery to talk of the child's freedom.

The same should be said about economic and social freedoms. They can be enjoyed only by those who have effective access to them and for whom that access is not positively hindered by all sorts of means, at times covertly and other times openly. What freedom of movement is possessed by someone who has no roads, no means of transport, or even the ability to walk? What freedom is there to choose a job or type of studies when there are jobs or places for students for only fifty percent of the population? What freedom of expression is there when there is active access to the media for only one percent and only passive access—for lack of literacy, lack of receiver sets, lack of means, and so forth—for over sixty percent? What economic freedom is there when access to credit is for the very few? What political freedom is there when one lacks the resources to create a political party and when the apparatus of the state and of associations maintain a climate of terror—or at least of generalized fear? It will be said that liberalism ideally desires nothing of this, that it seeks to offer equality of opportunity for all individuals and all inclinations. But in fact this is not so, and the least exercise of historicizing shows that freedoms and conditions of freedom are not given to but are won by people in a historical liberation process.

THE MEANING OF LIBERATION

Liberalization is one thing and liberation is something very different. Liberalization processes are only possible if liberation processes have gone before. Liberalization is a problem of and for the elite, whereas liberation is a process of and for the mass of the people that begins with liberation for basic needs and then builds positive conditions for the increasingly adult exercise of freedom and for the reasonable en-

joyment of liberties. The fact that certain liberation processes tend to become new processes of domination of the many by the few, is something
to think about very much. But it does not invalidate the axiological priority of liberation over liberalization in attaining freedom.

To want to pose the question of freedom outside of liberation is to
want to evade the real question of freedom for all. In the realm of the
personal, freedom is not actualized fully except by laborious liberation
processes confronting all sorts of more or less determinant necessities.
There is an internal basis and an ideal of freedom that up to a certain
point and in a generic way are given "naturally" to a person. But fundamentally this personal ideal is about capacities and freedoms that need
to be actualized to be changed into full realities, for whose actualization
quite precise conditions are required. With due distinctions, something
similar must be said about social and political freedom. Such freedoms
suppose a liberation from oppressive structures, which the classic liberals struggled against on the supposition that only the state limited or oppressed the individual, without realizing that there were social groups
that oppressed and exploited other social groups. It supposes, besides,
the creation of conditions where the capacity and the ideal of political
and social freedom can be shared equitably.

Liberation, therefore, is understood as "liberation-from" every form
of oppression and as "liberation-for" a shared freedom that does not
make possible or permit forms of domination. It makes little sense to
talk of freedom when opportunity for its actualization is reduced because of unsatisfied basic needs, drastic limitations on real possibilities
to choose among, and impositions of every sort, especially those depending on force and terror. But a mere "liberation-from" is not enough
since a "liberation-for" or a "liberation-towards" freedom is required, for
freedom can be full freedom only when it is the freedom of all. The
freedom of a few resting on the slavery of the rest is not acceptable, nor
is a freedom resting on the non-freedom of the majority acceptable.
Hence, freedom here too must be seen from its historicizing in the mass
of the people within each country and within the oppressed peoples in
the world as a whole. It is humanity that must be free, and not a few
privileged members of humanity, whether individuals, social classes, or
nations.

From this perspective, the question of the priority of justice over
freedom or of freedom over justice is resolved by the unity of both in
liberation. There can be no justice without freedom and no freedom
without justice, even though in the social and political order there is a
priority of justice over freedom, since one cannot be free unjustly. While
justice, in giving to each what is due to each, not only makes freedom
possible but also what is moral and just. Liberation from every form of
oppression whatever is a real process of "just-ification." This justification is the real means of promoting freedom and the conditions that
make it possible. Thus, liberation is a process of "ad-just-ment" with

oneself, in that it seeks to break one's internal and external chains. It is a "just" process in that it tries to overcome manifest injustice; and it is a "justifying" process in that it seeks to create adequate conditions for the full development of all and for an equitable use of the conditions.

In more explicitly Christian terms, liberation is a march towards the utopia of freedom through a real, prophetic liberation process, which implies liberation from sin, from the law, and from death (Rom. 6-8). Its goal is to actually reveal what it is to be God's children, what the freedom and the glory of God's children actually mean—a goal only possible through a permanent conversion and liberation process (Rom. 8:18-26) which follows Jesus by means of the personal reproduction of the "features of his Son, so that he may be the eldest of many brothers" (Rom. 8:29). A complete development of what is liberation from sin, from the law, and from death would give greater theological and historical clarity to how freedom is the result of liberation and how it is dangerous to pose the problem of freedom without regard to precise liberation tasks. This would demand a more extensive treatment of this question, but its mere suggestion points to the pressing need for processes of prophetic liberation so that the utopia of freedom can be really historicized.

Christian utopia, burgeoning from Latin America's prophecy and, in turn, oriented and ruled by it, pre-announces in a historical manner the creation of the new human being, of the new earth, and of the new heaven.

THE NEW HUMAN BEING

The new human being is delineated from the Christian ideal, but from a historicized ideal which proposes to take the place of the old human being that has been the worldly and even Christian-worldly ideal, proposed as such or at least as a practically irresistible focus of attraction. This is done starting from the conviction, nourished both from faith and from historical experience, that the ideal and/or the dominant focus of the human person maintained in Latin America is antichristian and does not respond to the challenges of reality. Not everything in that ideal is imported to the extent that one can speak of an inculturation of that ideal transmitting its own features to its historicizing. Prescinding for now from which ones are imported features and which are native, a sort of catalog of its traits can be made.

In regard to the ideal of the dominant old human being in the so-called North Atlantic and Western Christian civilization, certain features have to be rejected. These include its radical insecurity which leads it to take wild and irrational self-defense measures; its unsolidarity with what is happening to the rest of humanity; its ethnocentrism, along with its absolutizing and idolatrizing of the nation-state as fatherland; its exploitation and direct or indirect domination of other peoples and of their resources; the trivial superficiality of its existence and of the criteria by which types of work are chosen; its immaturity in the search for happiness through pleasure, random entertainment, and amusement; the smug pretension of setting itself up as the elite vanguard of humanity; its permanent aggression against the environment shared by the rest of humanity.

To feel the multitudinous effects of this Northern-Western human being on the Latin American human being, effects that are oppressive on the one hand and dissolvent on the other, causes us to prophetically reject its false idealism and to delineate a different kind of human being on the basis of that negation. But before this, we must reject the proposition that Latin America simply belongs to the Western world and to the Westernized Christian world. This is because Christ has been falsified by means of this ideologizing and used as a lure by a civilization that is not humanely universalizable. The attempt is to export it as the ideal model of humanity and of Christianity. When Hobbes wrote in *Leviathan* in 1651 that the causes of struggles among humans are three and that the three are written in human nature—insecurity, competition, and desire for glory—he was describing the experience of the emergent Western human being rather than anything necessarily innate to human nature. When official Christianity makes optional and intentional virtues out of what ought to be the outright negation of antichristian attitudes and deeds, then it is giving a biased reading of the faith that annuls its real truth and effectiveness.

Wealth and poverty as dialectical correlates

The return to the historical realism of the gospel proclamation, a historical realism that is by no means fundamentalist precisely because it is historical, obliges a return to the fundamental gospel theme of wealth-poverty. The biased reading of the faith has made it possible to reconcile material wealth with spiritual poverty, when the authentic reading, attested to by the church's greatest saints, is the opposite—reconciliation of material poverty with spiritual wealth. Now, the historical verification of the dialectical relation of wealth-poverty reclaims the depth of the gospel message, making poverty not a purely optional counsel but a historical necessity. Correlatively, this makes wealth not something indifferent, easily reconcilable with following Jesus, but one of the fundamental hindrances to setting up the kingdom. Poverty and wealth are not here spoken of apart from each other, but in their dialectical relationship: poverty as a correlate of wealth and wealth as a correlate of poverty.

Not only from the viewpoint of faith but also from the viewpoint of history, one sees in wealth and in greed, or desire for wealth, the fundamental energizer of a heartless and inhuman culture and the greatest resistance to the historical construction of the kingdom of God. The path of rapid and unequal enrichment has led to a Cainite rupture of humanity and to the formation of an exploitive, repressive, and violent human being. The relationship of human beings with wealth, a question so essential in the gospel, again becomes a central point in defining the new human being, who will not come into existence until there is an entirely new relationship to deal with the phenomenon of wealth and the problem of unequal accumulation. Asceticism and individual and group spirituality have tried to resolve this problem, but it must be taken up again because it has become a historical necessity to curb the dehumanization of both rich and poor in their dialectical confrontation.

Enticed by the allure of wealth, of wealthy persons and peoples, one loses the marks of one's own identity. To seek one's own identity in the imperfect appropriation of these foreign models leads to dependencies and mimicries that impede one's own self-creation. The culture of wealth proposes models and establishes means to attain them, and it does so in a way that outdazzles the possibility of seeking other models of fulfillment and happiness. It subjects to alienating dynamisms all those who devote themselves to adoring the golden calf which becomes the central idol of a new culture that in turn reinforces the central role that this golden idol plays in it. Where your treasure is, there is your heart, which comes to be shaped with the features of your treasure. Hence the importance of the choice of one's treasure. When one takes one's treasure to be the accumulation of wealth, the type of heart and of human being that results is subjected to a double alienation. This human being's own freedom is subjected to money's dynamisms which create needs and focus on things. And its own identity as a human being is subjected to a model created not for liberation but for submission. Certainly, wealth does have some possibilities for liberation, but at the cost of other possibilities of slavery for oneself and others.

All these evils, in great part induced from outside, are accompanied and reflected by others arising from within. Tendencies to machismo and violence are examples of these evils that degrade both men and women and are reflected in profound deviations in sexual and family life, or in a whole interdependent combination of submission, fatalism, and inertia. How much of this is ancestral or even natural and how much is a reflection of external stimuli is a matter to be investigated in each case. But to place the origin of all evils in outside agents would not be the right way to recover one's own identity, because this would make harder the task of constructing the new human being from within.

The ideologizing that corresponds to this set of real tendencies and deeds reveals itself as negative and nullifying of one's own individual and collective consciousness. This ideologizing presents itself as religious, economic, and political, and what it does basically is reinforce fundamental interests, latent or explicit. Religious fatalism, the economic competition of free enterprise and the urge for profit, the democratic system offered as a controlled and mapped-out participation of the mass of the people—all are examples of this ideologizing, which, although based on certain goods and values transmits greater evils.

In its negativity, the foregoing points to what should be positively the features of utopia. In the light of Christian inspiration that negativity indicates what the new human being is to be, in contrast to the old one. Since it is not primordially an intentional exercise but a praxis already underway, some of those features can already be appreciated in what is in existence.

The preferential option for the poor

The central point concerns the preferential option for the poor as a fundamental way to combat the priority of wealth in the shaping of human beings. There is a movement towards a greater solidarity with the cause of the oppressed, towards a growing incorporation into their world as the privileged place of humanization and Christian divinization. Such incorporation is not done in order to take perverse pleasure in miserable poverty, but in order to accompany the poor in their desire for liberation. Liberation cannot consist of passing from poverty to wealth by making oneself rich by means of the poverty of others. It consists rather of surmounting poverty through solidarity. We are, of course, talking about the poor-with-spirit, the poor who accept their situation as the foundation for constructing the new human being. Out of the materiality of poverty, this construction of the new human being arises actively from the poor-with-spirit, impelling them towards a process of liberation in solidarity that leaves out no human being. In other words, these are active poor, whom necessity spurs to escape from an unjust situation.

Hence, this new human being is defined in part by active protest and permanent struggle. This new human being seeks to overcome the dominant structural injustice which is considered an evil and a sin because it keeps most of the human population in conditions of inhumane living. This unjust situation is negative, but its negativity propels escape from it as from a catapult. The positive aspect is the dynamic of overcoming. In that overcoming the Spirit breathes in multiple ways, of which the supreme way of all is readiness to give one's life for the rest, whether in tireless daily commitment or in sacrifice unto death violently suffered.

Typically, however, the motive of this new human being who is moved by the Spirit is not hatred but mercy and love, for all are seen as children of God and not as enemies to be destroyed. Hatred can be lucid and effective in the short range, but it is not capable of constructing a really new human being. Christian love is not softhearted exactly, but it does propose very decidedly not to let itself be entrapped and hardened in selfishness or hatred, and it has a very clear vocation to service. The lords of this world set out to dominate and to be served, while the Son of Man, the new human being, has not come to be served but to serve and to give his life for the rest, for the many (Mt. 20:25-28).

Along with love comes hope. To be really new, the new human beings must be persons of hope and of joy in the building of a more just world. They are not moved by despair but by hope, because despair tends towards suicide and death, and hope tends to life and to giving. It may at times be hope against all hope, but therein can be seen joy and the security of one who is above humans and their thoughts, the impulse of a vocation to build the kingdom, which fundamentally is the kingdom of God, because God is its final goal and its constant motive. Latin America, which has so often been called the continent of hope, is exactly that as multitudes of persons full of hope, and not merely just as a pure natural potentiality not yet developed.

It is an open and untiring hope. The new human being is an open human being who does not absolutize any achievement in the illusion of making something finite into something infinite. The horizon is necessary as a limit that gives orientation, but it is more necessary as a permanent opening for the one who moves forward. To absolutize wealth, power, the organization, the institution, and such is to make idols of them, and it makes the idolater a dull and subjugated person. Such a one is the opposite of the person who is open to a God who is ever greater and to a kingdom that is to be historicized in an ever greater proximity to reality that, for various reasons, surpasses each partial achievement and surpasses it qualitatively through the interpretation of new developments that are logically and conceptually unforeseeable.

Thus one arrives at not only a new relationship among human beings but also a new relationship with nature. When the first inhabitants of Latin America maintained that no one can own the earth, that it cannot be the property of anyone in particular, because it is a mother goddess that gives life to so many people, they maintained a respectful and worshipful relationship with nature. Nature cannot be seen merely as raw material or a place to invest but as a manifestation and gift of God that is to be enjoyed with veneration and not ill-treated with contempt and exploitation.

To make all this possible, liberation theology outlines a new human being, at once contemplative and active, one who transcends both leisure and business. Activity is not sufficient and contemplation is not enough. Against the temptation of sloth hidden in the leisure of contemplation, the urgency of the task impels to efficacious action, for the seriousness of the problems admits no delay. Against the temptation of activism concealed as the constant creation of new opportunities, the emptiness and destructiveness of its promises demand the wealth of contemplation. Action without contemplation is empty and destructive, while contemplation without action is paralyzing and concealing. The new human beings are hearers and doers of the Word, discerners of the signs of the times, and accomplishers of what is offered them as promise.

Other historical features of Jesus' life ought to be projected also on this new human being who dawns on Latin America's horizon already in the poor and in those who have cast their lot with them. But those features pointed out here, especially when they make explicit reference to a God ever present, in whom to confide and to whom to confide the ultimate meaning of the seed sown, are those which unify and nuance those other features of Jesus' life that are taken on with distinct nuances, and especially with different concretions, according to the particular vocation of each person.

Between the negative superseding of the old human being and the affirmative realization of the new one, between the prophecy that denies by affirming and the utopia that affirms by denying, the Latin American praxis of Christian faith begins to open up new ways, right ways for all human beings, right ways to build a new earth and a new world.

THE NEW EARTH

The creation of the new earth implies the utopia of a new economic order, a new social order, a new political order, and a new cultural order. The so-called New World, far from being really new, became, especially in Latin America, an impoverished imitation of the old. Only now that the earlier model has failed is there a disposition to raise a really new world upon its negation.

This is not to remain on the level of voluntaristic idealisms. There are a historical inertia, quasi-necessary laws, and a weight of tradition that cannot be abolished, but that must be countered and, as far as possible, transformed by the force of the utopian ideal that arises from an objective and not merely intentional need to overcome the grave and universal evils of the present. The existence of historical evolution's own dynamisms, never completely dominated by any historical subject whatever, cannot be ignored. But that is no reason to accept an absolute historical determinism that leads to fatalism or that, at best, merely permits an attempt to improve the structural whole by the improvement of each individual or of some of the social groups. The alternative proposal of "every man for himself" in this world disorder may be the momentary solution for a few, but it is the ruin of the majority. Hence utopia, the recourse to the utopian ideal as the effective force assimilated by many, is necessary to counteract and even to direct what otherwise becomes the blind and mechanical course of history. It is not correct that the freedom of each will lead to the freedom of all, when the inverse is much more real: general freedom is what will make possible the freedom of each one. And that ideal of realizing utopia can become the principle of freedom and of spirituality incorporated through the subjectivity of persons into the determinism and the materiality of the historical processes. From this perspective Marx's passage in "*towardss a Critique of Hegel's Philosophy of Right*" could be read in a radically new form: "It is true that the weapon of criticism cannot substitute for the criticism of weapons, that material force must be overcome by material force; but theory also becomes material force as soon as it takes possession of the masses" (Marx, 1844). The utopian ideal, when it is presented historically as gradually realizable and is assumed by the mass of the people, comes to be a stronger force than the force of arms; it is at once a material and a spiritual force, present and future, hence able to overcome the material-spiritual complexity with which the course of history presents itself.

The economic order

In the economic order, Christian utopia, seen from Latin America, arising from real historicized prophecy in a determined situation, proposes a civilization of poverty to take the place of the present civilization of wealth. From a more sociological than humanistic perspective, this same utopia can be expressed by proposing a civilization of work to take the place of the dominant civilization of capital.

If the world as a totality has come to be shaped above all as a civilization of capital and of wealth in which the former more objectively and the latter more subjectively have been the principal moving, shaping, and directing elements of present-day civilization, and if this of itself has already contributed all that it had that is positive and is now causing constantly greater and graver ills, what must be favored is not its correction but its replacement by something better, by its contrary— that is, by a civilization of poverty. From the times of Jesus, whenever poverty is preferred to riches in order to enter the kingdom, a great rejection arises on the part of those who are already rich or have placed in riches the essential foundation of their lives. But what Jesus proposed as personal ideal can and must be expanded to socio-historical reality, with suitable adaptation.

The civilization of wealth and of capital is the one that, in the final analysis, proposes the private accumulation of the greatest possible capital on the part of individuals, groups, multinationals, states, or groups of states as the fundamental basis of development, and individuals' or families' possessive accumulation of the most possible wealth as the fundamental basis for their own security and for the possibility of ever growing consumption as the basis of their own happiness. It is not denied that such a type of civilization, prevailing in the East as well as in the West and called capitalist civilization deservedly—whether state capitalism or private capitalism—has brought benefits to humanity that as such should be preserved and furthered (scientific and technical development, new modes of collective consciousness, and so forth). But these civilizations have brought greater evils, and their self-correction processes do not prove sufficient for reversing their destructive course.

In consequence, seeing the problem in its worldwide totality from the perspective of real needs and of the expectations of the greater part of the world's population, that civilization of wealth and capital must be radically superseded. On this point, the church's social doctrine, especially in its new formulation by John Paul II in *Laborem Exercens*, is to be added in a very significant way to the established demands of liberation theology. Materialist economism, which shapes the civilization of wealth, is not ethically acceptable in its own internal dynamism, and much less so in its real effects. Instead of materialist economism, a materialist humanism should be proposed, which acknowledging and therefore relying on the complexly material condition of human beings, would avoid every type of idealistic solution to the real problems of people. This materialist humanism aims to go beyond materialist economism, since it would no longer be economic matter that finally determines everything else, as is the case in any type of civilization of capital and wealth, but human material, complex and open, which conceives human beings as the limited but real subjects of their own history.

The civilization of poverty

The civilization of poverty, on the other hand, founded on a materialist humanism transformed by Christian light and inspiration, rejects the accumulation of capital as the energizer of history and the possession-enjoyment of wealth as principle of humanization, and it makes the universal satisfying of basic needs the principle of development, and the growth of shared solidarity the foundation of humanization.

The civilization of poverty is so denominated in contrast to the civilization of wealth, and not because it proposes universal pauperization as an ideal of life. Certainly, strictly evangelical Christian tradition has an enormous distrust of wealth, following in this the teaching of Jesus, a teaching much clearer and more forceful than others might be that are presented as such. Likewise, the great saints of the church's history, often in open struggles for reform against church authorities, have incessantly preached the Christian and human advantages of material poverty. These are two aspects that cannot be ignored, because in the case of the great religious founders—for example, in the case of Saint Ignatius Loyola in his deliberations on poverty—explicit reference is made not only to the personal, but also to the institutional. But, even admitting and taking account of such considerations, which call into question wealth in itself, what is here meant to be emphasized is the dialectical wealth-poverty relationship and not poverty in itself. In a world sinfully shaped by the capital-wealth dynamism it is necessary to stir up a different dynamism that will salvifically surpass it.

This is achieved, for the moment, through an economic arrangement relying on and directly and immediately addressed to satisfying the basic needs of all humans. Only this orientation responds to a fundamental right of human beings, without the observance of which their dignity is disrespected, their reality is violated, and world peace is endangered.

In regard to identifying basic needs, even accounting for cultural and individual differences that give rise to distinct subjectifications of those needs, not much discussion is needed if one looks at the conditions of extreme poverty or destitution of more than half of the human race. Such needs must be considered to be, first of all, proper nourishment, minimal housing, basic health care, primary education, sufficient employment, and so forth. It is not proposed that this exhausts the horizon of economic development; it is simply a point of departure and of fundamental reference, a *sine qua non* of any sort of development. The great task remaining is for all people to be able to gain access to the satisfaction of those needs, not as crumbs fallen from the tables of the rich but as the principal portion from humanity's table. With the satisfying of basic needs institutionally assured as the primary phase of a liberation process, people would be free to be what they want to be, provided that what is wanted not become a new mechanism of domination.

Rather than capital accumulation, the civilization of poverty proposes as dynamizing principle the dignifying of work, of work that will have as its principal object not the production of capital but the perfecting of the human being. Work, viewed at once as the personal and collective means to assure the satisfaction of basic needs and as a form of self-realization, would supersede different forms of self- and hetero-exploitation and would likewise supersede inequalities that are both an affront and the cause of domination and antagonism.

It is not merely a matter of the new human beings ceasing to make wealth their basic idol to which they offer all they have—their ability to work, their moral principles, health, leisure, family relationships, and so on. It is, above all, a matter of making a society that, negatively, does not oblige one to make wealth the supreme value because without it one is lost. (What does it profit a man to save his soul, which is not seen and not esteemed, if he loses the world, which is seen and is most esteemed?) Positively, such a society is structured so that one is not required to keep looking for wealth in order to have all that is needed for human liberation and fulfillment. It is clear that a society not structured by the laws of capital, but one giving primacy to the dynamism of humanizing work, would be shaped in a way very different from the present one, because the shaping principle is totally different. The humanistic and moral failure of present society, of the present earth, shaped according to capital's dictates, has begun in various ways to move those in the more or less marginal vanguards to shape a different society, even though for the moment that is by escaping from the structures and dynamics of the society that presently dominates. The definitive solution, however, cannot be in escaping from this world and confronting it with a sign of prophetic protest, but in entering into it to renew it and transform it in the direction of the utopia of the new earth.

In part, this will be gradually achieved if a fundamental characteristic of the civilization of poverty, shared solidarity, grows positively stronger, in contrast to the closed and competitive individualism of the society of wealth. To see others not as part of oneself, yet to see oneself in unity and communion with others, combines well with what is deepest in Christian inspiration and goes along with one of the best tendencies of Latin America's popular sectors, which unfolds in contrast to individualistic, separating tendencies. This solidarity is facilitated in the common enjoyment of common property.

Common property

The private appropriation of common property is not needed in order to care for it and enjoy it. When the church's social doctrine, following Saint Thomas, holds that private appropriation of goods is the best practical manner for their primordial common destiny to be fulfilled in an orderly way, it is making a concession to "the hardness of their hearts," but "in the beginning it was not so." Only because of greed and selfishness, connatural to original sin, can it be said that private ownership of property is the best guarantee of productive advancement and social order. But if "where sin abounded, grace abounded more" is to have historical verification, it is necessary to proclaim utopianly that a new earth with new human beings must be shaped with principles of greater altruism and solidarity. The great benefits of nature—the air, the seas and beaches, the mountains and forests, the rivers and lakes, in general all the natural resources for production, use, and enjoyment—need not be privately appropriated by any individual person, group, or nation, and in fact they are the grand medium of communication and common living.

If a social order were achieved in which basic needs were satisfied in a stable manner and were guaranteed, and the common sources of personal development were made possible, so that the security and the possibilities of personalization were guaranteed, the present order based on the accumulation of private capital and material wealth could be considered as a prehistoric and prehuman stage. The utopian ideal is not that all are to have much by means of private and exclusive appropriation, but that all are to have what is necessary and that the nonacquisitive and nonexclusive use and enjoyment of what is primarily common be open to all. The indispensable dynamism of personal initiative cannot be confused with the natural-original dynamism of private and privatizing initiative. Nor is excluding others as competitors to one's selfhood the only way to work for oneself or to be oneself.

The new, utopian arrangement of an economy at the service of human beings and certainly leading to a new earth must be the economic arrangement oriented by the above principles and favoring the development of the new human being. At present it is a shared complaint that today human beings are subordinated to the economy and the economy is not subordinated to human beings. Although this phenomenon indicates, among other things, the predominance of what is common and structural over what is individual and integral, the way in which the phenomenon appears—dominance of the economic over the human—is not acceptable as utopian ideal, much less is it compatible with the Christian ideal.

Which of the two great economic arrangements available today, capitalist or socialist, is more fitting for the attainment of that utopian ideal?

In Latin America the failure of capitalist models, which have been clearly dominant here for decades, is quite clear. It will be said that they have not been sufficiently capitalist; but, if that is so, it has not been because of opposition to capitalism, but because of the objective inadequacy of imposing a capitalist system in a situation like Latin America's. Capitalist systems in Latin America have been unable to satisfy the basic needs of the greater part of the population, they have created bitter inequalities between the few who have much and the many who have little, they have led to a gigantic foreign debt imposed on human beings who in no way enjoyed or received benefit from the loans, they have often produced deep economic crises, and they have promoted an immoral culture of consumption and of easy profit. Sadly, all this has been done by persons and classes that consider themselves Catholic and who see no contradiction between their economic praxis and their Christian praxis. From this reality, the least that can be said is that only a radical transformation of the capitalist economic arrangement is minimally reconcilable with what the Christian utopia is. Marxism, insofar as it is the great contradictor of that arrangement, insofar as it profoundly attacks the spirit of capitalism and analyzes the mechanisms that sustain it, and insofar as it utopianly proclaims the liberation of human beings through the liberation of labor, plays a long-reaching prophetic and utopian role in Latin America and offers a scientific method for unraveling the profound dynamisms of the capitalist system.

Limits of socialism

On the other hand, the economic results—later we will turn to the political ones—of the socialist arrangements are not satisfactory either, at least for entering world competition. The recent attempts by the larger socialist nations to correct their economic systems with procedures more proper to the opposing system, without meaning the abandonment of what is principial in their own system, point to certain limitations that well deserve to be considered. On the other hand, it would be premature to condemn beforehand the failure of the reformed socialist models because of what is presently happening in Nicaragua, although it would be a mistake to ignore the real difficulties which that system has in the concrete way it exists, considering the places and the times. Even the Cuban model, although it has achieved the best satisfaction of basic needs in all of Latin America in a relatively short time, still has intrinsic difficulties that can be overcome only with a massive external support. Hence, there are also serious problems in the realization of the socialist model as the most effective instrument to historicize Christian utopia.

Nevertheless, it can be defended that in economic matters the socialist ideal is closer than the capitalist to the utopian demands of the kingdom. The socialist economic ideal rests on profound values of the human being, but it does not prosper economically precisely because of its moral idealism, which does not take into account the empirical state of human nature. The capitalist economic ideal rests, at least in part, on the selfish vices of human nature, and it is, in this manner, not more realistic, but more pragmatic than its opponent, and for that reason it has superior economic successes. It could be said, therefore, that if the new human being were to be attained, the socialist arrangement would function better, whereas under the dominion of the old human being, structures that are fundamentally unjust for the greater part of the world's population work better. For this reason, although one cannot be naive in recommending one or other mediation of the kingdom, the Christian utopia, which strives for a new human being on a new earth, cannot help inclining in economic matters towards formulations that are closer to socialism than to capitalism as far as Latin America and, more generally, the third world are concerned. It is not too much to recall that the church's social teaching has been drawing closer to this way of seeing things.

The objection can be made that the satisfaction of basic needs is better assured in the capitalist countries than in the socialist countries. But the objection is not so solid if one considers, first, that the capitalist countries take care of a much smaller part of the world population and, second, that this satisfaction is achieved at very high cost to a great part of that capitalist population and, third, that the system is not universalizable, given the limited world resources and the private appropriation of those same resources by a few privileged countries.

In both cases, although not equally because of differing situations, prophecy and Christian utopia need to be critical of the theory and the practice of the dominant economic systems. At times the church's social teaching has been too naive and tolerant towards the theory and, especially, towards the practice of capitalism for fear of losing perquisites and out of fear of the Marxist régimes. But liberation theology has also on occasions been naive and tolerant towards the theory and practice of Marxism because of a certain inferiority complex before the commitment of the revolutionaries. Without ignoring prophecy's and utopia's difficult relationship with the historical mediations, which should not be anathematized from an unreal purism, what finally is important to underline is that, whatever the case, the civilization of work and of poverty must take the place of the civilization of capital and of wealth. And it would seem—and this is a most serious problem—that the civilization of capital and wealth is imposing itself worldwide, both where there is private capitalism and where there is state capitalism. Hence, Christian prophecy and utopia have a permanent task of leavening to do.

THE NEW SOCIAL ORDER

Corresponding to that new economic order, a new vigorous and multipolar social order must arise in which it will be possible for the people to be more and more the agents of their own destiny and to have greater possibilities for creative freedom and for participation. Just as it is the people of God that should have priority in the kingdom of God, and not a set of institutional superstructures that takes its place; likewise in this world's history it should be the social groups that carry the weight of history, and they should do so on their own. In other words, the social should be given more weight than the political, without individualism thereby becoming the highest form of humanization. The social dimension should prevail over the political dimension, but not take its place.

Between individualism and statism a strong type of society should be built to overcome the licentiousness of the former and the dominating interference of the latter. It is not a question of compromising between two existing extremes, but of finding new forms to supersede both existing models by negating them. Of course, de-statization must not be understood as a neoliberal demand for a lesser weight of the state before the demands of so-called private initiative and before the laws of the marketplace. De-statization is, rather, a socialization that promotes a communitarian and social initiative that is not delegated either to the state or to parties or to vanguards or to bosses. It is a question of overcoming social apathy in the management of historical processes without for this reason lapsing into either gremialisms or corporativisms. Basically what is proposed is, positively, to give more life and decision to social enterprises and, negatively, to overcome the unruly dynamisms of political power. That is, the principal characteristic of this socialization would be the seeking of the community good from community pressure and through community means without delegating this force to political enterpises, which become autonomous and can never adequately represent the social.

There is no reason to confuse the public enterprise with the political enterprise, or to accept reservation of the whole public sector to the state and to political parties, to the detriment of social enterprises. . . . The social represents not a mean but a mediation between the individual and the political, so that the individual's essential communal dimension is primarily realized not in the political dimension of the state but in the public dimension of the social. At distinct moments in the Latin American political struggle there has been a certain disdain for parties in the interest of the popular organizations. But this tendency has not contributed all it could when it has proposed that the organizations take on state political power. And these organizations have again fallen into the ill-advised use of politics to further their real interests. Likewise, the church has often abdicated its role in social enterprise to become an appendage of political power, thus impairing its mission and weakening thereby its historic potential for the service of the mass of the people.

In regard to the permanent problem of freedom and equality-justice, the question does not reside in giving primacy to the individual over the state or vice versa. The union of liberty-justice-equality is better achieved in the mediation of the social, which is neither of the state nor of the individual. The mediation of the social permits individual-personal freedom that is not individualistic, at the same time that it permits political freedom—that is, freedom of individuals and of groups vis-à-vis the power of the state. What generates real conditions for personal freedom is, first of all, social freedom. In turn, it is not only the individual but the community that becomes the best real and effective guarantee against the domination and oppression of politico-state structures.

This implies that excessive and conflict-producing inequalities are to disappear in the real area of the social without thereby giving rise to mechanical equalities that do not respond to different preferences in values and to the diversity of contributions by individuals and groups to social well-being. An obligatory equality does not respond to reality and is not demanded by ethical or religious considerations. What must be excluded, for the time being, is the present outrageous difference between those who squander and those who lack enough to subsist—this, even though there be no causal or functional relation between the poverty and the wealth. What is indeed a pressing obligation is that all be assured satisfaction of basic needs. But beyond that minimal level particular choices and greater labor or performance are to be respected, so long as equality of opportunity is respected and the processes leading to attention-getting and conflict-provoking inequalities are avoided.

These positions would be normal and reasonable ones for making possible an adequate freedom-justice-equality. But the utopian ideal of Jesus goes much further. Paradoxically, the follower of Jesus seeks to take the last place as the surest way to reach the first. In this first place one is not dominant but a servant, one seeks not one's own honor but that of the rest. In general, what Jesus' message propounds is to exchange the real dynamisms of this old world, of this old earth, for the dynamisms of the kingdom as utopian ideal of the new earth and as negation—death and resurrection—of the old one. The New Testament's tremendous reservations about wealth, power, and worldly honor and its emphatic proclamation of poverty, service, and the humiliation of the cross can and should be translated to the visible and the social. They represent not only a possible ideal for the individual, but a model for society. That the realizations of this have not been totally satisfactory—for example, in the case of religious orders which are social groups which bring individuals together without leaving them at the mercy of more globalizing institutions—does not keep these from raising the question of the need to give social, historical flesh to the invitation from Jesus to follow him. Social institutions, unlike political ones, can be impregnated with that spirit, which would seem to be reserved for individuals, and so the great founders of the religious orders have intended.

THE NEW POLITICAL ORDER

The new political order, prophetically outlined on the utopian horizon, is based on the attempt to go beyond the political models that are the result and at the same time the support of both liberal capitalism and Marxist collectivism.

What is being proposed is not a "third way" between liberalism and collectivism in the economic area or between liberal democracy and social democracy in the political. Such a "third way" does not exist in the latest documents of the church, not even as ideal solution (see John Paul II, 1987, #41). In this historical phase, what there can be are different forms of one or other way, both in the economic and in the political sphere, some better than others in their applicability to a determined reality. It would not be hard to prove that some socialist political forms are much better than some capitalist political forms and, vice versa, that some capitalist forms are better than some socialist forms. This appraisal is indeed interesting. It is usually presented as an opening of one system to the other, which in practice brings them nearer to each other in spite of their fundamental differences. Of particular interest are recent rather widespread efforts to democratize socialism, but there is hardly any equivalent effort towardss a much-needed socialization of the democracies, perhaps because the more advanced ones had already done so in some way.

This two-way opening up of each of the systems could be evidence not only of the insufficiency of each but also of a possible leap forward to a now scarcely recognizable new political system. It is one of the few instances where one might appreciate a positive dynamism of history that goes against the blind dynamism of the demands of capital—subject to constant corrections by what might be called the dynamism of humanization-divinization. Signs like the increasingly connatural appreciation of human rights, of a larger democratic opening, of a more effective world solidarity, are, among other things, manifestations of the struggle between good and evil, between the closure of the systems and the openness of humanity. They are positive and hopeful signs that can scarcely hide the heaviness and inertia of their opposites but they nevertheless point towards possibilities of change via reform.

Revolution or Reform

In Latin America, however, the search has been and continues to be for revolutionary change rather than for reformist change. Hence, on occasions the effort has been made to take advantage of the subversive dynamism of the Christian faith, just as the dominant systems have tried to take advantage of the conservative dynamisms of the same faith. The reason is obvious. On the one hand, there is such a degree of structural injustice affecting the very structure of society, that it appears indispensible to demand a quick and profound change of structures—that is, a revolution. On the other hand, the prevailing dynamism does not in fact lead to a reform that might build a revolutionary change, but instead to a deepening and spread of the structural injustice, and this under the guise of reform whose path is development.

From this viewpoint, it can be affirmed both from theory and from verification of historical reality and, of course, from utopian prophecy, that a revolution in the present dynamisms and structures is needed, an anticapitalist revolution—"anti" to the capitalism found in the underdeveloped and oppressed countries—and an anti-imperialist revolution—"anti" to every type of external empire that tries to impose its own interests. The question is not, then, if a revolution is needed or not, but what revolution is needed and how to bring it about.

The revolution that is needed, the necessary revolution, will be the one that intends freedom deriving from and leading to justice and justice deriving and leading to freedom. This freedom must come out of liberation and not merely out of liberalization—whether economic or political liberalization—in order to overcome in this way the dominant "common evil" and build a "common good," a common good understood in contrast to the common evil and sought from a preferential option for the mass of the people.

The imposition of the dogma that liberal democracy is the best path for combining freedom and justice in any time and circumstance is simply presumptuous, and it often conceals accompanying advantages for an elite. Likewise, the dogmatic imposition of the so-called social or popular democracies as the best and only way to adequately join freedom and justice does not square with some of the forms in which they have actually appeared. It would be better to stick to the more radical principle that it is reality as experienced by the mass of the people, and not dogmatic principles or even historical models, that is to be imposed as selection criterion leading to genuine self-determination. The real measure of a duly ordered and quantified system of human rights takes precedence over the formal criteria of one or other type of democracy.

From this perspective, social liberation appears more necessary and urgent than political liberation in the Central American countries and in the greater part of the third world, something that is perhaps not the case in other situations in the first and the second world. Of course, they are not mutually exclusive and, even less, contradictory. But social liberation, which rests on satisfying the basic needs of the masses and supports the autonomous exercise of social life, is above political freedom, which intends equality of opportunity for attaining political power, and above what are called strictly political freedoms, as distinct from fundamental freedoms. This is because, in order to be enjoyed by most people, political freedoms require liberation from basic needs and they also require social freedom, even though these in turn demand areas of political freedom.

For all that, in the present stage of the kingdom's realization, with the greater part of the population living in extreme poverty and oppression, the socialist ideal appears more connatural to the profound inspiration of the Christian message than the capitalist ideal, although neither of them is identified with the Christian utopian ideal. Another matter altogether is the possibility of actually realizing each of these two ideals.

Many trials and attempts to formulate a Christian correction of capitalism have been made, and the results have not been good even for satisfying basic needs, not to mention the area of ethics—of forming a new human being and a new earth better conformed to the utopian ideals of the kingdom. Although in the church's social teaching useful corrections of capitalism have been formulated, frequently the mistake has been made of thinking that capitalism is fundamentally good and is the system more conformed to Christian values. On the other hand, while the influence of the Christian faith and even of the historical forms of Christendom in correcting capitalism (as it has existed in Latin America, where the official faith has been Christian since the time of the conquest) has not been completely ineffective, it shows notable weaknesses. These in turn have made the church worldly and capitalist more than they have made the structures and behavior of the world Christian and evangelical.

The attempt to make the Christian faith the yeast and leaven of Marxist positions has been put to the test much less. Something has been done in this regard, as Latin American revolutionaries from Fidel Castro to the Sandinista leaders and those of the Salvadoran FMLN have acknowledged. Liberation theology in different forms has sought to contribute important corrections to Marxism, as the church's social teaching had sought to do until recently with capitalism. Not that liberation theology proposes that the church relinquish its social and political function to movements, parties, or vanguards who will represent it. On the contrary, liberation theology demands a direct and independent commitment of the church to the defense of human rights and to the promotion of greater justice and freedom, especially for those most in need. But it does propose that the Marxist forms of revolution, and not only the human beings who bring them about, be profoundly transformed, because in their theory and, especially, in their practice Marxists tend towards reductionisms and effectivisms little in accord with the Christian utopian ideal. In turn, the experience of the best of Marxism has served to spur the church and has obliged it to turn—to be converted—towardss radical points in the Christian message that the passage of years and inculturation into capitalist forms had left merely ritualized and ideologized without historical value for individuals and peoples.

THE NEW CULTURAL ORDER

The new cultural order ought to free itself from the models of Western culture, for these leave much to desire when it comes to achieving the perfecting and the happiness of human beings. Only by removing and freeing oneself at least from the deception found in Western culture can one begin to seek another type of culture as a way to true human progress.

The consumer cultural order is a product of the consumer economic order. Hence it is not adequate for mobilizing a civilization of poverty, which must also have its corresponding cultural development. The cultural tradition will not be enlarged through constant entertainment changes. To confuse being entertained with being happy favors and promotes the consumption of products by inducing needs in the marketplace, but at the same time it reveals and induces the greatest inner emptiness. The civilization of poverty, far from provoking consumption and activity in the cultural sphere, tends to further what is natural and to facilitate attitudes of contemplation and communication more than attitudes of activity-consumption in some and of pure passivity-receptivity in others.

The huge cultural wealth amassed through thousands of years of human life diversified in multiple forms and in various times and places. It must not be allowed to remain overwhelmed by cultural modes that seek in what is new the affirmation and consolidation of human beings that are not new and that only endeavor to sell newness. It is necessary to reclaim those age-old riches, not so as to rest in them conservatively but to open up possibilities of new developments to surpass but not replace them. Many of the technological and consumer models are losing sight of and losing the use of—if not destroying altogether—the reality and the deep meaning of the great cultural achievements that have proceeded from a true cultural identity. It is through one's own identity that one can assimilate the values of other cultures without becoming lost in them. For example, the case of the inculturated assimilation of the Christian faith made by the liberation theology movement is a good demonstration of how a universalizable reality can be historicized and particularized, and at the same time be enriched.

Culture, first of all, must be liberating. It must liberate from ignorance, from fear, from inner and outer pressure, in search of a fuller and fuller truth and more and more fulfilling reality. In this liberation process, culture will become the generator of real freedom; it will not be reduced to selecting from among—rather than electing among—distinct conditioned and conditioning offers. But this culture will be oriented towards persons, communities, peoples, and nations who are constructing their own self-being in an effort of creation and not only of acceptance. Everywhere in the world there is a tremendous cultural imposition from powerful centers that universalize the world's vision and values with the most varied communications media. In various ways this cultural imposition keeps the huge masses of Latin America and of other lands alienated from understanding themselves and from understanding and valuing the world. Something that ought to favor a plural unity becomes an impoverishing uniformity. At the same time, the facility of the communications media leads to another kind of alienation. These media promote the leap from a primitive state of culture, which is at times a very valuable and healthy state, into sophisticated and decadent phases of a culture imposed more by its milieu—and by its attendant baggage—than by its own basic content.

Here too the question is one of seeking a culture for the majority and not a culture for the elite with much form and little life. That all, if possible, and not just a few, have life and have it in abundance should be the motto of the new culture on the new earth. This is a really utopian task, but one to which real prophecy stimulates—and the stimulus is seen in many places. This real prophecy repudiates and overcomes the blemishes of an alienating and, at bottom, dehumanizing culture.

A NEW HEAVEN

The creation of a new heaven supposes achieving a new presence of God among humans that will let the old Babylon be transformed into the new Jerusalem.

Certainly, all of the foregoing, expressed under the headings of new human being and new earth, is a very special presence of the Spirit of Christ in the world as sent by the Crucified and Risen One. But it needs to be made more explicit and more visible, which is what is expressed in the new heaven—not as something superimposed on human beings and on the earth, but as something integrated and structured with them.

So, by "new heaven" there must be understood here that presence of God on the new earth that permits and encourages that God be all in all and in everything (I Cor. 15:28), because Christ is that for all (Col. 3:11). It is, therefore, a new Christological heaven and not simply the heaven of an abstract God, univocal in his abstraction. Neither does it mean heaven as the final place of the risen in grace, but the heaven present in history, the historical and increasingly operative and visible presence of God among human beings and public human structures. The historical Jesus must be constituted not only the Christ of faith but also the Christ of history. That is, the visible and efficacious historicizing of the Pauline affirmation that he is to be all in all and for everything, that the real life of humans and institutions—with the essential differences that this life must have in humans and institutions—must no longer be the life that arises from its limited and sinful immanent principles, but the life that arises from the principles that make all things new, that create, regenerate, and transform whatever is insufficient and even sinful in the old creature.

In this view, the new heaven exceeds what is habitually understood as church, although not what should be understood as the city of God, and of course as kingdom of God. Nevertheless, the reference to the church is indispensable for adequately describing the new heaven, under and in which to live historically, while God's history continues its journey, or God continues to journey through history as historical Christ. Indeed, one of the principal forms in which this new heaven ought to be historicized is the church of Christ as historical body of Jesus crucified and risen.

It is not enough to affirm that the church makes the divine life present to us, transmitted sacramentally. This is important, but it is not enough. For the present, that sacramental presence of the church as a whole and of the distinct sacraments in which that fundamental sacramentality is actualized (Rahner), ought both to be revitalized beyond the ritual and formal until the effectiveness of the Word and the active correspondence of the one who receives the grace of the sacrament are recovered. To confuse the mystery, which is the sacrament, with a process given in the interiority of the person is to devalue the mysteriousness of the sacrament's efficacy through an unverifiable and ineffective pure affirmation. Even from this viewpoint, a profound renewal, without which revitalizing sacramental life is unthinkable, is indispensable, prophetically and utopianly.

But the church must go beyond the sacramental ambit or, at least, its sacramentality must be understood more widely. For this it needs to be permanently open and attentive to the newness and the universality of the Spirit which breaks the fossilized routine of the past and the limits of a restricted self-conception. Only a church that lets itself be invaded by the Spirit renewer of all things and that is attentive to the signs of the times can become the new heaven that the new human being and the new earth need.

The church as institution tends to be more conserving of the past than renewing of the present and creative of the future. Certainly, there are things to preserve; but nothing vital and human, nothing historical, is preserved if it is not maintained in constant renewal. Fear of what is new, of what is not controllable by already established institutional means, has been and still is one of the church's permanent characteristics. When one reviews the positions of the different ecclesiastical authorities previous to the religious renewal movements that have afterward proved to be fundamental for the church's advance (for example, the founding of the great religious orders, new forms of thought, new methods and even data of biblical research, and so on), not to mention positions taken in the face of scientific and political advances, it is hard to maintain that church authority and its institutional organs have been open to the newness of history and to the creative breath of the Spirit.

This opening to the Spirit of Christ from earthliness, which implies the following of the historical Jesus, is, however, absolutely indispensable. There is no ecclesiastical enterprise that can replace this need, for the Spirit of Christ has not delegated the totality of its presence and of its efficacy to any institution, although their historical corporeity is also a demand of the Spirit. What often happens is that the church's institutions are configured more from the law than from grace, as if church institutions ought to be configured more according to totalitarian-like sociological and political laws—disguised as God's will and proper obedience to God's will—rather than according to the dictates and power of the Spirit. On the contrary, this is not just about an ordinary spirit concocted by some charismatic, but it is the Spirit of Jesus which animated his own conception, was manifest at his baptism, and was evident in his person and in his living, and which he finally promised to send to us when he should no longer be with us.

It is in this context that the signs of the times become present, some in one epoch and some in another, some in certain regions of the world and others in another. It is precisely the signs of the times that add the element of the future and without which an essential element is lacking for the interpretation of the word of God and of one of the greatest forces of renewal. But these are signs of the times framed here and now in the utopia-prophecy dialectic, without which one would fall back into ineffective idealism.

From the present situation of Latin America, the church's renewal and its projection towardss the future must be as the church of the poor if it is to become the new heaven. On the one hand, to be a church that has made indeed a preferential option for the poor will be proof and manifestation of the renewing Spirit present in it; on the other, it will be a guarantee that it can become the new heaven of the new earth and of the new human being. The church has been shaped in great part by the dynamisms of Western capitalism as a church of the rich and of the powerful which at best directs towards the poorest the crumbs falling from the table of abundance. But the utopian exercise of prophecy can lead it to become—in a genuine "conversion"—a church of the poor that really can be the heaven of a new earth where a civilization of poverty becomes dominant and where humans are not only intentionally and spiritually poor, but really and materially so, that is, detached from what is superfluous and from the constraining dynamisms of individual monopolizing and collective accumulation. Money can be an incentive for material development for human beings and for states, but it has always been, and it remains more and more, a deadly poison for a genuine humanism and, of course, for a genuine Christianity. That this arouses a powerful rejection from the world, that this is a scandal and even an affront to the civilization of wealth, is one more proof of the continuity of these ideas and of this practice with the fullest way of the gospel, always attacked with the same reproaches.

It is in this sense that the church of the poor becomes the new heaven, which as such is needed to supersede the civilization of wealth and build the civilization of poverty, the new earth where the new human being will live in a friendly and not in a degraded home. Here there will be a great encounter between the Christian message without disfiguring glosses and the present degraded situation in the greater part of the world—certainly in Latin America, still for the most part a depository of the Christian faith. That faith has nevertheless little served to make this region a new earth so far, in spite of its having originally been presented as the New World. The signs of the times and the soteriological dynamic of the Christian faith historicized in new human beings insistently demand the prophetic negation of a church as the old heaven of a civilization of wealth and of empire and the utopian affirmation of a church as the new heaven of a civilization of poverty. Although always in the dark, these new human beings continue to firmly proclaim an ever greater future, because beyond the successive historical futures is discerned the God who saves, the God who liberates.

Ethical Reflections:
Human Rights, Property, Democracy

Ignacio Ellacuría

3. Fundamental Human Rights and The Legal and Political Restrictions Placed on Them*

TRANSLATION BY PHILLIP BERRYMAN

The possibility that the enjoyment of certain human rights could be restricted for reasons of a legal and political nature raises serious problems about the true nature of those rights, and more profoundly, about that historic reality that is the human being. In this article, rather than offering a general moral theory for dealing with such problems, I will examine in a more modest but committed fashion some of the moral considerations that apply to the conflict between Honduras and El Salvador. Dealing with the conflict in terms of human rights will suggest ways of preventing the recurrence of conflicts of this kind.

. . . .

---

*Ellacuría (1969b); see the Bibliography in the back of this book.

This article was prompted by the 1969 war between El Salvador and Honduras. Because of the scarcity of available land in their own country, Salvadorans had been emigrating to Honduras for decades. El Salvador's land mass (8,300 square miles) is approximately the size of the state of Massachusetts and has a population of about 5 million people. Honduras, with 43,200 square miles of land (59,000 total square miles) has a population of about 4.3 million people. Tensions arose when the Honduran government began to expel Salvadorans. (As many as 300,000 Salvadorans are estimated to have settled in Honduras.) Fearing that a mass influx of returning jobless Salvadorans would augment social tension, the Salvadoran military and oligarchy whipped up nationalistic fervor, which erupted at soccer games (hence, it was called the "Soccer War" in news accounts). Salvadoran troops launched a strike in July 1969 into Honduras, which retaliated by bombing and strafing San Salvador. However, most of the victims were Honduran peasants. In the original article Ellacuría discusses the conflict at some length, and in general finds the official Salvadoran position ethically justified insofar as the purpose of the war was to defend the rights of Salvadorans. P.B.

Three Issues Pointing to the True Character of the Conflict

VIOLENCE

The conflict has once more raised the issue of violence, which we cannot address here as a theoretical and general problem (cf. Ellacuría, 1969c). It should be enough to indicate how great an indictment of our world it is when violence is assumed to be morally necessary, not simply in exceptional cases but ever more frequently.

The critical situation that El Salvador has experienced demonstrates that making use of force cannot be ruled out, either theoretically or practically, from either an ethical or a Christian standpoint. Certainly in principle a Christian favors peace but not pacifism. Hence the Salvadoran bishops, who first urged peace, later supported the right to use force. Posing overall the question of violence is not changed by stating that in the case of El Salvador the decision to use force was made at the highest levels of government, for that would be a merely legal justification, and so not necessarily an adequate one. The justification for the Salvadoran government's decision lies ultimately in its right and obligation to overcome a situation of manifest injustice, from which it believed there was no other way to obtain deliverance. The need to use just force makes it obvious that we are facing a situation of injustice.

In this respect, if the recent conflict had achieved nothing more than unmasking a situation of grave injustice before the conscience of the world and of the two countries directly involved, it would have been justified by this very fact. Of course this situation of injustice is not limited to what the Honduran authorities have encouraged or allowed against Salvadorans living in Honduras; it is much more complex, and it forces us to question the socio-economic and political structures of both countries.

Therefore, the important point here is not to repeat or even revise the traditional doctrine on the right to self-defense and to what is called the just war. Remaining on this level would be to disregard the true importance and seriousness of what is happening. The problem of violence is much more fundamental than the purely ethical and legalistic problem of whether the use of force is licit or illicit.

CLASH BETWEEN JUSTICE AND THE LAW

We arrive at this same point, when we confront the problem from the standpoint of the possible contradiction between positive laws and justice. Obviously, in truly critical cases like this, it is too easy to hide behind a legal order, which may be the embodiment, if not of a positively unjust situation, at least of a situation which is now unacceptable. Laws are necessary, and normally they should be respected, even though they are insufficient. However, even good laws are, for various reasons, a lesser evil. There should be a true hierarchy established among laws, so that simply pointing out that an arrangement was legal would not mean that it would require no further justification. For although under normal conditions laws should not conflict with one another, when the situation is abnormal, it is very likely that such conflict will occur. Indeed, there may be a real clash between law, which defends the best feasible good, and justice, which regards that best feasible good as absolutely insufficient. In such a case, the structure itself must be thoroughly reformed, since it allows only solutions that gravely contradict justice. Such troubling reflections on the possibility of opposition between law and justice force us to deal with the conflict between Honduras and El Salvador in a way that is not purely theoretical and abstract.

El Salvador has justified its position by appealing to justice rather than to particular laws. This approach, however, must be pressed further. The conscious awareness of the nation is such that it will no longer be possible to tolerate the invocation of any laws whatsoever, if they are seen to be the product of a situation which on the whole cannot be regarded as just for the Salvadoran population in its entirety.

The same is true in the international order: the starting point for international laws is the assumption that the current international order is fair or at least is the best possible one under present circumstances. Obviously that is not the case here, and hence an uncritical appeal to current legislation would simply be maintaining an inadmissible situation. If this principle were universalized, as it should be, it would not be permissible to hide behind pure legality when the situation that had given rise to that legality and which is protected by it, is fundamentally unjust and intolerable.

We must be on guard against going to subjective extremes, and that tendency should be counterbalanced by a presumption in favor of the law. Appealing to justice over the law, however, should always be possible both in order to constantly revise the law and to challenge it in particular cases.

The problem becomes especially acute when under a particular legal arrangement, human dignity cannot attain what is its due, for the law is then impeding that which is ultimately its very *raison d'etre*. If there are situations that do not allow legislation that would protect not only minimum living standards but even the minimum provisions necessary for a person to live, those very situations would seem to urgently require transformation. This would be the case if it became quite clear that under present circumstances laws offering such minimal guarantees, such as laws preventing employment discrimination due to nationality, or minimum wage laws, and so forth, were impossible. Such a situation would demand radical change—unless it were apparent that no other possible situation would permit better laws. However, the claim that no better legal framework is possible tends to be made by those who have a lot to lose [from change].

NATIONALISM

Besides the issues of violence and the tension between law and justice, the conflict between Honduras and El Salvador raises yet another problem, that of *nationalism*.

Again we find something seemingly positive, the idea of nation and patriotic pride, which, however, can lead to fatal consequences with respect to giving human beings what is their due. In this case the positive aspect was clear in the Salvadoran position: the conscience of the nation was immediately and effectively put on the alert, since those being persecuted were Salvadorans, fellow citizens who were being persecuted because of their nationality. Ultimately what was at stake was the dignity of the person, but the protest would not have gone beyond a remote sympathy if the offense had not been tinged with nationalism. The underlying reason was the fact that rights were being trampled, but the motivation of the moment was the affront to nationalism. A consciousness of national unity was thereby awakened, and the government received support for both its military and its diplomatic action, as well as for its declared intention to address the violation of the rights of any Salvadoran inside or outside the country. Would all of that come about without an increase in patriotic spirit? The idea of patriotism, impelled by extreme circumstances, can make it possible to achieve national unity above and beyond party and class divisions. In principle, such unity can be regarded as positive, if it does not become a game of exploitation.

However, the reverse side of nationalism is likewise obvious. Salvadorans are expelled from Honduras under the pretext of nationalism. In the name of nationalism, people whose only crime is their nationality are persecuted. National pride is going to make it very difficult to come to a settlement above the national level. Hondurans will reject both the people and goods of El Salvador, simply because they are Salvadoran. On our side, we do not always avoid the temptation to discriminate against people, past or present, simply for being Hondurans.

Thus we see how a seemingly indispensable idea becomes destructive. It is not enough to say that the harm comes from exaggerating an idea that is good in itself, since that would leave open the question of whether such exaggeration is not irremediably connected to the very idea of nationalism. In other words, it is an open question whether nationalism is not one of those ambiguous realities which cannot achieve good without entailing limitations and evils. Is group cohesion achievable only through confrontation with another group? Are motives for internal cohesion so weak that they inevitably need outside pressure? These are key questions for educing the value of the idea of nationalism, which cannot be presented as something absolute before which all other values must be relativized. Rather, that notion of nationalism itself must be radically relativized, especially by broadening the scope of national unity to the issue of Central American unification and beyond the numerous artificial and unnatural divisions existing today—thus making it contribute towards the best kind of human development for all.

Here the position that El Salvador has maintained insistently, that one's condition as a human being is prior to one's political condition, demands that we reflect profoundly and examine the nationalism of our politics. Rather than simply defending and promoting the rights of its subjects, is it not the role of the state to promote and defend the rights of all human beings? Or at least, should the state not undertake the defense and promotion of the rights of its subjects because its subjects are human beings and not because they are its subjects? Should it not seek to broaden and strengthen the overall unity among human beings in all spheres, instead of multiplying political entities?

Thus we have before us three serious issues. While on the one hand they deal with the justification of a past event, they also demand that a new stance be taken so as to make the future more just. These two kinds of justification are distinct, but if they are honest, their fundamental guiding principles should be in harmony with one another. It would be dishonest to utilize certain arguments in order to justify conflict that took place in the past, and then forget them in the rebuilding that is to come. El Salvador needs to continue and develop the basic intuition that sustained it morally during the difficult moments of the conflict.

The three fundamental problems noted up to this point can be summed up as a general problem, namely that legal and political provisions and limitations often become absolutized. When that happens, they no longer energize those fundamental rights which are their own ultimate justification. Those legal provisions thereby hinder the full development of those rights without which human persons cannot come to be what they are.

That this principle has been forgotten is both the remote and proximate cause of the conflict. Reviving it and making it the fundamental guideline for the next steps we take, will both serve as a justification for past events and as a new consciousness in the search for a just state of affairs, which in turn will make possible those laws, and only those laws that safeguard and promote the fundamental rights of the human person.

Principles for Evaluating Legal and Political Restrictions on Fundamental Rights

The conflict between Honduras and El Salvador, characterized as it is by the three problems noted above, should be regarded as a *limit-situation*. This circumstance is what makes an ethical judgment difficult.

Law and morality assume that people and societies are ordinarily in a normal situation. As much as its normative nature is open to question—and should be questioned—a legal framework takes that normality for granted. Normality might be understood as undergoing gradual change, but a particular normality is always taken for granted. Extreme cases may be envisioned, but the assumption is that such extremity is a rare occurrence, and thus what is normal is regarded as the rule. Obviously this position favors those who do not go beyond the legally recognized normal situation.

However, this legally recognized normality often makes it possible to hypocritically ignore the real situation. Such a normality is in the interest of those who hold power, whether it be political, religious, economic, or military. It does not, however, always fit the real circumstances, but at most an ideal situation. Thus the legal framework does not really create the opportunity to fight effectively for those rights that are recognized in theory, but that lie outside what is recognized as normality. This pertains to so many pieces of legislation, that provoke extreme situations because they proclaim political freedom, while simultaneously subverting freedom for workers, labor unions, and others.

Extreme situations can always occur and, indeed, they are generally foreseen in some fashion by the legislators. The shocking thing in our age is the growing frequency with which they occur both individually and collectively, in the moral as well as the political realm. At the very least, such frequency is a symptom that existing legislation hardly responds to the real situation. More importantly, it is a symptom that something very serious is concealed in this situation, so much so that it clamors for a deep and rapid change in whatever makes the situation the way it is.

This may be happening, on the one hand, because the situation upheld by legislation has always been unjust for most citizens. On the other hand, it may also be the case that society has made such a significant advance in its development and awareness that only in appearance is it similar to previous forms of society.

An extreme situation is not merely a pretext for undertaking actions which under ideal circumstances would be illicit. First and foremost, however, these actions are a denunciation of the situation and of the legal order that promotes or supports that situation. In order to clarify both of these characteristics, we must go deeper into the idea of a limit-situation. . . .

LIMIT-SITUATIONS

The term "limit-situation" was given currency by Jaspers who used it to refer to those situations in which one cannot live without struggle and suffering, in which one inescapably has to "exist" and cannot simply vegetate, in which one rises above momentariness and fragmentariness and has to live as a whole to the fullest extent (1969, vol. 2). These are the situations which place our whole existence in question and flood it with light, so much so that it is in these situations and only in them that we grasp our true being.

If we transpose this individualistic concept into a social key, as a result of the limit-situation which El Salvador has endured, we see that the following has taken place: problems affecting the very being of the nation, which people sought to ignore, have emerged in high relief; positive forces previously not evident have sprung forth vigorously; on the whole the nation's awareness of its situation and of possible solutions has grown. This is one of the positive aspects of the recent painful conflict. The question is why this takes place in the limit-situation. We will see why by examining concretely what has happened from the standpoint of both Honduras and El Salvador.

First, let us look at the problem from the standpoint of Honduras, that is, by taking the situation of Honduras as a limit-situation. What happens in a limit-situation is that a particular situation reaches its limit, and thus exacerbated, reveals what it contained in latent form. This is not playing with words; it is reality.

In the present case, abusing Salvadorans is the easy way out of a situation of intolerable pressure. Let us leave aside the political aspect of the problem and focus on its social dimension. The social situation in Honduras is particularly intolerable. In such circumstances, a "bad conscience," whether it be conscious or unconscious, struggles to disguise a situation in order to avoid absolutely necessary radical change. The thousands of Salvadorans in Honduras were a handy pretext for disguising the social situation. They were a significant segment of the working people in Honduras and hence offered a ready explanation for the unemployment and poor living conditions of Hondurans. It is beyond the scope of this article to analyze the complex core of the conflict, but it is clear that the limit was reached in an unjust situation. The sad part is that people are made to believe that the ultimate dimension of the problem is that of nationalism.

. . . .

Something similar, however, must be said from the Salvadoran side. The fact that several hundred thousand Salvadorans were unable to find a decent livelihood in the country of their birth, is an irrefutable denunciation of an unjust situation. The causes and solutions might be open to discussion, but the situation in itself is ovewhelming—especially if we take into account the proportion of those who have left El Salvador in relation to those who have been able to remain. The least we can do is to come to a common awareness that we stand before a limit-situation. We have not reached this point without incurring a collective guilt, and we will not be able to escape from it painlessly. Thus we stand before a collective experience of something that otherwise would not have struck the national consciousness.

Precisely because it puts the one confronting it into ultimate tension, the limit-situation is a translucidation of something that seemed to be so opaque that it could not be assimilated. That is not the end of the matter, however. It is also a situation from which escape is impossible without a break with normality, whether that of legal or ordinary solutions. In the recent conflict El Salvador felt it had no choice but to take up arms, to inflict death on others, to create hardships for its own citizens, to use particular methods of propaganda and espionage, and so forth—all of which are evil responses even if they may have been necessary in order to accomplish what was regarded as absolutely correct and utterly necessary. This is not a case of the widely reviled principle that "the end justifies the means." The point is that an end that is not only good but even necessary can be attained only by the obligatory use of evil means, since the obligation to act cannot be postponed, and all effective modes of action that are available are evil. This is almost always the case in limit-situations.

That is why the limit-situation is a condemnation: the situation is unjust and is at the crisis stage—so much so that although a solution is urgently needed, all available means are evil. Returning to our specific case, if El Salvador had waited longer for international arbitration, the situation of Salvadorans both in Honduras and in El Salvador would have become intolerable, and the country would have failed to meet a grave and urgent obligation to Salvadorans. Not waiting, however, entailed an armed military action, some of whose consequences could only be evil, both on the battlefield itself, and more generally for many citizens. This is the second important aspect of the limit-situation.

In order to describe the first aspect of the limit-situation, that of condemnation, we may borrow the theological formulation of Thielicke. That is to say "legitimated" illegality presupposes a state of injustice in which the "fallen" nature of our world is present with particular and even paradigmatic acuteness. Then, in order to deal with the second aspect, that of moral ambiguity, we will have to utilize Thielicke's further formulation that in such a case we stand before a conflict with no easy solution, because we are in the presence of a clash of values, which forces us to be guilty one way or another. Here lies concealed the tragedy of the limit-situation: the necessity of evil that does not free us of guilt, at least in a psychological sense (Thielicke, 1975).

In the limit-situation arising from a clash of values that could be resolved in an ideal situation, but not in an unjust situation which is now established as normal and legal, we find the following characteristics: 1) it is obligatory to act; 2) all solutions are evil; 3) once embarked, we enter into the grip of laws that leave no room for personal moral decision; 4) we easily lose our mental clarity and proper disposition due to the momentum of the situation, which on the whole is an embodiment of evil. If these last two aspects partly relieve individual responsibility, by the same token they lead imperceptibly to hardening of the heart and dehumanization.

This last point is extremely important for both theoretical and historical reasons. Situations such as that of resistance to totalitarian régimes, revolution against unjust structures, revolutionary violence, family planning, and so forth demand a thorough rethinking of what a limit-situation is. In this article, it will be sufficient to take up only the two aspects we have analyzed: first, the presence of a limit situation itself is a condemnation of an unjust situation that demands radical change; second, when a person or a people enter into a limit-situation, decisions are always ambiguous and therefore those who make and implement these decisions must refuse to be swept up in the passions aroused by the very thrust of that situation.

In both respects what we observe is that fundamental human rights are being obscured due to legal and political arrangements resulting from a situation that is no longer tolerable. The *possibility of antinomy between justice and law* takes on renewed force in the light of the limit-situation.

THE NECESSITY AND THE LIMITS OF LAW

Law appears to be a tool necessary for life in common, and indeed the objective basis for the application of justice. On the other hand, it is a limitation of freedom and an impediment to personal development. I do not want to look like a utopian anarchist, but a brief reference to one of the central themes of Saint Paul's theological thought, that of the law vis-à-vis Christian freedom, relieves me of the need for lengthy justification. The fact that Saint Paul does not deal with immediate sociological or political implications does not rule out any such extrapolation. Law may be necessary. But its limiting character assumes a fallen nature, if we want to put it in theological terms; or a nature that has not yet attained its full development, if we prefer evolutionary terms. The discussion is not merely theoretical nor is it remote from our present case. What have we seen in the way many people assess the conflict between Honduras and El Salvador? Is it not a reifying and absolutizing of the legal order, as if devotion to law were an absolute good and had to be preserved above and beyond any other consideration? Or are they defending this framework only as a lesser evil because there is none better?

The solution is not to attack the legal order for being legal. The legal framework is necessary as a safeguard against the ignorance of some, bad will in others, and everyone's subjective excesses. As relations between ever more complex groups increase in complexity and prompt uncontrolled and uncontrollable chain reactions on the part of each subjectivity involved, the only remedy is to multiply laws and courts. Nevertheless, we should not forget that this remedy is by its nature subject to change in accordance with the situation to be remedied—and that is in the best of cases, when legislation is entirely aimed at achieving the best common good possible and not at protecting the established order.

We would fall into anarchy if there were no laws and protection by law; but we would fall into injustice if laws were absolutized and not subjected to continual revision. The failure of legislation made obvious in a given limit-situation pressures us to change the conditions that gave rise to the legal order which led to that limit-situation and to the failure represented in it.

Law is a precaution against the limitations of human beings and of the society in which we live. That precaution however, should be directed primarily against abuses by the powerful and should serve growth towards personal freedom and personal responsibility. When law is nothing but the opposite, we stand inside a legal structure which on the whole is evil.

This leads us to a piercing question. The present legal order that made it possible for Honduran authorities to deny the fundamental rights of Salvadorans in Honduras, did not allow El Salvador to come to their aid and did not allow impartial judges to provide a prompt solution for a very grave and pressing situation. Is it not this very same legal order that has generated the limit-situation of Salvadorans who leave their country in the hope of finding steady employment abroad? Is it not the same legal order that is governing Latin America's fundamental relations, both internally and with the United States? Let us remind ourselves once more that laws are the reflection of a situation that, independently of good will, has its own dynamism, and its true results can only be truly appreciated when the situation becomes extreme and approaches its limit.

THE HIERARCHY OF VALUES EXPRESSED IN A SITUATION

Each situation, moreover, is characterized by a hierarchy of values. It would be interesting to analyze the real hierarchy of values—beneath rhetorical affirmations—governing the overall behavior of Latin American societies and governments, particularly in light of the continual and numerous interventions and involvements on the part of the society and the government of the United States.

In the present case, judging from the OAS discussions in Washington, it would seem that the inviolability of borders and the avoidance of armed conflict at all cost is a fundamental value. What lies behind these declarations? How can anyone speak of national sovereignty as an absolute value when foreign forces are continually intervening directly and indirectly in many Latin American nations and laying down conditions for politics generally and for many particular decisions? What is the ultimate reason for avoiding conflicts? Is it love for true peace, or to maintain the established order, or to prevent "hot spots" that might allow new forces to become involved in the existing "balance"? Moreover, if these principles of the inviolability of sovereignty and the unacceptability of armed intervention are so absolute, would it not be just to apply them retroactively to the history of the Americas?

El Salvador invokes another hierarchy of values in dealing with the conflict. In both the way it has argued and in its behavior, El Salvador has claimed that defending the fundamental rights of the person should be regarded as the supreme value. This stance does not rule out invoking and working towards lower values. It simply means that a lower value can never be invoked if it prevents the attainment of a higher value that should be pursued. El Salvador has committed itself publicly to a great deal, and both inside and outside the country it is going to be held to account for what it demanded at a difficult moment: the defense of the fundamental rights of the person, above other values and whatever the sacrifice might cost.

This appeal, to the human being and to what is human as a fundamental value, opens the way for us to deal with the problem of *nationalism*. We have already noted that nationalism is a value and has brought with it important benefits. We cannot forget, however, that very serious abuses have been perpetrated in the name of nationalism throughout history and specifically in the recent conflict and its aftereffects. We can go so far as to say that nationalism is a good that entails significant evils both inside and outside the nation. Hence it is clear that nationalism is a political limitation, a true limitation on human beings as citizens of the world. As necessary as that limitation might be considered to be, it remains a limitation. The human being is limited to a particular nationality.

It is proper to the human condition that a vital universality can be attained only on the basis of a very concrete incarnation, and conditions are presently such that this kind of concrete incarnation entails a specific nationality. Nevertheless, the fact that such is the case cannot make us forget that this necessary limitation can stifle a fundamental value. Again we seem to find ourselves facing a limitation of a fundamental human right, this time of a political nature. Nationalities exist so that each and every human being can attain the full scope of his or her humanity—insofar as possible, although not in an absolute sense. When national identities hinder what they should be promoting, they are running counter to their own being and meaning. Some kind of universal State may still be a utopian dream, but exacerbated nationalism is beginning to be humanly intolerable in view of present historical possibilities.

PRIMARY AND SECONDARY RIGHTS

Those who uphold natural law make an important distinction that can help us in properly conceptualizing the problem. They distinguish between primary and secondary natural rights. Primary natural rights are those whose claims are absolute and which are always in force, since they are required by the most essential levels of the human being, the levels that derive from the very notion of the human being. Secondary rights are those required for primary rights to take effect, but they do not flow so directly from human nature itself. In Thielicke's interpretation, primary natural right is regarded as related to the state of pure nature in creation and is obvious to all, while secondary natural right is connected to fallen nature and is not at all obvious but has to be attained by reasoning (Thielicke, 1979, vol. 1).

This explanation of the distinction is extremely important and provides the key for resolving very difficult questions. Let us leave aside the question of how original sin might be interpreted today. The important thing is to emphasize that some rights are such by virtue of natural weakness, so that if human nature were strengthened, they would not have to be claimed as rights. It is likewise important to insist that if at any time these secondary rights should hinder rather than favor the full unfolding of primary rights, they would have to be suppressed. Finally, it is important to insist that if better ways of protecting primary rights were to be contrived in the course of history, these new forms would have to be regarded as secondary rights superceding the older secondary ones.

One such "older" secondary right, and so recognized in traditional ethics, is that of private property. It would be well to keep this very much in mind in order to avoid defending it as the perfect and definitive way of achieving the fullest development of the human person. That is not our topic here, although many of the causes of the conflict and its possible solutions touch on this point. Suffice it to indicate from this new perspective that private property is one of the limitations of a fundamental primary right, namely that of community property (Ellacuría, 1969a). Therefore, in dealing with private property we should observe all the same cautions we demanded of law with regard to justice.

The problem of nationalism should be considered in the same light. Nationalisms are historic forms which claim to be necessary *for the sake of* integral human development. However, they are secondary in nature and reflect a weakness in human beings that ought to be surpassed. Hence they should not be encouraged, or at least they should only be encouraged as historic forms which should not obscure the fundamental value they are to serve and should not stand in the way of being superseded themselves.

This is the case for several reasons. First, the idea of the state should not be confused with that of nation nor with the way states have acted and continue to act. Secondly, there is no reason to believe that presently existing nations are the ideal units for the human beings composing them to reach their maximum potential as human beings in a comprehensive way and as equals. Third, it would never be just that any human being be denied the fundamental rights that are his or hers as a human being because he or she is of a particular nationality; (of its nature nationality is a limitation that proves advantageous for some and disadvantageous for most—although, providing it meets certain conditions, it is still presumed to be a just limitation). Fourth, no nationalism can ever be absolute since it would clash with other nationalisms, thus making clear its secondary and relative character.

These observations are not intended to justify either the theory of limited sovereignty, as it was used to defend military interventions such as that into Czechoslovakia, nor the theory of a more or less covert imperialism, including the work of its police agents. Matters will have to take their course in history, but we should not think that a historic form ceases being so and becomes eternal.

The principle that sovereignty is limited is, as a principle, healthy, and should reflect the fundamental commonality of all human beings and of all peoples, as well as the necessary interaction demanded by the fact that our planet is becoming fully occupied. Today however, sovereignity's embodiments are basically of a repressive nature, whether through tanks or through dollars. Thus far human beings have not been aroused to a consciousness of solidarity among themselves and among peoples to such an extent as to allow a truly common history. The fact that this awakening has not taken place is largely the fault of nationalism. In the past nationalism was a force for human progress, both nationally and internationally, but today it is blocking a universal consciousness, which is both prior and superior to national divisions.

THE FUTURE AS VINDICATION OF A PAST ACTION

If such is the case on a worldwide level, what are we to say with regard to Central America? What murky interests keep alive the difference and opposition of the brother and sister nations of Central America? Has the Central American Common Market been conceived as an instrument for union and equity, as a common task of development for all, or rather as an instrument for exploitation and machinations? Certainly it is not the ordinary people who benefit from this disunity, which some try to compound with misconceived kinds of nationalism. This amounts to the political limitation of a fundamental right: that right is being blocked by something whose only mission is to promote it.

Thus we close the circle. The conflict between Honduras and El Salvador can be examined from different viewpoints. Here it has been examined from the standpoint of fundamental human rights, which are sometimes unjustly limited by legal arrangements and political considerations. The conflict sheds light on the overall problem of such limitation, and the problem helps interpret the conflict. Theory and reality are interacting, as they should. This general approach even now enables us to get beyond the surface of events and come to an ethical analysis of what *really* happened. Consequently we can strike out in a new direction, one that will enable us to overcome the causes of the conflict. . . .

If El Salvador should fail to achieve the kind of future implied in the stance it took in the moments of crisis, if it should allow the logical and ethical consistency of its initial stance to be broken, it will not be possible to take seriously the position the country took during the difficult moments of these past months nor to regard it as ultimately justified. During those moments [of the "Soccer War"] El Salvador rediscovered its true vocation, and it cannot betray that vocation now. To betray the future would be to betray its past. How the truth of its future is forged will reveal the real truth of the recent crisis.

Ignacio Ellacuría

4. The Historicization of The Concept of Property*

TRANSLATION BY PHILLIIP BERRYMAN

The debate aroused by the first real step towards implementing the Agrarian Reform, as represented in the Initial Project, evidences such a high degree of confusion in the way concepts are used that an effort to clarify matters and bring greater rationality can no longer be postponed. Scarcely has it ever been so nakedly obvious how ideologies serve as a rationalization to cloak and falsify real interests as it is in the present case. At stake in the Agrarian Reform are situations and interests, whose character varies a great deal depending on the position the observer occupies in a society that is highly divided. This is especially true in El Salvador where land and social forces have such special historic characteristics. As has been shown over and over, the situation of the vast majority is one of desperation, while that of the minority—which is very much associated directly or indirectly with landholding—is not only one of luxurious wealth but of true domination.

Everyone claims to want to resolve this situation. There is general agreement, at least on the verbal level, that the situation is untenable and must be changed. The only ones who disagree are those who might

---

*Ellacuría (1976d); see Bibliography in the back of this book.

In 1976 the Salvadoran legislature approved what was called the Initial Project of an agrarian reform plan enacted in 1975 as the ISTA Law (Salvadoran Institute for Agrarian Transformation). Although the Initial Project would affect property in only two of the country's fourteen departments and owners were to be compensated, it unleashed enormous controversy. Not only the landholders, but the whole private sector, headed by ANEP (National Association of Private Enterprise), vigorously opposed the measure. Most of the left—with the exception of the Communist Party—were also opposed. The UCA welcomed the measure as a significant step, and *ECA* devoted a whole issue to land tenure and the law, examined from a number of disciplines. While most of the argument in this article, which headed that issue of *ECA*, is directed at private sector ideologues, Ellacuría also criticizes the reactions of Marxists. (It should be recalled that Ignacio Ellacuría, the rector of the University of Central America, was also the editor of its monthly journal, *Estudios Centroamericanos*.) P.B.

think that an intensification of the contradictions could bring a radical change relatively soon. Arguments advanced in opposition to the Project must be understood in the light of this situation. Everyone claims to want to resolve it. No one seems to want the effects to last forever, although many do not want the causes to change.

Thus we face a problem that is both theoretical and practical. Can self-interested rationalization for the sake of one's own advantage be unmasked? How can that be done? How are we to contribute to detecting as objectively as possible what is happening, and how can we push the process in the right direction?

In order to resolve these questions, I will attempt to analyze and combat the ideologization at work in what is being said. Perhaps the foundation may thus be laid for creating a sufficient social awareness. Otherwise it will be very difficult to reach the desired objectives promptly and in a humane way. What I propose to do here is not enough to bring about social change, but it is necessary. This task cannot be left in the hands of neophytes or dogmatists. The question will not be resolved definitively here, but I will try to situate it correctly, by showing how complex it is theoretically. This procedure will not help accelerate action, but it is the best course for making sure that the action taken be appropriate.

Our overall approach is to examine the historical context of the concept of property and to show how the historical variability and the cultural context of this concept undermine its current ideological role, and thereby constitute a necessary condition for social change. A similar approach can be taken with such concepts as power, freedom, justice, and work (Ellacuría, 1973b).

The historicization of concepts as a principle of de-ideologization

The problem is rooted in the fact that human beings use their faculty for knowing not only to determine how things really are, but fundamentally in order to defend themselves in the struggle for life. This biological and material characteristic of the human capacity to know is what lies at the root of ideologizing. Thus individual and group survival, which of necessity becomes a matter of some being superior and dominating, determines and conditions the possibilities of objective knowledge, especially when that survival is threatened. In this sense, all knowledge is interested knowledge, and the fundamental interest of knowledge is life and the direction one wants to give this life. Human thought can overcome this radical conditioning only by recognizing it as such and confronting it critically. Nevertheless, no matter how much this condition is faced and overcome, the factor of interest always remains present and impedes the path towards objectivity. Reasoning by no means always helps us to avoid the trap of interest; that is why we speak of rationalizations. Unamuno long ago said that the important thing is not to be right but to be truthful. An untruthful use of reason may give the appearance of being scientific, when it is really a means of domination.

The problem is intensified when immediate and serious interests affecting individuals and social groups come into play. Such is the case of the Agrarian Reform insofar as it affects private property—and along with private property matters as crucial as work, power, freedom and justice . . . and ultimately one kind of life or another, one kind of society or another. There are basically two standpoints from which to view all these realities and the terms used for them: that of those who are on top and see their privileges threatened, and that of those who from a condition of oppression realize that they must overcome this condition and that right is on their side. If the situation is characterized in this manner, it is more likely that the arguments proposed by the oppressed are on the whole more valid. An ethical and social validity, if accompanied by the proper critical reflection will be close to social objectivity. The arguments used to defend the prevailing situation or the causes of this situation are, on the whole, more likely to be a purely ideological weapon, although taken separately each one may to some extent be objective.

Propaganda and ideological struggle are not the natural sites for objectivity; and although in principle the most correct social option offers the assurance that it is on the side of the truest interest, that is not enough. In the name of justice we can fall into idealism and falsehood, especially when the independence of theoretical work is denied, thus unduly politicizing it. Both an ethical stance and a critical stance are required; only with them combined can we gradually approach the truth, especially where human interests are most at stake. Ideas have their own logic, but it is not a matter of pure ideas, even where it might seem that only ideas are involved.

In order to challenge the role played by ideology, we must first define what the predominent ideology is, and how it is the ideology of society itself as it is structured at a particular moment. When Durkheim spoke of a collective consciousness as a body of beliefs and feelings shared by most of the members of a society, he was recognizing a fundamental social fact (Durkheim, 1958). However, this group consciousness, although reflective of most people, is constituted by the interests of the concrete form of that society, based on the interests of the ruling class. This is another social fact which it would be unfortunate to overlook. We must ask how this group consciousness is shaped and whom it serves.

The answer is not difficult if we can find out what purposes the educational system serves and who controls the media. When the oppressed try to counteract the dominant collective consciousness, they may not achieve the greatest objectivity, but they do set in motion a positive principle of critique, begin a more valid change, and in this sense, make possible a greater openness to objectivity. Moreover, success is more likely if the good of the whole is being sought, for that is the best way to find the good of all, even though when the whole is structured dialectically, the good of all cannot be achieved except through evil for some.

One of the most decisive of all the components of group consciousness at present is the concept of property or ownership. Before beginning to analyze it, we have to say what it means to speak of the historicization of concepts as a critical principle of de-ideologization.

It is almost a tautology to state that concepts are historical, especially when they refer to historic reality. A historic concept is here opposed to an abstract and universal one. We can inquire about property and its relationship to the human person, by assuming that property is always the same reality and always has the same effects on persons and on society. However, the historic concept, since it refers immediately to historic and changing realities which depend on the structural and conjunctural situation where they are present, means something different in accordance with the particular moment of the process and the context in which that process is taking place. Historic concepts are rather like classical philosophy's analogous concepts, which maintain a certain unity of meaning although they refer to distinct realities. Similarly, historic concepts refer to different realities in process: the reality referred to is the same, but the modes of the process vary. Thus, it is not the same to own the means of production in the context of medieval feudalism and in that of modern capitalism. Owning land is not the same as owning a building or a computer; owning land in a country with 21,000 square kilometers and four million inhabitants is not the same as owning it in a country with 200,000 square kilometers and two million inhabitants.

Historic concepts are not thereby equivocal concepts, any more than analogous concepts were: both the human and the orangutan are animals but their animality is different, even if we abstract from the human's rationality. Something similar is the case with regard to historic concepts and more generally with regard to methods for dealing with what is social and historic. One cannot make a dogmatic concept and a mechanical method the starting point—as often happens with analysts who are supposedly Marxists—and then force the data, if one has even bothered to keep the data in mind. If the hypothesis cannot be invalidated by data, it is not historic; one is falling into sheer idealism, no matter how much the realist or the materialist one might claim to be. Marxism has correctly insisted on the historic character of concepts and social realities, but by its very nature this historic character must move towards reshaping concepts that responded to other contexts and other moments in the process.

. . . .

More than in any other case, it is obvious that the truth of historic concepts is found in their becoming reality. For example, if it is claimed that property ownership promotes initiative, personal freedom, and so forth, but in fact causes the opposite within the whole of a particular social body, the property under consideration is not the kind needed by that social body. Indeed, property is its antithesis if it is causing contrary effects. These are operative concepts whose truth can be measured in their results, and whose content must continue to change even if their essential meaning is maintained. *Demonstrating the impact of certain concepts within a particular context is what is understood here as their historicization.* Hence historicization is a principle of de-ideologization.

Dominant ideologies draw their life from a basic fallacy, that of proposing certain concepts or images, values and guidelines for action as real and historic concepts, effective and operative values, and effective guidelines for action, when in fact those concepts are abstract and universal. As abstract and universal, everyone assents to them and they stand for realities which, as they operate in history, are however the negation of what they claim to be. For example, press freedom is said to be a fundamental right and an indispensable condition for democracy, but if such press freedom can only be exercised by someone who owns means of production that are out of the reach of the oppressed majority, freedom of the press is a fundamental sin and a deception that renders democracy impossible. If a newspaper or a radio or television station can only be maintained by a great deal of money and can only keep going with support from advertisers, who represent the forces of capital, press freedom historicized in this fashion is the denial of that formal freedom of the press with which we all agree in theory and in a universal sense.

If we therefore succeed in historicizing concepts, that is, in saying what they mean and what they conceal here and now, we are contributing towards the de-ideologization of a superstructure, that really serves to reinforce particular social and economic structures, and they in turn actually cause the opposite of what they claim to want to achieve. It is here that philosophy can offer its assistance as a principle of de-ideologization and also as an opening to areas for new action (Ellacuría, 1976b). With these general considerations in place, I will turn my attention to the concept of property, viewed historically from within the situation of El Salvador and in the context of the Agrarian Transformation.

The historicization of the concept of property

In keeping with what has been said, little is gained by beginning with an abstract definition of property. The historicization of this notion should start from an examination of the reality of property in El Salvador, and particularly agrarian property: how it began, how it is today, and what effects it has produced and is producing. Browning has shown how present land ownership came about, starting with Indian communities, which were despoiled of what was theirs in community, moving on to the abolition of communal land until there were enormous production units—enormous [then and now] in proportion to the amount of usable land in the country—alongside of which there are numerous small parcels, which are each insufficient to even maintain a family (Browning, 1971; Colindres, 1976).

From the outset, therefore, we should distinguish between different forms of property ownership. The indigenous natives had property, the Spanish conquistadors and the surviving communities had property; and the descendants of those who took advantage of the 1881 Agrarian Reform, enacted for the sake of those who had private capital, also have property.* There is no single form of property, and it can be said without exaggeration that the existing forms of private property in El Salvador, especially in the rural areas, are imported; ones that have been imposed through particular transformations in history, which are closer to pillage than to just acquisition—at least if we take the conquest into account. What is therefore really at stake when it is said that the right of property is being denied? The question should be answered from within El Salvador, on the basis of what property is historically in El Salvador, and on the basis of what we want our country to be. This is a historic question and it requires a historic response, not one that is abstract and universal. It does us little good to talk about the ideal advantages of one kind of property, if reality is showing us that this kind of property is leading to the opposite of what it claims to be seeking.

What the dominant ideology is defending is private ownership of the main means of production in agriculture, industry, trade, and finance. This form of property is extremely concentrated and entails sharp polarization between the few who have everything and the vast majority who scarcely have anything. On this score, some cynically justify their position by claiming that since there is not enough land in El Salvador to be shared among all rural workers it is better that property ownership continue as it is now in order to avoid arousing a massive hunger for land ownership. Would it not be preferable to argue that if there is not enough land for each individual, it would be better if the land belonged to everyone and were for everyone? Would it not be better to devise forms of real property that would not be strictly private property? If in El Salvador it is impossible for each and every individual to develop his or her personal possibilities through ownership of a particular form of property, why not conclude that this kind of property ownership is inadequate for the country, instead of assuming that a few should enjoy this possibility even though their enjoyment is at the cost of others who suffer the consequences? It is one thing to acknowledge that some kind of property is necessary for developing fully as a human

---

*See also Montes (1986c); chapter 14, *this volume.* THE EDITORS

person, and it is something quite different to stubbornly insist that this form of property must be private property [understood] as the Romans understood it and as it has been experienced in Northern and Western capitalism.

PROPERTY CONSIDERED PHILOSOPHICALLY

. . . [At this point, the article discusses the positions of Hegel and Wundt on property as illustrations of how philosophers approach the issue. Ellacuría concludes the section enumerating the major points:]

What they [Hegel (1952) and Wundt (1917)] say can be summarized as follows: a) the destiny and the particular way of being of individuals and peoples is at stake in property and in forms of property; b) this has been a fundamental point of concern in the great bodies of law; c) legislators increasingly try to channel the shifting reality of facts by focussing more on empirical possibilities than on some requirement regarded as absolute; d) historic processes have led to different ways of understanding property, and hence it is not a universally fixed concept but rather a historic concept; e) different forms of property have provided various benefits but also great evils and injustices; f) something indispensable for the development of people and for the well being of society cannot be left to the discretion of the most powerful groups or individuals; g) the problem of property has a fundamental ethical dimension and hence it can be resolved adequately only by means of a profound striving to be ethical both theoretically and practically; h) critical philosophical reflection can help devise a more adequate way of focussing on the problem of property.

THE CONCEPT OF PROPERTY IN THE CONTROVERSY BETWEEN ANEP AND THE GOVERNMENT

ANEP (National Association of Private Enterprise) regards itself as the representative of Salvadoran private enterprise—although FE-NAPES (National Federation of Small Enterprise) also exists. Since the promulgation of the Initial Project of the land reform, ANEP has launched a very expensive campaign in order to defend its interests and to attack the initial measures of the Agrarian Transformation. Obviously, ANEP representatives are using their economic might to defend what they are at present; the arguments they use serve to justify their present position. This is not a theoretical discussion seeking objectivity, but rather an abusive use of the media in order to defend themselves and attack others (Stein, 1976). They are not defending arguments but defending situations. That is not illegitimate if the situation being defended is proper, but there is no doubt that from the outset the whole procedure has been one of self-interest.

Property in light of the interests of private enterprise

What kind of property are they talking about? What are their arguments for defending property? ANEP says it has always struggled "to maintain an economic system in keeping with the principles of social justice." In brief, ANEP regards centralized planning as tantamount to setting up a totalitarian-tending régime, and it asserts that government bureaucratic action is leading to the destruction of the dynamic entrepreneurial spirit. Business people will feel forced to cut back their efforts to avoid being hit by expropriation and being despoiled of the fruit of their labor, for no one will be assured that his or her efforts will be rewarded. The fundamental criterion for potential expropriation should be productivity; hence reform should begin with land held by the state, and then move to privately owned lands that are abandoned, idle, or poorly cultivated. However, lands [already] efficiently cultivated fulfill the social function of private property, since greater production benefits more people, and thus the vast majority are brought into a more decent life and into sharing more justly in the production of the nation (*Diario Latino*, July 9, 1976).

On the issue of property, ANEP repeats in its Second Statement that the measure will lower agricultural production, thereby lowering the living standard of the population. Implicitly, it is thereby recognizing that any agrarian reform is a matter of destroying the power of one class in order to pass it to another. When productivity is high there is no reason for state intervention, although ANEP believes that the most burdensome and least productive areas of activity should go primarily to the government. State intervention will increase unemployment, affect investor confidence, and create a climate of disunity, mistrust, and lack of incentives, and thus will increase the danger of communism (*Diario Latino*, July 13, 1976).

In its Third Statement, ANEP insists once more on its entrepreneurial nature and claims to represent the most productive sectors of the country. References to the "myth of productivity," an expression that the UCA had used in its statement (July 10, 1976), did not please ANEP, which failed to understand what was meant by "myth" used in that context. ANEP believes proposals for cooperatives and collectivist experiments are at odds with productivity; and it is against bureaucracy—"the same white elephants of the bureaucracy"—that has already proven itself ineffective. Finally ANEP stands for the system of free enterprise and republican institutions, "the fundamental foundations of the democratic system, the system that the Salvadoran people prefer" (*Diario Latino*, July 15, 1976).

The government's primary response to ANEP was to reject the core argument of the large private business community since productivity in the Project area is among the lowest along the whole coast. The government then went on to expose the actual social situation in that area: while five owners together held 17,318 manzanas [1 manzana = 1.75

acres], 2,483 owners held 5,006 manzanas [or slightly more than 3.5 acres each]; currently illiteracy is 65 % in that area, 98 % of the houses are without toilets, 50.4% do not have adequate drinking water, and 35% of the houses are unfit. The unemployment figure for the area is 54.3% and thus the peasants can expect just 141 days of work a year. Moreover, 38% of the peasant landowners earn about 35 centavos a day [$0.87] from their land, while the 5 landowners each have daily incomes of 2,479 colons [$6,197]. In other words, each of the 5 landholders each day receives the same income that 6,968 families earn together (*Diario Latino*, July 12, 1976).

In its second response, the government argues that the large land-holders regard any change in the country's economic structures as something affecting their interests adversely, even when such changes "might bring the well-being and peacefulness that furthers the common good." It also argues that "the problems caused by the dramatic living conditions of the people cannot be resolved simply by focussing on pro-duction." "El Salvador might reach the point of producing twenty times as much as now, but if the unjust economic structures due primarily to the present form of land tenure are not corrected, a few will enjoy the luxury of not even waiting in line to eat while a vast majority will not even get a chance to wait in line." Yet the government is not proposing any sort of socialist solution, but rather is attempting to "bring about the participation of most Salvadorans in a market economy." It insists, how-ever, that "the problem of the country is not simply that of production, but that of determining to whom the income flowing from production goes." Therefore the government "has decided to do away with the frameworks historically used to pursue the economic and social devel-opment of the country, for their only result has been to aggravate the al-ready wretched social situation of the vast majority." Selfishness is present in the defense of vested interests; the document also calls pre-sent structure of land tenure unjust. Certainly production and produc-tivity are important, but it is especially important that there be "a just distribution of income among those who contribute to producing such income through their labor." "Recognizing that there cannot be compat-ibility between the interests of a minority owning everything and a ma-jority owning nothing, (the government) reiterates its historic and irrevocable commitment to take its stand with the latter, and also regrets that the former have not shown the ability to comprehend that although their interests might be affected in a transitory fashion, the Agrarian Transformation process constitutes a life insurance policy for which their children will one day be grateful" (*El Mundo*, July 16, 1976).

In its third response the government highlights its intention "to thoroughly change the antiquated structures that have kept most of our fellow citizens in backwardness for centuries, victims of economic un-derdevelopment and social injustice." It insists that it accepts private property but not as ANEP understands it, "based on the old theory that regarded absolutism, exclusivity, and perpetuity as conditions for property rights"; the government also insists that private enterprise must be fostered and strengthened, since nothing can replace human imagination, creativity, and drive. Given the people who belong to it, ANEP cannot but oppose measures like this one; indeed, its opposition is a sign that the measure would benefit the majority, who are not exactly ANEP's primary concern, although they should be that of the government (*La Prensa Gráfica*, July 16, 1976).

An ideologized use of the concept of property

The controversy between the government and ANEP clearly evidences an ideologized use of the concept of property. What the government has done is to historicize the concept that ANEP uses universally and abstractly—that is, ANEP uses the concept of property without taking into account *all* its real consequences in our country. Indeed, a form of property that produces the disastrous social effects we witness in our country, as underscored by the government and not denied by ANEP, cannot be regarded as the kind of property the situation needs. One need only observe the present situation of our society—which has been this way for many years—to realize that this kind of ownership which, utterly unregulated by any authority beyond unfettered free enterprise itself, does not serve the nation as a whole. ANEP should acknowledge that Salvadoran private enterprise, despite its much vaunted productivity, has been unable to raise the country above the very low indices that describe most of the people, although this same private enterprise has been able to assure that those directly involved in it enjoy such high living standards that they have no reason to envy the way of life in even the wealthiest countries.

1. ANEP claims to be defending certain values, most importantly that of private initiative: the capacity to create is one of the fundamental values of human beings, who make themselves human by freely productive labor of some sort. It is by no means obvious that the system they claim can arouse private initiative has really been effective with respect to most of the country. Nor is it clear that initiative and creative ability are necessarily bound up with private ownership and/or a concern to make profit and dominate others. Perhaps many people are unwilling to work unless they receive certain selfish gratifications from their work, but it should be acknowledged that this is not an ethically ideal state of things. Salvadoran private business people might not be willing to put their best energies to work unless they are to receive large, easy, and sure profits, but it should be acknowledged that such a situation should change and that such people ought to change. In order that such a change not remain simply in the realm of subjective and moralizing aspirations, however, the material conditions enabling it to take place would have to be posited, and that would be the responsibility of the state. Such a process would have to be gradual and it would

have to be a subsidiary process, but it is absolutely necessary, given the way things are now and everything that is at stake.

2. ANEP is correct when it insists on the need to increase the country's production and on the issue of productivity. But ANEP's position, if we historicize it, is quite weak, precisely where it is regarded as strongest. Although ANEP claims to encompass almost all Salvadoran enterprises, and thus employs millions of Salvadorans, it has not brought about a humane situation for those people. Moreover, if productivity is the justification for ownership, the day the government evidences higher productivity it will be justified in doing away with any right to private property. Furthermore, ANEP is very inconsistent when it proposes that expropriation should begin with the lands with lowest productivity, whether they belong to the state or to individuals. Finally, it has not been established that productivity will not increase with what is proposed by the government, which intends to increase it by following ANEP's very philosophy, although with some modifications. The government wants to increase productivity by making more private entrepreneurs and arousing personal initiative. Its corrective consists in bringing about a more just competition, preventing just a few from making use of almost all available resources and striving to enable the majority to have some access to the means of production. Is it this modification that bothers the representatives of agro-export capitalism?

3. The discussion has shown that ANEP values productivity over distribution, while the government places more importance on distribution than on production. ANEP seems to assume that greater productivity and production will inevitably lead to better distribution: things will go better for everyone when they are going magnificently well for a few. This implicit line of reasoning confuses just distribution with an increase in the number and amount of compensations, for the result may be greater divergence in both absolute and relative terms, as the case of Brazil proves very clearly. For its part, the government claims to be seeking a better redistribution of income and of sources of income, with which it hopes to bring about greater productivity and production. From the standpoint of the social function, the government's position is undoubtedly superior. And in economic terms, it does not seem that it would be difficult to improve on the current indices of productivity and the levels of production in the country.

4. Each side understands the social function of private property in a different way. ANEP seems to regard that function as assured when a particular level of productivity is attained, thereby enabling more people to participate in the production process. The government does not regard that function as assured if the facts taken as a whole show that the situation of most people is disastrous—and not simply one or other fact in isolation. The way the country is now running economically cannot be regarded as having a social function, if most of the country is living in inhuman conditions.

Both sides seem to agree that the social situation of the country is bad, and that the solution lies in private enterprise. The difference lies in the fact that the government sees the need to intervene in the unjust structure of land tenure in order to reach more advanced and more humanized forms of capitalism. The government furthermore maintains that the measure will reinforce the private property system. Why then does the entire ANEP, which on the whole stands to gain, resist these measures by supporting agro-export capitalists who will indeed be harmed? What have ANEP and its affiliates seen in the government's measure to make them protest so violently against a measure which in fact is in their favor?

If we examine ANEP's various pronouncements, they envision the following: 1) the system of private property is under threat: "If they begin with agriculture today, they will go on to industry tomorrow," and so forth; 2) productivity and production, and hence the economic vitality of the country, are going to decline, thereby affecting industry; 3) these measures are going to stir up greater pressure from the very poor, who can see that the government itself is recognizing their situation and proclaiming their rights; 4) we are entering into a process whose dynamics and results cannot be calculated.

The significance of the government's position

If we go deeper into these arguments it is not difficult to uncover the root issue above and beyond the government's intentions. Paying attention to the government's intentions may be helpful for purposes of analysis, but it cannot be the key to formulating the issue, since what counts here is not the idealism of intentions but the materialism of facts. Moreover, the government has been very open about its intentions and there is no need to resort to well worn dogmas in order to decipher the first stage of what occurred. In this first step, the aim is to significantly expand the number of property owners in a process that will strengthen and improve the capitalist system of private property. But what lies behind these appearances of a strengthened, improved system? In my opinion, there are two things very closely connected with one another: the state is asserting its power vis-à-vis a ruling oligarchy that has been until now turning Salvadoran governments into mechanical instruments of its interests; and state power is proposing to exercise control of a significant amount of very good land that will affect a representative group of Salvadoran capitalists.

The ISTA Law and its application in the Initial Project undoubtedly indicate that the state is becoming stronger and relatively more autonomous vis-à-vis the oligarchical powers. Today's dogmatists, who have studied Marxism from scholastic catechisms, assume that the government is merely part of the superstructure and, furthermore, that it is monolithic and can only defend the immediate interests of the ruling class. Thus, the purpose of any government measure will therefore be to defend their interests and to maintain the prevailing system, and hence improvements at any particular moment only serve to reinforce the system and its mechanisms of domination. There is some truth to this, prior to any theory, and it applies to both socialist and capitalist countries. However, it is also obvious that due to its formal structure and its own drive, once it has become strong—and this takes place automatically as a result of the growth of society and is manifested in the national budget—the state cannot simply conform to the interests of a single class, which as such has another structure and other patterns of conduct. The two are not identical and cannot be so, although the separation can be greater or less. When, for example, the communist government of Poland tries to raise prices on consumer goods, it is following the dynamic of the whole, but it enters into conflict with the interests of consumers, who belong to the lower strata. There is a duality between what it is as state and what it is as the defender of the popular interests—how it is overcome is not our business here.

With the Initial Project, the government of El Salvador has shown that it is not merely the automatic stand-in for the oligarchy, and that it does something more than simply put itself at the immediate service of the most exaggeratedly capitalist interests. What ANEP has clearly realized—and what the corkscrew analysts, who do not realize when the cork has been replaced by plastic or metal, do not want to acknowledge—is that it can no longer simply control the government; we may be entering a period in which the government will recover some of its responsibility as the holder of state power, not entirely free from the ruling powers, but not identified with them either. When it reaches a certain degree of development, the state cannot be simply the sheer reflection of the ruling class, especially when other classes begin to represent a problem. What the state will do with this incipient independence remains to be seen, just as it remains to be seen what its former masters, who still retain all their power, can do about it. One cannot have illusions, but neither can one ignore that qualitatively this is something new that deserves to be fostered, as reformist as it might appear. In a situation like that of El Salvador with its distinctive size,* its present social situation, the present state of collective awareness, and the importance of technocrats, this development deserves special consideration, and we should not be too eager to force it to fit the idealism of universal doctrines.

This observation leads to another closely connected issue. Until now it has been maintained as a dogma of Salvadoran capitalism that private property is untouchable and that any government that sought to touch it would be pronouncing its own death sentence. The assumption is that

---

*It should be noted that El Salvador is Central America's smallest and most densely populated country. THE EDITORS

while private property and hence the present distribution of economic power is to remain untouched, the privileges and possibility of exploitation will not only be maintained, but the government will continually be held in check by that manipulating ability that corrupts the armed forces and the legislative, judicial, and executive branches. Whenever someone writes the history of how our native capitalism has intervened directly in political coups, in the appointing of presidents, in formulating some laws and blocking others, and in managing court verdicts and sentences, this hypothesis* will be abundantly proven. The fact that the government has even dared to redistribute the ownership of 58,744 hectares and to limit private ownership to a maximum of 35 hectares (86.4 acres), means that it has dared to touch a fundamental property dogma on which all others rest. This is a very important step, and one can fail to see it only through willful blindness. Perhaps those who are involved in politics in order to seek state power are not interested in recognizing this, but one who analyzes facts should prove it and say so aloud, for the analyst's intention and concern is not to favor a government but to foster a process at its deepest level, whatever the appearances may be. Those engaged in politics in a mechanistic or orthodox way, and political organizations that have their own prescriptions and had not foreseen that a step of such great magnitude could be taken, should not ignore the importance of this moment. Nor should they disregard those who are directing the attack by ANEP and its spokespersons.

Both aspects are undoubtedly ambiguous, but the only way to achieve something positive is to weigh in on the positive side of the ambiguity. The negative side is that state power will be strengthened not for the sake of social change but to be ready to unjustly repress those striving for social change in other ways. It may also promote a new capitalist spirit which in the long run would reinforce what has been judged to be the unjust structural cause of the present situation. Only by supporting true popular organizations and gradually shifting towards community forms of property will we be able to assure that the positive side of the Initial Project measure prevails over the negative side. But it is even more negative to provide weapons to the forces most resistent to social change and to ally oneself in practice with their immediate interests. It is sad to see how the aims of ANEP and of certain leftist forces coincide, even if only for this moment: they coincide in denying the validity of the agrarian reform, one side because it is too much and the other because it is too little. Only if this measure were to lead to the triumph of the most reactionary forces would it cease to be useful for this period, for that would take the country backward not only socially but

---

*For a later perspective, relevant to this hypothesis, see Martín-Baró (1982b): chapter 16, *this volume.* THE EDITORS

also politically. On the other hand, utopian solutions can trigger collective suicide or the conformity that follows defeat. Only direct action on the material structures of production even on a small scale will lay the foundation for a social change that moves from structure to superstructure. Action to alter the ideological and organizational superstructures without any change in the structures of the means of production and ownership amount to empty dreams and adolescent hopes, especially if they are not able to become a material force through the incorporation of a group consciousness. We must take seriously what is entailed when the property system is affected in any way; not to realize that is superficial and opportunistic.

PROPERTY IN THE AGRARIAN REFORM LAW AND IN THE INITIAL PROJECT

We have historicized the ideological aspects of the controversy between ANEP and the government. Now we must historicize the idea of property as it appears in the basic law and in the implementation decree. What kind of ownership do they actually propose? In historical terms where would this new kind of property lead, if its historic logic were consistent with its theoretical logic?

The main characteristics of the ISTA Law

In its foreword, the ISTA Law speaks of the state's obligation to assure that the inhabitants of the republic enjoy economic welfare and that the principles of social justice be upheld.* This general principle is immediately made specific by the statement that "changing the structure of land tenure" is ISTA's main purpose. Its primary activity is "to acquire through the means stipulated in this law, the properties necessary for carrying out changes in the structure of land tenure."

Lands belonging to ISTA and to the state and those lands that ISTA acquires voluntarily and by expropriation will be used for implementing the process of Agrarian Transformation. It is stated that implementing these projects is of public utility and social interest. The passage of law grants ISTA a certain supervisory function over land ownership, even over land not affected by the projects. The importance accorded to ecological considerations is significant, since concern over ecology assumes that the common interest has primacy over that of individuals.

The ISTA Law certainly recognizes that a piece of land is private property by the very fact that it is properly registered, and it assumes that any property is legitimized in this manner, without even questioning how it was acquired. Moreover, expropriation is to be compensated

---

*All quotes in this section are from this agrarian reform legislation.

and the criteria for that compensation will be very generous, since the most important of these criteria is "the value declared by the owner or possessor for tax purposes, or the official estimate made in keeping with laws regulating tax matters."

The primary beneficiaries are "peasants who are working the lands as tenant farmers or wage laborers, or peasant associations, those existing or in process of being organized on the property when it is acquired by ISTA." Revenues from the property, while it is temporarily in ISTA's hands, should go to all the peasants permanently associated with the property. There are four possible beneficiaries: family groups, cooperative agricultural associations, peasant community associations, and in exceptional cases, joint share enterprises. When those who are granted lands are families, they are usually obliged to work the lands directly, join a cooperative association or a peasant community association promoted by ISTA, and contribute personally and economically to work and services in the interests of all. They must also live in the area. Lands will be assigned to family groups as a "family property" for a period of twenty years.

When Cooperative Associations are awarded lands, they will be obliged to work them through their associates and will have to keep labor contracting for wages to a minimum: "these associations will only be able to employ wage labor during particular periods. In any case, wage laborers will have prior rights over any other person to be incorporated as new associates in these associations."

For Peasant Communities the property system is even more communitarian: "these associations will be made up of people who hold their labor, industry, services, and other goods in common, with the primary purpose of directly and jointly exploiting rural properties as well as trading and industrializing their products. They must share the profits or losses from each economic activity among the members in proportion to what they contribute."

In general, ISTA is assigned major rights and duties, more for the sake of unified planning than to enable the state to control private spheres. Nevertheless it is worth noting that ISTA acquires the lands first, and it always remains a kind of residual owner to whom the lands return in case the immediate owners to whom they have been conveyed fail to meet their obligations. The underlying notion is that the land ultimately belongs to everyone and to whoever represents everyone, although the state can supply land to those who deserve it in the form of limited ownership. Provisions that ISTA should deposit its funds in non-private banking institutions whenever possible point in the same direction.

The decree intended to set the Initial Project in motion follows the same orientation with regard to property and the need for the state to intervene to regulate it. Its first consideration reads: "In accordance with the constitution, the economic system of the republic should be in keeping with principles of social justice, which tend to assure for all the country's inhabitants a life worthy of a human being, and hence private property is recognized and guaranteed in its social function." The aim of this action is a positive change in the structure of land tenure, in order to create a just property system, with production units that are socially and economically viable, and that may assure a better distribution of income obtained from the rural area, an increase of production and agricultural productivity, and peasant training and organizing.

The Project affects 58,744 hectares (145,097 acres), and the limits of ownership are set between a maximum of 35 hectares (86.45 acres) and a minimum of 3 hectares (7.4 acres). The formation of peasant associations is to be encouraged, and these associations should try "to create an attitude of solidarity in the obligations and risks of agricultural, herding, and forest enterprises." These peasant associations will be granted preference in benefits and aid. The preeminent role that ISTA is to have as the Project gets underway is continually emphasized.

The concept of property underlying the law

In broad strokes, these are the main characteristics of the new legislation with regard to property ownership. It unquestionably marks a remarkable step forward not only in comparison to the positions held by business groups but also beyond what might be expected of a state apparatus like the present one. While it might be possible to regard the Law as just one more piece of legislation, its embodiment as envisioned in the Project gives it a degree of reality that deserves special consideration. What would implementing the Project mean for property in El Salvador?

1. The absolute and primary character of private property is disregarded; property is not viewed as the first commandment, so that if it were violated the economic and social life of the country would go to ruin. The state enters as the necessary guarantor and ultimate arbiter of what must be done in the realm of social structures. What the country must do will not be left to the large owners to decide or to the so-called free play of market forces. Property is such an important element in the shaping of society that its regulation cannot be left to the free-wheeling management of those who possess the most nor to the blind course of economic forces. That the state has become aware of this, even belatedly, means that something qualitatively new is at work. The calamitous condition to which unrestrained private property has reduced the country has not only made state intervention necessary, but it has imbued the state with a consciousness and an action that is not merely the automatic reflection of the economic interests of the ruling classes.

2. The law's position is that only a profound change in the structure of land tenure will make it possible to bring about the needed economic benefits and the social justice that is due and to which all citizens have a right and which the state should safeguard. The present land structure

is therefore to blame for the economic and ethical failings of Salvadoran agriculture. One of the most serious causes of the present situation is land ownership, and therefore only by changing its structure can progress be made. The primary aim of the whole process—at least according to the legal documents—is to break the oligarchical system of land tenure. The proof is in the fact that the Project mandates a much lower maximum holding than that proposed by those forces who regard themselves as the most radical in the country. It is also much lower than what is commonly regarded as very revolutionary in other agrarian reforms. It is true that the ratio of maximum (35 hectares) to minimum (3 hectares) is more than ten to one, but there is no question that 35 hectares of land do not provide the basis for the kind of political power that can control and shape society.

3. The aim is that those who work the land become owners and active agents in the agrarian transformation. It is only a step from this point to the adage "the land belongs to those who work it." It is here that the law becomes quite severe in its effort to do away with or reduce as much as possible the system of labor for wages. Wages are presently one of the main instruments of exploitation and the legal means for accumulating surplus value. For the ISTA Law the ideal is that there be no wage laborers, but rather that workers retain the product of their labor, as much as possible. Moreover, workers are to live on their land and not be parasites benefitting privately from income generated by production that is social. This may be the most revolutionary point in the Law, even though the critics from both right and left failed to see it. The fruit of labor should go primarily to the laborer.

4. Although the ISTA Law accepts private property as a legal way of owning a production unit that fits between the maximum and the minimum, the property it recognizes is not limited to individual private property since it also proposes other kinds of ownership, which are truly personal but not private. The minimum ownership unit is not the individual but rather the family unit. Thus a single person cannot be regarded as the only or main owner, and land cannot cease being family property, for at least twenty years. Moreover, other kinds of ownership beyond the family sphere are also recognized. It would seem preferable that even medium size enterprises not be state property both for the sake of productivity and to ensure higher quality through competition. We need not interpret this ownership position as a tribute to selfishness, for property may be viewed as enhancing personal self-realization in service to the community. Moreover, both cooperative and community forms of ownership provide a solid means for seeking greater solidarity among human beings. Self-realization through private property, although poorly understood, undoubtedly has been instilled in our group consciousness to such an extent that in conjunction with the inclinations of human selfishness, it has become a kind of second nature. However, it is equally true that if shared work is combined with shared life, the

result will be great progress towards creating new persons within a new society. Human solidarity cannot be built only on the basis of sharing in work. The personal conversion required will become flesh only when accompanied by the appropriate material changes.

5. The law implicitly recognizes that all citizens, and not simply one social class, should share in the ownership of the major means of production—and not just land. The enormous importance conceded to ISTA as the ultimate owner of land marks a considerable step forward in the way ownership is conceived. Although those awarded lands are true owners, they cease being so when they fail to fulfill the social function of ownership. Thus the way is opened, although in a very rudimentary way, towardss making the major means of production, and especially those of nature (land, sea, air, water, and so forth) the property of all. Of course there must be safeguards against either totalitarian or arbitrary exercise of the social function of property by the state, and for the moment such safeguards may entail differing forms of ownership. However, it is clear that at least in principle it is better that the sources of power be in the hands of those who formally represent all rather than in the hands of those who represent themselves or a small exploitative group. If the state belongs to all and is for all, there will be no dictatorship by the state. In any case the dictatorship of a particular group is worse (and the dictatorship of the bourgeoisie is inherently worse than the dictatorship of the proletariat). This notion seems to underlie the idea that non-private banking institutions should be accorded preference since they better represent the common interest.

6. In both the Law and the Initial Project, the principle of just distribution has primacy over the principle of productivity. This means that ownership and labor are seen correctly in terms of their social function. No one questions that production and productivity are essential to the life of a country, although revolutionary ideologues and organizers, who are preparing to take power but not to exercise it, should take it more seriously. From a human and social viewpoint, however, fair distribution has a higher priority than productivity. Fair distribution should not be regarded as something flowing from whatever eludes the grasp of large property owners. It should be conceived more radically as the kind of just distribution that flows from a just ownership of the means of production. Furthermore, if all the productive capability of all Salvadorans is stimulated, the quantity and quality of production will no doubt increase, provided that production capability be properly planned and regulated by rational state action.

7. The ISTA Law points towards a correct interpretation of the social function of property, in accordance with the core of Christian teaching on this question, as we will demonstrate below. A piece of private property fulfills its social function when it is used in accordance with the common purpose of all the earth's goods, which is to satisfy the needs of all, and when its distribution, that is, the distribution of what this prop-

erty produces, is structured along the same lines as the production: If production is social, distribution should be social. Nowhere is it declared that such distribution is best achieved through wages or taxes.

All these good qualities of the ISTA Law and the Initial Project are still purely legal fictions. Only if they are implemented, will they be true and really mean what they say. Actions will declare whether or not the formulations are true. In this sense the scope of the Project is not so important, although given the size of El Salvador and the political situation now, it is actually quite significant. It is not particularly important that no new projects can be undertaken until the current project is completed. Indeed, the process could be speeded up through other legal measures. In any case, three years is not a long time in the overall development of a nation. What is really important is how decisively this first effort is undertaken and that there is the will to stay with it until land tenure is entirely restructured in El Salvador. That is why it is so necessary that this first effort be successful. Given its size and population, El Salvador could restructure its whole present land tenure to benefit the entire Salvadoran people in a relatively brief period of time. The task will not be easy. Besides the very real difficulties involved in getting it going, there will be other difficulties caused by those who want things to get worse and by those who want things to remain as they are. It is extremely distressing to see that in this matter the most capitalist forces and those who claim to be seeking the interests of the people coincide in opposing the Project.

This is not the proper place to analyze the political consequences—which as such are superstructural—that this process is going to have: whether it is going to reinforce the capitalist system, foster reformism, or set in motion an irreversible historic process, which of its own dynamism will lead to profound social change. Given the nature of this article, it here suffices to underscore that what is partially at stake is the ownership of the means of production, and thus what is also going on, simultaneously with the strengthening of the state, is the weakening of one of the most oligarchical sectors of the country. This is plainly a structural process, one that should be irreversible. Ultimately the point is not whether it helps a particular government or is at the expense of particular individuals. For the moment it is the state—not a particular kind of state—that has to come out on the winning side, and one kind of property, that of large land holders, that has to come out on the losing side.

The need for structural transformation

The historicization of the idea of property as it exists in the Salvadoran countryside and as it exists—in dialectical counterpart—in the ISTA Law and the Project shows that the kind of property system prevailing in our country and the way it is defended are an ideologization. Present land tenure has brought about and continues to bring about the opposite of the claims made to justify it. Trying to change the *structure* of this tenure system in order to accomplish what is supposedly the fundamental objective of property is the best way to unmask the true intentions and true positions of each and every group. Obviously this is only the beginning of a process—indeed, of a process that is ambiguous, as I said before. What remains is to promote its positive aspects to help speed it along; to likewise promote all those real conditions that are required (including group consciousness, the assimilation of the process by peasants, and the right kind of organization) without which the redistribution process would not be viable, given the enormous resistance being put up by the present ruling classes.

Capitalists should not forget that even from their own standpoint, the present social situation, and more specifically that in the rural areas among the peasantry, is unsustainable. If property is necessary for freedom, the vast majority of Salvadoran peasants lack the indispensable condition for freedom. If property is the fruit of labor and is based on it, we would have to conclude that the age old labor of Salvadoran peasants is not a human labor, because it should have long ago produced for them a property tenure that they do not have. Consequently, to weaken the current form of property tenure would not be against the public interest and would disturb social peace only for a minority, since the majority would not be stabilized by acquiring what they do not have. If uncontrolled forces are aroused, they will have been incited by those who do not want to see the common good. Furthermore, the particular situation in El Salvador, which could barely provide a manzana of land to each family, shows that here the individualistic pattern of property holding is not viable.

Our conclusion in this section is clear. We must recognize that the line of reasoning used to defend the prevailing form of land tenure and more generally the present status of the major means of production, is false and must be de-ideologized. If reality itself proves that the reasons used to defend ownership are false or if ownership is defended in order to attain ends that a long history refutes, obviously the reasons and aims do not represent matters objectively, but rather are excuses used to defend self-serving positions. Although something is said to be white, the real aim is that it be black, especially when we are dealing not with the will and interest of an individual but with the will and intention of a social group. Although people are using capitalist terminology, they are not even willing to accept what a moderately progressive capitalism demands, much less a capitalism that could respond to a historic necessity as an obligatory step towards a new form of society. Objectivity absolutely demands that results be examined in parallel with intentions, so as to demonstrate not only the limits and shortcomings vis-à-vis the ideal but also any true contradictions.

What if the Project fails? The Project may fail for lack of technical "know how." In that case it will not be the principles that are at fault but the operating circumstances. It may fail due to the resistance of capitalist forces. In that case, those forces will either find humane ways to lessen the pressure or the situation of the country will retrogress to an even crueler capitalist dictatorship. It may fail due to the weakness of the state; such an outcome would prove that the state apparatus has still not attained a minimal degree of independence from the ruling classes. None of these outcomes, however, would disqualify a process which, were it well implemented, could move El Salvador qualitatively in a new direction.

The historicization of the Christian idea of ownership

What more can a Latin American theological reflection say about this problem of property, as it appears historically in El Salvador? This is not an idle question because people very often appeal to God in these matters, especially because Christianity is still a social force in our country. The problem of property is so intertwined with human salvation in history, that those who find themselves challenged by salvation history cannot but be concerned about this problem. Long ago Pius XI looked into ways to restore and improve the social order in conformity with the law of the gospel in *Quadragesimo Anno* (1931). It is primarily from this gospel law that Christians must seek guidance for the social process. Christianity does not have any technical solution for temporal problems either theoretically or practically, but it does have a light and a strength without which the solution to human problems remains incomplete.

Given the limitations of space, I will here only treat the core of the property problem under two headings: first, a review of the traditional sense of the church in broad strokes: second, the position of the historic Jesus on the issue of property.

CHURCH TRADITION ON PROPERTY

Considerations in this section divide into three brief subsections: the first, devoted to ancient tradition, the second to scholasticism, and the third to pontifical teaching.

Ancient tradition
One of the earliest Christian texts,* written almost at the same time as the gospel of Saint John, provides a basic outline: "You are not to

---

*In this subsection Ellacuría uses Sierra Bravo (1967) and Rubianes (1975), without citing the patristic references. Most of the English translations used here of those citations are from Avila (1983); only the texts that could not be located in English are translated from Ellacuría's article. P.B.

reject the needy; rather you are to share with your brother in all things. And you are not to say that something is your own; for if you are fellow sharers in what is immortal, how much more so in mortal things?" Already we find one of the features typical of Christian thought on property, its relational character. The important thing is not so much what one has, but what one has in relation to others; the crucial issue is wealth vis-à-vis poverty, the separation that property ownership can cause between human beings. The reason for this position is clear: unjust inequality militates against bonds of brotherhood and sisterhood and against community. This reason has a theological foundation: since we are co-participants in the things of God, should we not also be so in human things?

Similarly, around the year 200 we find that Clement of Alexandria, who lived in the richest city in the Roman empire, went therefore right to the center of the problem. He said, "It is God himself who has brought our race to a *koinonia* by sharing Himself, first of all, and by sending His Word (Logos) to all alike, and by making all things for all. Therefore everything is in common, and the rich should not grasp a greater share. The expression, 'I own something, and I have more than enough; why should I not enjoy it?' is not worthy of a human nor does it indicate any community feeling. The other expression does, however: 'I have something, why should I not share it with those in need?' . . . God has given us the authority to use our possessions, I admit, but only to the extent that it is necessary: He wishes them to be in common. It is absurd that one man live in luxury when there are so many who labor in poverty." By their very nature human beings are in communion, as is God, and it is their communication with other human beings that makes them so.

Writing around the year 225, Cyprian of Carthage, who came from a wealthy family, was insistent on the same point. Christians should act like God the Father, and thus everything that comes from God should be used in common (*quodcumque enim Dei est in nostra usurpatione commune est*), since God does not want anyone to be excluded from using these goods. A property owner who acts in this manner "imitates God the Father."

The great church fathers continue in the same vein. Living in a society of extreme inequality and injustice, they harshly condemn the economic differences which run against human brotherhood and sisterhood by negating the common destiny of the goods of the earth. Saint Basil says "If each one would take that which is sufficient for one's needs, leaving what is in excess to those in distress, no one would be rich, no one poor." "The bread which you keep belongs to the hungry; that coat which you preserve in your wardrobe, to the naked; . . . that gold which you have hidden in the ground to the needy. Wherefore, as often as you were able to help others and refused, so often did you do them wrong."

Saint John Chrysostom underlines a new issue, the necessary causal and structural connection between wealth and poverty: "With how many tears was your magnificent mansion built, how many orphans in the street, how many widows cheated, how many workers without their daily wage?" We should read his classic text in this same spirit: "Tell me then, how did you become rich? From whom did you receive it, and from whom he who transmitted it to you? From his father and his grandfather. But can you, ascending through many generations, show the acquisition just? It cannot be. The root and origin of it must have been injustice." That must be a starting point since it belongs to the core of the gospel: "The rule of perfect Christian living, its most exact definition, its highest peak, is to seek the good of others. . . For nothing can make us imitators of Christ as much as caring for our neighbor." Saint Ambrose stresses this same polarizing of rich and poor: "How far, O ye rich, do you push your mad desires? 'Shall ye alone dwell upon the earth?' (Is. 5:8). Why do you arrogate to yourselves, ye rich, exclusive right to the soil? . . . For all has the world been created, which you few rich are trying to keep for yourselves." "Nature therefore is the mother of common right, usurpation [the mother] of private right."

Many more texts could be cited. We would be guilty of literalism, however, if we simply transferred them to our situation or we offered them as a scientific analysis of the problem. Taken as a whole, however, these texts represent a series of fundamental statements that are unquestionably valid as expressions of Christianity. They may be summarized as follows: **a)** material goods are common goods for all humankind, for they originate from the same [earthly] source, and they have been created so that all human beings in community might seek their full development in solidarity; **b)** some goods may be distributed privately, but what is private about them is their current use and not radical dominion over them, which continues to be that of the human community; **c)** the abuse of private appropriation is what brings about these great differences between rich and poor that are contrary to human dignity and Christian brotherhood and sisterhood; **d)** there is a principle of injustice actually present in the vast differences between rich and poor, since some are rich because they have plundered the poor, or at least they have not done for them what they should; **e)** those who reject imitating and following Christ as much as possible, the essence of Christianity, cannot be Christians; and those who are more concerned about themselves than others, who look out for themselves more than for others, are indeed rejecting it; **f)** this whole matter is not one of "charity," (as commonly misunderstood), for if from the Fathers' standpoint inequalities should be corrected by giving to others what one does not need; this act of giving is an imperative for justice, something strictly due, for ultimately what is given is not one's own but what is common to all.

Without question, the right of all human beings to share the goods of this world is prior to, and more basic than, the right to possess something privately. Community owning of goods is more essential than holding them privately. Hence, when any form of holding them in private undermines their proper common ownership, it should be done away with since such ownership has no justification. At most it might be tolerated temporarily in order to avoid greater evils. It is not common ownership that requires justification but private ownership.

Scholastic Tradition

Saint Thomas should be regarded as the most typical representative of scholastic thought. In his *Summa Theologica*, he holds that by natural law there is no distinction in possessions (II-II, q. 66, a.2). It does not follow, however, that all things should be owned in common and that private property is against natural law, since it serves as a means that human reason has discovered to make goods fulfill their purpose in the most orderly way possible. Reason must be used in order to see which kind of property and which modes of ownership are most just and rational in each case, since this point cannot be resolved once and for all. Given the situation with which he is familiar, Saint Thomas thinks it is licit and necessary for human beings to possess their own things, and he offers three reasons: one is more careful with what is one's own than with what is held in common; there will be more order if responsibility for taking care of things is shared; in this manner, peace among human beings is better preserved. Even so, things appropriated in this manner should not be held as one's own but as common goods; the proof will be that they truly become common goods when others are in need. This is clearly observable in situations of great need when things return to their original stage of being common, and when because of need it is not a sin to take something that another holds as his or her own, since it is then common (*propter necessitatem sibi factam communem*, II-II, q. 66, a.7).

This has been the scholastic tradition, as we can observe in Vitoria, Soto, Bañez, Molina, Suárez, Lessio, Billuart, and others. "All of them . . . firmly establish the universal destiny of the goods of the earth and the fundamental and primary right of each and every human being actually to use those goods for their own fulfillment" (Rubianes, 1975). Nevertheless, the scholastics believe it is licit and fitting to divide up things as well as take control over them, but they attribute the need for such dividing to sin and the decline of humankind. Given fallen nature, it was better to take the route of private property. These authors regard private property not as an ideal but as a concession to the weakness of human nature; it may indeed augment that weakness. In any case, for them "the right to private property is based neither on divine positive law . . . nor on natural law. It comes from what the classics call the law of nations, which as such is only a matter of relative necessity and can change or be changed through human consent, just as it was introduced" (Rubianes, 1975).

Only later when scholastic thought was in full decline and under the influences of an individualistic mind-set did capitalism come to stress the importance of private ownership, even seeking to make it strictly a part of natural law or of the core of Christian thought.

Papal Teaching

We find a continual advance in papal thought from Leo XIII to the present, with occasional hesitancies, which should be correctly interpreted (Antoncich, 1976). The basic fact, already grasped in *Rerum Novarum*, is that social and economic development has produced a tiny circle of wealthy people living in luxury and has imposed a yoke of quasi-slavery on a vast multitude of wage-earning proletarians (Leo XIII, 1891). But Leo XIII does not think that socialism is a good way to resolve this situation, and so he insists on the natural character of private property, and he is also insistent on the individual character of the human person.

Pius XI goes further in *Quadragesimo Anno* (1931). He cautions that we should not succumb to state capitalism, but we should also move well beyond individualistic capitalism; in the former the state denies human freedom, but in the latter capitalism denies human solidarity and the fact that things are primarily destined for each and every human being. Hence Pius XI both acknowledges private property and recognizes the need for the state to be on guard to assure that private property be in harmony with the common good. He likewise recognizes that private property is not absolute or unchangeable since it has taken different forms throughout the ages. . . . The encyclical offers a stern criticism of capitalism because of the abuses it has committed, which amount to a denial of the destiny of the goods of the earth and of the dignity of the human person. The banner of social justice must be raised to challenge these abuses.

Pius XII emphasizes "the ineradicable demand that the goods of the earth, that God has created for all human beings, reach all in an equitable manner, in accordance with the principles of justice and charity." The right to private property "remains subordinate to the natural end of material goods, and cannot be disassociated from the primary and fundamental right, which concedes the use of those goods to all. . . . Only thus will it be possible to assure that the private property and the use of material goods can bring fruitful peace and solid life to society, instead of being the precarious conditions that cause struggle and envy, and people are left to the merciless contest between strength and weakness." When the distribution of private property stands in the way of the primary purpose of the goods of the earth, the state may step in to regulate the use of property and goods, and if there is no other way—he said this in 1944—it may decree that they be expropriated, provided there be fitting compensation (Rubianes, 1975).

John XXIII (1961) reaffirms the right to private ownership—even of the means of production—but he also accepts public ownership. He likewise points out the great advantages of socialization, which seems to be the direction history must take. He trusts more in the positive principles of socialization than in those of private ownership. Work, personal education and training, social security, and so forth are a better and more humane protection than private ownership.

Vatican II (*Gaudium et Spes*), underscores a principle that is very important now for discerning why those who insist on productivity above all else are wrong. The fundamental purpose of economic development is the growth, not of products, power, or profits, but of the human being. This aim is not achieved by allowing economic activity to proceed in accordance with its own blind mechanisms or by allowing a few, whether individuals or nations, to decide for everyone. The goods of the earth are of a social nature by their very nature: they do not simply have a social function added on, but in themselves they are inherently social before they are private. So they can be privately used only if that is the best way for them to fulfill their social destiny (Vatican Council II, 1975).

Paul VI, in *Populorum Progressio* (1967) earlier insisted on the universal and common destiny of the goods of the earth, by pointing out their universal dimension: "All other rights whatsoever, including those of property and of free commerce, are to be subordinated to this principle. They should not hinder but on the contrary favor its application. It is a grave and urgent social duty to redirect them to their primary finality." "Private property does not constitute for anyone an absolute and unconditioned right. No one is ever justified in keeping for his exclusive use what he does not need, when others lack necessities" (Paul VI, 1967). He condemns capitalism not only in its deeds but in its principles, three of which he does not regard as justified: regarding profit as the main engine of economic progress, holding that competition must be the supreme law of economics, and defending private ownership of the means of production as an absolute right without limits or obligations. In *Octogesima Adveniens* (Paul VI, 1971) he defines more precisely the Christian assessment of socialism, Marxism, and liberal ideology.

Over the course followed by papal teaching, we can observe a gradual progress in recognizing explicitly and in keeping with modern developments, the theoretical way that Christians have dealt with the reality of poverty from the first centuries through the time of the great scholastics and up to the present. There have been hesitations and momentary backward steps. But we cannot fail to acknowledge the significance of a persistent common stance, and it should be regarded as being of permanent value. The church does not have and cannot have its own approach for scientifically analyzing reality, for that is not its mission. In this sense, what is called the social teaching of the church cannot be proposed as a third way between capitalism and Marxism. That does not mean however, that the church's positions are ineffective in history, if indeed they are followed to their ultimate consequences. Simply proclaiming those positions makes it clear that situations like those of El Salvador are unjustifiable from a Christian standpoint. Once these positions have been proclaimed, one cannot continue to defend the present form of private ownership as one desired by the gospel. Clearly, if this message becomes the collective awareness of the Salvadoran majorities, an important factor for promoting deep social change will have been introduced into the process of history.

Such a development would entail a proper historicization. What, we may ask, is entailed in such a historicization? The first requirement is a careful reading of the context in which the documents were written; it also assumes that the documents are re-read from and for the situation to which they are to be applied. With this contextual reading done, we must see whether they are true or false from the standpoint of the concrete totality that is being sought. If, for example, the deep sense of Christian tradition is that all human beings share the available goods in an equitable way so that freedom be just and justice be free, it would not be correct to invoke a self-interested literalism in order to block or ruin a historic process because it was not entirely in accord with other aspects of the Christian message. If no process is perfectly in tune with the gospel spirit, we must choose the one coming closest to that spirit.

Thus the historicization of the Christian message requires mediations. The first step in historicization will enable us to know the true meaning of what is being announced; the second mediating step enables us to put this true sense into practice. Little purpose is served by wanting something if the conditions for achieving this something are not present. The first step in the church's own activity, aimed at bringing this about, is to change that true knowledge into group consciousness, into a social force operating on those social structures that negate what the Church proposes as bringing about the Reign of God in history. There is a second more difficult and more ambiguous step: that of supporting or rejecting concrete political movements. This is the difficult connection between faith and politics, something that has always been present in the history of the church, and will always be present, if the church really wants what it preaches to become real in history.

This two-sided historicization will uncover areas where false ideologies are at work and will show how we can engage in a de-ideologization. The fundamental matters to be historicized are as follows: a) the earth's goods are destined in common for all human beings and all peoples, and hence all human beings and all peoples have a primary right to them; thus they should be a principle of communication and solidarity rather than of division; b) private ownership is justified only when it is the best possible way to make the goods of the earth fulfill their primary purpose and to achieve solidarity among human beings; c) the historic abuse of private property has led to a situation contrary to what was intended when it was instituted—creating intolerable differences between those who have property and others who do not, and placing most of the human race in a situation of extreme deprivation and need;

d) we must find a solution to overcome the present state of things without descending into forms of totalitarianism; e) however, it would be even worse if such totalitarian and exploitative power were left in the hands of the owners of the principal means of production, and therefore proper involvement by the state is ever more necessary; f) productivity and profit cannot be the main energizers, either objective or subjective, of economic activity, for they lead to dehumanization and an economicism whose consequences are disastrous; g) justice should prevail over any other kind of consideration, and hence the obligation to promote justice should not be put on the same level as the right to defend private ownership; h) not only is the oppression of the poor by the rich anti-Christian, but so is the existence of vast differences among those who claim to be brothers and sisters, children of one Father, redeemed by the same Lord, and called to constitute one body.

There remains the whole problem of scientifically analyzing why the situation is the way it is and how to resolve it through coherently structured policies. We should also ask why the church's social activity has not been as effective as it should have been—even taking into account the limits of its mission. However, this does not prevent us from seeing in the church's message a very important influence for social change and a principle that is indispensable for assuring that new systems be more humane. Here also historicization rightly carried out will help us avoid falling into dangerous ideologizations.

PROPERTY IN THE LIFE AND WORK OF JESUS

Here also I will proceed in summary fashion. Leaving aside everything found in the Old and New Testaments about property, I will center on the life and activity of Jesus. The issue emerges primarily as a contrast between wealth and poverty. Seen this way it is obviously one of the most weighty themes in the proclamation and realization of God's reign. Although they do not use critical analysis, the New Testament writers in general and Jesus in particular regard the relationship between wealth and poverty as one of the crucial points in our common human life, in our striving for perfection, and in our relation to God.

It is clear that among the divided social groups in Palestine during Jesus' lifetime, he stood with those who had neither wealth nor power, with those who were most oppressed (Jeremias, 1969; Brandon, 1967; Belo, 1975). His basic position is characterized by what is radical in his mission: his stance vis-à-vis God's reign (Sobrino, 1978). One who is totally devoted to God's reign, to incarnating that reign in human history, must be poor, and indeed will be forced to be poor. The Son of Man will have nowhere to lay his head. An exaggerated apocalyptic expectation of the reign might lead to extreme attitudes towards the goods of this world; however, without going so far, the proximity of God's reign, and the urgency and scope of Jesus' task will demand a great deal of freedom towards the goods of this world and particularly towards wealth. Standing in radical opposition to each other are the reign of God and the reign of money (= *Mammon:* the authors of the New Testament took this Aramaic word directly into Greek in order to stress the religious aura around money—those who adore material wealth take on a demoniacal character which prevents them from entering the reign of God). Jesus did not come from the most down and out classes, but he did work with his hands, and so did some of his disciples. He was not a rigorous ascetic, nor did he show contempt for personal relationships.

Jesus' position towards wealth can be summarized from his two basic positions: a) wealth is a serious obstacle to our entering the Reign of God, and by the same token it makes it difficult that God's kingdom "come" to us; b) the possession of wealth entails the grave danger of oppressing the poor, and by distancing people from them, it makes it very difficult to bring about brotherhood and sisterhood. We will examine these two positions separately and then together.

Although the explanation of the parable of the sower probably comes from the early church and not from Jesus himself (Mat. 13: 18-33; Mk. 4: 13-20, Lk. 8: 11-15) (Benoit & Boismard, 1972), both the original anecdote and the subsequent layer of interpretation shed light on our problem. If the seed is the reign of God, one of the obstacles to its bearing fruit, that is, to the realization of God's reign, is wealth, even if it is not mentioned in so many words; if the seed is the Word, that is, the gospel of the reign of God, then God's call is strangled by wealth, as the three synoptic evangelists explicitly state. Thus they repeatedly stress how hard it is for the rich to enter God's reign; the rich young man refuses to give his goods to the poor, even though giving up wealth for the sake of the poor is essential for entering God's reign, which in the text is presented as eternal life (Mt. 19: 16; Mk. 10: 17; Lk. 18; 18). Jesus exaggerates the difficulty by referring to the camel forced to unload at the narrow gate: "It is easier for a camel to pass through the eye of a needle [gate] than it is for the rich. . .". That exaggeration indicates the inherent difficulty caused by wealth [excess of goods], independently of the subjective attitude of rich people. Wealth and the reign of God, commitment to the former and entrance into the latter, stand radically opposed to each other.

The second position is demonstrated when the rich are confronted by the poor. That *opposition* is present in the beatitudes, is expressed in the song of the Virgin in the presence of her cousin Elizabeth, and is given dramatic form in the parable of Lazarus and the rich man. It is true that in the gospel it is not only the rich who oppose Jesus but also the powerful oppressors in the religious, cultural, social, economic, and political sectors (Ellacuría, 1976). However, this whole group, whose interconnections are sometimes clearly visible and sometimes latent and more indirect, is partly linked together by wealth and partly by the causes and consequences of wealth.

It is the evangelist Luke who most highlights this opposition (Magnificat: Lk. 1: 46-55, and Beatitudes: Lk 6: 20-26). All of chapter 16 in his gospel points towards this issue; it reminds us that we cannot serve two lords (God and Mammon); it shows us how the pharisees scoffed at Jesus' words, because they were "friends of money." Finally, it presents the parable of Lazarus and the rich man—first the contrast on earth: a rich man, dressed in purple and linen, who had his fill every day and had dazzling parties in full view of a poor man who crawled around covered with sores and who wanted to eat scraps from the rich man's table; then, the contrast after death: Lazarus in the bosom of Abraham joyful and content, while the rich man is subjected to torture and has no chance of consolation or redemption. In this parable the evangelist shows that the gap that was not bridged on earth, because the rich man was not capable of sharing his goods, is a decisive gap and brings on his perpetual condemnation.

These two fundamental aspects are interrelated. The reign of God and wealth have nothing to do with each other, because what lies behind the reign, both as God's proclamation and human achievement, stands opposed to what lies behind wealth—and Luke likes to call wealth "unjust". One of the main reasons they have nothing to do with each other is that wealth divides human beings from each other, and arouses the demon within, who separates the human being from God and human beings from one another. The fact that human separation from God and divisions among human beings are essentially interconnected is the ultimate explanation why wealth is opposed to the reign. What separates human beings from each other separates them from God. Bridging this abyss opened by wealth and caused one way or another by injustice and cheating of the poor is absolutely necessary for actualizing God's reign among human beings. Humans have no access to God and God has no access to humans, as long as the injustice connected with wealth stands in the way.

We do not have to make a detailed analysis of what Jesus did on behalf of the most oppressed and against the oppressors. We need only establish that such was his reason for coming into this world (Lk. 4: 16), and that his struggle to establish God's reign caused his death, which was brought about by the violent and powerful of his time—who, looked for pretexts to put him to death legally. They thought that in this manner they were not staining their hands, when their hearts were already filthy. Like Jeremiah before him, Jesus could say (Jer. 20: 7-8):

> *You duped me, O Lord, and I let myself be duped;*
> *you were too strong for me, and you triumphed.*
> *All the day I am an object of laughter;*
> *everyone mocks me.*
> *Whenever I speak, I must cry out,*
> *violence and outrage is my message.*

We can summarize what Jesus' work—his life and death—and his teaching have to say about property as follows: a) the very thrust of wealth in itself—understanding this "in itself" as its essential relation to poverty—inherently tends to break the bonds connecting humans to God and among themselves; b) there is in the human heart a special relationship with the world of wealth, requiring a deep humanization—impossible outside of God's reign—if the demoniacal potential of wealth is not to end in the diabolical possession of the human being; c) we must take a stand towards this adversarial opposition between rich and poor, taking on some of the basic objective values of the poor and struggling so that they can recover their dignity which has been battered by the oppression of the powerful; d) God is especially present in the world of the poor and hence there is in that world a saving power which is extremely important for establishing the reign of God; e) Jesus' rejection at the hands of the powerful and his condemnation to death offers a criterion for what constitutes activity in keeping with the option for the poor.

The turning, or conversion, of Christians to this historic Jesus in their attitudes and actions, the real historicization of these attitudes and actions, is thus the effective principle of de-ideologization. Such conversion shows who is really with Jesus and who is against him, no matter what may be said outwardly with the lips or inwardly with ideas. Different groups can ideologize Jesus—and they are doing so. Only a deep and true faith in him will save any of them from their ideologizations. Without him there is no salvation—not even historic salvation, much less salvation history.

Taken together, tradition and the message of Jesus reveal a deep cohesion. Christian thought about, and evaluation of, property is basically clear. The attempt to use Christianity in order to bolster a situation characterized by injustice, on the grounds that some presumed natural rights are at stake, is an undeniable ideologization. In Christian terms it is a blasphemy: using God's name not only falsely but for evil. A Christian historicization of what is meant by the correlatives of wealth and poverty leaves no room for false ideologizations. One who seeks to escape from the history of salvation within the historic reality of human beings is ideologizing.

More than forty-five years ago Alberto Masferrer [well known Salvadoran educator] wrote: "Feudalism essentially means the monopoly of land in large concentrations whose only owners are the masters, and on which those who provide their labor in exchange for a subsistence exist as serfs or tenant farmers. As there were once dukes . . . they still exist today, without that title, on large plots of land which are called plantations or ranches. Their power and privilege depends on how much [land] they own and how many tenant farmers can live on it." . . . "Feudal lord—regardless of the lies that may be written in legal codes about freedom and equality, and the rubbish religion and morality may proclaim about fraternity and charity. The fact is that one who has bread has life, and the master of the land is the owner of bread par excellence . . . If he wants, I will think like him, I will believe like him, I will vote like him. . . ." "Sadly in the conflict between life and property, laws have taken the side of the latter, and of its symbol, which is money. The gross fiction, disproved a thousand times every day, assumes that money is always the result of work, of one's own honest labor, and hence that it is like an emanation from the individual. . . . On this fiction, one of the most gross of such fictions to which the incurable idolatry of human beings has rendered worship, there has been erected the Temple of Property, where Money, the Only and All-powerful God, is pleased to hear the moans and curses of the victims of monopolization" (Masferrer, 1928).

These lines date from 1928. Masferrer was de-ideologizing by historicizing the notion of property. His own thinking repeated in another language the very condemnation of wealth made by Jesus of Nazareth nineteen hundred years earlier. "Monopoly of land! It is really difficult to find a more bothersome expression and one that means greater absurdity and injustice. By what right can human beings monopolize land? All the more or less acceptable arguments used to defend private property are seen to be gross hoaxes when it is a matter of justifying monopoly over land." Masferrer's voice went unheard—such is the sad fate of prophets. Then came the events of 1932 [aborted uprising and slaughter of an estimated 30,000 peasants]. The fact is that unless there is a just solution, the land tenure system will continue to put the country through agony. Let us hope that we can begin to firmly take the first steps to prevent this sick country from exploding.

Ignacio Martín-Baró

5. Reparations and Democracy*

TRANSLATION BY ADRIANNE ARON

One of the thorniest problems that has to be confronted by Latin American states hoping to establish democratic governments is the necessity of dealing with the sequelae of the political repression carried out by earlier governments of "national security." This is a palpably real problem in countries like Argentina and Uruguay, a problem shaping up as critical in the immediate future of Chile, a problem that someday will have to be dealt with in Guatemala and El Salvador, and just beginning to surface in Peru and Colombia. The presumed peaceful transition from dictatorship to democracy, when it is not mediated by a war that establishes democratic forces as the victors, encounters great difficulty when it tries to deal with justice, and even when it takes on the simple matter of working with the past. But to paraphrase an old saying, it is surely the case that people who cannot confront their history are condemned to repeat it.

To this end, an assessment must be made of the magnitude—both quantitative and qualitative—of the damage produced by counterinsurgency campaigns or state repression, for only then can we appreciate the deception involved in wanting to wipe out history and start over. Only by taking a full inventory do we see that the past that would be put behind us with such haste is not only alive in persons and groups—victims and victimizers—but operating still, within the same social structures that existed before.

First, of course, there is the emptiness left by all those thousands of persons who have been murdered or "disappeared," an emptiness that still grieves and oppresses their families. But there is also the living wound of all of those—probably as many or more than the number who died—who survived by suffering the cruelty visited on their own flesh in cruel prisons, and by endless interrogations and refined tortures. Finally, there is the trauma of those countless people who were threatened, harassed, and persecuted and who, in order to save their lives and those of their loved ones, had to renounce their ideals and principles—or at least hide them—to flee, to seek refuge, and even to exile themselves from their own country.

---

*Martín-Baró (1990i); see Bibliography in the back of this book.

138

All this damage is of such magnitude that it becomes almost ingenuous or cynical to act as if it can be forgotten overnight, because fundamentally the problem is not one of isolated individuals, whether few or many; it is a problem whose nature is inexorably social. The damage that has been produced is not simply in the destruction of personal lives. Harm has been done to the social structures themselves—to the norms that order the common life, to the institutions that govern the life of citizens, to the values and principles by which people are educated and through which the repression has tried to justify itself.

People invoke a variety of arguments to defend the idea that all this damage should be completely forgotten, and those who committed it, unconditionally pardoned. In some cases, the argument of "owned obedience" is called up. Here, a few people of high rank are singled out as being the ones who are solely responsible for the damage, and of course they are always considered now as individuals, not as representatives of the state or of the armed forces. The second and most common argument is that of the political necessity of getting beyond the past, so as not to perpetuate the conflict, and this requires pardon and social reconciliation. On occasion, this argument gets wrapped in the cloak of Christian forgiveness, as if this way out were the only one consistent with Christian teachings. Finally, from time to time the argument of "greater might" is tried or insinuated, saying that if pardon and social forgetting are not forthcoming, there is the danger of the military rebelling against the democratic system and bringing back dictatorship. Consequently, as much for social convenience as for political realism, we would have to relinquish any thought of laying blame on those who committed offenses in the name of national security, and to be quit of all claims for reparation for the personal and social damage they have produced.

This is not the place to belabor the historical backwardness of the "owed obedience" argument. Suffice it to say that the Nuremberg judgments lose all validity, turning into a simple vengeance on the part of the victors, should their ethical, legal, and social logic be "inapplicable" under present circumstances. In this sense, the famous case of Lieutenant William Calley, one of the people responsible for the massacre at My Lai, already constitutes a bad precedent.

The second argument is without doubt the strongest, and must be granted a measure of validity. There is no doubt that the evolution of human society requires the capacity to overcome differences, to pardon offenses, and even renounce certain well-founded grievances in the interest of peace and the common good. Nevertheless, the problem turns on whether that pardon and renunciation are going to be established on a foundation of truth and justice, or on lies and continued injustice. It is clear that nobody is going to return his youth to the imprisoned dissident; or her innocence to the young woman who has been raped; or integrity to the person who has been tortured. Nobody is going to return the dead and the disappeared to their families. What can and must be publicly restored are the victims' names and their dignity, through a formal recognition of the injustice of what has occurred, and, wherever possible, with some material reparations. As for the "disappeared," restitution must be made by a full disclosure of what happened, and if possible, a return of the mortal remains of the victim—or of the person himself or herself, in the case of those children who were stolen from their families. Christianity calls for pardon, yes, but a pardon based on truth and justice. Even the most traditional morality only speaks of reconciliation when joined with the "offer of compensation"; that is, the recognition of wrong committed, and of "atonement through acts," which is to say, reparation.

The third argument—of "greater might"—is unfortunately the one with the most political weight, although it is also the most fragile. Because, basically, what it recognizes is the falsely democratic character of a social order mortgaged to the power of the military and subject to its will. A democracy that respects the argument of "greater might" will always be under the sword of Damocles—a sword wielded by those who through their control of violence can decide on the acceptability of a legal act or a political orientation, according to their group interests, or even personal interests. Such a democracy will always be constrained, censored, castrated—contradicting its own nature and vocation from its very roots. Further, this argument represents an offensive perversion of the military institution itself, for it presupposes that the military could never be wed to justice or could never function honestly. In other words, it writes off the possibility that the armed forces would be capable of facing up to and accepting the same principle of justice that would apply to any other person, group, or social institution. Do we really believe that this principle can lead to the establishment of a truly democratic society? Would it not be selling as a historical possibility for democracy something that constitutes precisely a condition of its impossibility?

Those who clamor for social reparation are not asking for vengeance. Nor are they blindly adding difficulties to a historical process that is already by no means easy. On the contrary, they are promoting the personal and social viability of a new society, truly democratic. What it comes down to is, how can justice be exercised in our societies if the people who are the principal violators of human rights can freely flaunt before their own victims the idea that what they did was "the right thing," something they might even have to do again? What right would we have to punish or imprison someone who steals another's goods or who kills out of personal motives, if we ignore the damage done by those who stole human lives and committed mass assassination out of ideological zeal?

Just as personal traumas require therapy so that they can be worked through and overcome, our societies in Latin American require the socio-political therapy of a just reparation for the genocide being committed in the name of national security and, indeed, in the name of Western civilization.

Segundo Montes

6. Is Democracy Possible in An Underdeveloped Country?*

TRANSLATION BY PHILLIP BERRYMAN

A sociologist must deal with democracy . . . because democracy must be the sphere of action for social groups and forces. However, speaking about democracy in Latin America also means referring either to an entelechy or to a utopia in the ongoing history of the continent—although it might be that democracy itself is a utopia.

Gabriel A. González has recently written an article analyzing democracy in El Salvador (González, 1979). After presenting the concept of democracy, he discusses the crisis of political democracy, the collapse of traditional democracy, and the fallacy of the democratic tradition, in order to note the consequences of this process. The author asserts not only that democracy in El Salvador lacks "authenticity" despite the laws that enshrine it, but that its very essence is lacking since the values on which El Salvador's society is structured are power and wealth. Indeed, "as long as a social stratification based on class and oligarchy is in place, the very institutional foundations for organizing the nation do not exist," because "there is no will, thought, or collective interest as a nation"; and "there can be no political authenticity unless there is conscious capability to decide," and that is impossible given the structure of domination over the peasant masses, for the very act whereby they become conscious is regarded as "an activity undermining established society."

I do not intend to contest González' thesis. In fact I accept it as valid and as a starting point. My effort will rather be to continue to develop this position to see whether it is really a crisis which we could call, perhaps incorrectly, a conjunctural crisis or one of growth, or whether it is rather a structural crisis; or better whether what we have is a crisis of democracy or simply the lack—conjunctural or structural—of even a formal minimum of democracy. Hence my question here will be: is democracy possible in an underdeveloped country like El Salvador?

Rather than presuming to rise to a very high level of generalization, I am going to deal with a specific country, El Salvador. However, my

---

*Montes (1980a); see Bibliography in the back of this book.

141

concern in this study is not so much its specific features but rather certain social characteristics that flow from its state of underdevelopment and dependence. Hence, if there are other countries where social conditions are similar to those of El Salvador in terms of underdevelopment and dependence—and I believe there are many in Latin America—I think the conclusions of this study could be applied to them, since they do not derive from the specific traits of one territory or one body of people, but rather from the social characteristics imposed by underdevelopment and dependence.

In order to discuss the question formulated, I must take up the concept of democracy and then see whether it is applicable to a country with particular social and historical characteristics. Consequently, my article is made up of two parts: in the first and theoretical part, I will try to establish an objective criterion for defining democracy; in the second and practical part, I will try to compare the requirements of this concept of democracy with some of El Salvador's social conditions in order to see whether or not they are compatible. Finally, my conclusions will summarize what has been said throughout the article in order to offer an alternative solution.

Towards an Objective Criterion for Democracy

Some official documents, such as the constitution of El Salvador, talk about democracy, but in very general terms which are often taken from universal statements and which make generic pronouncements flowing from compromises acceptable to all political systems. Consequently they do not refer to any specific system. Thus the Constitution [of 1962]* states: "El Salvador is a sovereign state. Sovereignty resides in the people and is limited to what is honest, just, and fitting for society" (Article 1). "The government is republican, democratic, and representative" (Article 3). "All public power flows from the people. Government officials are its delegates and have only those powers that the law expressly gives them" (Article 6).

As they appear in the Constitution, the concepts of "democracy" and "people," borrowed from a modified liberal conception, are still very abstract, and it is difficult to verify whether they can be put into practice or not.

A great deal has been written about democracy, and to get very involved in arguing over concepts would both be quite rash and would go beyond the limits of this article. . . . [Instead] from among writers who

---

*The Constitution of 1962 was replaced by a new constitution in 1983, three years after Montes wrote this article for ECA. Some articles from that new constitution are cited in Chapter 7, *this volume*. P.B.

have dealt with the issue of democracy, I have chosen a few who represent different schools of thought in order to consider the criteria they propose and to try to find some element, common to them all and essential to the concept of democracy, one that can be accepted in any interpretation.

GEORGES BURDEAU

Georges Burdeau is regarded as an eminent authority at least within the functionalist school. His is an open functionalism, and he is trying to combine functionalism and Marxism in order to find a general political science applicable to Marxist régimes as well. From among his many and varied works I have chosen *La Democracia* (Burdeau, 1970), not only for its brevity but also for its clear and succinct thought and because it offers us an interesting analysis of democracy and its real historic embodiments in modern times, the period which most concerns us. I am not going to write either an exegesis or a summary of his book, but rather I am going to take some of the elements the book offers, in order to examine whether his requirements can be applied to our specific society.* I will do the same with other writers whom I will examine after Burdeau.

Starting from the classic definition of democracy, "government of the people by the people," he adds, "because if it is always the people who govern (in a democracy) it is not always actual people themselves." Consequently, we must go deeper into the meaning of "people" in order to understand how the concept of democracy has evolved.

In the French Revolution, which proclaims democracy, the people are considered to be composed of "citizens." Its language refers not so much to the "people" as to "nation," an abstract concept, which assumes a "people of citizens, made up of identical beings, that is, of a classless people," who make up a state, which safeguards the freedom of these citizens. That is the spirit behind the "Declaration of the Rights of Man and of the Citizen." That kind of democracy, however, is "difficult for the governed, of whom it demands qualities so pure and so diverse, that Rousseau believed it could be truly realized only in a people of gods."

Such an idealization of democracy serves the bourgeoisie, and it is they who emerged victorious from the French Revolution. The people, composed mainly of proletarian masses, is very far from these ideals of citizen and god, and actually is an oppressed, marginalized, ignorant, and exploited people; this is not an abstract human being but one "in context." He continues: "The characteristics of the contextualized human being are diametrically opposed to those that define the citizen, and this difference has a profound impact on the style of democracy. While citizens bear the prerogatives of human nature and tend to

---

*All quotations in this section are from Burdeau (1970).

impose them on the surrounding environment [those who are] contextualized human beings must await from their environment the occasion for achieving that nature." That is to say: freedom is the attribute of the citizen, while human beings in context are awaiting their liberation. For a people of citizens, democracy safeguards the governing of existing society; for human beings in context, however, it would be tantamount to creating a new universe.

For Burdeau, true democracy is not the abstract democracy of citizens, but the real and concrete democracy of human beings in context, the majority, the real people, who cannot by any means assume it but have to conquer it, for "authentic democracy is possible only when the people, on whom political power rests, are able to exercise it directly, or at least to control its exercise." This is also the spirit behind Article 21 of the Universal Declaration of Human Rights. Such a democracy, however, requires certain prior conditions, namely the elimination of the most extreme differences between social classes and numerous other unjust inequities. Political democracy, says Burdeau, is founded on social democracy, that is, on a just and equitable participation in social and economic benefits, which is "the outstanding feature of the way forms of government have evolved during the contemporary period."

Social democracy should flow from something of a national consensus, since a "desirable social order should not flow from a caste, an intellectual elite, or an economically privileged social category. It should, as it were, gather in a bundle the aspirations of most members of the whole." However, the people reach this level of maturity only when certain social and economic conditions of equality and justice are fulfilled.

Apparently, however, in society this national pact should not be expected to come about spontaneously, and hence to some extent it will be imposed by the state in order to make social and political democracy viable. "Government should accept the responsibility for introducing democracy into society. Democracy thus understood can be called democracy by imposition, since authority is regarded as the instrument for implementing the requirements of democracy."

Can social democracy—a requisite for political democracy—really be established through the free play of ideas and of democracy, or will it be imposed by a bourgeois state? Burdeau goes on to present the Marxist position, which answers in the negative and holds that the bourgeois state is set up in order to defend the interests of the ruling class, and that concessions are wrenched from it by the working class, which is the true representative of the masses. The people will always lose out in the bourgeois democratic game, since the bourgeoisie has more resources and better ones, for taking advantage of that game. Consequently, democracy cannot be achieved apart from "a shift of power, which is inseparable from a revolutionary phase of the dictatorship of the proletariat."

The way towards the liberation of the proletariat and the establishment of social and then political democracy will be the seizure of power by the people, either through the transformation of political parties into ideological and mass parties, or through revolution leading to the dictatorship of the proletariat, as a prior step on the way towards the establishment of democracy.

Marxism's ideal and goal is the establishment of a true democracy, one without state oppression, which will disappear when the political is reabsorbed into the social, as stated in the *Communist Manifesto*. That ideal and goal, however, are a long way from the revolution, and it will be necessary to go through a prior stage, ruled not by democracy, but by the dictatorship of the proletariat.

The reasons justifying the establishment of the dictatorship of the proletariat are both extrinsic and intrinsic to the revolutionary process. These reasons are the capitalist encirclement threatening the process which can be defended only by the state, and the indispensability of the state apparatus for building socialist society, which is the prologue to the collective community. However, the long period that the dictatorship of the proletariat endures does necessitate that the concept of democracy be redefined so as to apply to this phase. The state and political power remain in place in this phase but it is a "state proper to a homogeneous society, and remains a superstructure, but now it is in harmony with the infrastructure. It is a real and genuine democracy; power belongs to the people as a whole. If the effort to build socialism requires intervention by government power, the power undertaking that responsibility can only be the power that comes from the people."

Of course [Burdeau continues], the dictatorship of the proletariat must be led by the communist party which, as the most conscious and most representative segment of the people is "the only authorized interpreter of proletarian ideology." During this dictatorship the party's mission will be not only to represent the interests of the people, but to educate the people to become conscious and to become involved in the process of socialism; this is all the more the case insofar as the alienation produced by the bourgeois capitalist régime has rendered people unfit for the socialist mission until they are reeducated and liberated.

Although the parties controlling Marxist régimes have officially redefined the concept of democracy, Burdeau does not see genuine democracy in those régimes: "given the domination state power has acquired over the masses, such uncontrolled power without any counter balance is simply that of the rulers." He regards the dictatorship of the proletariat not as a democracy but as a "closed power," which "can be termed popular monocracy, since political power is concentrated in a single party imposing its will on all branches of government."

In concluding his book, Burdeau states that the meaning of democracy is not immutable, and that the variations in its meaning are caused by the very practice of democratic institutions. "If this observation is justified, we are led to conceive of democracy as a movement rather than a static condition." The liberal revolution gave democracy a meaning that favored one class, but the dispossessed classes gradually moved in and even rebelled to the point of taking power, thus modifying the notion of democracy. Let me finish by quoting a final paragraph from this author, "We have been especially concerned to show that by giving power to the unprivileged masses, contemporary democracy inevitably turns that very power into the force that creates a new society."

If I have devoted a lot of attention to Burdeau, it is not only because he is important, but because I believe that his analysis, which takes account of different social and political moments in history and takes cognizance of various theoretical frameworks, can help us conceptualize the term "democracy." Nevertheless, I think it is a good idea to present other viewpoints, although I will have to do so more briefly.

KARL MARX

The proletarian revolution that led to the establishment of the Commune of Paris enabled Marx and Engels to observe the first embodiment of the socialist project that they had envisioned in their writings. In his introduction to Marx's work, "The Civil War in France" (1870), Engels offered an analysis of the bourgeois state and class oppression and presented the Paris Commune [government] as an embodiment of the dictatorship of the proletariat: "Look at the Paris Commune. That was the Dictatorship of the Proletariat."*

In that work Marx analyzes the revolution in France that gave rise to the Commune, presenting also the economic and moral corruption of the republican government [afterwards] headed by Thiers in refuge at Versailles. In contrast to that bourgeois, exploitative, and bloodthirsty government, Marx presents the government of the Paris Commune as an example of democratic government, whose representatives were elected by universal suffrage and who were "responsible and revocable at short terms." [According to Marx] They offered a model to be imitated in all industrial centers in France, a "communal *régime*," which would "have to give way to the self-government of the producers." Thus, the Commune "supplied the republic with the basis of really democratic institutions," since "it was essentially a working class government, the product of the struggle of the producing against the appropriating class, the political form at last discovered under which to work out the economical emancipation of labour." The Commune's social measures "could but betoken the tendency of a government of the people by the people. Such were the abolition of the nightwork of journeymen bakers; the prohibition, under penalty, of the employers' practice to reduce wages by levying upon their workplace fines under manifold

---

*All quotations in this subsection are from Marx (1870) as included in *The Marx-Engels Reader* (1972).

pretexts . . . [and] the surrender to associations of workmen . . . of all closed workshops and factories. . ."

The Paris Commune was wiped out by the armies of Versailles, with the consent and help of the Prussians. Noting the barbarity of the slaughter unleashed against the people and the Commune and the accusations against the people for starting fires and destroying property as they defended themselves and fled, Marx denounces the hypocrisy of the bourgeoisie, "which looks complacently upon the wholesale massacre after the battle," and yet "is convulsed by horror at the desecration of brick and mortar!" The bourgeois, he says, is the successor of the feudal baron, "who thought every weapon in his own hand fair against the plebeian, while in the hands of the plebeian a weapon of any kind constituted in itself a crime." Let us conclude with a closing passage from Marx: "The soil out of which [the International Working Men's Association, whom he is addressing] grows is modern society itself. It cannot be stamped out by any amount of carnage. To stamp it out, the governments would have to stamp out the despotism of capitalism over labour—the condition of their own parasitical existence."

The Paris experiment failed, however, and it was only with the victory of the Russian revolution that the dictatorship of the proletariat was established and thus we could analyze it. Nevertheless, it is in that institutionalization of socialist revolution and implementation of the dictatorship of the proletariat that it becomes problematic to call it democracy, although that was the dream that had inspired the struggle.

VLADIMIR LENIN

The State and Revolution (Lenin, 1917) is an enormously important work, not only because it was written by Lenin on the eve of the Russian Revolution, but because of its inherent value as political analysis. I will limit myself to a couple of points in Ralph Milliband's critical analysis of the work (Milliband, 1977-78).

According to Marx, socialist revolution leads to the disappearance of the state, but that stage seems to be very distant, as Lenin himself acknowledges. Nonetheless, the revolution must initiate the process of breaking up the state that was erected on the bourgeois foundation. Milliband states that "exercising socialist power continues to be the Achilles heel of Marxism."

The first point to discuss is that of the power of the post-revolutionary state, which is as strong as, or stronger than, the bourgeois state it replaces. Lenin answers that "the day after the revolution the state has not only begun to die, but is already in an advanced state of decomposition."[*] He does not mean that it is weak, and indeed it must

---

[*]All quotations in this section are from *State and Revolution* (Lenin, 1917) as included in Lenin (1975).

be very strong, but it is no longer a state of bureaucrats, but it has become a state of armed workers. This is a voluntary centralism, all the communes are voluntarily united into one nation: a really democratic state, the state of the soviets of deputies and workers. The soviets are sovereign and all powerful, but their members can be recalled at any moment, since popular sovereignty is in command. The bureaucracy will continue to exist but under the strict control of armed workers. The other state power, the army, will be replaced by the armed working masses, as a step towards the participation of the entire people in the militias.

The second problem is that of the "political mediation of revolutionary power," that is, the power of the party in the process. Milliband regards it as a serious flaw that in this work Lenin speaks very little about the Communist Party, even though in other works, especially those written after the Russian Revolution, he regards it as very important. Here he only grants it a leadership role in educating the proletariat so as to lead it towards the seizure of power and socialism. Actually for both Marx and Lenin and for all socialist revolutions, the Communist Party is the true political mediation, so much so that Trotsky was led to say, after the split in the party, that "the party organization first replaces the party as a whole; then the Central Committee replaces the party; and finally an individual dictator replaces the Central Committee."

After the Revolution, Lenin stated categorically in 1919: "Yes, dictatorship by one party!" and in 1921 "the dictatorship of the proletariat is possible only through the Communist Party." This response raises doubts about the withering away of the state, and he replies, "We will have time to celebrate more than two congresses before we will be able to say: 'Look how our state is withering away.' It is still too early. Declaring the withering away of the state prematurely would violate the perspective of history."

Thus the problem of democracy, as the participation of the whole people in the affairs of the nation, is not fully resolved in Marxism, either by a withering away of the state or by the dictatorship of the proletariat, which tends to be prolonged in the dictatorship of the party, and to make Trotsky's statement prophetic. At least this has been the real history of socialism in Russia, especially in Stalin's time, and thus socialism is even further away than when Lenin warned that it was rather far off in the future.

However, it is not only the control of power by the party, the Central Committee, and a dictator that has made this democratic socialist future more remote. A new factor comes into play in the process of history as the revolution is diverted to serve particular interests. Antonio García (1973) believes that the economic and social development of the Soviet Union has expanded the bureaucracy, the intelligentsia, and the industrial workers, who have become true middle classes and a majority, and it is they who participate most in the party and fashion a structure in which they are privileged. Indeed, the party is composed primarily of people from these middle classes, as well as the bureaucracy and the higher levels of the educational system and the professions. Thus they control political power which in turn controls economic power, and they are not going to allow that control to be wrested away from them for the sake of the more marginal classes in society, who have not benefitted from the revolutionary process to the same degree. Party dictatorship has actually become the dictatorship of certain ruling classes, and that fact will make more difficult the process of educating and integrating the masses, and will make even more remote the movement towards the withering away of the state and the participation of all in a genuine democracy. On the basis of empirical research, García believes that something similar has taken place in the countries of the southernmost cone of Latin America within a different system, that of capitalism.

MILTON FRIEDMAN

Finally, representing the very different perspective of the liberal school of economists at the University of Chicago, Milton Friedman, states: "I hold. . . that there is a close connection between politics and economics, and that only certain combinations of political and economic arrangements are possible; in particular, a socialist society cannot also be democratic, in the sense of safeguarding individual freedom" (Friedman, 1966). In keeping with this thesis he tries to prove that political democracy cannot exist in a socialist system since there is no economic freedom, and as proof, he points suggestively to state control over the economy. These same arguments can nevertheless be turned against even the most open capitalist systems.

In many works, Friedman (e.g., 1966) argues for utterly unfettered liberalism and opposes government economic planning, price controls, subsidies to business, and so forth; in other words, he advocates keeping the government out of the economy as much as possible and carrying *laissez faire, laissez passer* to its ultimate consequences, for ultimately he believes in social and economic Darwinism, in which everyone has the same opportunities, and the most competent and best adapted win out.

The reality, however, is quite different, even in countries like the United States, where in fact everyone does not have the same opportunities for education or for accumulating the capital necessary to get ahead, or equal access to credit. Political democracy is indeed connected to economics, as Friedman recognizes, and it is deeply bound up with the hegemonic economic groups. To speak of true economic democracy and effective equality of opportunities in the developed countries is really an illusion, if not a myth. That is all the more true in peripheral and underdeveloped countries, such as El Salvador and many other countries in Latin America. Friedman would certainly not grant them the honor of calling them economically democratic. And if we take his position to its logical conclusion, if there is no real economic freedom there is then no political freedom under capitalism either. In other words, there is no democracy—and that we know from experience as well.

To summarize what has been said thus far, in conceptual terms democracy means government of the people by the people. That concept, however, is historical, and it has to do with a people which is likewise in history and in an actual context. Such political democracy presupposes as an indispensable requisite, a social democracy, that is, a degree of equality in social benefits and a share in governing society. If individual forces are simply left to themselves, however, social democracy cannot be attained nor can political democracy; it must be imposed by the state. In a bourgeois capitalist régime, however, the state is at the service of a ruling minority and it is not going to impose that kind of democracy. It must therefore be the people themselves who take power and impose it, and to that end they must become organized. Until now the historic possibility has been that of socialist revolution, in which the organized people take power. Initially, however, things move not towards democracy but rather towards the dictatorship of the proletariat, led by the party, which runs the risk of installing itself in power and postponing indefinitely the shift towards democracy. That is all the more true, the more the people are alienated and unprepared to participate in government.

Do the conditions required for democracy exist in El Salvador?

All the writers cited in the previous subsections agree that political democracy is conditioned socially and economically. Burdeau holds that political democracy requires a social democracy, that is, a fair distribution of social and economic benefits eliminating huge class differences and enabling all members of the population to participate in government. The Marxist tradition holds that politics is part of the superstructure which is conditioned by the economic structure, and that private property gives rise to the social relations of production between opposed classes, leading the state to defend the interests of the ruling class; consequently, only a revolution that abolishes private property can lead to a democratic government. From a very different position, Friedman also asserts that there is a connection between the political and the economic, and therefore he holds that democracy cannot exist in socialist countres, since there is no economic freedom. He does believe, however, that there is economic freedom in advanced capitalist countries. For now let us leave aside García's idea, since in El Salvador the middle class has not grown and asserted its hegemony, as will be seen in the course of this article.

In El Salvador we have the opposite of what can be called a social democracy based on a fair distribution of social benefits. Salvadoran society is divided into statistically differentiated groups or strata—without entering into a theoretical discussion of the term—a phenomenon that I have quantified and analyzed elsewhere (Montes 1979a; for a later analysis, see also Montes (1989a) in Chapter 13, *this volume*). The very lowest stratum, made up of peasants and those who live in marginal urban areas, includes more than 80 percent of the total population of the country. These people fully merit the term "marginal," in the sense that they receive hardly any social benefits, as is evident in their moving from place to place, family breakdown, overcrowded living conditions, miserable housing, unemployment, sub-subsistence economy, exclusion from the educational system, and low level of aspirations. At the other extreme is the privileged group, not even 2 percent of the population, the group that really benefits from the system and controls political power. Between these extremes are what we could call the middle classes, who are scarcely more than 15 percent of the population, but who are divided into three levels, the lowest of which is statistically different from the other two, but also from the [80 percent] marginalized level.

Such a social stratification is quite remote from the "social democracy" needed for making political democracy possible. As I have been able to demonstrate [earlier] in the work cited above, it is the economic variable that explains the other variables, although it is in turn partly explained by the educational variable among heads of families, which is itself conditioned by the economic level of their parents. In accordance with the writings surveyed above, we can anticipate that, given such an economic and social structure, most Salvadorans will also be excluded from political participation.

Starting with the economic structure of El Salvador, let us examine whether there is a social democracy, in order to be able to understand the ideological and political structure, and to see whether democracy is possible under such a system. The Salvadoran economy basically revolves around agriculture, not only because most Salvadorans make their living from it, but also because agricultural products are the most important export sector. The land holding structure is highly concentrated in large plots of the agriculturally best lands, owned by a few large landholders, while the agriculturally marginal lands are divided up into a vast number of small plots. The result is a high level of unemployment, due to both the kinds of crops that can be grown and to the gradual proletarization of the rural population. This whole process is worsening as time goes on. Whenever the question of land ownership is broached—even within an overall scheme for modernizing capitalism—Salvadoran society goes into convulsions. That happened once more when President Molina's proposed Agrarian Transformation drew the whole national oligarchy together to oppose it in a political struggle for hegemony lasting three months (July-October 1976). The result was that the oligarchy defeated the government and took absolute control over it, as *ECA* denounced in its November 1976 editorial (Colindres 1977; *ECA*, 1973; 1976a; 1976b; see also Ellacuría, 1976d, Chapter 4, *this volume*). Other sectors of the Salvadoran economy have been built up on the foundations of agriculture as Colindres (1977), Dada Herezi (1978), and others have shown.

The existing economic structure leads Ibisate (1979) to ask "Is 'Salvadoran Capitalism' Capitalist?" [See also Montes (1983a), Chapter 12, *this volume*.] He argues that it is neither truly capitalist nor truly Salvadoran, given its dependence on world capitalism, its lack of planning, its coexistence with residual precapitalist and feudal forms, and the lack of a national economic structure. "The primary sector exports to the outside and the secondary sector imports from the outside. What both sectors have in common is 'ownership' and 'foreigner' and hence the so-called 'national economy' is a function of, or is oriented towards these two terms of reference. If this judgment is accurate, our capitalism seems to be a combination of 'mechanization and feudalism, open to the outside'; the lord of the fiefdom has been split in half, leaving one inside and one outside. This is a very peculiar case of a 'mixed economy'; it is also 'mixed' because it divides society into two parts: 'those who want to buy and cannot, and those who can and do not want to,' because they do so outside. This situation reflects a combination of economic and social underdevelopment. If the public sector gives in and is subjected to this structural situation, it will be unable to achieve 'national security,' nor to lead Salvadoran capitalism down the capitalist road itself" (Ibisate, 1979). One consequence of this kind of exploitative economic structure is the fact that the bulk of government revenue comes from indirect taxes which fall most heavily on the impoverished majority, but primarily benefit the most privileged strata, as Luis de Sebastián (1979) has shown.

The other variable explaining social stratification in El Salvador is the educational level reached by heads of households. The Salvadoran educational system also generates stratification in the very way that the benefits of the system are received, and it is quite in line with the existing economic and social stratification. At the bottom are officially recognized illiterates, who together with functional illiterates (those who did not get beyond the second grade) make up the 80 percent of the population who can be regarded as "marginalized from the education system" (Montes, 1971a). The next strata, whose numbers decline as they go up the schooling pyramid, are differentiated by the level reached. That is, the educational system, as can only be expected, reproduces the social and economic system which favors a minority, to the disadvantage of the great majority, thus preventing social change through education. The unequal and unjust distribution of the national budget among the different levels brings about this stratified pyramid which reproduces the existing social and economic system (*ECA*, 1978). If the economic structure conditions social forces and their relations, an economic structure like that of El Salvador has to generate social classes at odds with each other and a series of tensions and social conflicts.

On the one hand, in order to maintain its exploitation of the masses the economically dominant class must make use of all the superstructural elements at its disposal and remain basically united, at least during moments of crisis, and on the other hand it must both prevent the masses (especially the peasants) from becoming organized and it must divide the majority by creating certain middle classes as a "buffer" between the classes that are at odds. These middle classes are conveniently stratified and divided, but they tend to be identified with the dominant class and its interests. Lopez Vallecillos (1979) has just published a study of the different social forces in the country, how they are divided, and their alliances during the last fifty years, which develops this idea more fully.

Until a few years ago El Salvador was strictly an agricultural country and had a more homogeneous social structure with a simpler kind of conflict. During the 1950s, however, an industrialization process began and intensified in response to the Central American Common Market. The mainly urban industrial work force grew, as did its organization and a degree of class consciousness. The failure of that Common Market at the end of the 1960s led to a crisis in the industrial sector, and its initial impact was on that work force. The intensification of the economic crisis during the 1970s, especially during these last two years, in conjunction with a hardening position on the part of the oligarchy, put intense pressure on those workers who sought to defend themselves by strengthening their organizations and their determination to fight, especially this year [1979] when the economic crisis exploded. Samayoa and Galvan (1979a) develop this point further.

The issue of structure leads us to the level of the superstructure. An economic structure that is so oppressive and exploitative of the vast majority can be maintained only through violent coercion. For that purpose the ruling groups must be able to count on having political power at their disposal. The central concern is not the nation or the people but the private benefit of a few who hold or control power and the necessary means of repression. In the words of González (1979) quoted at the beginning of this paper: "this is the case because there is no will, thought, or collective interest as a nation."

A national security régime is then imposed, one that is undemocratic and unconstitutional, in order to defend and prop up this unjust structure (Campos, 1979). The most fundamental human rights are violated in order to repress and intimidate the people, in defiance of all international condemnations (Ungo, 1979). The state is militarized as the only way to safeguard the status quo (Andino Martínez, 1979).

Another aspect of the superstructural level is that the system is reinforced by the creation and diffusion of ideologies to justify it, and they then became a form of social coercion on the side of the ruling groups.

From the colonial origins to the present, the exploitative system imposed by the Spaniards has been bolstered by those ideological and religious values which deepen exploitation, hinder conflicts based on class or ethnic group, and introduce individualistic relationships of a paternalistic, emotional, and reverential nature. [In turn] these relationships are expressed in the social and political system of *compadrazgo* [strong ties between parents and godparents acquired at baptism] and clientelism, which is still in force. The ruling groups have inculcated this spirit in the people for centuries and have benefited from the meek subservience of the people (Montes, 1979b).

As I have already noted, the educational system not only has not served to encourage social change, but it has become one of the most potent tools for the reproduction and internalization of the system itself.

Finally, the mass media, which could have become an instrument for liberation and for consciousness raising among people, have instead always been in the hands of the dominant groups who have turned them into extremely effective means for increased alienation and exploitation. As Stein says, "this concentration of power is a necessary function of what occurs in other spheres of our society: . . . it favors the interests of capital and of the régime, sometimes going so far as to allow calumny and defamation; . . . we have systems, networks, and practices that have led to a country uninformed and misinformed. . . where the concerns, activity and experiences of the majority are not presented . . . where the drive to do business runs roughshod over the ethical and technical possibilities for development and fulfillment: . . . where advertising only emphatically reinforces these tendencies by proclaiming limitless consumption, unendingly promoting the ownership and use of luxury goods, entirely counter to the fact that the majority lacks even necessities and thus also counter to the austerity a poor country like ours needs" (Stein, 1979).

As is obvious from what has been said, El Salvador is an underdeveloped country, and its underdevelopment is not merely economic, but it is all encompassing. Underdevelopment embraces all aspects of its social reality. Furthermore, this underdevelopment is not simply a fact, but it is a deliberately maintained condition, precisely for the sake of the dominant interests. In my study of social stratification I tried to demonstrate this point by dealing with both internal and external exploitation and domination. I believe I should amplify this point a little.

Salvadoran underdevelopment is not independent, but is dependent rather on a higher-level structure of domination—by the capitalist bloc. Like so many other dependent countries, El Salvador has been assigned a specific task in the international capitalist division of labor, namely the production and export of raw materials and of a tiny bit of elementary industry and the consumption of manufactured goods, capital, and technology furnished by the hegemonic centers. In order to assure this exploitation of Salvadoran wealth and labor, certain conditions that guarantee high unemployment must be maintained in order to keep wages very low. Any effort to organize the exploited majority must be broken up, and an ideology legitimizing and sustaining the system must be propagated. However, a small profit margin must be left for the very smallest national groups so they will identify with this dominant structure and so they can consume the manufactured goods coming from the hegemonic centers. . . . .

This point is very important since the unjust and antidemocratic system under which the country suffers is not just produced within the country, but it is the result of a whole strategy by international capitalism. If El Salvador should seek to free itself from its internal oppressive structures, in order to begin a process of social democratization as a step towards a process of political democratization, it would find itself blocked by the international capitalist system, whose interests would not be served by the process, especially if there were danger of a chain reaction.

Conclusion

From what has been said thus far, I believe it can be clearly concluded that in El Salvador, or in any other country with a similar social situation, the conditions required for democracy as understood in the section of this article on "objective criterion", do not exist.

If one accepts Friedman's position, our lack of economic freedom makes political freedom and democracy impossible. If we follow Burdeau, there is no social democracy based on a degree of fairness in distribution, and hence the foundation required for political democracy is missing. If we look to Marxist theoreticians, the social and economic reality is the result of a system of exploitation which has created a superstructure to maintain that system for the benefit of the ruling class. In any case, it is obvious that the people do not rule but rather are ruled by a minority who have structured society for their own benefit.

The question of whether democracy is possible in an underdeveloped country like El Salvador nonetheless remains open. In my opinion, as long as the existing system remains in place democracy is impossible because democracy would lead to the destruction of the system, and the hegemonic groups, both inside the country and outside, are not going to permit that. The whole system is set up in such a way as to eliminate whatever threatens its continuance. (Here I think it is useful to recall the experience of the Agrarian Transformation in 1976 and the system of repression that intensified as a result of that failed attempt). Furthermore, as we can see throughout the second part of this analysis, all institutions are set up in such a way as to prevent a change in the system, and to thwart any effort to overthrow that system. Consequently, it is impossible that democracy be set up from within the system itself.

What remains is the other alternative, that is, that the people should be organized and take power through revolutionary victory, and then set up a socialist system. Let us briefly examine this possibility.

From the geopolitical standpoint, within the Western capitalist system, that alternative is difficult and would have to contend with a whole apparatus arguing against it. That is even more the case since the Sandinista victory in Nicaragua, because if El Salvador were to move towards the socialist system, the impact would be felt throughout the area. Countries on its border and others in the whole area would be changed and destabilized.

Let us admit, however, that such a shift could take place. According to Marxist theoretical frameworks, after the revolution it would not be democracy but a dictatorship of the proletariat that would be implemented next, not democracy—in order to prepare the way for the establishment of socialism and democracy. The social reality of El Salvador that we have examined in the second part of this study enables us to predict a rather long period of dictatorship by the proletariat, given the marginalization and alienation of the majority of the people, and combined with international difficulties, such a deep level of underdevelopment would very much hinder and retard the raising of the masses to the economic and social levels necessary for participatory government by the people.

On the one hand, El Salvador's underdevelopment and the degree of its abject poverty would require a very long period of time as a preparation for democracy. On the other hand, a revolutionary party would have to undertake the huge task of leading and educating the masses, and that would risk making the party so important and so powerful that in the long run it would impede its own mission of paving the way for democracy and handing power over to the people. Indeed the very development process, as García (1973) noted, would gradually create a middle class majority, which would control power for its own benefit, indefinitely putting off the integration of marginalized classes.

Nevertheless, there is no reason why the historic experiences of socialist revolutions and dictatorships of the proletariat must exhaust all the possibilities for reaching democracy by this route. That is, all socialist revolutions do not have to emulate the USSR, China, and other Marxist régimes. There can be new experiences and new ways to move from revolution to democracy.

The Cuban case may offer us some insight since there the process has been more rapid. The dictatorship has been more benign and has included more participation by the people, and the people have risen more rapidly in their preparation for democratic participation. We should also keep our eyes on the Nicaraguan case and how it evolves, to see whether it develops a new model for achieving democracy. It is possible that in small Latin American countries the preparatory process for democracy can be substantially accelerated. In any case, both Cuba and

Nicaragua are further along than we in this task—or this utopia—that lies ahead, the task of democracy.

Postscript [from the Author]: I finished writing this essay on October 12, 1979. Three days later young officers led a military insurrection in El Salvador and issued a revolutionary Manifesto. There has still not been enough time to analyze where this change is really leading. It is logical to remain skeptical that the coup will lead to true structural changes and that power will pass to the people. Nevertheless, we cannot be closed to possibilities *a priori* and on the basis of theoretical frameworks, when only history can provide the answer. S.M.

Segundo Montes, Florenín Meléndez, and Edgar Palacios

7. Economic, Social, and Cultural Rights in El Salvador*

TRANSLATION BY PHILLIP BERRYMAN

Attempting to analyze economic, social and cultural rights (ESC rights) in El Salvador is complicated and demanding. It involves not only a legal analysis, dealing with both domestic and international law, and with how ESC rights are embodied in legislation and with the mechanisms created to protect them, but also a socio-economic analysis and a reflection on the sociological and political dimensions of these rights. In the attempt we also need to keep in mind the armed conflict that has engulfed our country for years, and our situation, both politically and economically, as underdeveloped and dependent.
....

Economic, Social, and Cultural Rights as Fundamental Human Rights

A general conception of human rights informs our analysis. Fundamental human rights are identified and their conceptual unity established by virtue of their connection with human dignity. Taking the dignity of the human person as one of the highest values is the ground from which fundamental human rights derive. Hence, ESC rights [economic, social, cultural] are genuine rights, and their legal standing

---

*This chapter consists of three extracts from a book of the same title (Montes, *et al.*, 1988b). These selections are reprinted by permission of the publisher (San Salvador: IDHUCA). The first section (pp. 15-25 of the original) introduces—without detailed argument—the concept of human rights that informs the research and analysis carried out by the Human Rights Institute of the UCA (IDHUCA). The second section (pp. 69-73 of the original) presents a summary of the legal analysis offered in Part I of the book. The third section (pp. 107-13 of the original) summarizes Part II, the socio-economic analysis of the state of economic, social, and cultural rights in El Salvador in recent years. In the book, this analysis is supported by detailed empirical data which can be consulted as needed. THE EDITORS

cannot be called into question...and they are part of an integral vision, interrelated and interdependent with other categories of fundamental human rights. Indeed, ESC rights, like those of other categories, can be considered in their totality as the concrete embodiment of such ethical values as freedom, equality, justice and peace, which complement the value of human dignity. At rock bottom, then, there is an acknowledgement of the right to be regarded as a human being, a being of supreme dignity, a bearer of rights and obligations, and therefore to be treated as such by the state and society.

Without this primary acknowledgement of human dignity, there is no genuine possibility that authentic fundamental human rights will be either acknowledged or put into practice effectively. When we thus regard dignity as among the highest values, it follows that ESC rights are closely linked with the values on which the validity of rights in general rest. And despite serious legal problems that arise when the attempt is made to conceptualize, to classify and especially to protect ESC rights, they have become part of the wide range of fundamental rights now recognized by states and by the international community. . . . Unless they are really in force, we cannot speak of a complete and comprehensive acknowledgement of human rights, . . . and the current absence of true mechanisms for defending them does not mean that we can ignore their fundamental character as human rights. They are neither a vague kind of right, nor are they to be ranked higher than other fundamental rights. Rather, together with certain civil and political rights (CP rights), they make up the fundamental rights of the human person, affirmed as such by various legal systems and international conventions.

CIVIL AND POLITICAL RIGHTS AND ECONOMIC, SOCIAL, AND CULTURAL RIGHTS

A preliminary to a complete analysis of ESC rights is an analysis of CP rights, because in modern history there has been a more or less steady rise in human rights—initially CP rights—as norms legally recognized by states. Early on there were declarations in which states formally acknowledged that the individual primordially had certain rights and public freedoms that the state must respect. Later, in the late eighteenth century and throughout the nineteenth century, these became embodied in constitutions. Thus at the outset of our history it is civil rights and political freedoms which emerge as the rights of individuals vis-à-vis the state, and it is not until some years later—in 1917—that certain ESC rights are recognized as authentic rights inherent in the human person.

This difference in the way recognition of different categories of rights has arisen is due primarily to the class interests prevailing at the close of the Middle Ages and at the rise of the modern liberal state in the eighteenth century. In that era the liberal state sought to make concessions to the individual. The context of those conditions was that of freedom which the state would not infringe upon—by pledging to stay out of the private sphere of persons. Thus as initially conceived, the liberal state takes on a formal and legal obligation towards individuals, which is an obligation to *not* act in opposition to the exercise of acknowledged rights.

The state's stance of abstention at first makes it passive with regard to human rights. The state assumes no other obligations than that of not acting, that is, of allowing individuals to act in their interpersonal relations and in their relations with government bodies without any restrictions, except those established by law. . . . Thus, if these rights are truly to be in force, what is required is that government bodies for the most part refrain from acting. Nevertheless, some of these rights entail certain obligations which require positive action on the part of state institutions. That feature is characteristic of ESC rights.

CP rights are sometimes called "first generation rights," because of the period when they emerged and because they were acknowledged in legal codes before ESC rights were (Martí de Vases, 1983). They emerged under the strong influence of natural law thinking, liberal currents of thought, and various social, political, and philosophical movements, among which we should mention the English revolution, the French and American revolutions, and the constitutionalist movements of the nineteenth and early twentieth century. From the outset, however, they emerged as rights of the human being in the abstract, as the rights of the citizen, as the rights of a category of persons determined by their situation in relation to the interests of the state, and not as rights of human beings in their real and concrete situations. Despite this, some of these rights, especially civil rights, were framed as rights proper to all human beings in virtue of their very condition as human beings.

Given the nature of CP rights, it has not been too difficult to define them conceptually, or to determine who has such rights; and they are clearly defined today. A conceptual problem really does arise, however, when we begin to examine ESC rights, since the effort to incorporate them into positive law raises certain issues about their nature and composition . . . . Even within the group of ESC rights we encounter problems when we try to conceptualize some rights in relation to others, (for example, economic rights vis-à-vis social rights).

It is in fact really difficult to separate out social rights, especially when we take into account that all human rights, both by reason of their possessors and by their very essence, have a strong social component and are ultimately social rights, no matter whether they are intended to assist individuals or social groups. From the moment the individual becomes the direct beneficiary of fundamental human rights, the legal norms protecting his or her interests as a human person become social norms, but that is compatible with trying to conceptualize and characterize social rights in the strict sense—as those rights intended to protect the various social groups and the whole of society. This question of how to define and distinguish economic and social rights is already present when we try to analyze ESC rights as a whole, and it hinders an easy understanding and development of those rights.

Finally, while it is true that civil rights and public freedoms emerged as rights at a particular moment in history and were influenced by the interests of a privileged minority holding economic power at the expense of the dispossessed majority, and that those rights emerged partly in order to protect private property as it was then constituted, we cannot thereby diminish the credit due to some thinkers, especially in the eighteenth century, who helped put fundamental human rights into positive law. They established the extremely important precedent of incorporating into the laws governing the incipient modern state the formal recognition of some of the most important political freedoms and civil rights of our own time.

Thus, whether they be civil, political, economic, social, or cultural, human rights taken as a whole are an expression of certain higher values which taken together safeguard human dignity. Only when states recognize those rights can they be truly effective as rights of the human being, and that can be the case only when they are conceived in an integral fashion, since some of them cannot really take effect unless the full effectiveness of the others is also assured.

Hence we can assert that CP rights demand that ESC rights be put into effect and safeguarded, and these latter rights need civil rights and public freedoms if they are to be effective. Human rights taken altogether are universal, indivisible, and complementary.

Towards Democracy in El Salvador

In accordance with the legal considerations on ESC rights in El Salvador,* we can state that even though these rights have not developed and been extended as much as their character as fundamental rights would require, they do not thereby cease to be true fundamental human rights in the realm of law.

Their legal character is not even altered by the fact that some of these rights are "of gradual application" in contrast to others, such as the right to be protected against hunger, the right to education, and the right to health care, which are all "of immediate application." These are genuine rights and as such they entail the correlative duty on the part of the state to safeguard and comply with them. While it is true that some of the ESC rights, such as the right to work and the right to housing do not entitle their bearers to use legal mechanisms to demand that they be

---

*As previously noted, the entire presentation on ESC rights in El Salvador can be found in Part I of Montes, *et al.* (1988b).

satisfied immediately, they do not thereby cease to be fundamental rights. We should bear in mind that the specific features of each right determine its nature and how it is to be implemented in the legal life of states.

Hence we cannot determine the nature and essence of a fundamental right by the way it is applied in practice. Rather we must look to its very makeup and its place in the scale of higher values that accompany the human being at every moment and in every circumstance.

We have stated that some ESC rights are "of gradual application," because complete compliance with them depends on the state's access to both internal and external resources. This does not thereby reduce them to programmatic statements to which states like our own merely pay lip service, even though they have acknowledged in constitutions and in international human rights treaties that these rights exist formally as basic human rights. . . . On the contrary, in acknowledging these rights, the state assumes the obligation to use the resources required to assure that the most basic social and economic needs of the Salvadoran family are met in a gradual, planned, and systematic manner.

Consequently, the Salvadoran state, whether or not it is under international economic pressure or dealing with an internal conflict, must utilize rationally and carefully its internal resources in order to carry out its ultimate constitutional commitment, which is that of guaranteeing and safeguarding human dignity and the welfare of the Salvadoran family and the whole of society. This legal obligation flows directly from the very nature of ESC rights, and the state must respect and implement them by authentically adopting economic policies, that objectively address the real social needs discernible in our country at this historic moment. The obligation, then, is that of setting in motion adequate and effective policies which, by using resources properly and rationally, can lead to the greatest possible satisfaction of social and economic needs in El Salvador.

As has already been observed, the state should also safeguard these rights because of the interconnection and interdependence they enjoy with certain civil rights and public freedoms. The fact that as basic human rights they are all of a piece makes them essential values that must also be guaranteed . . . democracy demands that the fundamental rights of the person and of social groups be recognized and implemented, and that only through an adequate interpretation of our constitution, and of the provisions of international law which are in force in our country, will we be able to determine exactly the obligations that flow from the various ESC rights formally recognized in El Salvador.

Consequently, fundamental ESC rights, such as the right to protection against hunger, [and rights] to health care, to housing, and to work must be regarded as fundamental rights of Salvadorans since they are legally recognized in our country. Hence from the standpoint of the democratic state, under the rule of law, fundamental ESC rights should be guaranteed to the maximum, whether they are to be applied immediately or gradually. The state's obligation to safeguard these rights is a consequence of the requirements for a decent human life for all human beings and for Salvadorans as a whole.

Furthermore, although our country's constitution does not explicitly acknowledge all the ESC rights that have been incorporated into positive law, such rights are not thereby excluded from being legally applied in El Salvador, since they are included in international treaties which are in force. Ultimately these rights are part of our legislation as stipulated in the constitution itself, and indeed they rank higher than secondary legislation.

Precisely in order to reaffirm those rights which are not incorporated into the constitution, Salvadoran lawmakers should expressly acknowledge that they have the rank of constitutional rights. Similarly, in the realm of international agreements there is a need for legal protective mechanisms in keeping with humankind's present situation and level of development. Specifically, with regard to our region and country, the OAS system for protecting human rights should become concerned in an objective manner about the adoption of true legal instruments for protecting ESC rights in the Americas (since they are fundamental human rights). And the OAS should create suitable mechanisms for safeguarding these fundamental rights.

. . . .

In our country as in any other, we must assert that if there is an effort to lay the legal and moral foundations for democracy—that is, for that system which favors human rights—ESC rights must be formally recognized as fundamental constitutional rights, and their full implementation in practice must be assured by the presence of genuine legal safeguards and through the initiation of effective economic policies. For democracy finds its full justification only by assuring that the fundamental rights of the human being and the whole of society are really in effect. Certain imprecise legal concepts, like the "general welfare" and the "common good," find their meaning and their raison d'être when the rights of the human being and of society are really in effect. . . . Democracy is morally justified and has a legal foundation only when it objectively responds to the interests expressed by the ESC rights and by the CP rights of all without exception. Otherwise, democracy is reduced to a legal and political system for making decisions, but it is utterly illegitimate.

Therefore the system needed in order to assure that fundamental human rights be truly in effect must assure that a new conception of social justice, equality, and fairness be adopted in practice. It should bring about and consolidate an economic order that can respond "essentially to principles of social justice," tending to assure a life worthy of human beings for all without exception (OAS Charter). It should lay the structural foundations for assuring economic and social development, and thus assuring the progress and welfare of the whole society. In this sense the OAS Charter (Art. 32) stresses that "development is the primary responsibility of each country and should constitute an integral and continual process towards the creation of a just economic and social order that will permit and contribute towards the complete fulfillment of the human person."

Finally, it must be borne in mind that in addition to what is required within states, certain external conditions which are indispensable for fully satisfying and truly implementing fundamental economic and social rights are also required. In particular a new international economic order must be set up, one that will make just and equitable international economic relations possible for all states, but in particular for underdeveloped countries. In addition there must be adequate international cooperation in economic matters in order to make it easier for states to consolidate the structural foundations on which the economic, social, and cultural rights of peoples rest.

In conclusion, the ESC rights of Salvadorans are legally protected within our legal framework, but they must be safeguarded in practice; otherwise the state will not be meeting its international legal commitments in this area, nor will it be consistent with its constitutional mandate as laid down in our magna carta, namely that of "assuring that all inhabitants of the republic enjoy freedom, health, culture, economic welfare, and social justice."

Economic, Social, and Cultural Rights in El Salvador

The first part of our study* consists of a legal examination of existing legislation in El Salvador with regard to human rights. It begins with an interpretative study of the constitution and the articles that refer to the various ESC rights, and with a consideration of the scope of the legislation, and how obligatory, how normative, and how binding that legislation is. We then examine the various international charters, statements, agreements, and conventions that the Salvadoran government has signed and ratified, and which are therefore binding in the country and have a higher priority than secondary laws, as is stipulated in the Salvadoran constitution. In fact the principles and rights proclaimed in those international documents have been incorporated into the constitution, at least in their more salient features. In our legal analysis a distinction is drawn among the state's obligations in this area: some rights are to be applied immediately and cannot be postponed nor can their violation be excused. Others are to be applied gradually, although with urgency, and they also cannot be postponed nor can their violation be excused, at least with regard to beginning and gradually moving

---

*Pages 26–67 in Montes, *et al.* (1988b) are omitted here. P.B.

forward, although making them a reality for all citizens is contingent on the resources available to the society and the state and on other serious circumstances.

In the second part of this study* we present the real situation of ESC rights by using official published data and by examining, category by category, each of the most important rights included in the current binding legislation. We treat the last two decades separately in order to observe the effect that the crisis and the war have had on either compliance or violation. In a rather descriptive manner we have also inquired into the possible causes and/or structural and conjunctural conditioning that is in some fashion manifested in these data.

These two analyses—legal and socio-economic—provide us with an almost contradictory contrast between the ideals and obligations, as formulated in the constitution and other legally binding agreements, and the reality, as demonstrated through the data and the indicators. In reading the legislation we cannot but admire the principles underlying the constitution starting with Article One: "El Salvador recognizes the human person as the origin and end of the activity of the state, which is organized for the attainment of justice, juridical security, and the common good" (Art. 1, par. 1). We also admire the norms and obligations expressed in the remainder which deal with the rights under discussion, and we admire the commitments made by the state and society to implement those rights. By contrast, the empirical data, that reflect how much these principles and rights are in force or violated for most of the population, present a society different from the one sought in the constitution and in national and international legislation. Rather it seems—assuming that both refer to the same society—that in El Salvador the situation is permanently unconstitutional. . . .

If the human person is acknowledged to be the origin and end of the state's activity (Art. 1, 1983 Constitution), that human person is not recognized as a person or as human in the situation reflected in the social and economic data published by the official government bodies themselves. If "consequently, it is the obligation of the state to assure that all inhabitants of the republic enjoy freedom, health, culture, economic welfare, and social justice" (Art. 1, par. 2), that obligation has not been implemented for most citizens, nor can we perceive even gradual progress towards fulfilling those obligations.

Life is the primary, basic, and supreme end of the human individual. The data, however, show that, although there is a great deal of life in El Salvador, it soon begins to be frustrated by the high rate of infant mortality and the relatively short life expectancy. Food that is scarce and of low quality, illnesses that are easily preventible and could be cured

---

*See pages 77–113 in Montes, *et al.* (1988b).

with current medical practices, the scarce and unhealthful hygiene where most people live, especially in overcrowded urban shantytowns, the poor housing—all this taken together forces a large part of the population into living conditions that can hardly be considered human or up to the minimum standards acceptable in civilized (even underdeveloped) societies today, or acceptable in terms of the principles and obligations laid down in legal documents. Even worse, this life consequently begins to shrivel up as soon as it begins, and increasingly it becomes premature death for most of the population.

The means for obtaining the resources needed to meet basic needs are property and labor. With regard to property, matters have been worsening, not only as a result of the conquest and colonization, but also since independence, to the point where most people in both the countryside and city do not own their own means of subsistence. The reforms implemented during the present decade have not sufficed to provide most of the population, especially in the rural areas, with land to work or with other resources of their own. Nor does the demand for labor meet the supply, and hence a large proportion of the economically active population fluctuates between underemployment and unemployment. The minimum wage and the income most families receive are insufficient to provide even those goods most necessary for a human life. When people do not have their own means of subsistence or are out of work, or when their pay is not enough to meet their basic needs, they cannot attain all the other fundamental rights such as the rights to housing, food, health care, education, and rest.

It is often claimed that education and training are basic means for increasing production, productivity, and development, as well as institutionalized channels for upward mobility, and that they in turn can improve human resources so as to make it possible to move from being a backward society to being a modern one. Nevertheless, education and training are conditioned by the resources available and by the concrete and real—not simply theoretical and legal—opportunities within society as a whole and for families and individuals. The data supplied in the second part of our original study indicate not only low levels of education, but also the lack of resources for making qualitative leaps and thus entering into the circle of modern and prosperous nations.*

Taken altogether, such data tell us how far our society really is from the ideals and commitments formulated and acquired in the legal realm. Once again it can be said that the concrete and real situation is unconstitutional—one in which human rights are systematically violated in the economic, social, and cultural realms. Moreover, an examination of the data shows that, although in many aspects the situation has been

---

*See also Montes (1980a), Chapter 6, *this volume.*

worsened over time by the civil war and the deep crisis of the country during the present decade, what we are talking about is nonetheless prior to the crisis and is rooted in elements independent of that conflict. That real situation can certainly be understood as the ultimate root of the crisis and the civil war, which broke out when the majority of the people saw that their most elementary problems could not be resolved through peaceful means.

Economic, social, and political forces, left to the free play of the market—supply and demand and competition—have failed to resolve the fundamental problems of society or to create the means and resources necessary to meet the basic needs of the majority. These forces have also been erecting structures that make it impossible to resolve the problems, thus producing a systematic and structural violation of ESC rights for the bulk of Salvadoran society, and consequently a permanent situation in which the constitution is violated. These violations thereby pave the way for and legitimize movements seeking structural changes to make compliance with such rights possible and viable.

Nor has the state been able to remedy the defects generated by the free play of social forces, to correct the failures of the system and its structures, and to put itself at the service of the majority and thus fulfill its binding legal mandate. An examination of budgets and the way funds are dispensed to different categories—and here we are not making any political judgment or value judgment—shows that the available resources have not been apportioned to serve ESC rights. Nor are they directed towards those areas where the system and its structures do not offer the possibility of meeting basic needs and rights. [Nor are these resources used] to soften harmful effects, remedy defects, and correct the [ineffective] tendencies and consequences of the system, and thus bring about basic equity in order to serve the good of the "human person as the origin and end of the state's activity."

The violation of CP rights, which was exacerbated at the end of the last decade, led to international condemnation and to the October 15, 1979 coup. In subsequent years such violation has become so widespread and serious that it has focussed attention on El Salvador, and has led the United Nations and other national and international institutions to monitor the country on a continual basis. This tragic and dramatic perspective on things may conceal something that is even more serious, and which is the cause and source of that violation of human rights and of the political crisis and civil war the country suffers. Although the civil war leads to death and destruction, even more deaths are due to poverty, unemployment, illness, the lack of housing and minimal resources, and the precarious conditions which cannot be called "human" in which most of the human Salvador population lives. Hence this can be regarded not only as a permanently unconstitutional situation, but also as a systematic and structural violation of the ESC rights of the vast majority. Any solution to the present crisis and war, therefore, will entail changing those structures and those conditions systematically not only in order to meet the commitment that is binding on the state and on society, but also to restore people's human dignity and compliance with their rights, and in order to deal with the structural causes that gave rise to the present conflict. The war might end militarily, but peace will not be attained unless these structural problems that are at the root of injustice are resolved.

SECTION III

The University and Social Justice

Ignacio Ellacuría

8. The Challenge of The Poor Majority*

TRANSLATION BY PHILLIP BERRYMAN

Alfonso Comín obviously sought to carry out his theoretical and practical work from within the [ranks of the] poor and oppressed—and not simply for the poor and oppressed—while striving for universality and solidarity. That is also the perspective of our university, at least in intention, and for twenty-five years it has been working out of, and within, the light that the oppressed majority of the world cast on the world. Some are blinded while others are enlightened.

When we look at matters from the vantage point of the poor majority in their universality and solidarity, we can discern that our world as a whole must move in a new direction. Both the negation of prophecy and the affirmation of utopia point towards a process of revolutionary change which will entail reversing the main thrust of world civilization.

The two major processes are labor and capital, each understood in its full scope, dialectically interwoven in the structure and advance of history. Until now and with ever greater determining power, capital has prevailed over labor in countries of both private capitalism and state capitalism. It is the drive of capital that really dictates the law for almost all processes, with greater weight in some than in others. For the most part, it has not been human beings, classes or social groups, nations or groups of nations who have decided to put themselves at the service of the production and accumulation of capital. Rather it has been capital, especially internationally but also within nations, that puts at its own service human beings, social classes, and nations—not to mention the entire workings of the economy, the most decisive part of the social body. Human work, meaning almost everything human beings do consciously and purposefully to transform reality, is especially subjected to capital's driving forces.

Before condemning (and not on the basis of *a priori* ethical criteria or reasons) this historic—and not merely economic—order based on

---

*Ellacuría (1989a); see the Bibliography in the back of this book.

This is the text (with introductory remarks omitted) of a lecture given on November 6, 1989 by Ellacuría in Barcelona as he accepted, on behalf of the UCA, an international award named after the Spanish theologian, Alfonso Comín. THE EDITORS

171

capital, we must credit it with certain achievements that are important in human history, especially in the realms of science and technology but also in that of politics. Scientific research has advanced and has made numerous contributions which in themselves are quite positive and absolutely indispensable for resolving the huge problems that the human biological species and life in society are inevitably generating. Important advances in the ethical and political domain have also been made and institutionally recognized. These advances can be summed up as the theoretically universal acceptance of human rights. Of course there are other advances in the ideological and cultural realm, although in this area it is very debatable whether the achievements made in a world of vast capital accumulation are superior to those gained at other moments in history. It is not only concern for objectivity that should lead us to recognize these values but pragmatic need so that the future we desire not turn into primitive escapism.

"Beginning anew" cannot be confused with "beginning from scratch." Even less, however, can it be confused with "continuing or pushing ahead with the same thing," for the present accomplishments of this capitalist civilization and those accomplishments of the foreseeable future, evaluated in universal terms, continue to contribute a) not only to widening the gap between rich and poor, whether in regions, countries, or human groups, and thus the creation of more and more poor (while the numbers of the rich increase arithmetically the poor increase geometrically); b) not only to making the processes of exploitation and oppression more harsh, albeit in more sophisticated forms; c) not only to the gradual ecological breakdown of the whole planet; d) but also to the conspicuous dehumanization of those who, pressured by the nervous and harassed productivism of having or amassing wealth, power, honor, and the ever changing gamut of consumer goods, opt to give up the difficult task of gradually achieving their own being.

Let no one be too quick to say that poverty is worse, and that you are either on the top or on the bottom, and that if you have nothing you are nothing. The starting point for the critique of the capitalist civilization is not moralizing idealism but a compelling materialism. The poverty that is worse is that which comes from being dialectically opposed to wealth. Such poverty is produced by a civilization of capital, not by a civilization of work.

Work in this sense is not just any work, however. The work which capital needs in order to thrive is not that work which fills leisure but rather that which is the negation of leisure. I do not thereby intend to frame the question in an aristocratic Hellenizing fashion. Work and leisure should not be opposed. Whether or not work produces value and ends up being embodied in commodities and capital, it is primarily a personal and social need of human beings for their personal development and psychological balance as well as for the production of those resources and conditions that enable all human beings and the whole human being to live a life freed of needs and free to realize their particular life-projects. Therefore the kind of work in question is not controlled exclusively nor predominantly either directly or indirectly by the drive of capital and accumulation, but by the real drives towards perfection in persons and the humanizing and enhancement of the living environment of which they form part and which they must respect.

Many men and women of both yesterday and today agree with this general proposal to replace a civilization of capital with a civilization of work. Such a civilization would not mean doing away with capital and its driving forces but rather with ending its primacy in both capitalist and socialist countries and letting labor have the primacy. Perhaps this was one of the fundamental ideas of Alfonso Comín, deriving from both his Christian perspective—his unblemished Christian faith—and from his Marxist perspective. Christian faith is irreconcilable with a capitalist civilization. The theological core of *Laborem Exercens* (John Paul II, 1981) can be centered around that statement—and I believe it is also irreconcilable with the postulates of Marxism other than the rejection of the private accumulation of capital. Because he saw matters in this fashion, Comín and his thought were a preview and a challenge to both theory and practice.

Much remains to be done. Only in a utopian and hope-filled spirit can one believe and have enough energy to join with all the poor and oppressed of the world in order to overturn history, to subvert it and send it in another direction. But this huge task—what on another occasion I have called "co-pro-historic analysis," that is, the study of the dregs of our civilization—seems to indicate that this civilization is gravely ill and that in order to prevent it from ending in destruction, we must try to change it from within. Helping to stimulate and nourish a collective consciousness of the need for substantial change is in itself a first great step.

There remains a further fundamental step to take—that of creating economic, political, and cultural models that may enable a civilization of work to replace a civilization of capital. All kinds of intellectuals, that is, those who are theoretical critics of reality, have here a challenging task that cannot be postponed. Criticism and tearing apart are not enough; a constructive criticism that offers a real alternative is also necessary. A good deal of such constructive criticism is observable in socialist states which are undergoing a deep crisis of reconversion. Only a pathetic historical shortsightedness would enable one to interpret that crisis as simply a shift from state capitalism with its own political, social, and ideological structures to a private and class-structured capitalism. A good deal is also observable in some revolutionary movements in Latin America, including the Sandinistas in Nicaragua and the FMLN in El Salvador. But little constructive criticism can be observed in strictly capitalist countries, and what can be observed is marginal. Those countries think that they have been vindicated by *perestroika* in some socialist countries and the exodus of people from others. They believe it is the other side that has to change and imitate them. They do not want to match the democratization of socialism—which for many reasons is insufficient—with a correlative socialization of the so-called liberal democracies. These countries are particularly unwilling to undertake a socialization that would not stop at their own national or regional borders, but would extend to the whole of humankind, which they want to "democratize" simply in order to bring it more fully into a civilization of capital.

Not only must we unmask the ideological trap in this tidal wave of ideology. We must also produce models which in a fruitful interchange between theory and practice may really generate ideals intended to stimulate—not escape from the task of building history.

Our university, on which those in charge of the Comín foundation have so generously decided to bestow this award, is trying to do something along these lines. I am convinced that is why you are granting it this recognition. The university is living in the midst of a situation where history itself is going through a crisis, or at least where the crisis of present universal history is evident in all its gravity. In this situation the civilization of capital and empire has been manifesting some of its gravest evils. In response, a very serious movement of protest and alternative has arisen and has not been defeated after ten years of harsh confrontation. The United States has engaged in that confrontation by spending over three billion dollars and sending hundreds of advisors to El Salvador. In such a context the university has sought to respond to this reality which directly affects the poor majority in El Salvador and on a more universal level raises issues whose implications are worldwide. . . . .

Our primary aim as a university is to contribute to this historic struggle. We believe we ought to play an active role in this struggle, and therefore we want to do so. We are striving to do so as a university, but that does not mean we seek to do so primarily by training professionals. That is important, albeit ambiguous, because the country needs rapid economic development. Rather, we also intend to make our contribution by creating a body of thought, models, and proposals which, by starting from a negotiation capable of getting beyond the surrounding reality can then attempt to bring this active negotiation into society's immediate awareness. That in turn will make it possible to move towards both conjunctural and structural solutions, in all realms of the national reality—political and religious, economic and technological, artistic and cultural. That task requires as much academic excellence as possible, for otherwise we would have little to contribute as intellectuals to such complex problems. It also demands a great deal of honesty, which not only relates to our calling to objectivity, but demands that we strive for the greatest independence and freedom. Finally it requires a great deal of courage in a country where the weapons of death are fired too often and in a very threatening proximity.

All that would not be enough unless we were clear on where we had to stand as university persons in order to find historic truth. It is often said that the university should be impartial. We do not agree. The university should strive to be free and objective, but objectivity and freedom may demand taking sides. We are freely on the side of the popular majority because they are unjustly oppressed and because the truth of the situation lies within them both negatively and positively. Our university as a university has an acknowledged preferential option for the poor, and it learns from them in their reality and in their many expressions which both draw matters together and point the way ahead. We take this stand with them in order to be able to find the truth of what is happening and the truth that all of us must be seeking and building together.

There are good theoretical reasons to think that such an effort is well grounded epistemologically, but in addition we think there is no alternative in Latin America, in the Third World, and elsewhere, for universities and intellectuals who claim to be of Christian inspiration. Our university is of Christian inspiration when it places itself in this preferential option for the poor, who in quantitative terms are the greatest humanistic challenge facing humankind.

From within this option, in theological terms we favor placing faith in tension with justice. It is an indispensable, although perhaps not sufficient, condition of faith, that it be confronted with justice; the justice being sought is profoundly enlightened in turn by faith lived in the preferential option for the poor. We do not regard faith and justice as two separate realities brought together by an effort of our will, but as two interrelated realities that form or should form a single structural totality, as liberation theology and other related theological movements have said repeatedly. We believe that a good deal of the preaching and the embodiment of the faith have had infelicitous effects when they have both ignored justice and the oppressed, impoverished popular masses. That has also been true of a good deal of the preaching and of the embodiment of justice when they have been more focussed on taking power than on benefitting the popular majorities . . . .

This is how our university works in a revolutionary fashion for the cause of liberation in El Salvador. In a university manner we want to accompany a process led primarily by the masses, although perhaps in a partial and imperfect way, and we wish to do so out of a Christian inspiration which regards a preferential option for the historic cause of the poor as obligatory.

In El Salvador the right and even the extreme right generally now recognize that the country's main problem is not simply poverty, but the extreme poverty that affects more than sixty percent of the population. Poverty also exists just a few kilometers from the center of international capitalism. That poverty is one of the best proofs of what the fruits are that are inherent in capitalist civilization—no matter how

much capitalism would like to see itself as a western Christian civilization and as a model of democratic life. The truth is quite the opposite:
capitalism is not Christian because it lives quite contentedly with, and is
the cause of, many forms of poverty and exploitation of others. Capitalism is not democratic because it respects neither the majority will of humankind nor the sovereignty of other nations, nor the overwhelming
votes in the United Nations, nor the World Court rulings.

As you know, currently in Central America we are facing a critical
moment in our history, especially in El Salvador and Nicaragua. In the
midst of great difficulties, Nicaragua is trying to find peace once and for
all, and along with peace a democratic process that has no reason to
copy democratic processes that take place in other countries. In any case
they are seeking, and we should help them. I know that the Alfonso
Comín Foundation has already given its support to the Nicaraguan process, but at this moment in El Salvador we are also facing a very important moment—I want to remind you of the cruel murder of some labor
union comrades with a car bomb a few days ago, done with the purpose
of disrupting the negotiation process between the FMLN and the government. I believe that throughout our region we are moving into a new
phase, one in which the maximalist revolutionary aims have diminished
somewhat, and the maximalist counter-revolutionary aims have also diminished. These two overall projects are coming closer to each other,
and they are going to face one another, perhaps no longer in a violent
way with weapons, but in tough, difficult negotiations in which the
claims of the poor majority will really be negotiated vis-à-vis the de-
fenders of the elite minorities. As you know, the FMLN has broken the
third round of negotiations, in justified protest over the murder of the
Salvadoran union members. For we work not only with theoretical proposals, but in this task we also work face to face with both sides, trying
to inject rationality on behalf of the poor majority who are treated unjustly. Our present situation is absolutely exceptional, and I ask you
who are here as individuals and perhaps as government officials to turn
your gaze towards Nicaragua and El Salvador and help us.

Ignacio Ellacuria

9. Is A Different Kind of University Possible?*

TRANSLATION BY PHILLIP BERRYMAN

The University of Central America (UCA) was established on September 15, 1965 in order to enhance university endeavors in El Salvador through what might be called a Christian inspiration and energy. For a variety of reasons the typical patterns in universities calling themselves Catholic were not useful as guidelines for this task, nor were there any other models available that were sufficiently detailed and operational. The "no" was clearer than the "yes": no to other ways of being a university, no to other attempts to heal the malaise of the Latin American university—attempts which were proving ineffective. Little by little this path of the "no" understood as a creative process was destined to bring about a new awareness and a new way of understanding the task of the university.

First came facts, admittedly facts that were stammering and ambiguous. Out of facts themselves and out of the new liberating consciousness that began to appear in Latin America during the sixties, a different kind of university began to emerge, or at least the intention of establishing a different kind of university. That intention was officially formulated in a speech delivered on the occasion of the contract signing with the Inter-American Development Bank (Discurso del BID, 1971). It was afterwards expanded in the university's organizational manual (UCA, 1972). It was also put into practice in a series of statements by the university's faculty and student organizations, and in a wide variety of research projects.

Now after ten years and with both the achievements and obstacles before us, a minimum sense of critical responsibility demands that we look back at the distance covered in order to see whether in view of the facts—not intentions—we can speak of a different kind of university. Have we accomplished something along this road? Do the real difficulties encountered during these ten years prove that in our situation a different kind of university, one that by its very structure and proper role

---

*Ellacuría (1975d); see the Bibliography in the back of this book.

as a university is actually committed to opposing an unjust society and building a new one, is in fact impossible?

In this essay I am going to respond to these questions under three headings: 1) the attempt to create a different university; 2) an examination of our university with that aim in view; 3) the Christian meaning of the university

. . . .

Attempting a Different Kind of University

The criterion for measuring the ultimate significance of a university and what it is in its total reality is its impact on the historic reality within which it exists and which it serves. Hence it should be measured by a political criterion. At first glance this statement might seem to lead towards a politicization that would disfigure genuine university endeavor insofar as it is a theoretical effort to know and then on the basis of this knowing, to lay open the possibilities for doing. That need not be the case, however, and to that end we must look into the university's political dimension very explicitly, for the university unquestionably has such a dimension, and it is very important for giving it direction. What will make such a university different then will not be that it does not carry out its political mission, but that it does so in another way. That is the issue. If we do not face it, besides leading to continual internal contradictions that create tension and ultimately make university work impossible, the university itself is left without a compass, and even worse, it is at the mercy of pressures over which it has no control.

There is no need to insist too much that the university has a political dimension, that is, that the university is a factor in the political situation. We are speaking primarily about the university here and now, in El Salvador in 1975, where there are only two universities. They are in charge of all the higher education in the country. Under present conditions the quantity and quality of resources of all kinds at its disposal make the university an important component of the social structure. It is no exaggeration to say that the university wields the greatest ideological power in the nation, although it finds it extremely difficult to unleash that power and translate it into social awareness. To a great extent the university responds in each case to the greatest social pressure exerted on it and/or pressure from the state, and consequently it is shaped politically by these pressures, while at the same time and with a variety of direct and indirect means it can exert pressure on the power of society and the state. In itself it is a power to be reckoned with, especially if it could be given the cohesion it should have. For example, the UCA has three thousand students, two hundred and fifty professors, and an annual budget of about three million colones [$1,200,000], and it is unquestionably a very important social force in El Salvador, at least in theory. The country's universities are also the major source of professional people who, consequently, are the major contributors to maintenance of the social system. They can produce the instruments for national policies in economics, education, technology, health care, and so forth, as well as the people who are to handle those instruments. Finally, the fact that they are a ripe field for the activity of political movements indicates indirectly that the structure and thrust of the university can be politicized.

The political potential of the university is obvious at a glance. Nevertheless, what the university actually is can only be seen through its impact on the social and political situation. Any other approach is abstract in the pejorative sense: it would deny the concrete reality of the university and would amount to neglecting one of its most serious possibilities as an institution meant to serve the public.

However, there are two inadequate and deceptive ways of carrying out this political mission. One of them is to help strengthen the prevailing system by responding positively to its demands or at least by not hindering it, by being devoted to knowledge and technical matters in an ostensibly neutral manner. The other way is to challenge the system head on, especially that part of it that is the state, in the manner of an opposition political party or the popular organizations, whose political activity is determined by their primary objective which is to take over state power. Because of its own critical character, and because of its fundamental need to be rational and ethical, the university cannot be reduced to taking the side of any given political or social system indiscriminately. Nor can the university abandon its proper university approach to dealing with political reality, ultimately because of that same propensity for the rational and the ethical.

It is quite clear that Latin American universities have tended to fall into one or other of these false forms of politicization. In some instances, as a reaction to overpoliticization or worse and with a clear intention of favoring those already favored, universities have striven to anesthetize students, ostensibly in order to attain the greatest degree of impartial scientific rigor, as though social reality did not also need a high degree of scientific rigor. In other instances, in an effort to respond to the most urgent and immediate ethical demands, people have undertaken political action without the proper tools or sufficient power, obviously thus shortchanging their scientific and technical training. Can there not be a different way of fulfilling the university's inescapable political mission? This is the question that leads us to raise the issue of a different kind of university, one that as university and in a university manner responds to its mission in history, one that demonstrates its political effectiveness in a university manner by imparting shape to a new society and to a new form of state power.

What might be the university characteristics of this new way for accomplishing the university's political mission? That political mission has already been defined in the documents cited above. What I would like to do now is to be more specific and precise about what constitutes the university's way of playing a role in liberation in order to determine whether the university can in fact play that role and to determine the limits proper to such activity by the university. From the outset we cannot admit that the only conceivable way for the university to engage in political activity for the liberating transformation of society would be by ceasing to be a university in order to become a revolutionary political organization. It is certainly risky to claim that one has been unable to do what one has not done because it has not yet been possible or because problems of the moment have prevented it. It may be that what looks like something conjunctural is actually structural, in which case the different impeding conjunctures would only be so many crises masking the same structural obstacle. Before making such an admission, however, we must define clearly the specifically university features involved in the political mission that a different university is obliged to carry out.

Defining these features is helpful in two ways. First it helps the university pursue its own specific identity so that neither pressures nor siren songs can pull it off course. Second, it provides a criterion for judging whether from its own being, that is, without departing from what it is and without disfiguring its own reality, the university can make an effective and irreplaceable contribution to the process of national transformation, even when the dominant social and political structures are opposed to such a change.

In seeking [to identify] the specifically university features of the university's political mission, we are going to inquire into a) the horizon of university activity; b) the specific field of this activity; c) its way of acting; d) its basic disposition; and e) its immediate object.

THE POOR MAJORITY AS THE HORIZON OF UNIVERSITY ACTIVITY

In inquiring about the *horizon* of university activity, we are asking about the ultimate standpoint and deepest purpose of this activity. We could answer that it is the national reality or, in more human terms, the Salvadoran people. That answer has the unquestionable advantage of being structural and of going beyond individualistic considerations, but it does not take into account the national reality and the Salvadoran people as presently structured. The national reality and the Salvadoran people are manifest not only in terms of established injustice, institutional violence, and international dependence, but also as a divided society in which the two sides have clashing interests; the dominant minority cannot identify its interests with those of the oppressed majority, for as they confront each other, they are indeed at odds and actively so. That does not necessarily mean that common interests cannot be found between the two sides "materially" or "conjuncturally," but it does denote a fundamental separation, one that makes it necessary to take sides.

A university of Christian inspiration cannot doubt whose side it must take. If at a particular moment it is not possible to overcome the differences by doing away with them, such a university must take the side of those sectors who are not only a majority—a majority so overwhelming that by its very magnitude it can be regarded as the authentic representative of the interests of the whole—but also an unjustly dehumanized majority. In this sense it is not the ruling classes but the scientifically determined objective interests of the oppressed majority that must be the criterion guiding the university.

The idea here is to make the university take sides, or rather, to opt for one of the inescapable ways of taking sides. Any decision and any action supports a stand "for" one side or the other. This does not occur in an entirely pure manner, since the same action may serve clashing interests, but the horizon ought to be clear, as should the fundamental option, in order that the university be able to play a meaningful role in ongoing history. The matter cannot be viewed statically or mechanically, but must be seen dynamically and historically. That is, the action must suit the present moment, but only insofar as this present moment is preparing one kind of future or another. The future depends on the present, but the present is not merely preparation for the future: it has its own rights and its own needs. That is why interests may coincide at a particular moment, and yet the processes are not thereby identified with one another. When lines cross they are identified at one point, even though they are going in different directions.

It follows that the university cannot take as the fundamental criterion and ultimate horizon for its activity the subjective interests of students and professors, unless these subjective interests coincide with the objective interests of the oppressed majority. The argument that the students pay money to the university does not mean that they have an absolute right over the direction taken by university endeavors insofar as this direction entails an ultimate horizon, for the simple reason that they do not even pay the full cost of their education, let alone the whole cost of university activity. Even if they did pay the full cost, they would still not have an absolute right—not having an absolute right does not mean that they do not have relative rights—since they would not have this ability to pay if it were not as a result of a particular structure of society, and that fact by itself would limit and relativize such a right. A similar argument can be made with regard to the subjective interests of professors and even more justifiably, since they are paid for their work and are not always identified with the broader interests of the university.

A completely different issue is how to discover and pursue the objective interests of the great majority from a university standpoint. Here the contribution of professors and students ought to be decisive, particularly if they can gradually identify their own private interests with those of the unjustly dehumanized majority.

If this horizon of the poor majority is taken seriously, if it is really adopted as an ongoing criterion for how the university is organized internally on all levels and in its activity towards the outside, the university would have an essential component it needs for continuing to discover the specific character of its political mission. This horizon is by no means exclusive to the university: it should be the criterion of any institution which in an ethical way wishes to move in the right direction in our ongoing history at this particular moment. In the university, however, that criterion will resonate in a particular way and the university will serve it in accordance with its own distinctive nature, whose special features can be noted in the characteristics we are now going to discuss.

CULTIVATING THE NATIONAL REALITY AS THE SPHERE OF UNIVERSITY ACTIVITY

The proper *field or sphere* of university activity and its own set of instruments is culture. The term today is not a very felicitous one, since culture tends to be understood as the birthright possession of the cultured classes, that is, of the oppressor classes and of the individuals who are at their service and who are supported and sustained by those classes. Stripped of its class connotations and of its purely contemplative connotations, however, it can and should be retained. The reason to retain culture [in the university] is precisely in order to emphasize the university's identity and prevent it from veering off course in its political task. In a proper division of labor the specific nature of the university should be maintained; otherwise we would regress to an absurdly ahistorical primitivism, which would deprive those who have no voice of one of their basic supports.

Of course, culture must be understood differently in this case. That is not difficult to do. When we speak of culture here we conceive of it in the sense it has in expressions like agri-culture, that is, as a cultivating of reality, as an activity of cultivating and transforming reality. What the culture of the university should seek to do is to make its members rational cultivators of reality. Culture has an essentially praxic meaning, insofar as it derives from the need to act and should lead to an activity that transforms both the subject and his or her natural and historic environment.

The material elements of culture include a rigorous *knowledge* of nature and society—neither nature alone nor society alone but both as necessarily interwoven—and it includes a mastery of the *techniques* for transforming nature, human beings, and society. Such knowing how to do and so doing with wisdom are not atemporal, but they should take their orientation from the horizon proposed above. This does not mean any lessening of knowledge or technique, at least not necessarily, but it means simply a principle of selection, which in each instance should be derived from the national reality as it unfolds concretely in history. The study of that national reality is one of the fundamental dimensions of culture, that is of national culture.

Obviously culture requires a rigorous and continual analysis of the national reality, extending from the past which partly constitutes us to the projected future towards which we must move. If culture is cultivation, the first thing to be known is the reality that must be cultivated in order to know how it must be cultivated. Moreover, the national reality in its present historic fullness is indeed the locus in the fullest sense, and it gives ultimate meaning to everything that is done and everything that happens. Our country's collective consciousness can be scientific only if it is based on this analysis of the national reality. How, therefore, can the awareness of its own reality not be part of the culture of the country? Since culture is here understood as operative, however, what must gradually be sought is a collective consciousness that has been properly prepared and made operational in a fitting way. This position is not one of idealism vis-à-vis ongoing history because the pursuit of a clear consciousness does not mean that consciousness, and especially group consciousness, can be achieved independently of social structures and of everyday collective activity. The point is that doing by itself does not always generate the appropriate consciousness and that there will be no adequate culture unless the nation's consciousness has been made ready.

It is the historic reality of the nation—the dynamic reality of a nation being made and to whose making many factors contribute—that is the bearer of national culture. Culture therefore embraces not only systematic knowledge of the national reality, and not only the anticipation of its future step-by-step—in this sense a five-year development plan, for example, fully belongs to what we here understand as culture—but culture is also tracing the routes and making ready the means for the journey.

In this pursuit of national culture the university is clearly not the only generator: rather it is the critical and technical processing plant. However, the university should certainly strive to amplify the deep feeling of the people, the meaning of their needs, interests, feelings, yearnings, and values. Thus national culture does not mean national folklore, although folklore can express some important aspects of the people's being. An accent on the aesthetic side of national culture may be narcissistic and tranquilizing, when what is required is that it become effective for building a new human being on a new earth. Culture should be watchfulness on the alert, tension towards the future, transformation.

In its active sense, culture should strive to establish new values and towards that end it must unmask present values. It should often be easy to uncover instruments of domination in those values. Certainly few things are as necessary as a cultural revolution in these countries which from pre-Colombian times have not been allowed to be what they are. Such a cultural revolution would entail thoroughly examining the current system of values that has been internalized, destroying it if necessary, and developing new values that really respond to the new possibilities of Salvadorans at this particular moment of history and in this specific geographical context.

Culture becomes ideological struggle from this vantage point. That may look like a borrowed term but it is not, for culture has been a matter of combat with other dominant cultures from time immemorial. Culture as knowledge, while it has often served as a tool of domination at the service of whoever pays best, has also been, and is inherently, a critique of what is, as well as a jolt to arouse people from tranquil slumber. Creative culture entails breaking—although the first barrier it often encounters is the previous culture that has been fossilized.

It is in this manner that the university can become the critical and creative consciousness of the national reality (Discurso del BID, 1971; UCA, 1972, p. 8). The notion of "consciousness"* does not mean a movement that is purely ethical, subjective, and volitional; it explicitly denotes 'con-science': there is no university conscience unless there is university science and university method and style, which will be historical and changing, but which have their own specific structure. Finally, both the critique and the operational quality demanded of this science, which deals with things from as situated and in order to transform them, must be drawn from this creative science and consciousness, just as they should themselves be nourished dialectically on the truth that comes from involvement in both natural and social reality" (Ellacuría, 1972e). Culture as critical and operational consciousness is what the university should be required to provide. Knowing how things are and knowing how they ought to be; knowing what is being done and what should be done in the unity of con-sciousness, which is ultimately the operative and historical unity of a people seeking itself with help from all.

We thus come to the crucial issue of the "who" of this consciousness and of this culture. Culture as here understood is a "culture-of!" That is, it belongs to a particular people in history linked in its march through history with other peoples and it is what this people cultivates. If that is the case, the endeavor of the university is obviously not easy, for it risks being an endeavor that is neither of the people nor for the people. That is so, not primarily because the ordinary people do not make up the university population, nor because the university fails to come down to levels that the vast majority can understand in their own terms, but because of the difficulty inherent in promoting a culture of the people without getting away—through the use of the requisite theoretical tools—from the very reality that one is seeking to cultivate and raise to awareness. The difficulty of the endeavor, however, should not prevent us from acknowledging that culture and the people's culture are the

---

Conciencia in Spanish denotes both "conscience" (moral) and "consciousness" (awareness) which tend to be conflated. *Ciencia* has a somewhat wider sense than the English word "science," encompassing scholarship and systematic knowledge. P.B.

field and specific set of instruments for university work. Consciousness and culture are not absolute, detached, and on their own. They are always someone's consciousness and culture and in each case we should be very clear who this someone is.

Furthermore, this culture should be fostered at its very roots and within all fields. The history of a people cannot be left exclusively in the hands of those who cultivate the people politically, those who seek power for the people, let alone those of another political stripe who also cultivate the people. Culture is much more; culture is that total condition in which people live, not that for which they die. It should be a culture that breaks with every bond of domination, a culture advancing towards an ever greater liberation, but also a culture truly lived at each step along the way. The final goal affects the paths taken, but does not do away with their autonomy, and naturally does not eliminate the steps taken each day. If the university does something important in this area of cultures it will have made a very serious contribution to the life of the people.

THE EFFECTIVE WORD AS THE METHOD OF UNIVERSITY ACTIVITY

The *way* of acting and the fundamental *method* of university activity might be described as the efficacious word. That might look like very little, and it might seem that our peoples need not words but actions, and that words can do little in a world determined by well established powers and structures firmly in place, and about which science and consciousness and their transmission through the word have little to say. The word and culture made word, might be acknowledged to have some impact on the awareness of individuals, but it is difficult to see how they have an impact on the structural movement of history. Everything depends on what is meant by effective word and how we assess the real possibilities for university activity.

"Word" is here understood as the communication, reception, and comprehension of culture as it is re-elaborated in the university, in the sense described in the previous section. Thus culture and word are inseparable; the culture of the university cannot remain cloistered there. From the outset it is cultivation and activity, or at least the source of activity. Who or what can assure that this word be effective, and that it can do what it says?

To begin with, the word must be powerful. This power will derive support primarily from its degree of rationality, and when appropriate, of scientific validity. Increasingly, knowledge is power, especially if such knowledge is effective by its very nature; it will be effective when it proposes the best and most effective means towards particular ends, and when it proposes the best solutions for pressing problems.

This knowledge communicated and received reveals its effectiveness in various domains. In technical matters, it can be shown to be unquestionably superior for accomplishing some practical tasks. When it comes to analyzing a situation, then making that judgment the situation demands and determining the means for changing it, it is more difficult to accept such knowledge because interests and ideologies may be interfering. In making an ethical assessment both of overall directions and of particular public actions, a university respected for its theoretical objectivity and for its impartiality towards the interests of the ruling classes and of government authorities can have a major impact on important events.

Speaking more generally, if a culture in the sense described in the previous section is created and this culture is communicated to the nation and to national consciousness, its impact will be unquestionable. Things may move slowly because history has its own pace, which is not the same pace as that of individual lives, but it will make history. Moreover, what does not become history, and more specifically, historic structure, is in danger of being for others merely an evanescent blossom even if it is very important for oneself.

The word made history is the particular way that the university word becomes effective. It entails communication with what, somewhat loosely but with some truth, can be called group consciousness, independently of however such a consciousness might work. It also entails that the word take flesh in historic structures which generate new actions, new attitudes, and new achievements. If something like a collective consciousness is achieved and if that consciousness is gradually embodied in institutions, effectiveness is assured. What I am talking about is not any idealism about history that would prize the autonomy of consciousness above all else. The university must realize that it is just one component in the social structure, and that its role is not so much to implement things technically or politically as to propose principles for such implementation, and understanding by those principles, and the dynamic instruments for accomplishing things—and not simply to propose theoretical formulations.

AGGRESSIVENESS AS THE DISPOSITION OF UNIVERSITY ACTIVITY

The fundamental *disposition* for university activity whose horizon is the real situation of the oppressed majority, cannot be one of conformity or conciliation. The university must have an aggressive disposition. In our situation, aggressiveness is an important feature of university activity. In our situation the university is one of the few institutions that can really be aggressive—and it should be.

Reason is inherently aggressive when faced with prevailing irrationality. Confronting historic irrationality, that is, a structuring of historic reality in a flagrantly irrational way, the university as critical cultivator of reason cannot but feel and be aggressive. From this standpoint, its aggressiveness is a matter of condemning the irrationality and making an effort to overcome this unreality of the irrational. It is not as though the irrational did not exist, or that everything real were rational; the point is that its existence is so false that only a new realization can end its falseness. It is not simply that reason is absent, for that would not arouse a positive aggression; the problem is a positive irrationality, and an irrationality that is shaping society and history, and thereby people's personal behavior.

If besides being irrational, this situation is one of positive injustice, aggressiveness is even more necessary. That is the case in our situation. Very peaceable and highly respected people have repeatedly spoken out about institutional violence and institutionalized injustice. The tiny redoubt of idealism that the university may represent due to the youthful idealism of its student body and the relative isolation of its professors from the directly dominant structures, makes it more possible for the university to be aggressive institutionally as well as personally towards the prevailing injustice. If in addition, it is agreed that the horizon of the university is that of the oppressed majority, and that horizon is not restricted to being a merely theoretical framework but is rather something experienced, an aggressive stance is inevitable.

This aggressive disposition, as we call it, which can be expressed in terms of struggle, is not an invitation to irresponsibility nor to the use of non-university means. We are not defining the means of action but the attitude to be manifest in university activity. The university should be aggressive with regard to culture and by means of the efficacious word. University protest does not require shouting or violent actions to make its protest. But it is quite the opposite of a passive and contemplative attitude; it is active and nourishes hope; it wants to struggle for a better future, knowing beforehand that this future will not come as a gift. It knows that university protest is going to engage it in ongoing conflict with those who defend other viewpoints, and especially other interests, and that it cannot retreat when faced with pressures and obstacles. It is in this context of rebellion against injustice and irrationality and of resistance to those who prevent the university from carrying out its mission that the need for an aggressive disposition must be viewed. We do not live in a society that is disinterested and in equilibrium, but in one that is torn and in conflict, one in which solidarity can be conceived as possible only through a dynamic process that overcomes its polarizations. That can be achieved only by advancing in such a way that objectivity is not at odds with aggressive assertiveness.

STRUCTURAL TRANSFORMATION AS THE OBJECTIVE OF UNIVERSITY ACTIVITY

The *objective* around which the horizon and aim of university activity are focussed is the structural transformation of society. That is, the university's activity is not aimed primarily at changing persons but at

changing structures. In principle, changing persons and changing structures are not two mutually exclusive missions, but putting the accent on
one of them significantly affects the direction of university work. The
proposal here is to put the accent decidedly on the problem of structures.

The reason is obvious, no matter how much it has been taken for
granted that the university should be aimed primarily at persons and at
educating persons, namely professionals exercising their profession. If
in fact what the university is pursuing is ultimately the transformation
of the national reality, and if that national reality is formally of a structural nature, anyone who is not struggling to work on those structures
will not find that reality. This is true from a general standpoint, if you
will, independently of any particular experience, although it is
grounded in any and every possible experience. Reality in general is
structural, and social reality is particularly structural. This is also the
case, however, for reasons that are demonstrably empirical. There is no
other way to reach a dimension like that of the national reality except by
setting out in pursuit of its structures; the national reality cannot be attained through its parts or through the individuals who make it up, and
even if it were thus attainable, it would not be operational.

This point is extremely important for giving direction to each and
every university activity, and especially for unifying university endeavors, which is also a matter of structure. The most striking consequence is
that it negates the notion that the main objective of the university is to
train professional people. In our country there are clear ethical reasons
for such a negation; we cannot invest a notable portion of scarce national resources to favor even more the tiny number whom the social
system already favors. The only justification for focussing the university
on training professionals as the primary thrust of its activity would be
with the understanding that only with well trained professionals can the
structural transformation of the nation be brought about—but we would
thereby be reasserting that structural transformation is primary. Since,
however, in the present system we cannot expect that a university oriented primarily towards professional training would make a serious
contribution to deep and rapid structural transformation, not even this
derivative justification can be considered valid at present (see Ellacuría,
1972d). This does not mean that training professional people is not one
of the structural requirements of that university that can and must be directed towards transforming the country structurally.

Another consequence is that the university's research and social
outreach, that is, the projection of the university towards society, ought
to be guided by this focus on the structural, and on the structural in process of transformation. Obviously transformation here is not limited to
transforming consciousness, although collective consciousness also has
something structural about it, but that it should include transforming all

kinds of structures, culminating in the transformation of socio-economic and political structures.

This accent on the structural may jeopardize the personal; however, the salvation of the personal cannot be realistically conceived by leaving aside the structural. Hence the question is: what way of structuring society permits the full and free development of the human person and what kind of personal activity should those persons undertake who are involved in transforming structures? The major instruments with which the university works are collective in nature and have structural implications. That is the case with science, technology, professional training, the very makeup of the university, and so forth. To personalize this set of instruments does not mean destructuring and privatizing it but simply pursuing one's own fulfillment in a historic praxis of transforming structures, and by thus objectifying an effective universal love, recovering the real sphere for authentic personal commitment.

If we review these characteristics together (vast majority as horizon, cultivation of the national reality as its field, the effective word as its proper mode of action, aggressiveness as its disposition, and structural transformation as its objective), we can easily recognize a clear political mission and a strictly university character in this definition of the university's activity. If in fact such a university is able to move forward, if such aims are actually embodied in appropriate internal structures and appropriate channels of communication with society, we can truthfully speak of a different kind of university, one that can efficiently fulfill an important political mission.

Historico-political reality is the appropriate place for correctly interpreting university activity. If it is not focussed to the point where it becomes utterly concrete, the university is playing its role thoughtlessly and employing its great potential irresponsibly. Similarly, if it does not firmly strive to be faithful to its very essence as a university, that same charge of thoughtlessness and irresponsibility can be made. That is why we have spent some time sketching what constitutes specifically the work of the university, both in itself and in its political aspects. There is no contradiction between university and politics; indeed, they are mutually necessary and they energize one another. In our concrete situation today it would be suicidal to abandon the possibilities of the university out of a concern for changing the country, and not to use properly the political potential of those possibilities.

The matter is clear in principle. Is it clear in our specific situation? Do the real conditions under which our university is unfolding permit what we have just proposed as a historic necessity and an ethical obligation? Do the conditions exist for making a different university possible or are the issues being evaded intentionally? What can we observe in ten years of experience of the UCA?

Can Our University Be Different?

In talking here about "our" university we mean the UCA, and when we talk about a "different" university we have in mind the university as described in the previous section. Nevertheless, the question is not about a particular case. Although the immediate object of the discussion is to analyze critically whether this university can carry out the mission which is considered proper to any university in Third World countries, the scope of the question is broader and it includes any universities that may be in similar real situations. To focus on a concrete case to support the argument does not necessarily mean reducing matters to a particular case. That is true whether or not the concrete case serves as a paradigm, for the deeper reason that the truth of history can be brought to light only through a praxis within history. What do these past ten years teach us? Have they fulfilled a part of what has been proposed as the proper mission of a different kind of university? If that has not been accomplished or has been accomplished in a mediocre manner, why is that the case? Even under the same present conditions might it be possible to do something different from what has been done thus far? We confront a question that is basically ethical. If the university cannot justify its claims in reality, taking refuge in good intentions would constitute a grave hypocrisy, one that would conceal base interests. If we are not doing what we claim to be doing, even if it be due to outside pressure, the only justification for continuing would be a notion of the lesser evil, but to appeal to the lesser evil as the foundation for committing one's life would be the saddest of justifications.

This next consideration divides: the first section deals with the obstacles and the second section with the real possibilities. Our assessment will derive from the clash between the impediments to and the possibilities for our university.

CONJUNCTURAL AND STRUCTURAL IMPEDIMENTS TO THE UNIVERSITY MISSION

The aim in this section is to provide not simply a conjunctural analysis but a critical analysis of the real difficulties encountered in the university's endeavors during these past ten years. What has happened reveals a structural framework above and beyond particular conjunctures or moments. The important thing is this structural framework, even though it always wears a conjunctural mask. The nature of the social reality of the university, depending as it must on the society in which it exists, the basic "bourgeois" structure of universities like ours, and our groping "trial and error" efforts, are the three headings under which we can group all of the structural and conjunctural obstacles which have impeded and continue to impede the university's mission, understood as the struggle for the radical transformation of a people.

Social factors shaping the university

It is utterly obvious that the university is a social reality and consequently is conditioned by the structure of that reality which is society. Any effort to regard itself as outside society, as something immune to the enticements and pressures of society, is affected by ideology and indeed militates against really attaining a certain distance from society when the proper time comes. In a socialist country the university is something essentially different from the university in a capitalist country, even though they have many elements in common and these elements look the same. Among the many factors conditioning the university in our own case, three can be singled out as the most obvious.

The *first conditioning factor*: It is the university's dependence on economic factors which, in our situation is *per se* a hindrance to the university's mission. The university needs a good supply of economic resources. These resources may come from what the students contribute, from the state, and from private financial entities. In all three cases the need for money tends to be a hindrance. In justice we cannot say that during these ten years the sources of our financing, including the Inter-American Development Bank loan, have entailed direct coercion of the university's work, some sort of crude *do ut des*. That might seem to be the case with the students since what they are demanding with their resources is simply professional training so they can find a place in society. However, this pressure from students is not, or has not been, decisive, from this perspective—later on we will take it up from another point of view. Private capital did not lay down special conditions with its initial major contribution, and the failed effort to provide the university with a board of trustees can be seen as a providential failure. Moreover, it cannot be said that the UCA set out to teach anyone. It was opened to provide a service to the Salvadoran people from a Christian viewpoint, and by its structure as a university and its Christian inspiration it could not be made to take orders from capital on how to understand this service to the Salvadoran people. Finally, the state has not tried to exert pressure directly, although on some occasions it has felt "compelled" not to contribute financial aid for the practically indispensable service that our university provides in our country. The university has sometimes felt forced to protest the flagrant discrimination it has suffered, for although it may not have a legal claim to assistance from the goods of the nation it has real claims. The fact that thus far pressures have not been too great does not shed much light on the future. The university cannot function without economic resources, and obviously those who provide such resources are not going to work against themselves. The rationality of university activity might be explained to them, but their interests need not coincide with reason, at least in the short run. Can a university remain free when it is dependent on economic resources that can be halted at will? Will a university seeking radical change be able to be supported by those who see no advantage for themselves in such a radical change?

The *second conditioning factor:* we face the social and political resistance of ruling interests. This is not the same as dependence on economic factors; it is more subtle, if you will, but quite effective. Those who wield power always hold a potential threat over those who can check that power. This pressure can take different forms, ranging from systematic campaigns against the institution and some in it to more directly coercive and threatening measures. There are many ways to encroach on university autonomy* both institutionally and personally. Under the pretext of avoiding the excesses of university autonomy, the worst excess takes place; namely, the limiting of university autonomy because of either class interest or partisan interest. Under this same heading comes the resistance from students who do not want to be disturbed with regard to their interests, whether present or future, and who prefer technical training that does not challenge them either on their present involvement in society or their future ethical incardination in the country's structure and functioning. We should also keep in mind the resistance from professors, which is more passive than active. Insofar as professors are involved professionally in carrying out their responsibilities in a business that serves the ruling classes, or at least in the present societal structure they become "professional" people of the dominant system—although this is normally not the case of those who work full time in the university. Even when that is not the case, we encounter the same obstacle in another sector of the faculty who, because they teach more technical subjects, either do not become aware of their political responsibility or do not see how to relate it to the technical nature of their own discipline. Finally, another factor to keep in mind is that of the university authorities, who may think that the development of a greater political consciousness among the various groups in the university will jeopardize the smooth running of the institution. In short, the nature of the pressure, coming as it does more from those who have power than from those in need, is one of the most compelling reasons why the university does not take the direction it should.

The *third conditioning factor:* It is the lack of proper resources. El Salvador is not oversupplied with technical capability, and naturally the university cannot compete with those who are able to pay for the most

---

*Latin American universities generally enjoy legal autonomy; for example, the military or police cannot enter their precincts. Hence, even in military-controlled countries like El Salvador the universities have been sanctuaries for ideas that could not be expressed elsewhere. P.B.

highly trained technical people. Our university continually experiences the pressure that private businesses and even government agencies put on our professors by offering higher salaries. In addition, the initial effort to launch and establish the university has hindered us from freeing personal energies and economic resources for what should be our main task. Nor would it be unjust, let alone unfair, to say that the university has not always proved able to get the most out of the resources at its disposal, whether personal (professors and students) or institutional (curricula, material facilities, real possibilities for action, and so forth). Moreover, it is ethically quite questionable that the money spent on the university's physical plant has been put to its best use, if we keep in mind per capita income levels in the country, and the psychological impression these buildings may convey—both on those who connect their own professional image to the physical image of the university and to those who do not have access to this university that claims to be devoted to serving them and which, nevertheless, presents a facade that they can only regard as distancing.

"Bourgeois" structure of the university

It is likewise undeniable that the underlying structure of the university is "bourgeois," independently of its intentions of change or revolution. Bourgeois structure is here understood to mean a structural reorganization required by and oriented towards a capitalist system. From this standpoint, it is difficult to deny that the university's bourgeois structure or that this bourgeois character is to some degree inevitable. Indeed, most of those involved in the university, whether students, including their family circle, or professors and administrators, do not feel that a profound structural change is urgently needed for the sake of their own interests. Indeed, such change would not bring them great material advantages. Secondly, at the university there is little real contact with the oppressed majority. Whatever such identification there might be for university people is with the interests of *another* class and not as the defense of their own. The amount of time the university devotes to making contact with the oppressed and in bringing what the university does to the oppressed has been almost insignificant. Third, the knowledge mastered and transmitted does not originate in the needy real world of the bulk of the Salvadoran people, nor is it even neutral and antiseptic. It is generally the watered-down knowledge cultivated by dominant countries so that they can remain dominant. Here again the university's physical plant exhibits the style of life and thinking of those of us who do their work in it. That plant is in keeping with a bourgeois mentality and at the service of bourgeois mentalities.

A trial-and-error process

The trial-and-error process of searching, although it has been more conjunctural in nature, has been another reason why the university has not been able to become a "different" university over the course of the past ten years. Although the basic aim was clear very early if not from the beginning, making it a reality had inevitably to be a matter of process, and that entailed an apprenticeship, with some errors along the way. There must be interaction between working out an idea and its embodiment. We had to realize both the idea and the conditions for the idea at the same time, and we had to abandon a previous framework and work out a new one. The obstacles encountered were not purely external. Fears, reservations, and lack of vision from within the university hindered progress. Things had to be this way. This new kind of university activity was being launched from a starting place that truly contradicted it. This was not only another model, but a model that to a great extent sought to depart from the traditional models of both so-called private universities and national universities. Gradually a team of people who believed in the new idea was formed, and the new idea gradually convinced those who had reservations, either because they were working with out of date notions of what a university should be, or because they feared that this university would be a reactionary bastion. Perhaps only now can the university be said to be basically constituted and only now can it devote more energy to getting things done rather than to getting itself going, although it is only in this new doing that the university will gradually become itself in the full sense.

REAL POSSIBILITIES OF ACHIEVING A NEW KIND OF UNIVERSITY

The aim in this section is to examine whether it is actually possible to strive for the kind of university we first intended, now that we have seen the hostile factors conditioning it structurally and conjuncturally, as revealed during the university's earnest efforts for past ten years. The procedure will be first to move from necessity to possibility: such a university is necessary; therefore it is possible. Although at first glance such an argument may look purely logical, it is in fact utterly historical. Then we will indicate the various ways this possibility can be made a reality.

The new kind of university as response to a need

The starting point should be the need for what the university represents and its importance for shaping the national reality. As a tool for training professionals, the university is a necessity in our society. In all likelihood, society is not going to want a university to foster critical consciousness nor to be a force pressuring for change. But a society must want a university to provide it with professional people who will serve the system. Since any society will regard the production of professionals as an enormously important industry, it will invest in that industry a good deal of its most important resources. These include personal resources of professors and students, instrumental resources in the realms of science and technology, artistic expression and communication and, finally, resources in the influence and the prestige that society grants the university at a given moment. When there are only two universities, as is the case in El Salvador, the need for each one and their particular impact on society is significant from every angle. The university is thus not only a fact but a necessary fact.

Something so meaningful and so powerful cannot be entrusted to those who are technically irresponsible or politically immoral. They would be irresponsible if they left society so unprepared technically that neither now nor in a politically different future would it have at its disposal the resources necessary to develop the country beyond subsistence level. They would be politically immoral if they tended to perpetuate a state of things that favors a minority at the cost of the majority. The university can do a great deal of damage to the country. Given that it already exists and is a necessary fact, merely neutralizing somewhat its potential evils and preventing it from becoming a blatant instrument of domination is in itself an important service, and in a given historic context that may be ethical justification enough. Furthermore, it is also an important contribution to provide technical and professional people with enough knowledge to resolve even indirectly some of the most pressing economic needs of the country and so prevent a serious near collapse from which recovery would be difficult.

An important conclusion follows from what we have just said. For the sake of a profound social change, we must get the most out of something that is necessary and that offers some of the greatest potential for action in our countries. Of course, those who believe that the universities have not contributed much towards liberation in our countries and who judge that what is possible can most realistically be judged from what actually has been done are not entirely wrong. However, it is certainly necessary—ethically necessary—to try to make the most out of something that is already there, something that can become a center of reactionary resistance and which also offers some of the greatest potential for really affecting the nation, not with a view to taking over state power—except indirectly—but certainly with a view to helping shape society. These possibilities are rooted not only in the particular potential of the university, which in the intelligence domain has no peer in any other group or institution, at least in countries like El Salvador and those with a similar makeup, but also in a certain ambit of freedom created within the university. Freedom is here understood in the sense of positive, though only partial, liberation from the "needs" of business and the state, and freedom in the sense of constituting an ambit or an enclosure where some distancing and critiquing are possible.

Between current realities and new possibilities

We should realize that we will have to travel some distance until the new order becomes a reality. This journey must be made possible in two senses: we have to gradually make possible the goal pursued and, as long as the new situation does not yet exist, we have to make it possible

to live "in the meantime." This has nothing to do directly with the debate over whether the pace should be reformist or revolutionary. Our
concern here is not with theoretical or even hypothetical questions, but
with real questions. Given a particular reality and a real process, the
question is what demands this reality makes within this real interim
process. Only two potential situations would make this question idle: if
we could envision either the possibility of imminent radical change or if
there were an effort to make such a possibility imminent—which in itself might be remote—by sharpening the contradictions, and by doing
so violently. The first possibility looks unreal, and the second raises serious ethical reservations. In any case, university efforts as such could
hardly be regarded as decisive in either of these two cases. By its very
structure the university should either aim more at training for the
longer run or at consolidating a new order already fundamentally just.

Training aimed exclusively at taking political power would leave
society broken into pieces during the "meantime"; and it would also
leave it in pieces technically and culturally when it came time to establish the new order. These two aspects are both distinct and obvious
enough. Only irresponsible people could imagine that it would be possible to restructure a society without technical preparation—a society
with enormous real problems that would be very difficult to solve. Here
"political idealism" may play a very dirty trick on those who have never
had to make anything work, not even as a model, and whose thinking is
so reductionist and fanatic that they reduce human beings to purely economic and political dimensions. Moreover, the "meantime" is real and is
grinding people in its gears, people who have to go on living and not
just dying. Thus it is mandatory that some people work towards making
that life as human as possible in basic areas like health, housing, food,
and so forth. To believe that people who are exclusively political, just
because of their purity or political idealism, can resolve real problems,
which are not merely political, is an idealist illusion. El Salvador in particular would not be able to subsist through such a chaos, not a chaos of
transition, but a chaos of people in power who lacked adequately
trained cadres.

Such training [of cadres] for the "meantime" and for the coming of
the new order need not be understood as preventing its arrival by tranquilizing the tensions that propel towards change. That could happen,
although a critically alert university need not be intimidated by such a
danger.

For the present, university endeavor can offer scope for the action of
those who are struggling politically for a structural change in society in
a number of very basic ways. It can provide ideological cover so as to inhibit pressure from reactionary ideologies, by showing both the rationality of the new positions and the irrationality of those opposed but
currently prevailing positions. From the moment that a position has no
rational support, it will be revealed as unjust, and sustainable only

through unjust force and violence. There is so much self-serving obscurantism in our country that a systematic and clearsighted effort to dispel the clouds could be very helpful on behalf of change. Along the same lines, weakening both personal and professional resistance can be very useful. Between not fomenting the needed changes with all one's might and resisting those changes with all one's might, there is a wide range of possibilities, and the university through its rational analyses can do a great deal to make actual aggressive resistance less virulent. Finally, in countries like El Salvador the university can step directly into various power centers in order to keep repression from being unleashed with impunity. Other institutions like the church—and unfortunately few others—can have a similar influence. Because it is non-partisan, that influence can be very effective at certain moments, and it should be kept in mind.

In a more positive sense, the university can supply the best objective analysis of the overall situation and can discover and begin to organize appropriate techniques for dealing with the various problems in that interim situation, prepare cadres for analytical work, find solutions and implement them. In the area of developing awareness, it can diminish irrational fears precisely when it subjects those fears to reason, and it can make the goals ideally sought reasonable by de-ideologizing attacks against them. The objection against what has just been said—and it is ever valid—is how little has been done along these lines. We thereby come to the question of our university's real possibilities for doing what it says it ought to do.

Identifying the real possibilities
Those real possibilities can be deduced from what has been done thus far and also by studying the real potential at our disposal.

Taking into account the problems involved in launching an effort this ambitious in an unsympathetic environment and with very limited means, what has been done thus far is no little matter. Thus we have some assurance that with financing and start-up problems overcome, we can talk of real possibilities rather than mere illusions. Leaving aside questions of the physical plant and administrative infrastructure, we can note certain aspects which can be regarded as anticipatory of what could be done.* With no attempt to be exhaustive we may list the following examples of such anticipations: 1) beginning to create among a good number of people a new awareness of what a new kind of university

---

*For example, the fact that the institution is non-profit without being any less efficient, the willingness of many staff members to refuse higher salaries outside the university, pay scales considerably higher than those normal in our country, and accepting ostracism by a social élite who regard the university and its faculty as its adversaries.

should be; 2) proposing, although in an admittedly incipient form, a new model of institution that seeks to move beyond the norms currently proposed by our society; 3) theoretically analyzing some basic issues facing the country and bringing them to public attention; 4) commenting critically on certain serious events in the country on both technical and ethical grounds; 5) confronting very serious developments in the country with an independent voice; 6) providing society with a significant number of upright professional people who are working for deep and rapid change, primarily in education and the public sector; 7) serving as a voice for those who cannot make their own voice heard, although in a limited and sporadic fashion; 8) providing immediate help to the neediest through social outreach programs; and 9) opening a new horizon for the next decade, with the assumption that what has been done thus far should not be simply extended but substantially improved.

These modest accomplishments, which manifest a certain spirit and assure that there is a desire to do better, also raise the question of whether what is proposed can actually be achieved, given both the real potential at hand and the difficulties noted. Rather than proceeding theoretically at this point, the thing to do is to indicate the mechanisms that can make it possible to make the proposed new university a reality.

In principle it does not appear that the change in the university's direction will come about through the simple admission of poorer students. In our situation it is misleading to believe that the university is communicating with oppressed people just because some who do not pay or who pay very low tuition fees are admitted. Statistics prove irrefutably that any university student in the country is privileged since those who get to the university amount to about one percent in El Salvador. Any university student here is privileged and should be held accountable as a privileged person. In terms of the university's mission, the important point about the character of the student body is not *where they come from* but *where they are going*. The university should be very selective on this issue: it should only admit and keep those students who are at least capable of becoming committed to urgent and deep social change in the country. Just as there are procedures for measuring intellectual performance, there should be procedures for determining as unfit for the university those who come with no public consciousness and no social concern and who have proven incapable of acquiring that concern throughout their [previous] education. Admission should be based on an assessment of who will do most for changing structures in the country with their technical training and ethical commitment. The sliding scale in tuition should be regarded as a tentative step towards equalizing opportunity and broadening the base for choosing candidates. Thus it has not been set up in order to favor those less privileged—who as we have just noted are *not* less privileged when compared with the situation of the vast majority—so that they can move up within the consumer society. It is simply a mechanism to prevent us from losing good candidates, candidates called to carry out the mission the university has set for itself.

The same point should be made even more emphatically with regard to teachers. Although university professors constitute a body and in a body not all members carry out the same functions, certainly in a sound and well organized body there is no room for alien and counterproductive elements. That statement does not in any way entail dogmatism nor any attack on freedom to teach since commitment to structural change in the country does not predetermine what should be taught or how. The only thing ruled out are professors unwilling to commit themselves to the social function of the university in this country. People can fail to meet that commitment because they are not well enough trained technically, but they can also fail through lack of ethical commitment to their own social reality. Professors should be chosen with extreme care, precisely in order to grant them maximum freedom in their work and great responsibility in university activity. It is to be hoped that the university mystique will continue, a mystique in which ideals can spread since the university as a body has both the calling and the means to free itself from society's pressures, because it is not involved or need not be involved in society's oppressive mechanisms.

Students can be selected not to be a set-apart élite, but rather to be universally committed to the oppressed majority, and professors can be selected both for their technical competence and for their mystique of service. But these are not enough unless the university is really autonomous, and not simply in the sense of legal autonomy, although that is necessary. What is needed is real autonomy, independent self-sufficiency. Independent of what? The answer is easy: independent of whatever pressure the dominant society uses in order to domesticate the university. The implication is that the university should depend as little as possible on financing under the control of people who want either to maintain the prevailing situation or to strengthen it with minimal improvements. Unless the university resolves the issue of its funding sources in a structural way, the scope of its independence will be far from desirable. The most radical way to solve this problem structurally is to charge the beneficiaries the full cost of what has been spent on them. Such a suggestion scandalizes superficial demagogues. Why, however, should huge amounts of money be given away to students who constitute the most privileged one percent of the nation? Will they as a rule return the surplus value of their work to the nation? Can we consider it just that in less than a year most of them will recoup with interest everything they invested in their university education? University students should return not only everything advanced to them but even a part of what they will be earning later, which derives not only from their own ability but from the capability the university gave them. This is just as true for so-called national universities as it is for our own. We cannot continue to bestow further privileges on the already privileged, which will in turn reinforce the system of privileges. The mechanism for resolving the problem may not be easy. How can those who currently do not have the means to pay be required to pay in advance with resources they will only later earn as a result of their university education? Certainly there is no easy, across-the-board solution, given dropouts and so forth. But [a solution] in principle might be that along with their diplomas, the newly trained professionals could each receive a statement detailing the real cost of their education and hence of what they owe the university. They would be morally obliged to gradually pay back to the extent [possible] as they began earning more because of their diplomas. The aim is not to make the university a profit-making institution, but simply to make it [a financially] independent institution that could really be devoted to its university mission and obligation.

In addition to this way of assuring real autonomy, we should consider another way: namely, working hard for the greatest independence from all those who favor the present system because it favors them. In our country, the system's ability to apply pressure beggars description. Its methods of pressure are more crude than those that Marcuse critiques in countries where the consumer society is in full swing, but they are no less real. Only a constantly refocused critical vigilance can prevent such pressures from undermining the university's resolve— whether these pressures cajole or threaten. I am not talking about failing to do what must be done out of fear and caution, but rather of more subtle temptations, which can turn university autonomy into a mere game that society can easily handle. Indeed society can simply regard criticism as proof that the system provides freedom, or have it as a "vaccine" immunizing it against any ideological structure that might challenge it. Only contact with the poor majority and with the poverty of the majority can be an effective fundamental for the university's independence from the social elitism prevailing in the university "milieu." Only if this critiquing becomes an efficacious awareness of the oppressed majority will it no longer be a kind of preventive medicine against change; only if this critiquing is impelled by real pressure from the oppressed will it become something authentic and truly efficacious.

Only on the basis of such real autonomy will the university be able to be a university in the sense outlined at the beginning of this lecture. Autonomy is not sought for any other purpose but to enable the university to be what it must be from an ethical standpoint here and now.

Whether the new mission of the university is fully carried out, however, will depend primarily on what it is prepared to do in its own proper sphere of activity. The university must embody and implement its professed dedication to changing social structures in its threefold functions of teaching, research, and social outreach.

It should do so especially in research for it is there that the independence and relevance of university endeavor is rooted. It is research that will enable the university to know the situation of the country, what it needs and what means can address those needs. This is one of the points that reveals most clearly the historic character of universities. It is commonly said that poor universities cannot be devoted to research and that at best they are in a position to gather the results of research by others and pass it on to their own clientele. But one can ask: is not the national reality strictly an object for research? Cannot the national reality well researched provide essential guidelines for further research? Can institutions foreign to the country be more capable than a university committed to getting to know the national reality, what its requirements are, and the most apt ways to fulfill those requirements? It is impossible to move a university in the right direction without first determining what the national reality is, where it is going, the forces at work in it, what goals are attainable, and adequate means for achieving them. Hence research should be political and historical, not because it should be reduced to what is usually understood as politics and history, but because the political and the historical provide us with the framework needed for economics, technology, culture, and science. All these dimensions, and others as well, are part of what constitutes the national reality in its historic process, and it is out of that national reality that they must be interpreted.

If that is the case, the university should unite the whole thrust of its research around establishing and implementing what can be called a "national project" [*proyecto de nación*]. The term is intended to be understood not simply in a theoretical or idealist sense, but as a project which, along with its ethico-political dimension, necessarily entails investigation of the clearly structured aspects of how it is to be achieved. The political situation, the socio-economic situation and potential solutions (along the lines of agrarian reform, banking reform, tax reform, and so forth), the educational and cultural situation are all areas where the issues must be analyzed, criticized, and condemned when necessary, but they should also be taken up with a view to solutions. Together with the overall problem of the general direction the country should take, and an appropriate structure for it, there are the particular problems into which that overall project can be divided.

Unquestionably, therefore, research should have a political thrust to it, namely the same political thrust that the university itself has. That is why the university itself should take charge of research and not be at the mercy of demands made by others. Thus it would be a good idea to unite in their ultimate aim all research projects undertaken in the university. Isolated they might not seem to amount to much, but organized as an overall project, they could become quite important. It would then be possible to use research done for master's and doctor's theses, which ought not to be left entirely to the discretion of the students, but which should be made to fit in with the real overall interests of the country. If the university were to make a priority out of research work in this sense, it would have a unique impact on society. And whether it was working could be verified by looking at the resources devoted to it, at the overall research plans, and at the results of current research. Other institutions can carry out partial research, but it is not likely that any can combine the conditions that the well conceived university can offer. Neither all professors nor all students are equally fit for this kind of work, but there is such a variety of specialization, ability, and resource-hours that taken all together they might produce unimaginable results. What is required is the right kind of leadership to organize and move things along in order to assure that resources are used properly.

Research understood in this fashion would make it possible to undertake a profound reform in teaching. That may seem exaggerated, but what is an apparent exaggeration turns out to be a great illuminating principle: what should be taught and what should be learned is the major subject matter of the national reality—what that reality is, as seen from the standpoint of economics, history, philosophy, literature, engineering, psychology, political science, and so forth. That does not mean that politics, psychology, or engineering need lose any of their true specialized character. But if such major disciplines do not contribute towards understanding the national reality better and transforming it, they do not deserve to be in the university, for such a university would be an intolerable luxury in a poor country. The university must radically reshape its teaching on the basis of what the national reality is, and be oriented to what that reality should become. Along with its activities, the teaching university should strive to create a new human being. But this new human being, this new professional person will only be new if his or her whole course of studies is completely re-worked. The newness will not necessarily be found in new techniques employed but rather in the way that such techniques are handled—all aimed at creating something new intellectually that the country really needs. This all requires that degree programs be carefully chosen, not on the basis of the claims made by society as it is, but on a rational calculation of the claims of the society to be established. It further requires that programs be restructured and that professors be re-educated, and of course it requires both greater productivity and greater quality on the part of all who work in the university. The reform of teaching is not primarily a problem of pedagogical methods but, far more serious, it is the revolutionary problem of understanding teaching from the standpoint of the national reality and in terms of radically changing the national reality. What each teacher in the university needs is not so much pedagogical methods *per se*, but a mastery of one's own discipline. From that mastery it is a short step to relate the discipline directly to the social structure and to the course of history. All subject matters do not allow this to the same extent, but that must be the thrust of them all and what unites them.

This is also where that other stepchild of university endeavor, *social outreach*, finds its rightful place. In our university neither research nor social projection is what it should be, and that shows how far we are from what we claim we want to be. Social outreach should be understood in the strict sense as that part of university activity that reaches society directly, or more specifically and assuming the proper horizon of this university, what directly touches the vast oppressed majority in the way of "culture," or more understood generally, the university's direct impact on the social structure. Given the particular characteristics of this structure, social outreach requires an aggressive involvement in our divided and polarized national reality: not by simply preparing ever better analyses of what is wrong in the process, and not by simply letting the concrete cry of the people resonate through avenues that make their claims truly present in the university, but by becoming directly involved in the national reality.

Such social outreach should be understood primarily in terms of consciousness. Utilizing its own specific means, the university should try to be one of the major elements shaping collective consciousness. Something like collective consciousness already exists and is an important element in the activity of society as a whole. The university should utilize the power of knowledge in order to shape this collective consciousness; that is, if knowledge is understood in operational terms as transforming power and not as sheer uncritical repetition. If we could unmask their situation for the masses, make them aware of their rights and obligations in establishing a more just society, persuade them that they have power, provide them with an analysis of their reality and show them ways out of their present situation, that would all constitute a great deal of progress on the way towards national transformation. It is possible for the university to do all that if it carries out the needed research and makes use of popular means of communication. So-called "university extension" should not be conceived simply as bringing the university to certain groups that normally do not have access to it, but as a way of reaching the collective consciousness of the nation directly. There is no apparent ethical reason why the university should not have access to mass media (newspapers, radio, television) when such access is granted to private companies which are motivated by profit and gain. The irresponsible activities of others cannot annul the university's obligation to put itself at the service of the people and at the service of a popular project towards which all forces of proven good will should be summoned. The university should sow its seed over the fields of the nation and not only in cloistered gardens.

Of course this is a difficult task, one with an ideal, but it is not impossible, and hence it is obligatory. It will be attainable only if a university community which really proposes to do so is established. Such a university community will be conscious of its real possibilities and of its obligations towards society and will know how to consolidate the real strengths and the potentialities that are currently being neglected. This cannot be achieved through pressure from above, but must be achieved through the ever richer contribution of people who are convinced and committed. Although there are numerous channels for serving others, that of the university provides an exceptional possibility. It is not the channel of action by the government or of political or state power, the channel of political parties, whether they are opposition or not, it is not the channel of popular organization, nor the channel of the church's mission, nor the channel of private enterprise. It is a different channel which has its own peculiar features, which it need not give up in seeking to wield effective power towards transforming the nation. Why not make the effort? Why not take advantage of its relative autonomy in order to widen the scope of national freedom? In the liberation process of Latin American peoples, the university cannot do everything but what it has to do is indispensable. If it fails in this endeavor it will have failed as a university and betrayed its historic mission.

The Christian Meaning of the University

Legally the UCA does not depend on anything or anybody. It stands by itself. It does not depend on any church hierarchy, nor does it make obligatory any religious confession or even any kind of religiosity. It sets its own objectives in accordance with what it wants to do and not on any outside orders that might coerce it to follow any particular pattern. What does it mean then, to speak of Christian inspiration as our university has done many times? Can such Christian inspiration really help the university move forward instead of being a hindrance? What is this business of the Christian meaning of a university, which must first of all be a university, and which does not acknowledge any imposition by a religious confession?

Both the university and Christianity are realities in history. As obvious as it might be, that observation is significant when the consequences become apparent. When we inquire about the relationship between the university and Christianity we cannot proceed by way of fixed concepts, that is, by seeing whether the concept of university can mesh with that of Christianity. Such a procedure moves from reality to playing with fantasies. We have to inquire about the real possibilities of a specific university and the concrete way Christianity is understood here and now. It is not difficult to perceive the deep harmony between what has been proposed here as the aim of the university, and what Christianity seeks, if Christianity is understood out of the most vital reality of Latin America and is interpreted by a Latin American theology. The issues of how a First World university ought to be a university and how Christianity ought to affect it do not concern us here for the moment. Our concern is to show how Christianity can energize our university endeavor without impairing it in any way.

A university's Christianity cannot be measured in terms of doctrines defended, sacraments distributed, or piety practiced. Universities do not exist for such things, and to be involved in them is a waste of time for a university. The university has its own structure and here and now it ought to have its own ends and its own very specific means. The important thing then is to show how its Christian inspiration can promote and energize those ends and means, even without imposing any religious obligation. The university can certainly ignore the old stereotypes that a Christian vision of humankind and reality are "unscientific" as well as those that seek to keep Christianity from having an impact on structure and history.

The Latin American vision of Christianity leads to an understanding of the historic process of salvation as a liberation of history. The notion is not that salvation history is limited to salvation within history, but certainly that its liberation is through salvation within history. This liberation is a process embracing the whole of the human being and the whole of history in pursuit of the freedom and fulfillment of all human beings. However, as a historic process it comes out of a particular situation: those who take a "scientific" approach to ongoing history will call that situation oppressive and dependent, and those who take a "theological" approach to history will call it structural and historic sin. Those who refuse to undertake an analysis of reality as it is, and who ignore the structural roots of this reality are deliberately closing their eyes for self-serving reasons, that may be obvious or concealed. Likewise, those who refuse to become engaged theologically and make the assessment that this reality merits on the basis of the sources of revelation, are shutting out the light of the gospel for self-serving reasons; they thereby refuse to follow the redeeming path that that light shows us in the midst of what is a reality of sin. A university like ours, precisely as a university, cannot forget the "here and now" situation in which it is exists and from which it must separate itself in its striving for change. A university that claims to be of Christian inspiration, because of that very fact, cannot ignore that this situation is deservedly judged to be one of injustice, institutional violence, and structural sin. For different reasons and from different angles, the university and Christianity, understood in historic terms, here and now offer a common starting point and a common direction: injustice and sin should be abolished through a process of liberation.

Liberation has to do with both structures and persons, both the requirements of nature and options in history. By its very character the scientific analysis of reality tends to focus on structural evils and reform of structures. By its very nature the theological analysis of reality, without ignoring the structural character of evils and their solutions, focusses more on the relation between person and structure. The two viewpoints are complementary, and hence Christianity can and should offer to university endeavor a clear concern for the personal dimensions, because it is aware that mere change of structures does not thereby necessarily bring about a deep and total change in personal reality. To state the same point in more positive terms, we must seek simultaneously to build a new human being and a new earth, although the newness of the new human being will not attain fulfillment realistically and collectively except through active participation in striving to build a new earth. However, the formal standpoint from which Christianity projects its liberating work is not that of power or domination but that of service. Certainly as university it shares in a certain power, but that is the power of hope, of affirmation in the future, and of struggle against evil. The university of Christian inspiration is not a place of security, selfish interests, honor or profit, and worldly splendor, but a place of sacrifice, personal commitment, and renunciation.

In our particular situation, given the present phase of the historic process of salvation and of liberation, both university work and Christian work are matters of struggle and combat. Long ago Saint Paul said the same thing in another context, but he certainly insisted that the struggle entailed by Christian activity in a world of sin was real. Christianity seeks the salvation of all and the liberation of all, but it does so primarily through the liberation of the oppressed. In the realm of persons, it seeks their liberation from oppression of any sort whether from within or without; it seeks in the realm of "social classes" to do away with classes, not by eliminating persons but by eliminating the oppressive role they play in belonging to a particular class. An oppressor class must be forced to cease being oppressive since that is the source of all kinds of injustice. Injustice must be combatted, not supported.

Correctly understood, Christianity defends and promotes a series of fundamental values which are essential to our current process in history and therefore very useful to a university endeavor committed to that process in history. In one fashion or another Christianity regards the poorest as both the redeemers of history and the privileged of the reign of God in opposition to the privileged of this world. Christianity struggles against those things that dehumanize, such as the yearning for wealth, honors, power, and the high regard of the powerful of this world; it strives to replace selfishness with love as the driving force in human life and in history and it is centered on the other, on commitment to others rather than in demands made on others for one's own benefit. Christianity seeks to serve rather than to be served; it seeks to do away with unjust inequalities; it asserts the transcendent value of human life, and the value of the person from the standpoint of God's son, and hence it upholds solidarity and kinship between all human beings; it makes us aware of the need for an ever greater future and thus unleashes the active hope of those who want to make a more just world, in which God can thereby become more fully manifested. Christianity regards the rejection of human beings and of human kinship as the radical rejection of God and, in that sense, as the rejection of the source of all reality and of all human actualization. Since all these values are not merely professions of ideals but fundamental demands that must be lived out and implemented, the university finds in its Christian inspiration an energizing principle that little needs to be spelled out in confessional terms.

A university inspired and shaped in all its activity by these values is a university of Christian inspiration, and it will be un-Christian or anti-Christian whenever it ignores or violates these values. This is not a matter of intentions but of verifiable deeds. If in its activity the university does not proceed by starting from our actual world as institutional sin, it is ignoring the real foundation for salvation history; if it does not struggle against structural evil, it is not in tune with the gospel. The university's Christian character cannot be measured by professions of faith, adherence to the hierarchy, or explicit teaching of religious topics—although in our countries a center for theological reflection and publication is very necessary—but by its concrete direction in history. The university is measured by which master it serves, fully aware that one cannot serve two masters, and that one of the masters one cannot serve is wealth, understood as a god opposed to the God revealed to us in Jesus Christ.

A university is a Christian university when its horizon is the people of the very poor who are demanding their liberation and struggling for it. [Thus, it is] a university whose fundamental commitment is to a change of both structures and persons with a view towards a growing solidarity; a university which is willing to engage in dangerous struggle on behalf of justice; a university whose inspiration for making ethical judgments of situations and solutions and for the means to use in moving from such situations to solutions is the inspiration of the gospel. It is also—some of us believe—the different university that our country needs.

Ignacio Ellacuría

10. The University, Human Rights, and The Poor Majority*

TRANSLATION BY PHILLIP BERRYMAN

The basic assumption of this article is that the appropriate theoretical site for focusing on major social problems in order to correctly interpret them and find practical solutions is that of the poor majorities, as a rule. I say "assumption" because this is not the moment to establish and develop the point. However, even if it cannot be developed further, or even if the way it was developed and established did not lead to total agreement, the existence of majorities of poor people should nevertheless in itself be regarded as a challenge to the ethical conscience of humanity and specifically a very urgent challenge to the university in the realms of both theory and ethics.

To understand this point we need only look at [what characterizes] the world's poor majorities. By this term I understand: 1) those true majorities of humanity—that is, the vast bulk of humanity whose standard of living is such that they can scarcely satisfy their most basic needs; 2) those majorities whose material living standard does not permit them sufficient human development, who do not have access in an equitable way to the resources now available to humanity and who are marginal in relation to certain élite minorities who, although they constitute a small part of humanity, dispose of the greater part of available resources for their own immediate benefit; and 3) those majorities whose dispossession is not due to natural laws or personal or group laziness but rather to historic social arrangements that have relegated them to situations in which they not only lack, but are deprived of, what they should have, whether because of exploitation in the strict sense or because they have been hindered indirectly from enjoying the fruits of either their labor power or their political initiative. Assent to the first characteristic alone would oblige us to recognize that we stand face to face with an immense challenge to both theory and practice. However the ethical urgency becomes more pressing to the extent that we agree that the other two characterizations are accurate. I myself believe that

---

*Ellacuría (1982i); see Bibliography in the back of this book.

fundamentally the accuracy of all these characterizations is beyond question, although to explain the matter completely would require analyses and theories that are open to debate.

As I see it, this is the perspective from which the problem of human rights in general should be focused. Again, since this is not the main topic of this article, I am simply going to state a truth so simple and immediate that it is a truism, but one full of enormous consequences. These vast poor majorities are those who most suffer actual violation of their fundamental human rights and those who are objectively demanding that they be able to enjoy those rights. Hence the question is: How can the poor majorities be not deprived of their fundamental human rights and be able to enjoy those rights? For present purposes, the question can be limited to how the university can contribute by assuring that the fundamental rights of the poor majority are respected.

First, however, it would be a good idea to raise a prior question: Should the university as university be formally and explicitly devoted to defending the fundamental human rights of the poor majority, or is that a task which at best should occupy it tangentially and secondarily? The answer must be, "Yes, the university should not only devote itself formally and explicitly to having the fundamental rights of the poor majorities respected as much as possible, but it should even have the liberation and development of those majorities as the theoretical and practical horizon for its strictly university activities, and it should do so preferentially."

The reason is that in this area the university has very explicit obligations deriving from the very nature of the university. My argument here is not the general one that all institutions should work towards the common good, and that, in the present situation of our societies, the common good obliges each institution to defend and promote the human rights of the poor majorities. Rather, the basis of my argument is the specific and peculiar nature of the university; namely that the university is the theoretical and technical cultivator of truth and knowledge, so that its role transcends the mere training of professionals to serve the needs of a particular social system.

To elaborate this point a bit more, allow me to begin with a classic line from St. Paul's letter to the Romans: "The wrath of God is being revealed from heaven against all human impiety and injustice, *that of those who repress truth with injustices*" (Rom 1: 18).* Leaving aside any possible theological meaning, let us focus on the repression of truth by injustice and on the assertion that rebellion against truth and attachment to injustice are related (Rom. 2: 8). This is the problem of the university as seeker and communicator of truth. It is also the problem of the university as the

---

*This translation of scripture follows Ellacuría's Spanish citation. P.B.

womb of education for a whole people. In a social system where injustice prevails, it is not only difficult to proclaim the truth but it is almost impossible to find the truth, to study reality, to develop knowledge that is true and just. It is not hard to find and disseminate a truth that is incomplete—incomplete in the sense that it does not get at the root problems of real human beings and at the deepest structural roots of a socio-economic and political system. There will be innumerable obstacles, however, when this truth tells "the" truth about the human being, about the poor majorities, and what underlies and what is inside the whited sepulchre of our society. The difficulty I have in mind is not only the external danger (attested by the murders of the University of El Salvador's rector, Félix Ulloa, of dozens of professors at the University of San Carlos in Guatemala, and of more than two hundred Salvadoran school teachers during the last two years), but also the difficulty inherent in finding the truth, and educating people towards the truth that must be sought and made a reality.

Let us look at this point more concretely in two tasks which it is assumed the university must accomplish and which have to do with development and economic growth, namely the training of technical people and of ruling élites in general, and the transmission of particular bodies of technical knowledge which are essential to a society once it has moved into the circuit of the buying and selling of goods and values (which are certainly economic). This assumption can lead to a fatal trap that has been criticized countless times. First, a society does need trained leadership elites, since without them there is no way to stimulate the development necessary for meeting the basic needs of the poor majority. The result, however, is that those who wield economic power are reinforced in their power, and these leadership elites, many of whom were trained in the university, help them rationalize exploitation. Or it may happen that a class of technocrats arises and seeks to fortify and perpetuate its position, so that its members become a minority in their own right, separating themselves from the way of life of the poor majority. Secondly, these people acquire certain techniques and an overall framework of knowledge, values, and behavior patterns which are assumed to be necessary for development and certainly for a life that is at least more satisfied, if not happier—given its tremendous counterpart of neurosis, exhaustion and boredom, meaninglessness and disorientation, and so forth. Moreover, these techniques, knowledge, and attitudes nourish and perpetuate a system which serves not the poor majority but the minority, the powerful, those who initially managed to accumulate more capital and educational resources. In short, professional people and technical "know how" are necessary in order to eliminate underdevelopment, but they also perpetuate the marginalization and underdevelopment of the vast majority of humanity. It is an obvious fact that never in the history of the world have there been so many people so poor, so dispossessed, especially in comparison to such a few who are so rich and predatory.

These two aspects show us clearly how difficult it is to really accomplish the basic tasks of a university that remains within the context of a social system that is fundamentally unjust towards the poor majority. Within a fundamentally just social system, it would be much easier from an ethical standpoint for the university to develop the kinds of knowledge and educated people, the techniques and technicians, needed in order to sustain such a society and move it ahead.

Here in this intrinsic tension between truth and injustice is the origin of the need for the university to be devoted negatively to the struggle to end injustice and positively to support the struggle for freedom. Truth and freedom are intimately connected: ultimately, it is more that truth leads to freedom than that freedom leads to truth, although the interrelationship can in no way be disconnected—each is necessary for the other. Truth and justice are also connected negatively, however, only insofar as injustice is the great suppressor of truth. The relationship is dialectical in nature, since truth will really become possible only in the struggle against injustice and in forcing it into retreat. Although here again the struggle against injustice and the pursuit of truth cannot be separated nor can one work for them independently of each other.

Viewing the problem from a slightly different perspective, we can say that the existence of the poor and oppressed majority in itself represents the most powerful existential and material negation of truth and reason. Overcoming this massive, unjust, and irrational fact of the existence of the poor majorities is one of the greatest challenges facing the intelligence and will of the university; namely, that of helping these majorities find an adequate theoretical response and an effective practical solution. A dialectical view of the problem impels the university to seek to fulfill its proper university mission and its mission as a social institution from this perspective of the human rights of the poor oppressed majority. That will require interpreting and transforming not only the reality at hand, but also the ideological framework reflecting and sustaining that reality.

The question is how to do so vis-à-vis a society that does not want that to be done and that not only resists efforts by the university to do so but demands that it do the opposite. The university cannot ignore those pressures under the risk that society will abandon it because it is no longer fulfilling a social need.

The University's Ultimate Objective: The Well-being of The Poor Majority

The university will have to set as its ultimate overall objective the attainment by the poor majority both of living standards sufficient for meeting their basic needs in a decent manner and of the highest degree of participation in the decisions that affect their own fate and that of

society as a whole. To propose this as the ultimate overall objective for
the university institution may look unusual. It may appear that it does
not specify what the university should be pursuing and that it also
encompasses more than what it can achieve as a university. That "may
appear" is based on prejudice and habits that must be overcome
however.

What is proposed here is that the betterment and liberation of the
poor majority, which necessarily entails their participation and organization, is what we initially have called the ultimate overall objective.
The assumption is that the university as a whole, and even more its various parts, can and should have other immediate objectives which are
not only not excluded, but are required in order to achieve the ultimate
overall objective. Hence what is proposed here is that each and every
one of the immediate objectives be integrated into, and subordinated to,
the ultimate overall and unifying objective. The only valid objection
would thus be the question of whether the liberation and betterment of
the poor majority can really be made the ultimate objective, one that can
energize the immediate objectives that might be present in each division
of the university, whether such divisions are understood in terms of persons or institutionally. If this proposed objective cannot even fulfill that
aim theoretically, it should be rejected as the ultimate unifying objective
and relegated to being a minor objective at best.

That objection, however, does not hold. The liberation and betterment of the oppressed poor majority is more than sufficient for energizing and unifying any legitimate objectives that the university as a whole
and any of its divisions may set for themselves. I leave aside ethical considerations for proving this point, although ethics has much to say, at
least as an ideal of what should not be and what should be in positive
terms. I also leave aside pragmatic arguments to the effect that the work
of the university is impossible in social contexts where the rights of the
poor majority are not respected. I am going to limit myself to purely
university considerations.

The ultimate overall objective of university activity should be such
that it integrates and energizes to the greatest extent the capabilities of
the various sectors of the university: personal (primarily teachers and
students) as well as institutional (departments, laboratories, research
centers, publications, and so forth). This integration and energizing
should affect theoretical work as well as attitudes and ideals. In the case
of people who have not made economic gain the driving force in their
lives but who rather feel fulfilled in cultivating knowledge or in having
an educational relationship with others, it does not seem difficult to
awaken creative attitudes and ideals to deal with the challenge of the
oppressed poor majority. Hence the greatest difficulty would seem to lie
in the area of the theoretical formulation, especially in the realm of
"pure" disciplines or in "purely" technical studies and practices. Even
here the difficulty is more apparent than real, at least in theory. There is

moreover a valid formal answer: the activity of the parts finds its ultimate meaning in the activity of the whole, and ultimately the parts are shaped and guided by the shape and direction of the whole. It remains true, nonetheless, that the reality of the whole does not annul the autonomy of the parts, and that in practice such autonomy can lead the whole to take a direction and assume a concrete shape little connected with what is said about it in theoretical and ideal terms.

That having been said, we can return to the main question of whether the liberation and betterment of the poor majority can be made the ultimate overall objective of the immediate theoretical objectives proper to the different sectors that constitute university activity. The answer can only be positive if it is agreed that the great "learning" field for the university's teaching and research is the national reality, and that the national reality can only be perceived in a comprehensive and concrete way from the standpoint of the poor oppressed majority, at least in underdeveloped nations like ours. This proposition contains two separate claims: 1) that the national reality is the theoretical objective of university knowledge, and 2) that the national reality cannot be perceived adequately unless the observer is situated in the "theoretical locus" represented by the poor majority.

Regarding the first claim, while universities endowed with great resources may know more about biology, mathematics, economic theory, philosophy, and so forth, none of them should know more about the national reality, at least as a whole, than the university which is established and placed within that national reality. Knowing the national reality and training for the national reality are inescapable obligations for that kind of social institution known as the university. However, knowing, analyzing, interpreting, and evaluating the national reality demands a wide range and high quality of intellectual resources. Reality is the grounding and determining principle of intelligence, and in our case the national reality, with its manifold aspects and its connection with universal historic reality, is the grounding and determining principle of what intellectual activity in the university should be. The necessary interweaving of theory and praxis, hypothesis and verification, universality and particularity, projection and realization, and so forth, which are essential to a correct methodology of intellectual labor have a most appropriate field for execution within this perspective of the national reality as the fundamental object of university activity.

The second claim, namely that the poor majority are the "theoretical locus" of the national reality par excellence, is what we stated at the outset as our fundamental assumption. That assumption can no doubt be questioned, especially if one insists on the "par excellence," but it is much less questionable if the position is not taken to extremes, and it is certainly reasonable enough to be made the object of a responsible intellectual option. In any case, we should not forget that in our countries, given the demographic weight of these majorities and the complexity and difficulty of the problems of all kinds that they present, even if they are not necessarily the perspective from which everything is viewed, they should be taken into account and should occupy much of the university's intellectual field of vision.

The University's Priorities in Light of The Poor Majority

Consequently, it is necessary to determine priorities for all university activities in accordance with the criterion of what is most conducive to satisfying the needs of the poor majority, and assuring them their proper place in the political and economic process. This principle enables us to determine the order of research priorities, what should be taught, the size of the university and how many students should be accepted, what majors should be given priority and how they should be studied, what values and professional training should be imparted, and what the structure of the university itself should be, since the participation that the poor majority should have in this field and in others is not always evident here.

None of this directly suggests the creation of some kind of popular university, whose students themselves would be the poor majority, or a university significantly devoted to what is usually called cultural extension. The former is rather utopian, since the university of the people does not seem to be within the university campus, and the latter is utterly insufficient. Of course the university should strive not only for an impartial and "objective" knowledge of the people's needs, but also for direct contact with such needs and with those in need who should be organized as active agents in the satisfying of their own needs. These needs and agents are indispensable for getting to know the national reality from the perspective of the poor majority. That however, does not mean that they, the poor majority, should undergo the professionalizing process of the university or some version of it. It means that the university mission should be subordinated to what these majorities objectively need.

In our experience there are two fitting approaches to achieving this aim. The first is the ongoing study of the social situation of these majorities from two and complementary angles—what they unjustly suffer, and to what they justly aspire. Such studies include both the condemnation of what is evil and the elaboration of rational solutions in the realm of both politics and production. The second way is to transmit to the nation's collective consciousness, and especially to that of the poor majority, both the body of knowledge that the university acquires in its studies and also consciousness oriented towards overcoming injustice and building a different society, based on freedom and participation.

It is obvious that the first of these approaches is necessary in societies where the poor majorities have not been able to become aware and organized enough to emerge from ideological as well as economic and political domination. It is unlikely that other institutions besides the university will address this need with sufficient critical capacity and ideological independence. Certainly there are other institutions that can do this, especially when condemnation is called for. However, the university can do that in its own particular way for which there are no ready substitutes. If it does not become aware of this need and does not critically explore the thousand and one ways in which domination spreads, it is quite possible that the university is itself contributing to this domination. In order to avoid surrendering to the interests and power of the ruling classes, the university must engage in its own careful critical studies. To struggle against those dominating interests, and particularly to unmask them scientifically, it must exert all its scientific and critical capability. It is even more difficult to work out the most fitting solutions for the poor majority in the realms of politics, economics, technology, and education. The university should help find such solutions, although it is not the only institution doing so, but its role in the implementation of these solutions is even more limited. Sometimes criticism will come more easily than creation, but a critique oriented towards subsequent affirmation can be a good beginning for finding appropriate solutions.

Other assumptions are involved in the second of these approaches, most basically, that the collective national consciousness, inhering in the diverse structural categories of people, is held in thrall by a variety of ideological mechanisms that work in favor of the system. It is also assumed that the university is in a position to have a direct or indirect impact on this realm of the ideological, which is one of the elements that shapes collective consciousness. Another assumption is that by means of an ongoing effort to find the truth the university has achieved a certain degree of knowledge and a certain way of evaluating that can deservedly become collective or social consciousness. Finally it is assumed that "consciousness" as critical knowledge of oneself is indispensable for those seeking true freedom. It is not easy to determine which mechanisms are most effective for translating the "science" gained by the university from the "theoretical locus" of the poor majority, so practical solutions should be sought on a case by case basis.

We can strengthen both approaches to the service of the poor majority in a university manner by saying that the university should strive to articulate reason for these majorities. On a number of occasions, the Latin American Church has expressed its devout wish to be the voice of the voiceless and it has sometimes done so, in a strikingly effective way, as in the case of the martyred Archbishop of San Salvador. When this has happened it has been because the Church has taken its place among the voiceless, listening to their reality, learning from it, and internalizing their message. Thus the Church has been able to draw together, amplify, and deepen that unheard voice and turn it into an effective public voice. In this respect, the mission of the university must be slightly different. It has more to do with reason than with reasons; it must be the public and developed reason of that popular reason, which although it is true reason, cannot manifest itself as such because the people have not been permitted to articulate their reason with reasons and reasonings. In proposing this mission for the university I am absolutizing neither so-called scientific reason nor popular reason, nor do we want to get into the complex problem of the relations between popular and academic culture. I simply want to say that in many of the positions and attitudes of the poor majority, both as they claim their rights and as they express their viewpoints, there is a good deal of truth and reality whose power can easily be overlooked. Those positions and viewpoints of the people can be purified and energized if university reason is willing to put itself at their service, not in order to manipulate or ideologize them but to better uncover their deep reason, to learn from it, and only then to relaunch that reason with more developed reasonings.

These viewpoints are especially valid for the topic of the relationship of the university to the fundamental rights of the people and of the poor majorities. The very denial of those rights, which in the first instance is embodied in the everyday life and the hopeless future of the poor majority, is in its immediate and obvious negativity, a negative principle of reason; in a second moment, the efforts of these majorities to become organized and participate are a positive principle of reason. By going more deeply into these two instances, and participating actively in them, the university can aspire to become the theoretical and practical reason of those who, even though they have reason on their side in one way or another, cannot back up that reason with reasons, because they have not been taught to do so or because the self-interested reasons of the ideological structure have distorted their immediate capacity for articulating their deep truth.

The University as a Place for The Pursuit of Liberation

If it wishes to respond to its mission as university and wants to be effective when it comes time to work for the human rights of the poor majority, the university must shape itself as a place of freedom. Speaking of the university as a place of freedom here does not refer directly to the insistently repeated demand for university autonomy and academic freedom. Although they are undoubtedly necessary, these kinds of freedom are not very meaningful without another prior fundamental freedom which is won by continually striving for liberation from the existing social structure. In a society where most people live in unjust and inhuman conditions, that social structure is oppressive by definition.

This striving for liberation should be primarily an effort of the university as such, that is, of the whole university structure. It has two essential moments: separating itself as critically and radically as possible from the demands of the system in which it lives and which to some extent it is forced to serve (the moment of liberation-from), and turning towards the liberating service of the oppressed majority (the moment of liberation-for). Neither is easy, for there is a whole range of allurements working against the first and a whole range of threats and repression working against the second. Both, however, are necessary, and neither can exist without the other. One cannot serve two masters at the same time in any case, for what is given to one is taken from the other, at least where interests are opposed and mutually exclusive. That is not always the case if we go from considering the whole to considering the parts that make up the whole, or if we move from a utopian and unhistorical perspective to a perspective centered on what is possible and on gradual approaches.

However, it is the whole university community that must strive for liberation in this manner. If that community reproduces the interests of the prevailing social system and of the dominant minorities, we can expect little from university endeavor. If students are coming to the university campus in order to secure a dominant and profitable place in an unjustly structured society, we find ourselves with a serious constraint on the ideal of the university's mission. Even worse, if teachers come to the university with the same attitudes and concerns of the other professionals who enter the labor market, very little indeed will be possible. If neither they nor the university as a whole are freed from the financial loans that society provides in order to force acceptance of its demands, the battle to take a stand on behalf of the poor majority is lost, no matter how much fiery and demagogic language of liberation and protest might be employed. We need not pose the issue in overly idealistic or ascetic terms, for the university community does need asceticism and idealism. The reason is that work in the university offers intrinsic gratification, one that arises from the possibility of internal self-realization, of self-giving, of personal creativity, of reproducing oneself in the people of tomorrow. If one of the purposes of work these days is to obtain a measure of leisure—the very term "free time" expresses something deep—it should be said that university work already is in itself or can become, creative leisure, free time, and privileged living. Although such work does not provide the so-called universal substance, the raw material of our time, the general equivalent that money is said to be, it actually offers things that are much more important and can provide what money cannot.

We cannot here go more deeply into this idea of the university as place of freedom. A reminder is enough, for it will be essential when it comes time to think of a university able to take its stand effectively and credibly to serve the fundamental rights of the poor majorities. The university, however, must do all this while remaining true to itself and not ceasing to be what it should be and becoming something else, whether that other thing be a factory turning out professional people, a safe corner for the inept, or a sanctuary for political activism.

The point is that the university cannot stop cultivating a whole range of intellectual resources with the facile excuse that the liberation of the poor majority urgently requires either the training of competent professional people at one extreme or revolutionary political struggle at the other extreme. To be devoted to [only] one or other of these extremes is to ignore the liberating potential of a process of knowing that is itself free and to ignore the burning need for a true knowledge, a difficult knowledge dedicated to serving the poor majority. In no way am I denying that this liberation requires political struggle of one kind or another, nor am I denying that there must be a good number of professional people who can competently respond to the real problems present in society. However, I refuse to give in to the temptation to stop cultivating knowledge with the excuse that it does not get immediate results. The consciousness-raising and liberation of the poor majorities demand a free and critical intelligence, but the freedom and critical quality of the intelligence can be achieved only through arduous intellectual work, although that work is not only intellectual. Creating new solutions in the realms of politics, economics, technology and management also demands arduous intellectual labor in order to get beyond importing models, shortsighted pragmatism, and mechanical repetition . There is an escapist kind of intellectual work, which may take very diverse forms and find varied legitimizing excuses, but there is also a committed kind of intellectual work. We cannot abandon that kind of intellectual work, for to do so abandons to adversaries one of our most effective weapons, which then serves only domination instead of being employed in the service of consciousness-raising and liberation. There are certain medium- and long-range kinds of work that the university should undertake in a strictly and specifically university manner even to the detriment of more urgent tasks whose appropriateness for the university can be questioned and whose immediacy may seriously jeopardize efforts with a much wider scope.

From this perspective we must free up resources for deeper studies, and especially for research. This research would not be all-encompassing since for that there are other research agencies that are so far ahead of us in this respect that we can never catch them. Rather, it would be a kind of research that can help resolve the huge problems of a national reality whose chief defining feature [now] is the existence of popular majorities who see their fundamental human rights violated and a blockade of the potential paths towardss a life emerging from true cultural and political self-determination. The university cannot substitute for this act of popular self-determination either culturally or politically, but it can help bring it about in a reflective and critical manner, and it can be watchful and halt all kinds of cultural and ideological impositions. In addition, the university can draw from the innermost lives of the people (more than from the past) what could serve as the basis for a new kind of civilization. A civilization yet to be formed, but which even now appears in outline; it is to be the negation of many aspects of today's dominant civilization and a response to very specific social and material conditionings. While it helps the popular majority to emerge from the abyss where it currently finds itself, university research must also indicate what the new world towards which we are headed might look like, not only as a utopia proposed to collective consciousness, but especially as a rational projection.

In short, the historic mission of the university should be shaped in accordance with the situation of the human rights of the poor majorities and in accordance with the stage or phase in which those poor majorities find themselves and out of which they are advancing. Although that mission is always basically the same, it can and must embody that sameness in very different ways, which may even at certain moments assume characteristics that are somewhat shocking and quite different from those that the university has traditionally assumed—characteristics more fitting for those systems not interested in change or in which the claims of the poor majority are not of primary interest. Of course there is no single response to these claims, but the university must find a way to respond to them creatively. Its response must reflect a genuine love for the poor majorities, a passion for social justice, and a courage to meet the attacks, the misunderstandings, and the persecution that will ensue because of its stand on behalf of the poor.

Ignacio Martín-Baró

11. Developing A Critical Consciousness through The University Curriculum*

TRANSLATION BY JOHN J. HASSETT

The Socio-political Reality of Central American Universities.

The image of the wise philosopher who, strolling along lost in thought, steps into a hole and falls head first, is a stereotype that nowadays is not quite so common as it was in the past. However, many of us as Central American academics do run the risk of falling into the depths of our own abstractions. Our very status as university people distances us experientially from the structures that condition and determine with ever greater frequency the lives of our people, just as our own particular daily work, for the most part of a theoretical nature, places us within a psychological stratum that is also far removed from the common man.

Hence, we need to make a special effort to reposition ourselves, if not existentially, then at least theoretically, within the harsh reality of the average Central American: a reality characterized by its economic misery, scarcities, and uncontrolled pressures and forces. A reality filled with life, but a life that is also impregnated with death. A deeply contradictory reality and, for this reason, it is one that is in a constant state of turmoil.

Many adjectives have been used to categorize the reality of our Central Americn societies: underdeveloped, marginal, oppressed, dependent. Each one of these terms implies a vision of our world that does not necessarily deny its other aspects, but places the emphasis upon a structural condition that is considered to be peculiar to us as a people. The expert on development will focus on such things as deficient productive capacity and the poverty of the country, and will use as comparative indicators gross national product, per capita income, levels of

---

*Martín-Baró (1974b); see the Bibliography in the back of this book.

220

illiteracy, the number of hospital beds, etc., stressing in all of this the low level attained in all of these categories. The expert on marginal societies will insist that such poverty corresponds only to a particular sector of the population, the majority of which has not been introduced to any of the benefits that modern civilization has to offer. The theorist on oppression will, in turn, point out that marginality is not simply a state of alienation but rather a condition that has reciprocal causes. In other words, that those who become integrated into society depend on those who live on its fringes and that the latter are indeed marginal because they are exploited, oppressed, and repressed. Finally, the dependency expert will stress that this situation, produced internally in our countries, is little more than a reflection on a national scale of reality on an international one, that internal oppression reproduces the external oppression that wealthy countries exert over poor countries, and that this structure of oppression and dependence has been engendered within a history of subordination of one group to the interests and dictates of another.

We are not about to engage in a debate about these theories. It will suffice to have mentioned them in order to remind us of the context of our own social reality. And the image of this social reality, just as these different interpretations present it, offers the following characteristics:

1. Ours is, above all, a *tragic* reality. Neither the most optimistic statistics nor the most ideologically contaminated explanations can disguise the situation of inhumanity and injustice in which our societies struggle. As long as we do not recognize the catastrophic state of certain societies in which the great majority of their people live in perpetual life-threatening situations, everything else, as a consequence, will be out of focus and totally lack any semblance to reality.

2. This catastrophic situation is, in addition, a *conflictive* one. Conflict defines our society in all its strata and levels and in all of its aspects. Racial conflict, economic conflict, political conflict, cultural conflict—in short, historical, societal conflict. The innermost part of our being is conflictive. It is absurd to wish to remain on the sidelines of this conflict: the very nature of the situation forces us to make a choice one way or another and, at times, even against our own personal needs and desires. Either we choose consciously and thoughtfully, or the choices in our life are made without our ever being aware of it. But in any case, our life and our action are inscribed within [the dimensions of] one of these two contending forces. There are no people on the sidelines in a social conflict; there are simply outspoken opponents and disguised ones, those who need no convincing and those who are useful fools. Too often, and more because of naiveté than because of ill will, we academics tend to fall into the latter group. All of us are committed: it remains to be determined to whom.

3. Our society, tragic and conflictive, finds itself in *a state of human alienation*, that is to say, in a state in which people are neither their own

masters, the masters of their own fate, nor beings in the process of becoming whose identity is the result of choices, but rather the product of something imposed from without. For this reason our society is not only alienated with regard to its own being but also, and for the same reason, it alienates the life and behavior of all those who compose it. This notion is equally applicable to individuals as well as institutions.

4. Finally, from the above it can be inferred that truth in our society is to be found neither in its past nor its present but only *in its future*. In the future and—as Dussel would say—in the other. It is otherness with respect to our current existence, the otherness hidden within people, in their destiny and in their culture, all that which today denies our reality, the only valid option that opens before us like an immense theoretical challenge. Of course, it would be absurd to pretend to forge that future with oblivion as our starting point. We need memory, a clairvoyant historical memory in order to precisely perceive all that has blocked, oppressed, and crushed our people. But in the presence of all interested parties we contend that Central America and all of Latin America have the truth of their peoples in the future and only in the future.

In the context of this society, universities actually form an essential pillar of the entire system. I am not saying anything new when I assert that our Central American universities, the public as well as private ones—although perhaps with some distinctions and shades of difference—constitute an effective instrument in strengthening and perpetuating the ruling system, as well as providing an outlet for the most mediocre of bureaucrats. There are two essential ways in which our universities actually serve the system: through cultural penetration and technocratic mandarinism.

I understand *cultural penetration* to be all those academic activities which, in dealing with our reality, utilize foreign modes of comprehension, propositions, points of view, systems, and solutions without taking into account the nature of our own specific reality and which consequently reinforce our situation of historico-structural dependence. It is not simply a question of adopting, for better or worse, a system of alien thought and science to treat our problems. It is a question of proceeding from a point of departure that is radically false. When one begins with a prefabricated science, that is to say, fabricated in another place, and not with an analysis germane to our own problems, all development becomes, by this very fact, tainted. This does not mean that we should create our own science or technology out of nothing. It does mean, very simply, that a science not generated locally is a science that is estranged, and, that such generation is never achieved by examining our particular reality through the use of previously prepared analyses. But it is achieved by seeking answers or help from science (or technology), beginning with our experience of our own reality as the principal question to be addressed. It is quite different to go to science from our reality than to approach our reality from the vantage point of a science that is ready-made. It alters the sign of subordination, of what is the means and what the end, of what is the point of departure and what the objective. In other words, this approach radically changes the horizon that gives meaning to a specific scientific endeavor. In the former we are talking about a form of thinly disguised cultural imperialism; only in the case of the latter are we dealing with a sincere effort towardss a science of awareness and, therefore, with an undertaking that is autonomous and culturally creative.

In the majority of cases the work that is carried out by our Central American universities is, to the shame of us all, an undertaking of cultural penetration and not one of cultural creation. It is not the goal of this essay to demonstrate the validity of this assertion, but it does serve as a presupposition on which I base the entire essay. Precisely because this phenomenon of cultural penetration occurs, our societies are dependent and they view themselves more and more in this way. This situation could not be explained, at least adequately, if it were not for all the profound fifth column cultural work that is performed by the university. The best test is, once again, reality itself.

The existence of a certain technocratic mandarinism is a another way in which the university strengthens and perpetuates the established order. By technocracy I mean, along with Roszak, "that social form in which an industrial society achieves the highest level of its organizational integration." In such a social form "everything aspires to be purely technical, everything is subject to a professional treatment." According to Roszak, the great secret of technocracy, which today is experienced in certain sectors as a kind of cultural imperative, is its ability to convince us of three premises that are interrelated: a) "That the vital necessities of humanity are of a technical nature"; b) that an analysis (highly esoteric) "of our needs has already attained a 99 percent level of perfection" and that c) "the experts that count are those who are highly certified." The basic strategy of technocracy, again according to Roszak, consists "in taking life to a lower level which the technical is able to control, and then, on this exclusive and false basis, proclaim an intimidating omnipotence over all of us thanks to its monopoly of experts" (Roszak, 1969).

I understand mandarinism to be the consecration of a certain social status that preserves a number of powers that separate, distinguish, and place it above the rest of society. For our particular purposes mandarinism should be understood as the mandarinism of technocrats.

Among us, the establishment of a technocratic mandarin class presupposes, in fact, the consecration of social classism. There are already numerous studies that document that education—including university education—actually produces a profound social differentiation, instead of socializing or democratizing our societies, or offering identical opportunities to all its members. Thus the scholastic pyramid is superimposed upon the economic one, which ultimately ends up being fortified and strengthened by the scholastic one. The exceptions only confirm this pyramidal superimposition which can be expressed in a positive correlation that is almost perfect.

This classist differentiation penetrates even the deepest levels of psycho-social structures through the transmission and imposition of social models that are of a very rigid classist stripe. The good, the valuable, and even the most natural is everything in reality that serves to describe the dominant classes: race, language, values, customs, tastes.

And between the academic economic separation and the social molding along classist lines and values, there begins to be transmitted subtly, but nevertheless forcefully, the mythical conviction that social differences are nothing more than the logical expression of natural differences. Society, then, is no more than an extension of nature, social differences are an extension of genetic differences and, consequently, there is nothing left for the individual to do but adapt to this "judicious order" imposed by nature and perhaps by even God Himself.

Certainly, our universities constitute the apex of scholastic institutions and fulfill perfectly their role of insuring class distinctions. Together with a diploma that certifies them as technical people, the university bestows upon its graduates the power to join the social mandarinate, the club of the powerful, the cult of the privileged.

In spite of what we might wish and taking into account all of the nuances and distinctions that one might want to make, this is the reality of our Central American universities. A painful reality but one that we need to recognize in order to confront it honestly and to truly transform it for the benefit of our people. How can we speak of socio-political awareness if we are not even aware of who we are or whom we serve? Our knowledge of ourselves is necessary, and only by having attained such self-knowledge can we ask ourselves how we might go about inventing a process to develop a critical consciousness within our country and in conjunction with its people.

Developing a Critical Socio-political Consciousness

In recent times there has been so much talk in Latin America about consciousness raising that the mere mention of the term is enough to actualize in one's mind its meaning and implications. However, since the term is not always used in the same sense and since—which is more serious—a certain assimilation of the term has occurred within our society, to the point of stripping it of all of its revolutionary negativity (in the dialectical sense as expressed by Marcuse), allow me to summarize in three points what, in my opinion, constitute the essential characteristics of an authentic process of developing a critical consciousness. I will synthesize these three points, asserting that consciousness raising is a psychological and social process. Of course, the important thing is to see what the word process means, and what this *process* consists of on the psychological as well as social levels.

First and foremost, raising consciousness is a process. It is, therefore, not an isolated event and even less a state; nor is it even a personal situation. Raising critical consciousness is the dialectical, personal, and collective movement of men and women confronting historical reality in its most basic dimensions. Consciousness raising is movement, dynamism, change. It is not a being but a becoming. A becoming whose essence emerges dialectically from the reflection and praxis that human beings exercise in their relationships with one another and, above all, in their collective relationship to nature. It seems important to underscore this dynamic aspect of developing a critical consciousness in order to unmask certain attempts at a magical mythification of the term. Consciousness raising is a process that implies movement and, even more, conflict. If our society is conflictive, it is only through conflict, which tends to be painful, that one can realize a process of becoming that embodies the distinct operative consciousness of a new society.

Secondly, developing a critical consciousness is a *psychological* process, that is to say, an internalized process felt by people at the deepest level of their psychic being. Through this process people forge a new awareness of their own reality and their relationship to the world, with the latter understood in a very broad sense. This process of knowing and knowing oneself is not merely passive but fundamentally active. Let us remember: raising consciousness emerges within the dialectic of praxis and reflection which confronts human beings and the world. It is a process of active transformation of the world, a reflex transformation of humankind. Psychology knows very well that beginning with certain data that are transmitted genetically, human beings become what they do to their environment and what the environment does to them. Piaget has shown clearly how the structures of intelligence are continually being shaped, beginning with the most elementary reflex and sensorimotor activities through which individuals initiate their interaction with the environment. Even B. F. Skinner, with all his technological mechanization of the psyche's activity, makes habits and behavior dependent upon the environment's reinforcements, that is, upon those transformations which the action of the individual brings about in the environment. In other words, what individuals become depends, principally, on what their action succeeds in accomplishing in the environment. Developing a critical consciousness, then, implies a very radical transformation of the human individual, a reflex and an operative consciousness that continues to emerge out of a dialectical process between human beings and the world in which they live.

Lastly, developing a critical consciousness is a *social* process. It would be correct to say that it is a psycho-social process as long as the union of these two terms implies neither a psychological nor a sociological reductionism. In my opinion, raising consciousness is, structurally, a social process before it is a psychic one. I believe that here is contained one of the greatest simplifications that has ever dealt with the concept of developing consciousness—a simplification that is frankly misleading. The process of developing a critical consciousness is social not only to the extent that personal consciousness only makes sense as a dimension that is fundamentally social—that is to say, within the context of a community of persons and in relationship to the world of that community— but also to the extent that the subject of consciousness raising is above all a community, a people. When Freire insists over and over again that no one educates anyone else but that we educate each other in a process of transformation of nature, he is clearly implying that this process of reflex transformation is a collective one, that the subject of reflex transformation is the community. If I understand correctly what he is saying, this social comprehension of the community as the subject of consciousness raising is based on the Marxist concept of the "maximum amount possible of consciousness" (Zugerechte Bewusstsein). Each social situation, the structure of each group, only allows the components of that group a fixed level of consciousness. Breaking those limits only implies breaking the structure of the group, to the extent that each group can only attain a knowledge of reality that is compatible with its own existence as a group. Here we are touching upon one of the most fundamental aspects of consciousness raising: without a transformation of the group there is no possible progress in our awareness; although, as reality demonstrates to us every day, many groups have not even attained that maximum level of consciousness that is compatible with the current structure. In any case, it is important to emphasize that the development of a critical consciousness is, above all, a group process and that in the best of all possible senses, it is a community process. Developing such a consciousness implies socialization and the transmission of culture, not in an adaptive sense, but rather in a creative and revolutionary one.

The necessary and fundamentally social character of consciousness raising leads us to the conclusion that every process of this type is essentially *political* in nature. Developing a critical consciousness is either political or it has nothing to do with consciousness raising. And this should not only be understood in the most elementary sense, but also, that the dynamics of consciousness raising lead necessarily to political choice, whether desired or accepted. This is undeniable; and historical examples do not allow for any ambiguity in this matter. The final politicization of the developing of a critical consciousness could even be taken as a criterion for the genuineness of a specific consciousness raising process, just as the conflict with the powerful was pointed out by Jesus of Nazareth as a practical measure of the authenticity or falseness of his disciples. But to state that this phenomenon is necessarily political in nature is not to limit it exclusively to being an indicator of the genuineness of a particular consciousness raising process.

It is a basic truth to state that the political constitutes an essential dimension of human reality. This is especially true if we accept the term both in its broadest sense of organization, interdependence, and citizen interaction as well as if we use it in its most restricted meaning of orientation, determination, and execution of the destinies of a society or social group. Both aspects are essential to the human being, because typical of humankind is to "become" a history through an organization that pursues specific goals. And this, which points precisely to the final and most important aspects of our being, this is the political dimension. Although what we normally call "political" scarcely operates within the realm of concrete circumstance, basically it is the political that is at work whether we recognize it or not. Those who are very conscious of this fact are the great economic interest groups that abound throughout our countries and who never disdain the political realm even though their principal pressures are exercised at its most elementary level (in those structures and factors that determine the life of a society).

If the political, then, is a special dimension of human reality, the development of a critical consciousness must be a simple ideological mechanism when it does not have a direct and immediate bearing on human reality. In this sense one can affirm that ignorance of the political is the negation of the process of raising awareness. What type of consciousness would it be that hides or separates humanity and the community from those forces, factors, mechanisms, and structures that determine the organization of our lives and the direction of our destiny? The most dangerous ignorance is that of individuals who are convinced they know everything. In a similar fashion, consciousness raising that makes an abstraction of political elements would be little more than a farce, an attempt to raise the consciousness of non-thinking beings, and, ultimately, a dangerous artifice for maintaining and increasing dependence and oppression. When Marcuse points out the assimilative capacity of the current system, he is in a certain sense indicating a danger that stalks not only those realities that arise as a direct product of the system but also, and principally, those that arise with the best intention of transforming the system and even of revolutionizing it. The process of developing consciousness has fallen within a short time into this danger, and today dictatorial governments, the newspapers of the SIP (International Society of Journalists), the Boy Scouts, and even Alcoholics Anonymous speak of consciousness raising.

An important point about developing consciousness is its connection with liberation. Consciousness formation and liberation are two concepts that explain different aspects of one and the same reality. It is worth stating with equal emphasis that developing a critical consciousness embodies a force that liberates just as all liberation is one that raises critical consciousness.

We have already pointed out that consciousness raising is not simply becoming aware of a certain fact, but rather it is a process of change, of active and passive transformation. This means that the arrow of consciousness, even though it flies from the longbow of a historic past, aims at striking a new and different future, a future whose image can only define itself negatively. It is precisely the community in this process of developing consciousness that—in the encounter between action and thought—traces a new historical undertaking: a new consciousness begins to project a new image of the community. Moreover, any historical undertaking in this direction that does not imply the radical freedom of a people is not an authentic one. And let us not mythify the concept of freedom: freedom is expressed and realized historically in concrete freedoms, and freedoms are obtained through a process of liberation. Because of this, any consciousness raising effort that does not unleash liberating forces is a false one. For this reason, we indicated previously that the raising of consciousness must be essentially political in nature. The development of a critical consciousness and of liberation are closely linked processes which form the spinal column of the historical movement of a people towardss its own authenticity.

Mechanisms for Developing A Critical Consciousness in the University

From this perspective of what our society is, of what the university is and represents and accomplishes within its walls, and of what consciousness formation is all about, we can now ask ourselves realistically what the mechanisms are that can facilitate a process of consciousness raising in the university. The analysis that we are about to undertake presupposes a conception of the university that defines itself through its choice in favor of the total liberation of our peoples, through the activity of scientific research, teaching, and social commitment. The operational feasibility of this academic option carries with it the danger of adulterating its radicalness. However, it is certainly necessary to run the risk, establishing those mechanisms of constant critical evaluation which will permit us to flexibly modify our objectives in accord with specific requirements and historical opportunities. Not descending to the world of the concrete is one of the most dangerous ideological frauds: it is easy to accept concepts and theories when they go no farther than what they are—mere abstractions. To avoid the concrete under the guise of purism, is a form of intellectual escapism and useless dogmatism. True, liberation cannot be reduced to simply walking down a street or stepping into everyday life, but there will be no liberation as long as concrete free actions do not occur in the street and in everyday life.

We distinguish between two types of mechanisms that can operate within the realm and mission of the university: one is complementary in nature, the other, structural.

COMPLEMENTARY MECHANISMS

Complementary mechanisms are those practical means that try to make up for the deficiencies produced in the process of achieving goals that the university has set for itself. Consequently, it is a question of completing by addition that which supposedly has been left undone after the basic academic programs have been put in place. For our purposes, it would involve filling in the gaps with regard to the socio-political development of consciousness that the university tries to provide.

The advantage of complementary mechanisms can be seen in the way in which, they broaden, to a certain degree, the scope of academic work. Perhaps they come through the service entrance, but when all is said and done, they do indeed enter the realm of academic rigor. If correctly applied, they can influence the student in a very decisive way, who will in turn become a kind of promoter for academic work that remains to be done and for the needs uncovered by the process of raising consciousness.

The major drawback of these complementary mechanisms is their marginality. Experience shows that they are given little attention by both professors as well as by the great majority of students, not to mention administrators as well. This marginalization reflects a disdain for them, not only with regard to their extrinsic usefulness but also with regard to their intrinsic importance. They are not considered to form part of "science," part of what matters, but rather they are perceived as something added on, something similar to diversions for our leisure time.

The marginality of these mechanisms carries with it another danger: the fact that they serve as an instrument for justifying the remainder of the university's objectives. In other words, their mere existence is considered sufficient to leave intact the structure and meaning of the work that remains to be done by the university. Stated in more popular terms, since we have already lit a candle to God, we can therefore continue to preserve our permanent cult to the devil. It becomes something like the theory of charity held by rich Christians who appease their economic immorality by giving alms to the poor on weekends. Thus, when these complementary mechanisms exist, the remainder of academic activity—"what really matters"—is able to maintain its sense of a system that both alienates and fortifies.

Furthermore, complementary mechanisms offer the drawback of not reaching everyone or of not reaching them with the appropriate intensity. On the one hand they are based on the false supposition that adding on makes up for deficiencies. On the other hand, merely adding new activities—without changing others—only produces the effect of a valuation which results in academic work maintained at a superficial level and which does not allow for a critical comprehension that can raise the level of one's consciousness.

The most common complementary mechanism is to add specific courses. This has been the typical approach of schools and universities which are supposedly Christian and which add a course on the social doctrine of the Church or something similar as a curricular requirement. Lay schools usually include a course on sociological problems, dialectical materialism, or something along these lines. With a focus aimed at developing a critical consciousness, these courses try to provide some knowledge of reality, of environmental problems, that might serve as a point of reference for other academic disciplines and endeavors. In fact, rarely do these courses exert a lasting influence on the student body— although there are exceptions. Most of the time they cause a slight uneasiness so that the most these courses achieve, when divorced from the total formative process, is the generation of a marginal realm of "social" concern within a state of undeniable and readily recognizable schizophrenia. In this sense, the consciousness of the central personality is not raised; rather a "psychic corner" of uneasiness is created, something similar to a psychic state of mind that responds to specific environmental stimuli: catastrophes, moving performances, opportunistic preachers, a specific demonstration for just compensation, etc.

Another type of complementary mechanism is so-called *social service* which at times—as in El Salvador—is required by law as an indispensable requisite for the procurement of an academic degree. Social service is conceived as a time dedicated to the practice of the profession in which the individual has been trained for the supposed benefit of society's most needy sectors. Its non-profit nature is subsumed within this concept of social service, to the extent that such services must be rendered free of charge or for a minimum charge that satisfies the basic needs of the professional.

Such social service can be done at the end of or during a career. Obviously, when it is performed at the end of a career, the service offered is more complete and more competent, that is to say, it tends to be a more valuable service. But, as a mechanism for developing consciousness, social service, at the end of a career, has no effect whatsoever on the career. Most of the time, as the professional accedes to his social service with its completely structured program, the possible impact of reality is already grasped in a biased fashion through a perceptive filter which renders this impact superficial, fleeting and, finally, ineffective. On the other hand, experience makes all too clear that social service at the end of studies is usually not viable—whether due to the subjective baggage of those who have graduated from the university or whether due to the objective baggage inherent in social organization itself, particularly that found in the professional schools which block any competitive practice that does not pursue the same profits that have been outlined as minimal. The fact is that, just as the National University of El Salvador has demonstrated time and time again, the professional ends up with a diploma without having performed even a glimmer of social service.

When social service is performed during one's studies, the disadvantage is that as a student one has not yet mastered the scientific and technical complexity of his field of specialization and, consequently, the service is more incomplete and deficient. But social service performed throughout one's career presents the advantage not only of a much greater viability but also of a questioning and continuous influence upon the rest of academic work. A partial but continuous activity in the most needy areas of our national reality produces a very profound questioning of the true value, meaning, and importance of other academic disciplines and research. In other words, social service conducted throughout a career makes possible a process of consciousness formation in the student, that in the long run, can affect faculty, courses, studies and, finally, the whole range of work carried out within the University. We would contend that in this way a road can also be paved to the liberation of the university, its structures and its alienating requirements.

However, it is important to maintain a certain skepticism with regard to the consciousness-raising value that social service can have, at least as an isolated entity. Besides the drawbacks already indicated for complementary mechanisms, social service implies to a certain degree the idea that the student must satisfy a specific quota of service and, with that once satisfied, can then turn his profession towardss personal profit. In other words, it would seem that social service implies a contract and that once it is fulfilled, the individual no longer has any obligations to serve society. In this sense, not only is there a profound prejudice standing in the way, as far as time is concerned, but also a schizoid conception that reduces the social to a simple sector or aspect of reality. The same phenomenon of perceptive imbalance occurs here as in the badly understood concept of charity which, to certain Christians means: "charity is giving alms to the poor"; even if it means turning one's back on their most basic needs for human justice. In this context, then, the "social" would be the isolated poverty of certain sectors and not a structural characteristic of our society. Obviously, social service understood in this way implies a serious insistence upon the justification of a professional career as it is currently practiced in our society— that is to say, upon a professional career that disregards the people's most basic need for justice and, in so doing, reinforces a state of structural oppression.

The last of the complementary mechanisms are all those scholarly activities that include diverse types of organizations and student movements, lecture series, panel discussions, symposia, publications of every type, etc. They present an enormous advantage in regard to their ability to develop a critical consciousness; those who get involved with them do so freely, and therefore within the context of a dynamic that is far more spontaneous and creative. Given the many limits that these types of activity usually encounter, it is undeniable that they lack the administrative red tape that usually hampers the dynamics of a consciousness raising endeavor. In this sense, often students becomes more aware of their personal contribution through their participation in a student movement, than in long and arduous hours of classes, laboratories, and exams. It is not uncommon for a panel on a particularly hot issue to

project a ray of light that is more illuminating for the consciousness formation of the student than the most pondered and most famous texts
written in the style of Samuelson.

These mechanisms reflect the very serious drawback of marginality.
Everything that we have said previously with respect to this question
can also be applied here to a maximum degree. University curricula in
no way take into account extra-curricular scholarly activities. Not only
do they not take them into account, but frequently they oppose and tor-
pedo them intentionally. On the other hand, student organizations that,
undoubtedly, provide the most effective mechanism for the purpose of
consciousness formation, present the danger of unleashing what we
might call "the paranoid deception." That is to say, they unleash a pseu-
do-revolutionary behavior, whose only dynamic emerges from the same
structure and peculiarity of the student group, but which has no roots in
social reality. The student is, then, a "revolutionary" while he forms part
of these groups, but he stops being one the moment he receives his degree or his first paycheck. This paranoid deception can lead to extreme
positions with regard to academic formation that ultimately will make
change impossible. Within the consciousness raising strengths of these
student organizations is also found their weakness: their lack of commitment to the established society gives them a tremendous freedom of action, just as the lack of economic worries on the part of the majority of
their members allows them to adopt positions that are extremely critical.
But this freedom and critical spirit have no more roots than the temporal
nature of the status of being a student. It is worth asking if, during the
time they are effective, they allow enough of a level of consciousness
formation that the lives of their members are affected in a lasting way.
My personal reply to this question is negative, if we consider this mechanism by itself alone. But even in this case there is no doubt that this
mechanism offers elements that are not at all insignificant with regard to
the notion of a team effort and, undeniably, it makes certain contributions that are capable of producing personal and group relationships
that can prove to be important in a given historical moment.

STRUCTURAL MECHANISMS

Structural mechanisms pursue specific objectives as an essential part
of the university's task. They are determinants with regard to the
university's organization and the work that it carries out, or, to put it another way, they constitute its spinal column. In this sense it is the structural mechanisms that will give the measure of what the university is
really pursuing. For our particular purpose, they can be understood as
those mechanisms that show whether or not the university is truly pursuing a process of consciousness formation and the liberation of people.

Obviously, *planning* is the first structural mechanism that has to do
with the university, and more specifically, with the process of

consciousness raising. Either the development of consciousness forms part of the primary objectives to which planning addresses itself or it does not. Planning consists in determining those policies and plans through which the university attempts to organize and rationalize its personnel and its resources in order to realize its objectives in the most effective way possible.

Planning requires a "thinking head," whether it be a Board of Directors, a Board of Managers, or an equivalent structure in each case. This head must identify the general and specific objectives as well as the strategies and organizational plans that, through the best possible use of available resources, will try to make such objectives a reality. One of the principal points with regard to consciousness raising is who constitutes this "thinking head." Let us not deceive ourselves: if at the head of "the" planning we have those who, in some way, represent the economic, political or social head of the country, it is unlikely that we can expect from them a system of planning that is directly linked to developing consciousness. People of excellent scientific backgrounds are certainly needed at the head, but above all, those with a profound understanding of the country's problems are needed and, if possible, those with an even greater radicalness in their concern for the people. In this sense, there have to be people with ability at the head and even those who have undertaken specific research on our national problems. Only this type of individual can set in motion a strategic plan that springs from the people's true needs for liberation and not a plan that tries to respond in a spirit of social assistance or development; that is to say, a plan that functions in terms of maintaining and strengthening the interests of the few.

We can distinguish two types of planning: one that is academic and the other that is budgetary. In the first place, academic planning's starting point must be a clear ideological choice. It is absurd to claim *a priori* a pluralism based on the affirmation that the university must be universal. This universalistic posing of the problem contains one of the most dangerous fallacies imaginable since it ignores the conflictive nature of our current society and seeks to ignore the fact that the university finds itself enveloped by domineering, oppressive interests. When our universities claim to be universal they are, in fact, little more than mere instruments in the hands of the powerful. In this sense, then, a strategic plan that seeks to raise consciousness and implement liberation must start with a clear choice on behalf of the interests of the people.

The programs of study that the university should offer, the type of orientation that such programs should have, as well as the concrete objectives that one hopes to address by offering them, all of these should be determined on the basis of these interests and needs of the people together with an evaluation of the university's resources. Consequently, an academic strategic plan that wants to be part of a consciousness raising process must specify the curricula of each discipline: what subjects should be studied, in what order, with what intensity, etc. If this practical clarification of the university's general objectives is not actually carried out, the principles will never go beyond being mere words that may sound somewhat beautiful but will remain, nonetheless, ineffectual.

One of the principal mechanisms for possible consciousness formation is to be found in this determination of disciplines and their respective curricula. Its importance is not reflected solely in its impact upon the student body but also, in a more fundamental way, in the configuration of the university's academic being. Whether a university is trying to respond to the needs of the dominant classes or to the needs of the oppressed can be readily deduced with sufficient precision through an objective analysis of the disciplines, curricula and the priorities they manifest. And, in this sense, it is important to avoid a great danger: often the needs of the people are confused with the demands and interests of the student body. One has to realize that the student body sitting in the university's classrooms is representative essentially of the country's dominant social class and that, therefore, its demands are no more than an echo of that class. Each and every university of the developmental stripe falls brutally into this bondage to oppressive forces.

A second important aspect of academic planning is constituted by the determination of the general and specific goals of each subject matter as the subject matter relates to the objectives of a specific discipline. The way in which the program of a specific subject area is developed is not unrelated to the effects of consciousness raising. Later we will insist upon the appropriate pedagogical methodologies, but let us say from the outset that developing critical consciousness demands that the most important programs in scientific education receive a special treatment based on data provided by our immediate surrounding reality and not on the basis of data and problems that pertain to foreign realities. It is a grave error to leave the development of diverse programs to the discretion of each professor as if in the final analysis that development were not integrated in the facilitation or obstruction of the work of consciousness formation. Hence planning must contemplate a precision in program structuring, and this precision must originate with someone who possesses a profound knowledge of our reality. Perhaps someone may ask what happens then to the active and creative role of the professor. The answer is simple: that role is to be exercised not so much in the problems to be treated as in the way in which they are approached and resolved, which, if one thinks about it carefully, is quite an important role.

Finally, if academic planning wishes to facilitate the development of a critical consciousness, it must strive to ensure that the real problems of the country are those that are at the heart of disciplines, their organization and development, subject matters, programs, and required research papers.

All of us are well acquainted with those planning committees that tend to examine a miserable reality from the point of view of a comfortable one, that want to resolve the problem of oppression from aseptic offices that smell of air-conditioning and English as it is spoken in Miami. No matter how much good will they possess, such committees lack the vital experience that is necessary to capture the most profound dimensions of reality. Understand: I am not claiming that planners must accomplish their work in shacks, although it would not be a bad idea to have them do so every now and then. What I am insinuating is that there is the need to include in some way the anguished voice of the people in the work of all planning. In other words, I ask that we suppress the myth that the best type of planning is a planning done objectively, unemotionally. The ongoing state of emergency in which our people live transforms such objectivity into an inadmissible sarcasm.

On the other hand, it is important to highlight in academic planning the value that has to be conceded to research and social forecasting. A good planning process has to be one that is flexible in its formal requirements, in order to adapt to the real demands of a national reality as well as to the many possible options that will permit the kind of innovation and creativity that we need so desperately.

As far as *budgetary planning* is concerned, it constitutes one of the essential conditions for verification of the objectives proposed by the academic planning process. It is important that resources be truly subordinated to the objectives proposed by the university's leadership. In this respect economic planning will be a test of the integrity of the university's intentions regarding the raising of consciousness. As a matter of fact, administration itself represents a serious threat within our midst to all work that is involved in liberation. Very often economic difficulty is used as the final argument to justify and excuse the fact that no progress is being made in the area of developing a critical consciousness. It is always asserted that such a condition is only temporary, but all of us know that some temporary conditions soon become permanent in nature. At other times, there exists a *de facto* subordination of academic work to the administrative, as if the most important thing in the university were to maintain order in regulating exams, grades, fee payments, etc. This is tragic because it curtails academic freedom. As a matter of fact, it would seem that "law and order" is the number one governing principle in many of our universities. Thus budget planning must lend viability and veracity to those academic planning objectives that propose to affect consciousness.

The second structural mechanism of great importance to the process of developing consciousness is *the politics of one's personnel*. Do appropriate criteria exist in our universities for the selection of academic personnel? Not just any individual is suitable to achieve those objectives concerned with consciousness raising, although not everyone should have to carry out the same type of consciousness raising work. It is precisely here that we should apply rigorously what we stated earlier regarding the university's ideological option versus a false kind of universalism. It is a lie to say that the university has been, at one time or another, open to everyone. And it is false to state that the university has ever been universal. This is the case because the common people have never found the doors of the university open to them. The university has been an élitist institution, and it is absurd to deceive ourselves with pseudodemocratic bombast which actually does nothing more than disguise our own reticence in placing the university at the disposal of the oppressed. There has been no universality of ideas or of problems or of people. Because of this, no one should be scandalized that we are proposing criteria for the selection of university personnel. These criteria should not only take into account the scientific and pedagogical quality of specific academics, but also their ideologies and fundamental values. In the final analysis we should not forget that the professor is the most immediate behavior model that the student has regarding what is or is not a professional and that professor is the one who either puts into practice or blocks the process of consciousness raising. For this reason, and despite the possible exceptions that may be offered, it has to be stressed that if the university chooses the development of consciousness and liberation as its mission, it must be selective with respect to the academics that it hires for its faculty.

Another different point has to do with the criteria used in the selection of students. In this case one has to evaluate the university's real possibilities as well as the possibilities of each potential student. There is a great myth regarding the democratization of the university, as if democratization were going to open the door of the university to everyone. If universities do not change, if they do not open their doors to everyone (which does not really mean to "everyone" but to "others") it will be tantamount to a multiplication of the number of potential oppressors in a given society. The principal point is to examine whose interests the university really serves. In saying this I do not deny that making it possible for students of lesser means to attend is a valuable mechanism for raising the university's own consciousness. But the experience of our national universities, where education is usually almost free (meaning that it is paid for from the national budget) should teach us all a lesson on the effectiveness of an open door policy.

The third structural mechanism that we should consider is that of *pedagogical methodology*. It is worth insisting upon, from the very beginning, the instrumental nature of pedagogy. The ultimate meaning of pedagogy is that of directing academic work towardss the adequate fulfillment of desired goals. In other words, pedagogy tries to link internally the university's programs and available resources with objectives.

In principle, pedagogy, together with a specific discipline, seeks the transmission of certain formal structures of knowledge, as well as the mastery of a range of methods, techniques, skills, and fields of information. But along with these structures of knowledge or with them as its basis, a value-laden and attitudinal structure is also transmitted, that is to say, an ideology (Martín-Baró, 1972g).

There exist many different types of pedagogical techniques: the lecture, seminar, laboratory, tutorial, and team research methods. And it is important that our university apply these diverse methodologies according to their different contexts. It should be very clear that the diversity of subject matters may make one particular pedagogical method more appropriate than another and, what is even more important, that not just any method can be used haphazardly to achieve specific objectives. All the methodologies mentioned above can be instruments in raising consciousness, but one cannot fulfill with all of them, for example, the objective of knowing reality.

On the other hand, both the pedagogical method used as well as its practical application define the parameters of consciousness formation. When Freire speaks of a pedagogy of the oppressed, he is affirming clearly that a pedagogy with or for the oppressed is not at all useful in ensuring liberation. There are those, in this sense, who deceive themselves. The fact that one makes certain statements or deals with certain problems in a lecture class does not mean that the work of consciousness raising has been accomplished. The development of a critical consciousness, lest we forget, is something much more profound than that. In saying this we do not deny that a class lecture can affect the level of consciousness, what we are saying is that consciousness raising does not emerge simply from the fact that one speaks of certain issues or problems.

A pedagogy will be more or less of the consciousness raising type to the extent that it puts into practice specific features. By itself, the more active, critical, community-oriented, and dialectical that a pedagogical method is, the greater chance it will have of being able to affect consciousness. The activity reflected in such a method will juxtapose the dynamic participation of the student with one that is merely passive; the participation thereby making the student a subject and not an object of the educational process. A pedagogy that emphasizes critical awareness is opposed to all forms of "banking" relationships (Freire) in which prefabricated subject matters are gulped down and the ideal learning process is reduced to the ability to memorize in order to retain and accumulate more and more data (which assumes an ossification of culture). A sense of collective identity opposes pedagogical norms based on competitiveness and individualism, which reinforce the most anti-social tendencies in people, fomenting in them a selfish perception of reality. Finally, the dialectical nature of pedagogy positions the group engaged in academic pursuits at the heart of reality's problems and not facing either feigned, invented, or idealistic ones or those that relate to other worlds.

When a pedagogical method can integrate these four conditions it has far greater potential for developing consciousness than when it manifests no more than one or two of these features. With this said it is clear that not all subjects facilitate a pedagogical methodology of this type. For this reason, a well-balanced program will coordinate diverse pedagogical methods with a vast array of subject matters and objectives. What is absurd to think is that a pedagogical effort towards liberation is being carried out when in fact most academic work undertaken employs those pedagogical forms that possess the least potential for raising consciousness, which is exactly what occurs with the lecture-type class.

I want to stress, in this respect, the consciousness-raising value of what I have called team research. Possibly the majority of the student body will not be able to carry out research with the required minimum of scientific rigor. Nevertheless this majority can participate in doing research and participate in it very actively. I think that research is one of the best methods for teaching and raising consciousness. The reason is quite obvious: by itself our reality is so incredibly subversive, so communicative in its data that just direct contact with it can produce a new awareness. In this sense, the number of courses that could be called participative research would have to be greatly increased as a principal requisite of university curricula.

Finally, the difference between an academic effort that is linked to the critical development of consciousness and one that is not, can only be appreciated in the real results that are achieved. Hence, the fundamental importance that *systems of evaluation* possess. The latter would be the fourth and final structural mechanism upon which I think it is worth reflecting here.

The most honest evaluations can all be summarized by measuring and, if possible, quantifying the realization of proposed objectives; in capturing the mistakes made as well as the gaps left, and in providing, finally, feedback that will facilitate the improvement of subsequent endeavors. Evaluation is not, then, a mere final measurement but rather a very important instrument of work; in psychological terms, it is a veritable reinforcement. Without continuous evaluation it is very difficult to carry out an effective educational mission.

As a matter of fact, evaluation has been rigidified in the most incredible way, altering as well its most genuine meaning and, what is worse, contradicting, and even blocking its objectives. Exams, for example, are, in principle, an instrument of evaluation; however, their results have become the real objective of work done by students. What matters is not the learning process; what matters is getting a good grade. What matters is not acquiring skills; the important thing is to pass the requisite number of exams. The degree represents, in this sense, the sum total of all results obtained in successive examinations and not evidence of a real learning process having taken place. Grades, then, become a curtain that hide reality; they block access to it and impede the penetration of consciousness formation that can occur in academic work. Grades are one of the most formidable obstacles that academics confront when they undertake an effort to raise consciousness. Reality does not interest the student, grades do.

Evaluation, however, can and should become one of the most effective processes for consciousness raising. To achieve this one will have to focus upon the evaluation, not in order to overcome difficulties that are purely artificial, but rather to measure the knowledge acquired from reality and in reality, and to demonstrate the ability developed to solve real tasks or problems. In this way, evaluation will not only be at the core of academic work which, to a great extent, could in fact do without the traditional system of grading, but also provide a continual measurement of reality for a particular academic undertaking. All evaluation should presuppose the opinion of the marginal and the oppressed as the voice of the people making itself heard above the values of what is carried out at the university. Seen in this manner, evaluation would not only be one more element in the development of consciousness, but probably it would be the most effective mechanism to ensure that consciousness raising does not remain just mere words and grandiloquent goals.

Complementary and structural mechanisms are not necessarily exclusive. On the contrary, a great measure of their effectiveness depends on their being applied simultaneously. It is very possible that the work that most faithfully reflects the essence of a university is that of raising consciousness. In other words, the scientific research, for example, that denounces problems and their causes critically and then elaborates possible solutions, can transform consciences and signal the road to liberation. If this is indeed the case, undoubtedly our universities should not overlook any means that might contribute effectively to a greater realization of this historic mission.

Limits of Consciousness Raising at the University

Just as it is important to start with an analysis of reality in order to know where our work at the university takes root, it is very important to reflect, however briefly, on the limits of this endeavor. That is to say, we need to be aware of where the work of consciousness raising at the university can and cannot exert influence. A position that is very dangerous is that held by someone who ignores the possibilities and limits of this task. As we said before, there is nothing more dangerous than the ignorant individual who believes he knows. In this sense, the Latin American university may have to recognize that it has sinned frequently and very naively.

We can distinguish between two types of limitations to the work of the university in developing consciousness: first, those limits that are imposed by academic reality itself and secondly, those that emerge from the realm in which such activity is undertaken.

LIMITS IMPOSED BY THE REALITY OF THE UNIVERSITY ITSELF

It is true that in our social environment the university constitutes a power of no little importance. But one must not forget that it is no more than a single power and in the confluence of forces it is not the most potent. In fact, the power of the university is contained in its capacity for thought, in its ability to be a critical and creative conscience. If the university does not think, if it does not exercise the power of science, it remains disarmed, inert. A university that does not think is a university that has failed in its mission. In this sense, it seems to me to be a serious error to try to convert the university into something that, because of its identity, it neither is nor can be. For example, the attempt to make it into a kind of political party.

We have to recognize that the university is a power that is much less powerful than economic, military, and even ecclesiastic power. Therefore, the university should try to increase its power precisely by focusing where its strengths lie; that is, in the realm of conscience. Conscience must imply science. And the university must apply its science to the analysis of reality's structural problems and present viable solutions as well as prepare those who can carry out such solutions. In this sense the university proposes, it does not dispose, and even less does it impose. If the university does not exercise its ability to propose, the truth is that it will end up not contributing anything of its own to the construction of a new reality.

At the same time, we should not lose sight of the university's limitations that are due to the academic personnel that fill its ranks. We academics, as much as I hate to admit it, make up a characteristic social group with values, guiding principles, and customs that are closer to those of the bourgeoisie than to those of any other social class. Therefore, we enjoy a maximum possible awareness for our group, beyond which we cannot go without changing as a group. It is very possible that the university's awareness, when structurally considered, is located at levels that are distinct from the level of personal awareness of its professors. In some cases, its awareness may be more profound, in others, more superficial. But, in any case, the university continues to realize itself and shape its goals through the work of its academic personnel—a personnel that also have many limitations, and not only as far as its awareness of reality is concerned. The truth is that many aspects of our society escape us—that is, we cannot grasp the very basic elements of our own problems. All of this marks a limitation for the university, even with regard to those tasks that are proper to it and where it possesses power. It is important, then, to become aware of those limitations that are due to the nature of our academic personnel.

Finally, we should not forget the limited role that consciousness plays with respect to our peoples. The university seeks for itself a critical and creative consciousness. We know that consciousness is dynamic;

hence, as we said before, it is the strength of the university. We know that consciousness has its own weight, and we hope that this weight will influence the scale of history. However, it is not typical for the university to become an active executor of what is indicated by conscience. It is not part of the university's role to execute those changes that it has inspired and advocated. That execution requires another type of power and another type of organization that the university neither has nor is competent to provide. It is important to underscore this limitation so that we do not ask of the university what it cannot give, nor presume to change it into something that it cannot be. Either we believe in the effectiveness of science and conscience or we do not. If we believe, we will have to allow it to function. If we do not believe, and we wish to change our societies, the best that we can do is leave the university and dedicate ourselves to something else.

LIMITATIONS BECAUSE OF THE REALM IN WHICH THE UNIVERSITY OPERATES

Outside of the limitations that are intrinsic to the university, we find others that arise from its particular situation and historical context. And the first limitations come imposed, naturally, by the socio-political structure. It is not worth deceiving ourselves about the margins of action permitted to our universities. The still very recent interventions by the political military power at several Central American universities are bitter lessons that must be learned. It is very clear that the current political powers, pressured more and more by concerns of economic power, are no longer very afraid of an open confrontation with the university—at least as long as the university is nothing more than an elitist and paranoid environment. This type of conflict may be in the interests of political power since it hides problems that are far more serious in nature. And to ignore such a set of circumstances is to bet on a sure loser.

In conclusion, there are also those limitations that originate in the socio-historical realm. In fact, the process of developing a critical consciousness functions within a people at a particular moment of their history, in a context that presents a specific balance of forces. There are no rules, either certain or fixed. But something is certainly evident: it is that specific historical periods, both at the international as well as at the national level, are different and offer opportunities that are very distinct. It will be up to the university, in its ability to read historical signs, to discern such signs and make the maximum use of them.

By Way of Conclusion

It is important to know our limits, just as it is important to know our strengths and potential. Even more important is knowing the needs of our people and preparing ourselves so that our universities can serve those needs. A university that, under the guise of some excuse or other, never undertakes an effort to raise consciousness nor enters into conflict with the established order in support of the oppressed can hardly be considered a Central American university. At least our people will not recognize such a university as one of their own.

It is, however, important that we analyze very carefully to what extent we serve the goal of liberation, to what extent the structures of our university seek to accomplish or not accomplish the work of consciousness formation. In the face of this overwhelming need to raise consciousness, we experience the need for a serious examination of our own conscience—a realistic unadorned examination, but one that will lead to some practical and viable conclusions. Our reflection must also entertain practical applications. A thought that is not capable of affecting reality is an empty thought. And our people are in no mood for either empty thoughts or flowery speech.

Power and Social Structure

Segundo Montes

12. What Is The Dominant Mode of Production in El Salvador? *

TRANSLATION BY PHILLIP BERRYMAN

The question in the title is not for an examination in an introductory economics course, nor is it asked out of naiveté. Nor is it the product of an ignorance of economics, if indeed economics aims at getting down to the fundamentals of the real socio-economic structure, which is highly complex and cannot be explained with simplistic or *a priori* principles. Raising a question like this one, analyzing it in depth, and discussing it in a scholarly way can be helpful for understanding the real situation better, and perhaps for rethinking certain assumptions tranquilly taken for granted.

My interest does not derive from a purely scholastic or nominalistic concern over concepts. I do not question those termed mode of production, capitalist mode of production, or dominant mode of production; indeed I accept them as they are generally understood (Bartra, 1973). The situation in which we find ourselves and the deep crisis running through our country force us not only to reexamine data and the analyses to which they lead, but also to question our initial principles (the thesis that the capitalist mode of production is dominant) if we do not want to reach the point of saying that it is reality that is mistaken. One can easily say that the Salvadoran economy is in a deep crisis, but reality does not entirely concur with that statement. The discussion presented in this article can help both to clarify the composition of the Salvadoran economy and to discover what part of it is in deep crisis, what its causes are, and how to deal with this crisis.

If asked the question in the title, economists will invariably acknowledge that different modes of production coexist in El Salvador (as well as in other, especially underdeveloped, countries) but that the capitalist mode is the dominant one. I will present this reply as thesis (which I will try to support). If I counter somewhat exaggeratedly with its negation, the antithesis (not to make it look ridiculous, but to give it a more

---

*Montes (1983a); see the Bibliography in the back of the book.

antithetical character), perhaps I can then achieve a synthesis that can push us further towards a more profound knowledge of our reality.

Thesis: the dominant mode of production is capitalist.

From the standpoint of economics, the thesis does not seem to give rise to any consistent and systematic doubt. It is clearly and explicitly acknowledged that different modes of production co-exist in El Salvador. Alongside the capitalist mode of production, there are in varying degrees other modes also which I will call "non-capitalist" without getting caught up in discussing whether they are feudal or not (peasant economy, tenant farming, servitude, craft forms, precarious modes of subsistence economy, and so forth). Despite the fact that various modes of production co-exist, the general consensus is that in El Salvador the dominant mode is capitalist, in both its international and domestic dimensions.

With regard to the external dimension the argument is that our economy is articulated with the world capitalist economy through the international division of labor. Our products are sold and we acquire goods and services from abroad within a capitalist system. Our currency is tied to world capitalism and is subject to its laws, thus pulling in its train our whole financial system. Our various kinds of exchange with the rest of the world, plus the behavior patterns and expectations generated, and the technology used in production, distribution, administration, and other aspects of the economy are all governed by capitalist norms, and imbued with its spirit and subject to its laws.

Domestically, the same pattern is reproduced on a different and specific level. The production of goods and services aimed at the world market (and to a lesser extent at the internal market) is carried out within a capitalist mode—or at least such a mode is making increasing inroads—whether it be in the concentration of capital, in applied technology, in administration, in the proletarization of labor, or in the social relations established. Although it may not be the most modern, the primary sector is the most important one for the country, and it reflects the gradual penetration of capitalism and the consequent gradual proletarization of the rural population (Montes, 1980c).

The rules of capitalism also govern the acquisition of goods and services for the internal market and their distribution within the country, or their processing for a new cycle of production or consumption. The circulation of money, the internal finance system, a good part of trade (at least that of goods and services acquired on the international market or in the domestic capitalist productive system), and the more dynamic parts of the secondary and tertiary sectors are also governed by the laws of capitalism. Economic statistics and econometric calculations, which are the essential foundation for the science of economics, are primarily, though not exclusively, focused on indicators and measures of the capitalist mode of production.

The assertion that the capitalist mode of production is dominant is based not only on what has just been detailed, not only on the overall thrust of the world and hence of our national economy's articulation with it, nor on the fact that the capitalist sector is the most modern and dynamic part of the national economy, but also on the observation that the capitalist mode is gradually penetrating and permeating the other modes of production, linking and articulating them with the market economy or eliminating them through competition.

Economics is a positive and *a posteriori* science, based on data. Analysis of the data leads to inductions which are subsequently raised to the level of more or less universal formulations striving to become laws, although only as probabilities. However, if the data are partial, or even worse, if the methodological and epistemological principles behind the selection of the data are not solid enough, we run the risk of building a house of cards or erecting a structure with no foundation. Although questioning those very principles may destabilize our apparent security, that questioning can also contribute towards laying a more solid foundation towards a better knowledge of reality, which is so complex. Formulating the antithesis and the reasons for it can thus offer a contribution to this scientific discussion and exercise.

Antithesis: the dominant mode of production is not capitalist

From the sociological perspective, everything seems to indicate that the dominant mode of production in the country is not capitalist. This is not to deny or dismiss the data supporting either the thesis or the claim that the capitalist mode of production plays a role in the country. Rather, an array of data indicates that if the non-capitalist mode of production is not the dominant mode, it is at least the *predominant* one. The sociological perspective which focuses on society and social relations does not look at reality from the viewpoint of economics and the statistics on which it is based. It leads us to assert that, in general, the bulk of society is scarcely affected by the capitalist economy (mode of production), its economic and social relations, its articulation with the international market, the statistics already mentioned, the balance of payments, international reserves (or lack of them), per capita income, and so forth. This is true so far as the conscious and direct effects of the capitalist economy are concerned, and in addition there is little by way of either unconscious or indirect effects.

Data on the Salvadoran economy offer some unusual figures and proportions. If we look at 1979, the last "normal" year, which was also the one when figures (transformed into current prices) reached their highest point ever, 25.8% of the gross national product came from the primary sector (farming and ranching 25.7%; mining and quarrying 0.1%); 31.7% came from the secondary sector (manufacturing 25.9%; public and private construction 5.8%); and 42.5% came from the tertiary sector (Indicadores Económicos y Sociales, July-Dec. 1981). This distribution by sectors may be concealing something, since no one can doubt that the primary sector is the most important, especially since it makes up the largest part of Salvadoran exports (70.9%). Moreover, the size of the tertiary sector in an underdeveloped country also conceals (or perhaps reveals) a part of the reality since it contains elements that are both not productive and non-capitalist. It may be that domestic service is not taken into account in this category. Certainly domestic service does not enter into capitalist social relations, but it may be one of the largest sources of employment, if indeed not the largest (unfortunately we do not have trustworthy statistics on this kind of work).

We find that in the primary sector (i.e., in farming and ranching), 84% of all properties are small holdings, to which we should add the relatively small percentage of areas with tenant farmer arrangements (6.3% in 1971). Among families in the rural areas, 54.4% worked on small holdings in 1975 and another 41.1% not only had no land but could not find steady work throughout the year, since only 37.1% of the rural EAP [economically active population] have full time work (Montes, 1980e).

In the manufacturing sector (the most important part of the secondary sector), of the country's 9,874 enterprises, 88.6% have four employees or less, and hence they are mainly craft operations (they are classified as "non-capitalist production"). If we include agro-industry we find in 1978 that of 10,065 various kinds of manufacturing enterprises 86.9% are similarly non-capitalist (Peña, 1982, 1982; CUDI, 1982).

In the tertiary sector of the economy, it is trade that has the highest percentage; (it is moreover the only one for which I have data). Among the 2,301 enterprises, 41.4% employ four persons or less (Montoya, 1982), and thus a good part of trade falls into the "craft" category and does not exhibit capitalist relations of production.

If the proletarization of the labor force, the sign of which is working for steady wages under contract, is a valid measure of social relations resulting from the capitalist mode of production, the figures given are telling us something about the antithesis we have formulated. The dominant mode of production is not capitalist, and actually the *predominant* mode is non-capitalist in each of the three sectors of the economy: a sizeable majority of the population does not have a steady wage paying job, does not possess even a minimal means of production, or gets its basic income from work that is not strictly governed by capitalist relations.

I think that the fact that workers are covered by ISSS [Salvadoran Social Security Institute] is an important indicator that they have steady work and are part of a capitalist mode of production. (The ISS is primarily a health care system for employees of the government and of the larger private companies and covers only a small number of workers in the primary sector.) In 1979 the country had an EAP of 1,575,633 people of whom only 203,429 or 12.9% were working in industry, which is the most capitalist part of the economy and the one that enrolls the largest number of people in the ISSS. That same year (when Salvadoran Social Security reached its peak) the total number of people enrolled was 225,489 or 14.8% of the total EAP, but only 87,325 or 14.9% of the manufacturing sector was covered. Since the percentages covered and the totals are almost equal, it is possible that the same relationship obtains in the other sectors. Furthermore the urban population is more likely to be covered by ISSS, and although almost all members are urban, no more than 30% of the urban population are covered by these programs (Innocenti, 1983).

Reviewing the data presented thus far, we see that the bulk of Salvadoran society does not participate in the strict sense, or fully, in capitalist relations of production since most people do not have steady wage labor, including membership in ISSS. In the primary sector (farming and ranching) no more than 37.1% of the rural population has full time work all year. The current reforms, and specifically the agrarian reform, have not changed the situation qualitatively, given its limitations in terms of land area affected, families benefitted, and the effectiveness of implementation (CUDI, 1982; ECA, May-June 1982). In the manufacturing sector 88.6% of the enterprises are not governed by capitalist relations, and the same is true of at least 41.4% of the trade and the service categories, especially domestic service which is so widespread and involves so many people. In any case, the fact that no more than 30% of the urban population (and only 14.8% of the whole country) is covered by ISSS reveals to us the nature of their work. Thus we see that most of the Salvadoran population receives its sustenance by taking part in non-capitalist modes of production, exclusively, predominantly, or complementarily.

Many of them—I daresay the majority, although I cannot prove it with irrefutable data—especially in the rural areas (which includes at least 60% of the population according to the most recent census), do not participate in the monetary and market economy. That does not mean that they do not use money from time to time or go to the market. Indeed many of them, at least temporarily, work for wages and receive money, but that is only as a complement to their subsistence mode. They immediately hand that money over in order to pay debts contracted, and so maintain their credit, in the local store which is governed by non-capitalist relations towards its customers. They also use their scarce money as an instrument of exchange (as cacao was used in former times) given current demands and customs, but they do not use it specifically as money in itself (monetary value). By the same token, they do not make significant contributions to the expenses of the state through taxes, either because they have no property, or because they do not participate even minimally in the market, where indirect taxes are charged.

Since this large portion (or majority) of society does not participate (except marginally) in the wage market, it does not participate in the consumer goods and services market either. It does not obtain its food, housing, fuel, medicine, and so forth in the market but produces them or obtains them (or most of them) from nature as simple gatherers of these things. These people produce or gather their basic food; their fuel is firewood from the hills; their housing is built from natural materials at hand or from trash; their lighting is that of the sun and sometimes a device they buy plus cheap fuel; their medicines are primarily natural remedies, and when they seek a more modern type of care they go to charitable institutions since they do not have money to pay for personal services (they are not covered by ISSS).

If the antithesis is valid in normal situations, it can be even more obvious in a crisis period.

Major crises not only shake structures, but they also challenge the theories or foundations on which they rest. The great crisis El Salvador has been experiencing during the last four years [written in 1983] can help us clarify what we are analyzing in order to understand better the Salvadoran reality. The various studies done during this period (CUDI, *Proceso*, *ECA*, passim) demonstrate a continual decline in all indicators so striking that observers unanimously predict that the situation cannot be maintained, that we have hit bottom, that economic apocalypse is on the horizon, and so forth. Nevertheless, such predictions do not come true. Either reality itself is mistaken, or the analyses are not correct.

The data are unquestionably correct. Hence we can only conclude that they are partial and that we should revise our original ideas. Accepting the proposed antithesis helps understand these factors better. That is, if the capitalist mode of production is not the dominant one, then the data invoked, since they only relate to the capitalist mode of production, support at most evidence that this mode of production is heading for disaster. But, given how little of the total economy it actually represents, the damage it has suffered can be repaired with many millions in foreign aid (mainly from the United States) (CUDI, *Proceso*, *ECA*, passim).

The Salvadoran economy, however, is not crumbling, and one explanation could be that the non-capitalist mode of production, which is the dominant (or *predominant*) one in the country, is not affected by the crisis, or at least not in an utterly decisive way. If the majority of the population does not participate in the market (at least substantially and basically), the lack of foreign exchange and goods, price inflation, and so forth, do not have a great impact on it. The same can be said of the balance of payments, the costs of fuel, manufactured products, meat, and milk, cutoffs in electricity and drinking water, the high cost and scarcity of housing, and so forth, all of which are goods and services to which the majority never had access. The fact that the current rate of open unemployment is more than 38% (*Proceso*, 1982)—and might be higher than 60% if underemployment and disguised unemployment were taken into account—does not affect the majority much because they were not involved in the labor market previously. These people endured similar and perhaps higher levels of unemployment previously. We could continue along the same line with other sets of economic indicators.

All of this obliges us to rethink our methodology and assumptions for gathering and analyzing data. The fact that most of the population is surviving runs counter to the data: If 3,000 calories are the recommended daily amount and one cannot live with less than 2,000, according to the FAO [Food and Agriculture Organization], and if in El Salvador caloric production and consumption are considerably below 2,000 (76% of the Salvadoran people do not have enough income to meet their basic food needs), either the population is dying or more calories are being consumed than those accounted for. The fact that they are not dying must mean that the available data (CUDI, 1982) do not take into account a whole series of foods being produced, gathered, and consumed in addition to those that enter into statistics. Something similar could be done with regard to data like the gross domestic product and per capita production, the real income and expenditures of the population, consumption of goods, and so forth. All this remains outside official data, since it does not enter the market and the capitalist mode of production to which most of the data refer. If indeed the non-capitalist mode of production turns out to be the *predominant* one, the margin of error (or if you will the lack of precision and inability to measure) is quite considerable, and it would explain why reality does not live up to predictions and calculations—and even less so when the national capitalist system is in crisis.

Seeking a Synthesis

At least methodologically, the synthesis must be the negation of both thesis and antithesis. That is, we cannot come to the conclusion that the dominant mode of production in El Salvador is either capitalist or non-capitalist.

There is a great temptation, not only in principle but also in our perception of the situation, to assert that there is not one dominant mode of production, nor a single economic system in the country, but that two parallel and independent modes of production coexist with one another, each with its own characteristics and drives. Nevertheless, this is also not quite true. There are indeed two such modes of production, but they are not parallel and independent. They are closely connected and mesh together. The capitalist mode of production needs the non-capitalist one, and keeps it going for its own use, and thoroughly permeates it (Montes, 1980c). The non-capitalist mode also, in the present situation, needs the capitalist mode for its own precarious subsistence, and in order to complement its own income, to go to the market from time to time to sell its surpluses, and to acquire goods it does not produce but needs, as well as acquiring a little money for exchange. Is it, however, the capitalist mode of production that most invades and subjects its opposite? Perhaps in times of serious crisis like the present, the tendency is reversed. If so, many things could be explained. At the very least we could assert that the Salvadoran economic system taken as a whole is neither capitalist nor non-capitalist (although it resembles and has elements of both), but that it, the Salvadoran economic system, is something distinct, specific, Salvadoran (without excluding others like it), underdeveloped, peripheral, dependent, or however one might prefer, and that within it the two modes of production coexist in intimate connection and issue in another specific mode.

Perhaps a comparison or image can help understand this phenomenon better. Cancer is a living organism, which is caused or induced by external carcinogens, but it needs a larger autonomous living organism in which it can be implanted and from which it draws life (the receiving organism may draw some benefit from not rejecting it). The cancer keeps advancing at the expense of the host organism and it extends its tendrils everywhere—extracting food and life, and completely invading it, weakening and strangling it until death ensues. When the host organism dies, however, the cancer also perishes since it needs the host in order to live; unconsciously in its ambition for domination and parasitical exploitation, the cancer "commits suicide." The Salvadoran economy was non-capitalist, but the capitalist mode of production was brought in from outside and implanted in this economy and grew at its expense. Little by little it has invaded and penetrated the original organism and gradually weakened it. The capitalist mode continued to develop and gain strength while suffocating the host, almost to the point of strangling it. However it needs the host in order to live; if it kills the non-capitalist mode of production, it will commit suicide and disappear as Salvadoran capitalism, since it is not autonomous. In the current crisis this symbiosis may be undergoing at least a temporary reversal.

Segundo Montes

13. Classes and Social Movements in El Salvador*

TRANSLATION BY PHILLIP BERRYMAN

Structural analysis of social classes

Using the analytical elements in Marx's historical works and Lenin's more abstract and theoretical formulations (Lenin, 1975) supplemented by critical new elements (Gurvitch, 1971), I will first attempt to quantify how many people belong to each class and stratum and their respective subdivisions (fraction, sectors, and subsectors). Then, I will address three aspects of El Salvador's current class structure: 1) the place in the concrete mode of production of the various classes and sectors and their resultant social relations; 2) the perception different persons and groups have of that social reality; and 3) class consciousness and the options to which it leads. (Perception refers to a subjective element; consciousness to an adequate correspondence between perception and reality that can inform both individual and collective action.) Through a study of class structure, in the light of these three aspects, we will be able to grasp the behavior of distinct social forces during specific periods of history.

QUANTITATIVE ESTIMATE OF CLASS COMPOSITION

Note: This section on the class structure in Salvadoran society has been omitted. Montes attempted to summarize the percentage of Salvadoran families that fit into each of the categories mentioned in Table 1 below. The attempt confronted numerous difficulties, such as imprecise definitions of the categories, incomplete data, inconsistencies in official statistics, inability to conduct certain kinds of surveys, the rapidly changing social composition brought about by the war, repression, and resulting migrations, and the distortions resulting from the monetary remittances received by many families from relatives in the United States.

---

*Montes (1989a); see Bibliography in the back of this book.

253

Table 1 (which nicely encapsulates most of the information originally pre-sented in this section) represents an estimate, based on data for the year 1980 (Montes, 1984a). Although it cannot be considered as more than a rough ap-proximation, since the total percentage adds up to > 100%, it does serve to give a sense of the distribution of families among the classes, a baseline for measuring subsequent changes. For Montes, the two "fundamental" classes were the domi-nant and the dominated, and in a capitalistic economy the characteristic frac-tions are respectively the bourgeoisie and the proletariat, which together amount to < 30 % of Salvadoran families [cf. Montes (1983a); Chapter 12, this volume]. He noted that events since 1980, including the war and the Agrarian Reform, had little effect on the composition of the dominant class (PERA, 1985; Thome, 1984; Colindres, 1977; Sevilla, 1984; Montes, 1988d). But there had been drastic changes in the dominated class, for it had been profoundly recast since 1980 by events. For example, in 1985, unemployment had grown to 27.4%, particularly among the semiproletariat who worked small agricultural plots. Typically 1.5 hectares (3.7 acres) in size, such plots had provided those semiproletarians with an average of only 49 days of work per year. Thus they needed to be able each year to sell some of their unused labor in order to supplement their incomes (Montes, 1984a; 1986c; 1988b; Sermeño, 1988). THE EDITORS

PLACE IN THE MODE OF PRODUCTION AND RESULTANT SOCIAL RELATIONS

The place occupied by different classes in the mode of production and the social relations that result are, in general, neither uniform nor homogeneous. The dominant class represents an exception. Its members occupy their place as owners of the means of production or, in the case of upper management, by virtue of their critical functions in the produc-tion process. Social relations are predominantly capitalist. Increasingly, due to the roles being played by administrative personnel, the real own-ers are removed from direct relations with the labor force.

The position of the dominated class in the mode of production is quite heterogeneous, as are the various resulting social relations. Prole-tarians occupy a specific, clear, and uniform place, and their relations with the dominant class are well defined by class struggle. Much the same applies to the fractions of semiproletarians, underemployed, and unemployed when they sell their labor. Semiproletarians—when they are not selling their labor—occupy a different place in the capitalist sys-tem since they own some means of production (albeit precarious and in-sufficient), which enables them to partly reproduce their labor power and to sell some of this production on the market. In doing so, they not only reinforce the system and its extraction of surplus value, thus aug-menting the overall reserve army of labor, but they also inadvertently ensure a sufficient supply of rural labor during periods of greatest de-mand at the plantations which produce exports (Montes, 1986c). The underemployed—insofar as they are not the same as the semiprole-tarians—and the unemployed constitute the greatest mass of the reserve

Table 1. Quantitative Estimate of Class Composition in El Salvador (1980)

Class	Fractions	Sectors	Subsectors
0.76% *Dominant*	**< 0.01%** rentiers **0.76%** bourgeoisie	agrarian financial industrial services	**0.28%** large owners **0.06%** upper management **0.42%** medium owners
26.7% *Middle strata* *Petite bourgeoisie*	**3.4%** "intelligentsia" **10.7%** salaried workers **12.6%** small owners	agrarian industrial services	
77.5% *Dominated*	**31.8%** semiproletarians **25.6%** proletariat **14.4%** unemployed / underemployed - - - - - displaced refugees recipients of dollars from relatives in U.S.	agrarian industrial services domestic service	
< 1.0% *Bottom stratum*	**< 0.1%** lumpen		

Note: Figures do not add to 100% totals because rough estimates had to be made by Montes from incomplete and approximated data. THE EDITORS

labor army, along with the displaced fraction. [This fraction did not enter into the analysis of Table 1.] As long as they do not sell their labor power, their social relations within the mode of production are different from those of the proletarians. . . . The domestic service sector occupies yet another place in the mode of production; working a longer day, they often live in the same house as their employers, and are paid partly in money and partly in food and other basic services. Their social relations are not properly capitalist but personal rather; that is, pre-capitalist, and more those of servant/master, often including sexual "rights" for the male employers their female employees.

Unless they are contracted for some kind of work, the displaced do not occupy any place in the mode of production—often they do not even acquire goods in the market—but rather serve as the reserve labor army. They survive on the edge thanks to international donations. Their social relations are the outgrowth of their dependence on humanitarian assistance and are linked to a growing ideological and political dependence (IDHUCA, 1985, 1986). Finally, there are the [about 24%] Salvadoran families who receive dollar remittances from relatives who have gone to the United States (Montes 1987a). These remittances are often a family's only monetary income, and on average represent 60% of the income of these families. . . . The fact that they receive remittances and exchange them for local currency differentiates their place in the mode of production. Their social relations vary according to whether they contract their labor power and how often they need to sell it, and to how involved they become in the market of goods and services. To a significant degree, however, this large group's social relations have more to do with the market for labor, goods, and services, and class and ethnic struggles in the United States than they do with the domestic market.

In the middle strata there is also great heterogeneity. The "intelligencia," as they strive for consensus and attempt to shape civil society, are essential to the ideological reproduction of the system and its mode of production. Salaried employees too are essential to this process, in the sense that they are instrumental in maintaining both civil and political society. All of these groups actually sell their labor and so they could be placed on a par with the proletariat, but objectively they occupy a different place (irrespective of their subjective perception and socio-political stance) not only with regard to their economic and social rewards but also in their work. The resulting social relations are those that derive from their being tools for keeping the proletarian class in subjection and for helping to extract surplus value. There is a contrast when we consider the position of small owners. Ordinarily, they do not hire wage labor, but they go to market to sell their products and, in doing so, they transfer surplus value to capital, as they also do in acquiring supplies, credit, and other kinds of goods, as well as in exploiting labor power, either their own or that of unpaid family members who work on that property. Their social relations within the work group are normally based on family ties and on their exploitation of minors, children, and more distant relatives, while externally those relations are characterized by competition and struggle with intermediaries and capital. Those relations do not become antagonistic, however, as long as their family property and economy are maintained and reproduced....

PERCEPTION OF SOCIAL REALITY

The position people occupy in the production mode and the resulting objective social relations are one thing; their subjective and ideologized perception of that reality—leading to alienation or correct consciousness—is something quite distinct.

While the dominant class's perception of reality is in general correct, . . . that of the dominated class is not always so, and it is much less uniform. Semiproletarians often do not feel that they are being exploited by capital. Having so internalized alienation, they feel that, as owners of the means of production, they and their interests differ objectively from the other dominated fractions. The proletarians, who tend to be clearer and more coherent, have been acquiring an increasingly correct perception (except for those in the "public sector," who regard themselves as "salaried employees"). Nevertheless, within this fraction there are significant nuclei of alienation, which may be due to (a) fatalistic and fundamentalist religious practices [cf. Martín-Baró (1987b); and Chapter 20, *in this volume*]; (b) benefits received as a result of the reforms; (c) political positions and support they may have been given; (d) pre-capitalist bonds between permanent plantation workers and owners, or between craft workers and those who employ them; or (e) a memory that things were better under the owner of the farm before the agrarian reform and the establishment of production cooperatives (that are often managed and controlled by outside government officials).

Among the unemployed and underemployed, we find a variety of perceptions of the objective reality: a fatalistic interpretation, a predisposition to degrading servility, and a more correct interpretation of the reality. Finally, the perception of the displaced and refugees, if not that of resigned fatalism, is that the situation is temporary and will return to what obtained before their migration. They see the problem as due more to the war than to the structural causes that bring about both war and the vulnerability of their lives (IDHUCA, 1985; 1986). Hence they are victims of an alienation that is being deepened by a number of factors: their dependency at subsistence levels, the fact that they are being manipulated socially and politically, their gradual integration into the system which keeps co-opting them, and the indoctrination to which they are subjected through their sons who are recruited for military service. Those who receive remittances from relatives in the United States are thereby placed in a situation of privilege, and they are well aware of it. However, they are not so aware of the exploitation suffered by these relatives in the host country; nor are they aware of the degree of exploitation to which they themselves are subjected in El Salvador by the market, both in the goods they buy, and by the agencies and persons who handle the shipment and exchange of money (Montes, 1987a).

However, it is perhaps in the middle strata that the perception of reality is most alienated and shaped by ideology (Montes, 1980a; 1980e). Many in the "intelligentsia" fraction—excepting a large teacher sector—not only do not perceive their real place in the production mode as its salaried employees, but they see themselves as privileged, as independent intellectual creators of consensus or of a new society. They are therefore grateful to the system and to the dominant class for the opportunity afforded to them to develop their personal qualities and to create or communicate ideology. Among salaried employees there is great variation, ranging from a high level of correct consciousness to a maximum degree of alienation, in their perception of their objective reality, where it impinges on the system, the owners of the means of production, or the state. The system, the owners, and the state set them apart from others and from each other, pay them well and honor them, and so they feel that they are important and obligated to reproduce the system of domination in the working class. Sometimes they become fanatic instruments of exploitation or oppression of the very class to which, strictly speaking, they belong and from which they come. Finally, small property owners tend to . . . share the consciousness of owners and are sometimes allied to business associations, unaware of the degree of exploitation to which they are subjected by those same organizations, which they may defend and with which they stand in solidarity.

It is hard to measure or become familiar with the perception of reality by the lumpen proletariat without doing first hand research. While we may assume that the bosses and leaders correctly understand their place and relations in the system, we may also presume that most of those at the very bottom suffer from a deep alienation, not only caused by the system itself, but also as it is sometimes induced and deepened by intimidation mechanisms and blackmail on the part of those on top who lead and control this social stratum.

CLASS CONSCIOUSNESS AND THE OPTIONS TO WHICH IT LEADS

Class consciousness is not the same thing as perception of reality, although it is based on it, or at least on perceiving correctly. Nor is it a mechanical, automatic, and inevitable consequence of the class to which people belong. Class consciousness is more structural in nature; it is forged and consolidated along with the development of the production mode and of social forces, and it is manifested in organization and struggle during periods of relative social and political stability (Menjívar: 1979; Cabarrús: 1983, 1985; Cardenal 1985; Montes: 1984a, 1986c).

The dominant class is the only one that has had a completely consistent class consciousness and has maintained internal unity. Although this consciousness may have remained latent during the decades of development and greatest prosperity, it was energized to exert pressure and to put the apparatus of the state and the armed forces at the service of the dominant class, when the interests of the dominant class were felt to be jeopardized. That happened during the attempt at "Agrarian Transformation," so the dominant class demanded that strategies of repression and terror be implemented against those who threatened its interests (ECA (1976); Ellacuría (1976d); and Chapter 4, *in this volume*). On the other hand, divisions, splits, and deep alienation created over many years have been the prevailing characteristics within the dominated class. The small groups that are organized and struggling for their rights have been an exception. In the urban proletariat only a minority were unionized, and even so they were divided into a multitude of associations, federations, and tendencies (Samayoa and Galván, 1979a; 1979b; Montes, 1984a). Unionization in rural areas was illegal; and while on the one hand small property owners and permanent plantation workers refused to participate in any way in popular organizations and some even served in repressive organizations such as ORDEN, on the other hand the participation of the rural semiproletariat and proletariat in popular organizations tended to be divided (Cabarrús, 1983; 1985; Cardenal, 1985). During the attempted "Agrarian Transformation" and the accompanying debate, the potential beneficiaries stood by passively on the sidelines (Montes, 1986c). Within the middle strata, the division and alienation usually characterizing these groups has been the prevailing tendency, although there were small pockets of consciousness and organization, mainly among the country's school teachers. . . . (UCA, 1971). Of course the national university (UES) has been outstanding in its level of consciousness.

Living conditions steadily deteriorated as a result of those structures that violate the economic, social, and cultural rights of the vast majority—the structures of death (Montes, 1988b; see Chapter 7 *in this volume*). This deterioration, exacerbated by explosive events which it also caused, was to generate growing awareness and a consolidation of social classes (at least of the most consistent and combative groups within these classes). Among the explosive events are included: a) the war with Honduras; b) the failure to obtain its proposed objectives and the disastrous consequences (repatriation of 100,000 Salvadoran peasants and the subsequent pressure on the land and on the already scarce market for labor, the closing of the border* with Honduras and the resultant commercial isolation of El Salvador from regional trade); c) the electoral frauds of 1972 and 1977, which blocked the possibility of political change through elections (Hernandez-Pico et al., 1973); d) the failed attempt at the "Agrarian Transformation" proposed by the government in 1976; e) the

---

*See Chapter 3 (*this volume*) for more on both the background and the consequences of the "Soccer War" that preceded this border closing.

wave of repression against the incipient and weak peasant organizations, the Catholic Church, and other institutions; and f) the corresponding frustration of every hope for economic and social change through peaceful means. All of these developments were to lead to a greater unification of the dominant class which felt threatened, and to an option for the path of armed revolution, mainly by sectors of the "intelligentsia" and middle strata. They also led to the expansion and gradual unification of popular organizing in a part of the peasantry, to the strengthening of the most conscious part of the urban proletariat, and to the strengthening and subsequent alliance of sectors of the middle strata, from Church authorities to important groups of intellectuals and salaried workers, even reaching into the armed forces. The vast majority, however, the masses, who were neither conscious nor organized, tended to remain on the sidelines, passive towardss the ever accelerating crisis.

Class consciousness and the option to which it leads both become more consistent in the class struggle itself; they become more clearly revealed in the behavior of the various social forces at critical conjunctures, especially in an organic crisis such as that experienced by the Salvadoran historic bloc today ....

Conjunctural analysis of social forces

It is not primarily because the link between the dominant class and organic intellectuals has been broken—first by the October 15, 1979 coup and then by the shift of some intellectuals, military people, and government officials to the revolutionary fronts (democratic or armed)—that the present Salvadoran crisis can be characterized as an "organic crisis" in accordance with Gramscian analysis (Portelli, 1978). That link could be, and to some extent has been, reestablished. Rather the reason that the crisis can be so characterized is that hegemony over society as a whole has been dissolved. It has not been possible to reconstitute civil society nor to attain consensus within the whole society which is divided over two clashing projects. While the historic bloc *in crisis* is striving for a consensus through anti-revolutionary ideology and repeated elections, which supposedly delegitimize the revolutionary alternative, the historic bloc *in formation* is also seeking a consensus through a project and an ideology assumed to be in accordance with the interests of the dominated class, and through repeated proposals for dialogue-negotiation. Neither bloc achieves a consensus. Nor has it been possible to rebuild political society since the war is still going on. Neither of the two contending armed forces can defeat the other in the foreseeable future, and each side has zones under its control (the fact that the amounts of territory are unequal is irrelevant since each has enough to avoid defeat and to destabilize the other side and society as a whole and to prevent the rebuilding of a single political society).

EXPLOSION OF THE ORGANIC CRISIS

In my judgment the critical moment when the organic crisis exploded was not the final months of 1979 with the coup and its aftermath, which the dominant class tried to co-opt through various pressure mechanisms to the point where the first "revolutionary government junta" resigned and the army shifted to the right (*ECA*: September 1979-February 1980; UCA, 1982).* Rather the crucial events, of which we will identify four, took place during the first months of 1980.

1. Under pressure from the United States the armed forces broke their ties with the ruling class, became allied with the Christian Democrats, and committed themselves to reforms in economic structures (agriculture, banking, and foreign trade) while also opting to engage in counterinsurgency war and militarization of the country. They unleashed repression not only against armed revolutionary groups, but also against any organizations that might support those groups and resist the peace the armed forces were seeking to impose.

2. Having failed to repair the alliance in which the armed forces would defend its interests unconditionally, the ruling class came together and recognized the need to recreate its own instruments of domination and hegemony, which had been delegated to the military and the "auxiliary governing class" since 1931. For that purpose it needed a political party to represent it and defend its interests within the various branches of government, since the official party [PCN—National Conciliation Party] no longer served it and, involved in another kind of alliance, was taking a political direction that undermined the hegemony of the ruling class. Hence, after efforts at controlling or utilizing the already existing right-wing parties, the ruling class decided to create ARENA, build it up, and put it into the political ring. ARENA's initial efforts during the 1982-84 period were aimed at blocking progress on the agrarian reform. Then ARENA shifted to limiting the breadth and scope of the reform in the constitution. Later it sought to control or neutralize the

---

*In October 1979, a group of military officers executed a coup against the Salvadoran government and proclaimed their intention of carrying out revolutionary reforms (no doubt prompted by the Sandinista victory in Nicaragua in July of that year). Two of the three civilians in the subsequent junta were from the UCA as were a number of government ministers and high ranking officials. However, contrary to the declared intentions of the military members of the junta, violence against popular organizations increased dramatically, and hence in the first few days of 1980, all the civilians in the original junta resigned en masse and were soon replaced by civilians from the Christian Democrat party. The civilians who had worked in the junta became the core of the FDR (Revolutionary Democratic Front), which in turn became politically allied with the guerrilla organizations. P.B.

executive and legislative branches in any possible reform measures and finally to take power in the legislature and on the municipal level in 1988 and to aspire to gain control of the executive branch in 1989 and thus reconstitute the whole apparatus of class domination through the state.* At the same time ARENA was creating its own mechanisms for coercion and reorganizing political society through paramilitary groups, as well as through ongoing pressure, demands, proposals, and contacts with the military.

3. The dominated class took to the streets in San Salvador on January 22, 1980 first to show its cohesion and strength after the establishment of the National Coordinating Body (CN). With that action, this class became aware of the multiplicity and diversity of the organizations, fractions, and levels within it, as well as the support and sympathy it aroused in large sectors of the population. After undergoing repression and slaughter, however, both on this occasion and at the funeral of Archbishop Romero [in 1980], the dominated class became aware that the only alternative left was that of revolution, and it opted for insurrection and prolonged people's war, which required recruitment, training, and weapons.

4. The middle strata split and opted for opposing options. While strong and significant groups of both the "intelligentsia" and "white collar workers" joined the revolutionary fronts, both democratic and armed, another large sector believed that Christian Democracy represented its interests and was the political expression of its "class." Some thought a third way was possible, with their option resting on the social base of the middle strata. Those strata, however, had no coherent structure, economic, military, ideological, or social, and thus the basis for the proposal of such a third way was entirely superstructural, in the most abstract sense of that term. This sector found its efforts repeatedly frustrated, despite the support and resources provided by external and international forces whose hopes were based more on voluntaristic desires than on structural analyses (Montes, 1984a).

---

*The 1982 election for a constitutional assembly provided ARENA with a working majority in the assembly. (See also Martín-Baró (1982b); Chapter 16, *in this volume*.) Only forceful intervention by the U.S. ambassador prevented ARENA from having its leading figure, Roberto D'Aubuisson, elected president of the country. In the 1984 presidential election, D'Aubuisson was defeated by Jose Napoleon Duarte, but ARENA had a majority in the legislature until 1985. During the mid-1980s ARENA used its strength in the legislature to thwart any moves to extend the land reform. By 1988 the Christian Democrats had been discredited, and ARENA won a narrow majority in the legislature and won three-quarters of the mayors' posts in the country, as well. Finally in 1989, Alfredo Cristiani, who was regarded as representing the more moderate sector of ARENA, won the presidency. P.B.

From this point onwards, forces and alliances have shifted, social forces have won minor victories and suffered defeats, civilian and military leadership has changed, and repeated attempts to rebuild the historic bloc have failed. None of these minor conjunctures have led to a reconstitution of either political society or civil society. That is, no group has reestablished hegemony over society as a whole, and hence El Salvador remains in a situation of organic crisis, manifested in the civil war and the lack of national consensus. Throughout these years the two fundamental social forces—the ruling class which owns the means of production and the revolutionary movement which claims to represent the dominated class and to defend its interests—have continued to become more united, stronger, and more consolidated, contending not only with each other, but striving to win the support of, and establish an alliance with, the "middle sectors." A good portion of these sectors, however, stubbornly goes against history and the behavior or limits of existing structures, striving to become the core and basis of a new historic bloc (Montes, 1984a). If from a theoretically and universally valid perspective, the "middle strata" cannot become a true social class, let alone the fundamental class on which a new historic bloc can be built (Montes, 1980d), in El Salvador their future is even more chimerical, given how small a place they occupy in the class structure, as we have seen. There is the enormous concentration of property in a tiny group at the top as well, and the extreme polarization socially and ideologically among classes over the war. To conceive of these "middle strata" as the core and fundamental social class for an alternative approach to rebuilding a historic bloc is neither viable nor possible. At most it might be possible to build an alliance or strategic union between different social forces, who might become a pressure group and even a strong social movement aimed at achieving peace and a political solution to the conflict through a broad consensus.

. . . .

BEHAVIOR OF SOCIAL CLASSES

The degree of consciousness of each social class and its fractions can be comprehended and assessed through the behavior and options they adopt towards the various events occurring throughout the organic crisis. Since previously I dealt with that question up to December 1983 (Montes, 1984a), here I offer some analysis on developments and behavior during the last five years.

The dominant class has continued to become more united, stronger, and more consolidated. It has defended its economic interests through leadership of the trade associations which represent private enterprise, and through sustained struggle against all reform measures. Politically, its instrument has been the ARENA party, which has continued to increase its political power to the point where it won a majority in the assembly and in municipal councils in 1988 and is now getting ready for the final battle to gain total control over the state apparatus in 1989. Its aim in doing so is to reconstitute its hegemony over society and to restore the historic bloc that serves it.

. . . .

For its part the revolutionary vanguard of the dominated class is not only keeping up the insurgency war and becoming stronger militarily, but it has managed to maintain the social base necessary for confronting its enemy . . . and has forced matters to the point where it must be taken into account as a social and political force in developments in El Salvador, and must participate in dialogues aimed at resolving the crisis. The rapid and steady growth of the insurgent social base has been slowed by counterinsurgency strategy, by tens of thousands of murders of the civilian population and the resulting terror, and by the exile of more than a million Salvadorans who are largely hostile to the existing régime, and sympathetic to the revolutionary movements (particularly emigrants in Mesoamerica). Further hindrances have been the co-optation of a part of the peasantry that has benefitted from the agrarian reform and the depoliticization and passivity of a good proportion of those displaced within the country. These displaced fled from the war, but since they are in areas controlled by the government and must depend on aid in order to live, they are vulnerable to the campaign of ideological propaganda waged by the system. In addition, the induction of their children into the military creates internal conflict (they receive money from their sons, and when the latter are killed or wounded they blame not only the armed institution that forced them to fight but also the insurgents who actually killed them). Hence they tend to come down on the side of the system or at least remain passive and "neutral" in the conflict. It is foreseeable that this great mass of displaced people, especially the new generation, will be forced to join the until recently small lumpen, due to the trauma they have experienced, their lack of preparation for the new life into which they have been forced, the inability of the system to integrate them socially and economically, and the degrading experiences of dependency and of being used, which undermines whatever self-respect and self-image they may have. Such a development would substantially change the Salvadoran social structure, by shifting a large portion into the lowest stratum. (Particular attention should be given to what happens to the growing number of war wounded and those discharged from military service to see whether they are incorporated into productive work and into society, or whether they are also forced to swell the ranks of the lumpen).

Not only has the régime sought to delegitimize and to combat ideologically those social and labor organizations sympathetic to, or in solidarity with the insurgency, but it has repressed these organizations and has continually attempted to weaken and break them up. Nevertheless, the insurgent movement has devised new kinds of alliances and support within the dominated class and in the middle strata. Firmly committed social bases have been reestablished in the popular sectors. At the very time the popular organizations such as the CRM [Mass Revolutionary Coordinating Body] were suffering attrition, new organizations, such as Committees of Mothers, the UNTS [National Union of Salvadoran Workers], and many others were being formed.

It is the "alternative center project" that manifests the greatest inconsistency and least continuity, in accordance with the structural constraints already mentioned. Such a project cannot be based on any true social class, and hence there is an attempt to establish alliances with fractions and sectors revolving around the "middle strata." Because such an alliance cannot resolve existing problems and because economic and social expectations are not met, and the war goes on, this effort encounters continual frustrations, despite ongoing efforts to repair the situation through "social pacts" with the UPD [Popular Democratic Unity], with UNOC [National Worker-Peasant Union], or with cooperatives in the agrarian reform. . . . However, simply because they are organized and have some freedom, and because promises remain unfulfilled, and because they are continually subjected to political and ideological manipulation by the government and by outside agencies such as AIFLD, these organizations develop a certain degree of consciousness, and struggle for their own interests. But they also lose membership and undergo crisis at the grass roots level, leading once more to a new effort at organizing, manipulating, and co-opting social and labor forces into supporting the régime.*

In concluding this section, we will briefly analyze something striking in the workings of different social forces in El Salvador. New organizations continually emerge and split, they are continually being created and then falling apart, and being re-established. This is true both of efforts to create a centrist bloc and other efforts to take a more firm class option. I believe that this situation is to be explained primarily by the very organic crisis that Salvadoran society is undergoing, the sharp polarization created by that crisis, by the fundamental forces of the two opposing attempts to form a historic bloc as well as the attempt to form an alternative center bloc, and by their struggle to win over the various

---

*In the 1960s, AIFLD (American Institute for Free Labor Development), an AFL-CIO organization supported by the U.S. union, helped establish peasant organizations as an alternative to militant left organizations. Both the UPD and the UNOC were attempts by the Christian Democrats and the unions in the United States to establish moderate peasant organizations to support the Duarte government and to undercut the appeal of the left. (Popular Democratic Unity was known as the UPD, while the National Worker-Peasant Union was UNOC.) In both cases, however, members of these organizations became dissatisfied and moved to the left. When they did so, they lost U.S. funding and support. P.B.

social forces in order to broaden their base in the reconstruction or construction of the historic bloc. The result is that the various organizations joined together and their pacts and alliances are systematically and continually being worn away and undone in two ways. On the one hand, one group is continually accused through an ideological, physical, and psychological campaign of being tools of or facades for the insurgency, while those allied with the "effort at a center bloc" are under attack from the right, which regards them as a stepping stone towards the victory of the Marxist-Leninist left, and from the left which sees them as a means and instrument of the imperialist project. In addition, there is the continual pressure and effort on the part of the hegemonic groups in each project to radicalize, utilize, and absorb such organizations, subordinating their autonomy and their identity as labor organizations or other associations to politics. On the other hand, it is their failure as organizations to attain their objectives and the lack of a solution to the organic crisis that leads some of them to be radicalized, thus justifying the accusations and attacks mentioned, and leads others to become disillusioned and to quit. In any case the result is that the organization is distorted and withers away, both with regard to its objectives and as an instrument for resolving the organic crisis. Nonetheless, since the crisis remains unresolved and the living conditions of the vast majority and the organized sector continue to deteriorate, the very process creates pressures which prompt new efforts to come together both by reconstituting existing forces and by establishing or reestablishing alliances.

THE UNORGANIZED MASSES

Nevertheless, the vast majority of the population remains atomized and unorganized, lacking their own means of expression and of struggle for defending their interests. They can express themselves only infrequently, when they might be polled directly or when they give their opinion indirectly through voting. When polled, they have repeatedly declared that they regard the economic crisis and the war as the most serious problems, which must be resolved through dialogue or some other rational approach (Martín-Baró, 1987a; IUDOP, 1986-1988). With regard to elections, one can observe an ever declining participation by the people, which cannot be explained simply by saying that this method for the people to express their will and their approach to solving the crisis of the country is wearing thin, although that sentiment is probably at work (Montes, 1985c; 1988d). In the last election, in March 1988, approximately 1,100,000 Salvadorans, who were living in the country and were of voting age, did not go to the polls. Either they were not registered (300,000), or they were registered but did not receive their voting cards (300,000), or they had the cards but did not go to vote (500,000). All these figures were taken from official data supplied by the Central Electoral Council. Altogether these numbers almost equal the number of votes cast; but hardly 40% of the potential voters actually cast valid ballots since 220,000 votes were invalid (Montes, 1988d). If we exclude those who had real problems registering or in getting voting cards and those who were prevented from voting by fear or by the lack of transportation on election day, there is still a high percentage who chose to abstain from voting—plus the 19% who for the most part found no satisfactory option within the limited range of what was offered, or nothing that promised to resolve the fundamental problems affecting society as a whole.

Nevertheless, the elections reflect both the degree of consciousness and the degree of alienation of social classes, their fractions, and strata or other subdivisions. Insofar as the data for each one of these classes and fractions is valid, it is incomprehensible that the ARENA party, representing the interests of the dominant class, [which earlier was estimated to include at most 0.76% of Salvadoran families] can get almost a half million votes (48.1% of valid votes, 38.9% of the total cast and 17.9% of the hypothetically potential votes), a figure higher than the number of people in the ruling class and the middle strata combined—unless a high proportion of other social classes and fractions (many belonging to the dominated class) threw in their lot with this ideological and political option which is opposed to their own class extraction (Montes, 1988d). However, it is also incomprehensible that in the 1985 election the Christian Democrat party, the exponent and representative of the "middle strata," which make up between 10% and 26% of the population, got more than a half million valid votes (52.35%) and in 1988 got more than 300,000 (35.1% of valid votes, 28.4% of the total votes cast, and 13.1% of hypothetically potential votes), unless again a percentage of the members of the dominated class felt so alienated that they believed that a party responding to the interests of the "middle strata," and the United States project, could deal with their needs and resolve the country's problems in a way that served the great majority. Certainly the 1988 election has shown that the process and experience under the political leadership of Christian Democracy has stimulated a certain consciousness in the popular milieux, unless the alienation is so deep for some of them that they have gone over to vote for ARENA, not in order to "sharpen the contradictions," but with the hope of finding some minor relief from the situation and crisis in the country.

PERSPECTIVES

Given the present correlation of forces both domestically and internationally, it is unlikely that the Salvadoran social structure is going to change substantially—either through victory by the revolutionary process, or through a series of reforms and adjustments, and even less through the consolidation of the ruling class and its political expression in ARENA, and its likely conquest of political power in the executive branch.

Nor can we foresee either a military or a political solution to the civil war in the near or the foreseeable future. If U.S. representatives predict that it will take six or eight years for the army to attain a clear and irreversible supremacy over the insurgents, who in turn increasingly propose a "prolonged people's war," and if a "popular insurrection" does not look feasible, we cannot foresee the possibility of either side resolving the conflict militarily. A political solution through dialogue and negotiation is being put off rather than taken up seriously. Moreover, the present international correlation of forces is not favorable to a political solution, unless the administration in the United States exerts pressure in that direction (should the Democratic Party win and embrace such a policy), or unless the participation of the Democratic Convergence in the 1989 presidential elections should bring in a large number of voters who could exert pressure for political agreements.

An alternative course of events that might lead out of the impasse would require that the fractions and other subdivisions of the "middle strata," and especially the dominated class achieve a true consciousness. To do so, they would have to overcome their internalized alienation in order to achieve a strategic coordination among the different social forces within them or emanating from them, so as to serve as a huge pressure group within an overwhelming social movement demanding peace and the structural changes necessary in order to satisfy basic needs and safeguard the human rights of the vast majority.

If democracy is the system proclaimed as valid and desirable, and if the term is understood in its full etymological sense, we must admit that real and true democracy has never existed in El Salvador and that the people have never had power, since the dominated class, that is, the vast majority, not only has not had power but has not even had a political party representing it, defending its genuine interests, and emerging from within it. Political parties coming from the tiny ruling class cannot represent the majority or really defend its interests; at most they can make symbolic concessions in exchange for votes. Nor are parties and representatives arising from the small and splintered "middle strata" genuinely popular, nor do they represent or defend the interests of the dominated class, of the vast majority, no matter how much they may claim to be and may present themselves as popular (contrary to what structural analysis and their specific political practice reveal). The true path to democracy entails the consciousness-raising, unification, and organization of the vast majority, the dominated class, along with a part of the middle strata who, although they may not recognize it, objectively belong to this dominated class. In this way these will all give voice to their own political expression through a party that represents and defends their specific interests by safeguarding first the rights of the great majority, the rights of the people.

Segundo Montes

14. El Salvador: Its Land, Epicenter of The Crisis*

TRANSLATION BY PHILLIP BERRYMAN

Land, generating wealth through agricultural exploitation, has been El Salvador's only natural resource thus far. No fossil fuels or valuable minerals have been discovered in any significant amounts. The sea has not been a source of nourishment, wealth, or trade and has not even been used to attract any appreciable international tourism.

Moreover, throughout its history the Salvadoran economy has been structured primarily around holding and exploiting land. The result has been an underdeveloped and dependent economy. Development depends upon the secondary and tertiary sectors gradually becoming predominant in the economy of a country. These more profitable sectors can lead to a greater and ever ascending reproduction of capital. To depend basically and predominantly on the primary sector—especially when it is agriculture and not mining or fossil fuels—is tantamount to remaining immersed in underdevelopment and being prevented from moving forward. Furthermore, the agricultural sector and the primary sector as a whole are controlled internationally by dependency relationships that are not subject to challenge or negotiation. Its products are subject to regulated quotas and prices in accordance with the will and interests of traders and consumers who, by excluding the producers from this phase which involves more profit, monopolize the processes that transform and prepare products for consumption. These traders and consumers also set prices and conditions for the products and goods that El Salvador and other underdeveloped countries need to acquire on the international market for their subsistence and production.

Under such conditions, land naturally becomes the epicenter of economic, social, and political conflicts in El Salvador. We could almost say that the history of the country revolves around the struggle over land. I have previously connected the periods of successive crops to the social and political crises those crops occasioned and to the process whereby the Indians lost their identity and the Salvadoran population became racially homogeneous (Montes, 1980c).

---

*Montes (1986c); see Bibliography in the back of this book.

In the first period or phase there was plenty of land for the subsistence of both Indians and Spaniards, particularly since there was not enough demand in European markets for our natural products (cacao and balsam). Moreover, there were few Indians and their numbers were declining, and there were few Spaniards. Communal property and that of royal land concessions to Spaniards existed side by side more or less peacefully, although there were small local conflicts over boundaries (Casin, 1972). This system rested on the exploitation of Indian labor, mainly through the *encomienda* and the *repartimiento* [systems whereby the Spanish crown granted lands and the rights to quotas of Indians to work those lands to the conquistadores] (Montes, 1979b). The incipient process of "ladinization" [assimilation of Indians into the *ladino*; i.e. non-Indian, population] took place primarily through mixed marriages.

Competition over land arose during the indigo period since this product, which came from the xiquilite plant, was in great demand in the European market as its textile trade became more industrialized. The struggle over land, excessive exploitation of Indian labor, plus the constant forced recruitment of young men for the armies and wars of the *ladinos* were all behind the uprising of the Nonualco Indians led by Anastasio Aquino. His defeat was followed by repression of the Nonualcos (Arias Gomez, 1964). This event led not only to the punishment and repression of the rebels and to their loss of land and other "privileges." The main result was extremely important for Salvadoran society; *viz*, the *ladinization* of the people of Nonualco as they relinquished their characteristic ethnic and social customs, which exposed them to the suspicion of having taken part in a rebellion against the system. The only way to evade death or repression was to leave the area or become *ladinos* in order to melt into the rest of the population, which was mestizo.

Initially, the next or "coffee" period led to the suppression of the Indian communities and generated competition over land suitable for its cultivation. Later it provoked another very serious social and political crisis, the peasant uprising in the Izalco area which was similar to what had happened with the Nonualcos (Montes, 1979b). This last remaining Indian area of El Salvador underwent a *ladinization* process for self-protection in the face of the repression unleashed after these Izalcos were defeated (Montes, 1986i). Thus the Salvadoran population became racially uniform both as a result of gradual intermarriage and the intensive and violent *ladinization* process.

The context of the most recent period is the fact that the country has reached its agricultural limit with products of high demand in the international market (coffee, cotton, and sugar) and has also reached the "industrial limit" possible within the model that has been promoted in Central America, thus augmenting pressure on agriculture. Hence the struggle over land has reached its climax and has increased rural poverty, forced people out of peasant life, and increased the pauperization of the rural people who still constitute the majority in El Salvador (Montes, 1980c). As a consequence of this phase the country's greatest social and political crisis has arisen, and in early 1981 it turned into open civil war.

In social terms, the crisis has led to the disappearance of the small remaining outposts of peasant life—of a "peasant economy" to some degree—which still survived to some extent in marginal agricultural lands, which are also the most conflictive areas. The result has been that the masses of the Salvadoran people have become even more homogenized due to the overall tendency to proletarization, which means that people cannot find their place in society, because the system is not able to create enough permanent jobs in either the countryside or in towns and cities—not only temporarily when they have been displaced and had to rely on humanitarian aid (IDHUCA, 1985).

Revolutionary Agrarian Reforms

In El Salvador thus far there have been two agrarian reforms that we could call "revolutionary." The first came from outside the [indigenous] society; namely that introduced by the Spaniards for their own interests during the conquest and the subsequent colonial period. The second was carried out in 1881-82 by the resident ruling class, the liberals, also for their own interests. In both instances, the Indians were the dispossessed.

Both the sixteenth-century conquest and later colonization had a revolutionary impact on land. At the outset, the Spaniards wrested control over their territory from the Indian population, conveying title "legally" to the Spanish crown. They permitted some of the communal property system but as a concession; moreover it was restricted to particular areas. Besides thus handing over the land to a foreign and alien power, they also brought in a tenure system previously unknown to the Indians— private ownership of land. On top of this they added a labor structure based on slavery—that of the "forced serf" system (*encomiendas*) and the "forced wage laborer" system (*repartimientos*), both in sharp contrast to the Indians previous work which usually had been free and communal (Montes, 1979b). As a result the Indian population weakened and declined, and the process of social and cultural *ladinization* began. At the same time, a new socio-economic relationship, that of "forced semiproletarization" was introduced. Now the labor power of the Indians was reproduced by them as subsistence products grown by them on their own communal lands; and they were further coerced into productive super-labor for the Spaniards in the *encomienda* and the *repartimiento*. Most of the mestizos and assimilated Indians barely survived by submitting to this superexploitation of their labor, in accordance with the prevailing social and labor conditions of the age (Cortés y Larraz, 1958).

The second "revolutionary" agrarian reform [about 300 years later] in Salvadoran history is the so-called "liberal" agrarian reform of 1881-82, which suppressed the communal lands of Indian communities and the lands near *ladino* towns that were also worked communally. The system of collective land tenure which had survived the coming of the Spaniards, even though restrictions were imposed and lands changed hands in accordance with the need to grow indigo for export, was now completely abolished as a result of the struggle for land. The social and political group, called "liberals" on the basis of their ideology, had wanted to acquire land but had been prevented from doing so since Independence because the land was still in the hands of the old creole landholders ("conservatives") and because the liberals did not have enough power to seize land or force the conservatives to share it. New land was now needed for coffee cultivation, which was rapidly becoming an important crop. The lands used for indigo were not good for the new product but the communal lands under the control of the communities were very suitable. The first revolutionary change was to unify the land tenure system entirely as private property, by suppressing any other kind of tenure; namely, the communal tenure. The second revolutionary change was the subsequent proletarization of the rural population, both Indian and mestizo. Since the people did not have the means, knowledge, or resources to own their land privately, they no longer had their own means for subsistence and had to depend on hiring out their labor power for wages (or some other vulnerable form). Coercive legal mechanisms, such as the "vagrancy law," the creation of the "rural police," and the institution of the "registry of deeds," reinforced the proletarization process.

The third radical change was the consequent *ladinization* of the population. While previously some Indian communities had continued to coexist alongside communities of creoles, mestizos, and *ladinos*, henceforth all would be peasants or rural workers no matter what their ethnic background (Montes: 1986i). This phenomenon goes beyond the merely ethnic or cultural realm since it is a result of more deeply rooted objective conditions. An Indian community can maintain itself as a community, as an integrated and differentiated social unity, only to the extent that it has the basic material conditions for its own existence—and not simply those that are cultural and ethnic. In order to maintain their subordinated levels of independence, to be able to organize their society, develop their culture and religious expression, and maintain some kind of power structure, in a word, in order to be a community, they needed their own community-rooted economic foundation—and that the reform took away from them (for example, by prohibiting Indian *cofradías**

---

*Cofradías were religious confraternities organized in the Indian villages in order to foster community identity and internal authority. THE EDITORS

from owning land). They might be able to survive as an ethnic and cultural group, almost as a piece of folklore, but not as a true Indian community, since each family had to subsist through its individual plot or by selling its labor for wages. This fact had a much deeper and more radical impact on the homogenization and *ladinization* of the Salvadoran population than the effects of the repression following the uprisings previously mentioned. From now on, there would be no more Indian communities strictly speaking, but just land owners, peasants, and rural wage laborers. The foundation they needed in order to be Indian communities had been destroyed.

As measured by all social indicators, these "revolutionary" reforms resulted in declining living standards for the rural population even before 1980. Employment, housing, education, health, applied technology, access to sources of credit, and so forth (Montes, 1980c), were for the most part lower than for those of the marginal population in the cities (Montes, 1979a). However, given the [limited] amount of land available and the numbers of rural people, it was already foreseeable that a capitalist or "reformist" agrarian reform could not solve the problem of Salvadoran agriculture (Montes, 1980c). Consequently, in an earlier article, even before assessing in depth the present agrarian reform, I proposed as a working hypothesis that an agrarian revolution was needed—both as a just solution for the people who had been despoiled of their lands, and as a resolution of the nation's agricultural problem (Montes, 1986f).

Reformist Agrarian Reform (1980)

Any agrarian reform fostered or implemented by the state is the product of a political decision. Whether or not it is possible to implement it will depend on the correlation of forces at each particular moment. The First National Congress on Agrarian Reform, held at the behest of the legislature in early 1970, led to the conviction that land reform had to be carried out. But that conclusion could not be implemented because at that moment the correlation of forces did not favor such a far reaching political decision. Similarly, three years later, following a seminar on this issue, the armed forces came to the same conclusion but again a favorable correlation of forces was lacking. Another three years later President Molina, who supposedly had the support of the armed forces as well as others, thought the time had come to set in motion a timid agrarian reform and that he had the necessary support behind him. How mistaken such analysis had been was revealed when the government and its allies were unable to successfully confront the combined opposition forces. Three more years were to pass before a military coup led to a new correlation of forces which cleared the way for the political decision to change the parameters of land tenure (Montes, 1980c).

Before pursuing the question further we should classify the present Salvadoran agrarian reform.* This reform is not "revolutionary" but "reformist." It does not introduce any structural element, anything radically and qualitatively new, neither in the relations of land tenure nor in the social relations flowing from it. Private ownership of land remains the only possibility, whether that be in individual or in cooperative form. In fact matters are further "privatized" through Phase III of the land reform. The reform only limits the amount of land holding permitted. The state acquires what is above that limit through a compulsory sale with indemnification (in cash and/or bonds), in order to sell the land to new owners whose holdings are similarly limited. An evaluation of this reform should indicate whether the status of the beneficiaries has undergone real qualitative change, as they have progressed from being wage laborers to something else, or whether, despite appearances and public statements, their condition as owners is more formal and juridical than real and qualitatively different, at least with regard to their social conditions and their chance of becoming true capitalist entrepreneurs.

We take it for granted that any agrarian reform involves a political decision, as stated above. Not only is that true in the present case but indeed its main objective is political. The 1980 agrarian reform in El Salvador was adopted primarily, if not exclusively, as a counterinsurgency measure to check increasing popular pressure and a growing guerrilla force by undercutting its demands and taking away its social base—especially after the victory of the Sandinista revolution in Nicaragua and the perceived imminent danger of a possible revolutionary victory in El Salvador. In this respect it is noteworthy that the experts advising this reform were the same as those who planned or implemented the land reform in Vietnam (Montes, 1980c).

The fact that such an agrarian reform had political objectives and was implemented during a period of instability and political fluctuation has made the reform conditioned on the vicissitudes of politics. It began during the rule of a transitory civilian-military junta. Two years later it survived under a provisional coalition government (1982-84), in which the forces that were furthest to the right and most opposed to the reform controlled the ministries that dealt with the economy and the agencies connected to the reform. Since June 1984 a constitutional Christian Democrat government has been in office, but its real power has proven to be quite limited in all respects (*ECA*, May-June 1986).

---

*The Agrarian Reform law was enacted in 1980 (Phases I and II in March, Phase III in May) under considerable pressure from the United States. Phase I affected the 300 largest farms and ranches. Phase II, aimed at medium-sized properties, and particularly the coffee farms, was never implemented. Phase III enabled people to claim (for purchase) lands they had been working under rental or sharecropping arrangements. P.B.

If, however, there is an attempt to implement agrarian reform during a period of civil war, it is foreseeable that the initial aims will be much constrained by the conditions that the war imposes on the nation as a whole. The deterioration produced by the war (whether in the military realm itself or in human lives) the destroyed infrastructure, the vast amounts of resources used in the war, the social and living conditions of the people, the decline of the economy and the currency, as well as other negatives, inevitably affects the agrarian reform. One indicator is the fact that the area in basic grains cultivated collectively under Phase I has gone down year by year from 29,063 hectares in 1980-81 to 9,780 hectares in 1984-85. Export crops have also declined, although they rose last year slightly above the previous year's level, but not above the level of earlier years. With the feeble qualification that "other crops" have increased, the total surface area cultivated decreased from 91,361 hectares in 1980-81 to 71,157 in 1983-84 and increased slightly to 72,914 hectares in 1984-85 (PERA, 1985).

A number of studies over a period of time have analyzed the Salvadoran land reform as a whole and by sectors in recent years (Strasma et al., 1983; Pleitez, 1983; Seminario, 1983; Thome: 1984; Olano y Orellana, 1985; Solórzano, 1986; Pérez et al., 1986). This present study is based primarily on an evaluation done for the Ministry of Agriculture and Ranching by one of its own agencies (PERA: 1985). This government study is the most complete and up to date evaluation with which I am familiar. The data are reliable, and we can assume that they have not been manipulated to demonstrate flaws in the agrarian reform, since this government agency was set up to improve the reform and make it work. We are thus going to consider five aspects we regard as important for seeing the implications of the agrarian reform.

SCOPE OF THE AGRARIAN REFORM

Our starting assumption has been that land is El Salvador's only natural resource. We must add that up to the point when the crisis began to worsen and war broke out, and before the agrarian reform was applied, more than 60% of the population was rural (1971 census), although admittedly the category of rural includes considerably fewer than the number of people and families who work and live off the land (Montes, 1980c).

I have taken Thome's figures to use in Table 1 below (Thome, 1984). They represent a higher estimate than that of PERA (1985) for the amount of land affected by Phase I, without counting land affected by Decree 842 (land ISTA owns or acquired in addition to those affected by Decree 154 and assigned to the agrarian reform cooperatives). Two alternative estimates are offered for the "retention rights," that is, the amount of land the former owners are allowed to retain. These will naturally be the best lands. The first is in keeping with the original law

Table 1. Cultivated Lands Affected by and Beneficiaries of Land Reform

AREAS ENCOMPASSED BY REDISTRIBUTION

| | Total Affected Hectares | Retention Hectares | | Available Hectares Distributed | | | |
		Original Set-asides	1983 Set-asides	Original Land	Percent of Total	1983 Land	Percent of Total
Phase I	223,217	25,750	172,747	197,467	13.70%	172,747	11.80%
Phase III	---	---	---	97,205	6.64	97,205	6.64
Phase II:							
Original	345,764	(219,375)	---	(126,389)	(8.63)	---	---
1983	192,250	---	(156,800)	---	---	(35,450)	
TOTALS				294,672	20.34%	269,952	18.44%

*Note: All data enclosed within parentheses are not added since the Phase II lands were never actually distributed.

PHASE I & PHASE III BENEFICIARIES

| | Rural 1982 Population | Rural EAP Population | Beneficiaries of Agrarian Reform | | | |
			Direct Recipients	Percent of Total	Indirect Recipients	Percent of Total
Phase I		65,134	27,456	42.12%	145,411	5.04%
Phase III		180,682	63,668	16.67	382,008	13.24
TOTALS	2,885,347*	245,816	91,104	37.06	527,419	18.30

*The figures represent 1982 data and calculations.

Note: Of the 1,463,359 cultivated hectares in El Salvador, the Agrarian Reform Law encompassed a little more than half of the total land holdings. Phase I and Phase III redistributions actually affected 294,672 arable hectares; Phase II of the law was not implemented.

which allowed them to keep from 100 to 150 hectares, depending on the quality of the land, with an average parcel of 125 hectares. The second is the maximum retention amount in accordance with Article 105 of the 1983 constitution, which set the limit at 245 hectares and would be applied to Phase II if it were implemented, but which if applied retroactively to Phase I would increase the retention rights of the former owners who could then claim that land.

Thus far [1986] the agrarian reform (excluding Decree 842) has actually affected 294,672 hectares—the lower quality lands of those potentially to be affected—representing 20.34% of the arable land in the country; but that figure could be reduced to 269,952 hectares (18.44%) if the article in the constitution is retroactive. Had Phase II been implemented in terms of the original decree, the amount of land subject to the reform would have totaled 421,061 hectares (28.97% of the arable land in the country); but the amount of land changing hands would be only 305.402 hectares (20.82%) had the new constitution been applied, or up to a maximum of 22.74% of arable land if the clause in the constitution is not retroactive for Phase I. In any case, even applied to the maximum, the agrarian reform affects only a small percentage of the land, which is our crucial resource, as I have pointed out. If, moreover, we examine the ratio of beneficiaries to the rural EAP—and the questionable criteria used to calculate it lead to an underestimation (Montes, 1984a)—only 37.06% have benefitted (very disproportionately between the two phases), while 18.3% of the "rural" population has benefitted indirectly (also disproportionately between the two phases). The upshot is that the agrarian reform, as proposed, cannot resolve El Salvador's fundamental problem. It can neither bring about an adequate land distribution nor can it benefit the rural population as a whole.

ACCESS TO CAPITAL AND FINANCIAL CREDIT

The problem of access to monetary credits for production was very serious before the reform and the crisis, especially for small farmers and basic grain producers, since the economy revolved around export (Montes, 1980c). While implementation of the agrarian reform has made large sums available for credit, despite the worsening state of the economy and national finances, it does not seem to have been enough nor to have met expectations and needs.

Although Phase I encompasses 73.6% of the land affected and Phase III encompasses 26.4% (PERA: 1985), nevertheless the Phase I lands received 90.15% of financing, leaving only 9.85% for those in Phase III. Moreover, the average amount of credit per hectare is much less in the latter group. The reason, among others, is that there is still a bias favoring export crops. Moreover, the beneficiaries of Decree 207 are less able to absorb credit, make investments, and offer collateral. Indeed, the fact that 44.7% of loans have not been paid back, 75.4% have had to be refinanced, and 24.5% have been declared to be in default, clearly indicates the difficulties inherent in the reform and in keeping it solvent (PERA, 1985). Actually the amount of Phase I land planted with credit loans has been declining steadily. While in 1980-81 it was 80,422 hectares (29.67% of those affected), it declined in 1983-84 to 58,345 hectares (21.52% of those affected), and rose somewhat in 1984-85 reaching 64.521 hectares (23.8%) of those affected (PERA, 1985).

EMPLOYMENT IN THE REFORMED SECTOR

Employment generated in Salvadoran agriculture left much to be desired before the reform. Scarcely more than 37% of the rural EAP had work year around (Montes, 1980c). One of the supposed aims of the agrarian reform was to intensify utilization of vast amounts of labor and thereby increase the rate of employment.

In fact, job creation has not improved much. This fact becomes more startling if we consider that only 26.5% of the EAP is in Phase I while 73.5% is in Phase III, where employment is so dismal. At the very least, Decree 207 has not only not resolved the problem of unemployment in the countryside but has left a very high proportion of the population with only minimal employment. Thus they have to supplement their income with other kinds of work. Given this level of employment it will be difficult for them to meet their obligations, even for their own subsistence, let alone their obligations to pay their debts (PERA, 1985).

SELLING THE PRODUCT

With regard to selling the product, we will leave aside export products, since the government has nationalized and centralized foreign trade, and COPAL [Cotton Producers' Cooperative] has a monopoly over cotton. Here we will deal with basic grains, not only because they constitute the largest part of production, especially among Phase III beneficiaries, but because they are sold mainly on the domestic market. The IRA [Agrarian Reform Institute] offers good prices to producers, but because it demands a certain quality, payments are not always made on time. Moreover, the COPAL offices are not nearby, and the farmers do not have their own means of transportation. So many of them look for buyers closer at hand who can pay immediately, even though they pay considerably less (PERA, 1985).

Although the reform sector includes 30.9% of the land devoted to growing basic grains, it produces only 27.7% of the total. Nevertheless, the IRA buys 33.3% of what is produced by all growers, but only 21.96% of what the reform sector produces. Farmers keep the rest for their own consumption or sell it to dealers who pay considerably less. The IRA's efforts to extend its coverage have thus far been insufficient for the interests of the farmers. In this connection I would like to cite Solórzano's assessment of the various points presented thus far:

> The economic results in the management of the cooperatives have been satisfactory, and their production levels are above national average, thus confirming that peasants in agrarian reforms in Latin America have fulfilled their function in working the land well, despite the non-economic motivations behind the reforms. . . . The cooperatives' financial problems lie primarily in the fact that simply owning land does not assure that one will appropriate the surplus generated in agricultural activity. Indeed agrarian reform can become a new and refined tool of exploitation. . . . When turning land ownership over to peasants is not linked to trading and the setting of prices, financing and providing supplies can become an instrument of exploitation, since the surplus generated can be transferred

to other sectors through "price fixing" of supplies, products, and exchange generated in the agricultural sector and used in other sectors to finance imports of raw materials, the expansion of money supply, foreign debt commitments, the fiscal deficit, etc. (Solórzano, 1986).

AGRARIAN DEBT

We have already indicated that the current agrarian reform is of a "reformist" nature and that it has been carried out by forcibly expropriating land and then paying the former owners, whom the state is committed to compensating partly with cash and partly with bonds. The state in turn charges the beneficiaries the value of the land plus interest over a thirty-year period. This is called the "agrarian debt" and is what the beneficiaries now owe the government. If the situation as presented in earlier sections already indicated that the beneficiaries had serious economic and financial problems, the following data reinforce that impression all the more.

The conditions under which the agrarian reform is being carried out, the vulnerability described above, and the vastness of the sum itself [the original debt was $725.8 million colones, with an annual interest rate of 9.5%], strongly suggest that the beneficiaries cannot pay this debt. In fact, as we have seen, many farmers have not paid back loans used for crop production. Indeed, "the total sum of payments made by cooperatives on the agrarian debt scarcely amounts to $8.3 million colones [at the time, approximately U.S. $2 million] (PERA, 1985). It is unclear whether this amount refers to total payments since the beginning or simply to the 1984-85 harvest period. In any case it is no more than 12.05% of the annual interest, with no payment on the principal. Hence under current conditions the agrarian debt cannot be paid. It is rather like the situation of the foreign debt of underdeveloped countries, especially Latin America. Solórzano's conclusions are worth citing:

> As the agrarian debt is structured, it is very difficult to conceive any circumstances under which the cooperatives can discharge such a heavy debt. . . . In the short run and under current conditions there is no foreseeable way in which the cooperatives can pay the agrarian debt. Nevertheless it is very important for the future of the cooperatives and the viability of the agrarian reform that alternative solutions be found. Moreover, dealing with the agrarian debt has important implications that go beyond politics and affect financing and revenue throughout the economy of the country. . . . The basic objective of the reform undertaken in March 1980, "a fair distribution of national wealth," will not be achieved unless the problem of the agrarian debt is resolved in favor of the small farmers. This problem should not be viewed in isolation, but within the context of a development policy for the country and particularly for the agricultural sector, that will allow for creative ways to reduce the heavy

weight of the agrarian debt and assure that the agrarian reform enterprises will be run efficiently and be profitable (Solórzano, 1986).

The fact that the agrarian debt is unpayable has forced the government, under pressure from peasant and labor organizations, to change conditions of payment and interest. Among other measures, the annual interest rate has been lowered to 6%, the payment period has been stretched out to a maximum of fifty years and a five-year grace period has been granted (MAG, 1986). Nevertheless, all indications are that such measures will also prove incapable of resolving the problem and will merely prolong the agony, by refinancing the debt and putting the burden on the beneficiaries and their descendants. It is similar to the way the problem of the foreign debt is being treated. The data examined here show us that the measure will fail to resolve the problem of economic agriculture in El Salvador.

New Variables Aggravating the Problem

As already noted, the political objectives of the agrarian reform and its implementation during a civil war have their impact on the reform, just like any other aspect of the national reality. Now, however, we should examine it from another perspective—that of the civil war and one of its most serious consequences, the huge number of displaced people and refugees.

The civil war is being fought largely, though not exclusively, in the northern part of the country. Traditionally this zone has been predominantly one of small plots of land producing basic grains, and its social and economic structures were still "peasant" in nature until the war began. The war and the dislocation it has produced have not only driven many people out of the area, but they have forced people out of the peasant way of life at an ever faster rate, in the few corners where such conditions still remained. The people leaving the area ceased being peasants not in a natural and gradual way, but abruptly, when they were forced to live in refugee camps or shantytowns, unable to continue their way of life. This process has destroyed this "small farming" mode of production and peasant social relations, further homogenizing rural workers or turning them into urban misfits, potential proletarians with no job opportunities, or candidates for the lumpenproletariat.

Along with the depopulation of these areas there has been a large scale abandonment, deterioration, and destruction of crops and of land devoted mainly to producing basic grains. In many areas production has fallen off to such an extent that once subsistence needs are met there is little or no food surplus for the market. This development has enormous repercussions on the national level because of the shortage of basic food. Other lands have to be used in order to provide a supply of these basic foods, thus cutting back on export crops. Or food has to be imported, thus worsening the trade balance and using up foreign exchange. The problem will become worse if peasant associations even partly carry out their threat not to plant for the market this year (1986-87) but only for their family consumption, due to the cost of supplies and the freeze on crop prices which led to economic losses for the producers (as a result of the "Program for Stabilization and Economic Reactivation," approved in January 1986).

We can foresee that these tendencies will prevail for a long time, first because the war is continuing and intensifying in the conflictive zones; and second, because the end of the peasant way of life is essentially irreversible, especially among the new generations who have been raised away from the countryside and agricultural work. . . .

A rather different, and to some extent, opposite tendency is evident in some of the zones of conflict. A kind of readjustment in the location of displaced families and of their working of the land has taken place. People from smaller population centers have moved into houses left vacant by those going to larger areas, sometimes with the approval of the owner, or rental, partnership or other arrangements with the owner, and sometimes simply by taking them over. Meanwhile their own homes are being occupied by people from even smaller settlements. The overall tendency is to move to settlements slightly larger and more secure, although elsewhere medium-sized towns are deserted and peasants are living in isolated huts. This process is observable not only in housing but also in the planting of crops on abandoned lands. In conflictive and abandoned areas land is cultivated freely (in some cases) by peasants who want to do so, or it is subject to regulated collective exploitation (IDHUCA, 1986).

As we have already noted in another study (IDHUCA, 1985), the process we have been describing leaves a relatively large amount of land available. Much of it will not be reclaimed by its former owners for various reasons. The result might be a concentration of lands that are marginal for diverse agricultural purposes but suitable mainly for basic grains, thus retrogressing to a more concentrated land tenure, which is contrary to the aims of the agrarian reform, especially those of Phase III. Everything depends on how the crisis and the war are resolved, on what kind of model is implemented, and other variables as well.

Conclusions

Our starting point was that land is El Salvador's only natural resource. That fact conditions not only its economy, but its whole society and politics, and is the epicenter of the crisis. Throughout the course of this work we have confirmed that thesis. The solutions attempted have not resolved the fundamental problem of the country or of its agriculture. The result of the war has been to aggravate the problem and to neutralize or even block the modest contribution that the agrarian reform might have been able to make towards solving such problems.

We can note certain constants that complicate our problematic situation and prevent a suitable solution. First, El Salvador continues to be dependent on agriculture and on the land factor. Moreover, there is continual resistance to implementing Phase II of the agrarian reform, which would affect the most important part of the country's wealth both quantitatively and qualitatively. The scope of that phase was weakened through Article 105 of the 1983 constitution, and the government has been passive or even negative about implementing its scanty and symbolic content, even though the period of time in which it should be carried out by force will soon be over (December 1986). The crisis and the civil war continue to show virtually no signs of ending in the foreseeable future. The consequences have been sufficiently noted here and in numerous studies. Moreover, the Salvadoran crisis has paralyzed industrialization and services and set some back, or even dismantled them, even though they were far from as advanced as they should have been for the development and diversification of the country and its economy. Finally, the country's underdevelopment and external dependence have deepened further. They have deteriorated to the levels of several decades ago. El Salvador has reached a degree of dependency that is in all respects unprecedented in our history.

The only thing remaining is to sketch what has been proposed as a working hypothesis: agrarian revolution. We have sought to prove that the country's only natural resource is land, at least for the present. If that is the case, it cannot be left up to the free disposition of individuals or interest groups. Land is our national legacy and should be used rationally and for the benefit the country as a whole, both now and in the future. It must be regarded as belonging to the nation and be under the control of the whole society so as to serve the whole of it. The country has one more extremely valuable resource: its labor force, its human resources which are abundant and hardworking but little trained— indeed, the vast majority are hardly trained at all. The future must be planned with both of these resources in mind, aiming at their rational optimization, keeping in mind the best use of different soils, the most appropriate crops, the extent of productive areas, and the technology most appropriate for our other national resource, our abundant but not highly trained labor. It may be that initially we cannot aspire to anything more than an acceptable level of subsistence—but for all Salvadorans. Having reached that point, we could go on to higher goals and levels of production, productivity, living conditions, and national wealth. This may be a utopia, but it cannot be rejected out of hand as a working hypothesis, especially since other solutions attempted or proposed have in fact proven incapable of resolving the country's fundamental problems.

Ignacio Ellacuría

15. The True Social Place of The Church*

TRANSLATION BY PHILLIP BERRYMAN

To inquire about the Church's true "social place" is not simply a matter of sociology, but is in fact a theological issue that is urgent both for the Church's self-understanding and for its pastoral activities. Naturally it is a sociological question and theologians and pastors would do well to review what the social sciences have to offer for understanding this issue. Insofar as the Church is a social institution—not only is it a social institution but it is excessively so—the Church is a social reality and is subject to all the laws of social realities, including, of course, all kinds of sociological conditioning. The issue is also theological, however, for how the Church receives the word of God, how it perceives and interprets the signs of the times and what activity it undertakes as its fundamental praxis will depend largely on its location in society.

New Awareness of the Problem

What does "social place" mean in this context?

The question assumes that there are different "places" in society. At the very least they are different; often indeed they may be opposed or in contention with one another. Perhaps one of the most significant limitations of Vatican II when it "sent" the Church out into the world again, was that it did not emphasize enough that there are very different social sites in the world, and that not all of them can energize faith and Christian life to the same extent.

There are different places in the world. People speak, for example, of a First World and a Third World (for various reasons the term Second

---

*Ellacuría (1982 l); see Bibliography in the back of this book.

It should be noted that *lugar social*, "social place" is something of a wordplay on *lugar teológico*, (Latin *locus theologicus* referring to theology's sources—scripture, tradition, the sense of the faithful). The term is essentially normative: where should the church locate itself in society? P.B.

World is not used much). It is obvious that institutionally the Church
has taken its place primarily in the First World, not only geographically
and materially, but—and this is more serious—spiritually. It shapes its
ideas and interests, or at least poses its theoretical and practical problems in accordance with what is uppermost in the First World. This
stance has no doubt brought certain intellectual advantages and a degree of modernization. It has also entailed disadvantages, however, not
only for understanding the vast majority of humanity, which is not like
the First World, but—and this is more serious—for understanding some
essential aspects of Christian faith, and for prioritizing correctly the
missions of the Church. That may sound shocking, but the fact is
undeniable. Moreover, it can easily be explained both sociologically and
theologically.

As understood here, "social place" has at least the following aspects:
it is first, the social place that has been chosen; secondly, it is the place
from which and for which theoretical interpretations and practical proposals are made; third, it is the place that shapes current practice and
into which people's own practice fits and to which it is subordinated.

For example, if we understand the poor as a social place, in order
that we may claim to be in that place, it is not enough to claim to be
among them geographically or physically, although that may be indispensable, a thing of great merit, and a magnificent witness. Much more
is required. This place of the poor should reflect a preferential option:
the ultimate object is that these poor people be first in God's reign in a
real sense and not simply in intention or rhetoric. Second, these poor
people should also be the *locus theologicus* from which God's word is
heard, the signs of the times are read, answers and interpretations are
sought, and proposals for change are made. Third, it is assumed that
these poor people have undertaken a praxis of liberation and that they
are accompanied by a Church that not only wants the Word to be
heeded, but above all else wants the Promise to be made into reality.

Obviously if "social place" be taken this radically, it is all important
that we find the Church's true social place, the place from which we can
encompass most correctly and fully the potential totality of the Christian
message and the universality proper to the Church's catholicity and to
the differentiated whole of God's reign. For what we are talking about
are universalities and totalities and not closed partialities.

"Social place" entails taking sides in a gospel sense and a degree of
preferentiality, but there is no intention of excluding anyone or any
whole people from the call to conversion and perfection. However, presenting the Christian message from the social place represented by the
politically or economically dominant classes is not the same as doing so
from the dominated classes. The dominant classes certainly look out for
the whole, but they do so from within their dominance. The dominated
classes must also look out for the whole, when they are enlivened by the
spirit of faith, but they do so from their domination. The argument here

is that their viewpoint, their place, is much more privileged than any other for finding the total truth of faith, and especially for putting this total faith into practice.

How to Find the True Social Place

If social location is so important for faith and for the Church, it is extremely important to determine in each case how to find this authentic social place, for it is obvious that some social places are inauthentic for the Church. This danger of inauthenticity comes out more clearly if we point to a characteristic feature of any social place. This place is where one really is, even though one may go forth from it to do one thing or another. Social place does not mean where one normally is, the site where one lives, where one has one's address, or where one is registered.

Jesus for example, went out to many places. He could dine with the rich, he could spend the night at Lazarus' house, he could go up the mountain and preach on the lake, preach in Galilee, or struggle in Judaea and Jerusalem—but in his mind, his heart, and his practice he placed himself with the most needy. Of course I know that it can most correctly be stated that Jesus was with God, his Father, but one thing does not exclude the other. First, being-in and being-with are not the same: Jesus was located in that social place constituted by the poor, and it was from that place, which purified and enlightened his heart, that he was with God and went about his Father's business. Second, this very being with God was not unrelated to his being with the poor, among whom he wished to establish his dwelling.

This reference to Jesus and to the business of God's reign, already provides us with a first general response to how to determine in each specific case what the true social place is for the Church in general, and for the different particular Churches. On this matter, Jesus' person and life is the fundamental principle of discernment. We do not have to be very insistent on this point, since it is evident that Jesus is the fundamental principle of discernment and that Jesus tended towards a particular social place for finding the Father within his historic life and for finding the best way to announce and bring about God's reign. We can take this for granted.

We must go further, however, since many who acknowledge this starting point then proceed to take very divergent paths, some of which in fact lead to social places that are inauthentic for the Church and for proclaiming the kingdom.

Both sociological and theological criteria can help us find the true social place. Both are necessary, although which takes priority it is not a matter of indifference. Even admitting such priority, however, does not mean that the series of sociological criteria are not essential.

SOCIOLOGICAL CRITERIA

Why must sociological criteria be taken into account, and which of them are more necessary, or at least more useful?

Without providing any general theory of what I have written on this problem elsewhere, it can be stated that issues connected with the kingdom of God, because of its very nature as Kingdom, need mediations* if they are to be interpreted and set in motion, and those mediations are very much connected to sociological factors.

The kingdom of God has to do, first, with historic reality, which is structural and which largely shapes personal destinies; second, it has to do with historic praxis which, without abandoning the personal dimension, must come to bear on aspects that are specifically social; third, it has to do with a whole people on the move, and indeed, with the whole of humankind at least in intention. Finally the kingdom of God has to do with structural sin and evil, which insofar as they are historic, require the utilization of sociological criteria both for interpreting them and for overcoming them. These are four powerful reasons why social factors must be taken into account in finding the Church's true social place.

The most basic element is unquestionably a deep human and Christian experience. As such, this experience does not need explicit or very sophisticated mediations, although it is a condition for such experience that one be in some way in a fitting social position. Indeed, it is possible to be Christian and to be receiving the light and warmth of faith in a systematic way and yet not to see, let alone experience, the true reality of the world. In that case the message of faith cannot enlighten that reality, since it is not present or it is present in a distorted way. The same can be said from a human standpoint: even a well developed ability to understand and to feel can be impaired because one's social place prevents one from perceiving the true reality.

As true as that is, it is just as true that the basic element here is a deep human and Christian experience.

The point is that the starting point is not ideologies, nor even purely theoretical ways of posing the problem. These may play a role but they are not what is most basic and decisive. What is basic and decisive here is human experience and Christian experience. In countries like El Salvador and Guatemala this experience has a nightmare quality, while in other countries people undergo something similar, although not as

---

*Ellacuría and other liberation theologians frequently speak of "mediations." The notion is that human beings can neither understand nor carry out God's will directly but rather need "mediations" such as the social sciences for discerning what is happening in the world, and then movements, programs, and the like for acting effectively. Such mediations are not identified with God's kingdom, but they are required for bringing it about. P.B.

sharply dramatic. This is the human experience of a brutal repression, which is not only claiming more than ten thousand victims a year but is also carried out with indescribable cruelty and sadism. This is the Christian experience of how the forces of the anti-Christ, of the beast of the apocalypse, fall on the lowly, simply because they have begun—or it is feared they are beginning—to really demand their rights, or simply to defend themselves against those who mercilessly plunder their lives, land, and belongings.

This is the primary datum, which immediately comes under the influence of what we may call sociological elements. Some of them conceal matters. The ideology of dominant capitalism, in the form of national security ideology, tries to distort the facts and disqualify that experience. Thus, as this ideology presents it, incidents of repression are unclear, no one really knows who is carrying them out. At most they are conceded to be the work of the far right, as though it had no connections with anything else. Besides, the conflict has a clear explanation: Soviet communism is striving to expand across the weak borders of the democratic world, and that is why there are popular uprisings, which must be crushed in the name of freedom for the sake of Western Christian civilization. Christian experience has also been led astray; it has been politicized to unacceptable extremes, and has been placed at the service of anti-Christian interests, namely those of revolutionary communists. Such obfuscating ideologies therefore deny that there is any political or religious persecution. Indeed, what is taking place is a crusade for freedom and against atheistic and totalitarian communism.

When faced with such an obfuscation of the root experience presented with ostensibly scientific terms, we must turn to other kinds of sociological interpretations. These tend to be, to a certain extent, Marxist.

It is simply not true that Marxism has been the primary influence behind the efforts of Christians to change the social location of the Church. The originating experience mentioned above undercuts such an explanation. Assistance from Marxist analysis comes at a second stage: it comes when people see the need to clarify theoretically what is happening in countries whose structure is barbarously capitalist, and why it is happening. Marxist analysis is one of the theoretical instruments that people seize at a critical time in order to unmask ideologically self-serving and distorting explanations and in order to clarify situations that they must understand in a way that really goes beyond the appearances.

They use such Marxist analysis—with some significant corrections of course—because other kinds of analysis, capitalist or supposedly neutral, are less explanatory.* They also use it after having found wanting from a theoretical standpoint the set of concepts used by the so-called

---

*The essays of Segundo Montes in this volume, especially chapters 6 and 12, represent examples of Marxist analysis used with such corrections. THE EDITORS

social doctrine of the Church. The Church's social doctrine proposes Christian principles for social realities, but it also employs social analysis which as such may be inadequate and questionable. Christians certainly welcome these principles, but Christian intellectuals are not always happy with the accompanying social analysis.

Even while emphasizing that the role of Marxism in rediscovering the true social place of the Church has been secondary, there is no point in underestimating the importance of Marxism both for clarifying theoretically the social authenticity of the social place, and for promoting certain practices that are more consonant with the real needs of the majorities who suffer oppression and repression. It would be wrong to deny the influence of Marxism in justifying why we must be on the side of the poor in a historic manner, and in determining who are truly poor socially and politically and why they are poor, and in offering approaches towards effecting basic social change. The pluses and minuses that may be due to such influence must be analyzed in each case. Generally speaking, however, we can say that Marxism, both theoretical and practical, not only in bureaucratized parties but in revolutionary movements, has had an important influence on something that is highly positive and deeply Christian, namely the re-locating of the Church's social place and the launching of the preferential option for the poor.

It is commonly said that the Christian needs no help beyond Christianity, beyond Christian faith, in order to discover and affirm that the Church's authentic social place, its preferential social place, is that of the world's oppressed majorities. We cannot go into the various groups of reasons that should be given in response to such a statement, but we should at least outline them.

To begin with, it must be said that thus far the Church has not placed itself overwhelmingly and preferentially in the social place most authentic to it, namely the Third World as a whole. The Church as a whole, and especially in qualitative terms, stands more in the First World than in the Third World. Even in the First World, the Church is situated more among the dominant classes and is more in tune with the dominant structure, than it is with the dominated classes or in tune with social change.

Second, it must be said that since ancient times the Church has made use of assistance from beyond Christian faith. It has made use of theoretical resources from Aristotelianism and Platonism in order to clarify theoretically the mysteries of faith. It has made use of artistic resources in order to transmit Christian realities and values to believers. It has used the theories and practices of capitalism—the market economy, it is generally called—for its own institutional development and maintenance. It has used physical force in order to safeguard the purity of the faith and colonialist structures to spread the gospel. It has needed the papal states in order to safeguard the primacy and even the supremacy of the papacy in a worldly manner. It has used social science to back up its social teachings.

Third, as we noted earlier, it must be asserted that the fact that the kingdom of God is historic requires mediations. Such mediations are not the exclusive property of Christians and indeed do not even come from Christian inspiration. Finally, it should be said that since ancient times God has spoken in many and diverse ways, and that although Jesus, dead and risen, is God's definitive Word, God continues to speak, among other ways, through what has been called the signs of the times, which in addition to the discernment of faith, must be accompanied by a careful theoretical discernment.

THEOLOGICAL FACTORS

While it is true that we need to take social criteria into account in order to find the Church's true social place both theoretically and practically, it is also true that such social criteria are neither the main nor the decisive moment. That main and decisive moment is provided by Christian faith and by a series of human and historic criteria flowing from that same faith.

We have already noted that the initial impetus came mainly from human and Christian experience. Faced with the horrible spectacle of human evil that is pushing most of humankind to the brink of death and desperation, human experience rebels and strives to set things right. Starting from that same human experience and viewing matters from the [viewpoint of the] Christian God revealed in Jesus, Christian experience sees that this horrible situation of evil and injustice is itself the denial of God's kingdom. That is, it is a denial of God and the human being, the very denial of the salvation that Jesus proclaimed and promised, a situation that has turned what should be a realm of grace into a realm of sin. From this perspective, Christian experience is original and irreplaceable.

This Christian experience has unquestionably had a decisive influence in the situating of the true social place of the Church among the oppressed majorities, and in prompting many Christians to actually take their place there. Here again, experience comes before reflection and praxis comes before theory, although such sharp divisions cannot be drawn between the one and the other, and it must be acknowledged that there is a reciprocal action in an ongoing energizing cycle.

This conversion in faith to the oppressed, who out of the stark agony of their repression, cried out for help to any person of good will and to those Christians who had made love for the neediest the main argument to support their Christian faith and practice, redounds to that faith and obliges Christians to re-read in a new way the old and new testaments, the Church's best traditions, and its own religious charism.

This renewed spirit leads once more back to historic reality, now viewed sociologically and theologically with new eyes. That in turn leads to a new practice which is both personally converting and socially transforming. Thus we discover the true social place of the Church, and now situated in the right place, the Church is renewed from within that place. Faith is committed in charity, and thus committed, it takes on new life and strength.

That is not to say that there may not have been excesses or defections. To deny, however, that the faith has been strengthened with new life or to deny that a broad sector of Christian communities, sometimes accompanied by their pastors, are giving an admirable example of martyrdom in the strict sense and of faith in Jesus Christ, is to willfully close one's eyes to the light. It is unjust to say that such people are in this new social place in order to engage in political action, when quite the opposite is true. Because they are standing by their side in a Christian manner, these people are helping to forward the historical cause of the dispossessed.

To some extent we can regard this preferential shift to the poor, this emphatic shift in the Church's social location, as a charism of the Latin American Church. This is not surprising, since many places in Latin America are the sadly privileged site of dire poverty and injustice. However, a firm precedent for this change of direction was already present in Vatican II. At the request of some bishops and cardinals, including Lercaro, Gerlier, and Himmer, who were shocked at how little attention the poor were receiving in the doctrinal discussion of the Church, a seminal text was inserted in *Lumen Gentium* (Vatican Council II, 1975): "Just as Christ carried out the work of redemption in poverty and under repression, so the Church is called to follow the same path in communicating to men the fruits of salvation."

These words did not go very far and were not very explicit, but they touched the heart of the matter. Prompted by the situation of the poor, these bishops brought pressure to bear; but the Council, disregarding somewhat this theological exigency based on reality, limited itself to considering the life of Jesus. There it insightfully looked at the two factors of poverty and persecution together, although it did not explicitly say that persecution befell Jesus because he situated himself in the social location of the poor and thereby incurred the enmity of the rich and the powerful.

Perhaps Vatican II did not say enough on this point. Certainly Vatican II was inspired to point the Church towards the world and to turn to the world as its mission. However, despite the clear deliberations of *Gaudium et Spes* (Vatican Council II, 1975), it did not take the full measure of this world, a world it should have defined as one of sin and injustice, one in which the vast majority of humankind suffers severe poverty and injustice.

Be that as it may, Medellín picked up from Vatican II, and thus the Third World truly emerged at Medellín as the Third World. At Medellín the historic reality and truth of Latin America now became a genuine theological *locus;* it became the underlying question to which the bishops of the continent tried to respond in the light of the gospel and in the light of Vatican II renewal. Now, however, this renewal became more radical and deeper, more concrete and committed, precisely because the bishops were no longer speaking simply of the world, but of the agonizingly painful world that is the Third World, representing most of humankind.

It is in this same context that we should view the enormous advance represented by Christian base communities as a theological factor in discovering and putting into practice the true social location of the Church. Christian base communities signify one of the greatest efforts to draw the Church into the midst of the very poor, so that it can be challenged by them and respond to their human needs in faith. In base communities the Church has learned how closely the personal and structural dimensions of salvation, the transcendent and historic moments of Christian faith, the reception of grace and the exercise of praxis, follow one another, and especially what the preferential option for the poor means for faith itself and for the holiness of the Church. This experience of base communities has made much more clear what the true social place of the Church is and should be.

Finally we have the significant phenomenon of liberation theology, which, as an effort at Christian theoretical reflection on the praxis of salvation viewed from the believing popular majority, has focused on what a Church of the poor and for the poor—a Church of the people—should be. This [it has continued to do] despite the misleading, and sometimes self-serving things said about that term. One of liberation theology's main questions has been that of the true social place of the Church, and it has sought to clarify theoretically the historic nature of the Church and to propose a kind of pastoral practice in accordance with that historic nature. Here also there has been an ongoing circularity between the experience and praxis of a Church committed to the poorest and theological reflection on that experience and praxis. One leads to the other and back again, in continuing cycles, in which both are mutually energized.

This whole series of theological and sociological criteria has helped situate the Church theoretically and practically in its true social place. That social place can be defined in general as that of the vast dispossessed majorities, but to do so in particular requires a deep Christian discernment. Here I have only traced the general lines, and I have made a few observations in order to put into writing the experience of some parts of the Latin American Church, understood as the Church of the poor.

Situations that are quite different would demand that the Church's pursuit of its true social place take different forms, but deep down those forms could not be very different, among other reasons because in the gospel there is an essential imperative that cannot be ignored. Moreover, the existence of dispossessed majorities everywhere and the fact that Western peoples have numerous responsibilities both past and present towards them obliges every Church to look at them preferentially in all of their concrete reality, or at least to consider this reality as an unavoidable horizon. That reality is, as a whole, that of a crucified humankind. Looking towards this horizon with the eyes of both faith and social analysis, we can come back to our more immediate surroundings and context. Then each particular Church, especially if it has the inspiration of living Christian base communities, will be able to shape itself by what the catholicity of the Church demands both universally and locally. Such catholicity is historic and therefore combines universality and concrete embodiment.

Ignacio Martín-Baró

16. The Appeal of The Far Right*

TRANSLATION BY PHILLIP BERRYMAN

The terms "right" and "left" used to designate political forces are always relative, both to one another and to a particular nation. Hence their ambivalence when they are used to make comparisons between different countries or to locate a particular political group along the worldwide ideological spectrum. Left in the United States might represent a moderate right in France and the Swedish right a radical left in El Salvador. If I use these terms here despite their potential ambiguity, I am taking everyday usage for granted and analyzing what one of these terms, the "right," means ideologically in El Salvador today. My aim in this work is to examine what the top level of the right wing forces or the "far right," is about, particularly by looking at a concrete instance, the Republican Nationalist Alliance, or ARENA.

The political right and left seem to be best defined by their option for a particular socio-economic system. In general, the right is made up not only of those who oppose all kinds of change but also of "progressive" sectors who champion certain social reforms, as long as they are carried out within a particular order and framework. Thus the Salvadoran right is made up of those groups and persons who uphold a social order based on the capitalist system, even when some of them admit that present Salvadoran capitalism needs serious reforms.

While it is their diverging postures towards the capitalist system that divides right from left, what divides the right internally into a "moderate right" and a "far right" is their stance towards reformism. Those of the Salvadoran far right do not accept in theory, let alone in practice, that El Salvador needs substantial social and economic reforms, and hence they vigorously oppose any policy seeking such changes. Historically, the Salvadoran right has remained united as long as the social system has remained unchallenged and unchanged under the firm control of the agroexport oligarchy and big business, whether industrial or financial. Since there were no visible splits in the bourgeoisie, the more conservative sectors or groups have not stood out. The far right, the last holdout of political conservatism, emerged with its own identity

---

*Martín-Baró (1982b); see the Bibliography in the back of this book.

only when the country, under mounting pressure due to internal problems and demands for radical change, was contemplating some kind of
reform in order to modernize or adjust the system to new circumstances.
What the far right in El Salvador represents, therefore, cannot be understood simply by contrasting it with the revolutionary movement, but
must also be seen in relation to attempts at reform that have taken place
in the country during the last two decades.

At these moments of danger from reform, the far right explicitly assumes its hegemonic role in the oligarchy, draws on its resources, and
refurbishes its political and social traditions. Therefore, although obviously it is directing its forces against popular and revolutionary movements, which it knows are ultimately the explanation behind any
demand for change, conjuncturally it reaffirms its own stance vis-à-vis
reform sectors, which it perceives as opening the way to revolution. . . .*

The Ideology of El Salvador's Far Right

In order to analyze the ideology of ARENA, as the current political
arm of the Salvadoran far right, I will first examine its statements and
propaganda, and then its symbols and the style of its public action.
Rounding out this ideological analysis will require going beyond this
conceptual and formal discourse to the concrete way the party and its
members act in various circumstances, since only that will reveal the
deeper meaning of its conceptual statements.

FROM INDIVIDUALISM TO NATIONAL SECURITY

The starting point for ARENA's ideological vision is its exaltation of
individualism (ARENA, 1981). The individual is to be regarded as the
beginning and end of political activity, the foundation of the people,
which is simply the sum total of individuals. The state is nothing but a
"means for the expansion and progress of the individual," who should
be the ultimate beneficiary of all social activity. In fact, "all the accomplishments that are the pride of humankind today are the result of the
creativity of the individual." ARENA accepts "the equality of all human
beings before God," but also underscores their diversity on earth. This
becomes very important when human rights come up, since the only

---

*Here the original article goes on to discuss in some detail the activity of those
in the "far right" in the 1976 conflict over land reform and in the aftermath of
the 1979 coup. In both instances they mobilized to defeat reform proposals. The
creation of ARENA as a political party in 1981 was the far right's response to
the announcement of an electoral process. P.B.

one who "is acknowledged to be worthy of freedom is that individual who successfully conquers freedom through his or her own daily effort to get ahead."

It seems obvious that the individualism that ARENA exalts is primarily that of the individuality of each person. Nevertheless, ARENA extends its exaltation of personal individualism to business individualism by opposing "private enterprise" to "public enterprise" in the same terms it uses to oppose the individual to the group. The transition from the individual to the enterprise takes place through the "individual right to the acquisition, retention, and use of property as a projection of the human personality" which in turn makes "private" enterprise an essential part of the individual. Accordingly, to defend private enterprise is to defend the individual's human rights. Thus, the individualism upheld by ARENA is an individualism within organized corporate private business, and the liberty demanded for private enterprise is a logical extension of the liberty demanded for the individual.

From this foundation of business group individualism ARENA focuses its ideological discourse on three values: *nationalism, anti-communism,* and *capitalism.*

ARENA's *nationalism* seems to be a matter of defending this "nation" which is regarded as those individuals who are integrated into the political and economic order existing in El Salvador until the present. According to ARENA, the value of a social system must be measured by its capacity to bring about the integral development of the nation. Therefore, the option for a democratic and republican system is a pragmatic question rather than one of principle. The choice is made because it is the quickest and most stable way to attain national development, which occurs when individuals are guaranteed the freedom to act and to pursue their own ends. Thus if the system prevailing thus far in El Salvador is good, it is so because it has brought about the integral development of this nation. That, however, means that the Salvadoran nation is made up solely of the "true Salvadoran people," sometimes called the country's "vital forces" or "productive forces," who are in turn identified with large private enterprise and individuals connected to it (that is, those who have achieved their own "integral development" through this system). Hence ARENA's nationalism amounts to promoting the productive forces of large private enterprise and defending them against any attack from within or without.

This kind of nationalism is closed to any conceptual division into management and labor "for in our practical activity and tasks we business people and workers could never be separated from one another in a democratic society" (ARENA, 1981). To accept such a division would entail acknowledging that there are other factors besides individual "betterment and work" which come into play in the "integral development" of the nation and hence of individuals, and that it is these factors that keep most Salvadorans enslaved in misery. Such a division would ultimately lead to questioning the very principle on which the nationalism of the Salvadoran far right rests, and hence would not allow the interests of capital or big business to be identified with the "noble interests of the nation."

ARENA's second great value is its militant *anti-communism*. On a deeper level, this is an anti-value since it is interested primarily in what is to be rejected, and only negatively in what is to be sought for the future. What ARENA means by communism is never defined except on a very generic level. For example, communism is identified with collectivizing tendencies, with the nationalization of any means of production, and with a certain kind of state intervention in the country's economic life. Thus the term "communism" is more emotional than conceptual, and with little qualification it is used interchangeably with other terms such as socialism, Marxism, Marxist-Leninism, and totalitarianism. During the political campaign for the March election, ARENA even called the "communitarianism" of Christian Democracy communist, thus indicating the real meaning of the term "communism" in the ideology of the Salvadoran far right. Communism is any system, movement, or ideology that is not fully identified with the prevailing system in El Salvador or that calls for some kind of social change. Communism is thus the denial of the nationalism that ARENA upholds. Therefore, in the discourse of the Salvadoran far right, Fidel Castro and Jimmy Carter, the Communist Party and the Jesuits, the FMLN and the United States Senate can all be equally communist.

This understanding of communism shows that the posture ARENA defends is in perfect harmony with the principles of the doctrine of "national security" (Campos: 1979). From the standpoint of "national security" the world is radically divided into supporters of the capitalist system and "the values of Western civilization" and their adversaries. There is nothing in between and no one can get around this division. Maintaining this system is the basic principle, the supreme value to which everything must be subordinated. Therefore the defense of this system and these values justifies any measure and any action, no matter how harsh. Hence the need to keep an eye on anyone suspicious and to apply the same yardstick to both peaceful and violent opponents, to activists and intellectuals, to open enemies or mere critics. Communism is a cancer that sneaks into every corner and it must be rooted out. This vision provides prior justification for any behavior by the armed forces for the purpose of maintaining traditional law and the existing order.

ARENA's third core value, *capitalism*, is not just any capitalism, but rather the kind of capitalism that has prevailed in our country. This economic system revolves around the inalienable right to private property, and the state's role is simply to protect and safeguard the free economic activity of individuals and firms. Any measure that threatens the right to private property or the freedom of private enterprise is an assault on the basic principles of the capitalist economic system, which is the foundation of national unity, and is therefore a threat to national security. Thus in practice the nationalism ARENA upholds is a nationalism defined by its anticommunism and by its profession of capitalist faith and which utilizes the principles and mechanisms of national security in order to preserve the system of profitable productivity and individualistic development which has prevailed in El Salvador for decades.

Even a cursory examination of ARENA's political propaganda confirms this ideological vision. Of ten major pieces of propaganda published by ARENA in newspapers in San Salvador in March of 1982, five attacked the destructive "accomplishments" of the nationalizing reforms carried out by the Christian Democrat government. Four others tried to prove with ideological arguments or with documents (a letter of introduction) that "the Communist Party and Christian Democracy are the same" and therefore that Christian Democrat communitarianism is as dangerous to national security as the communism of the guerrillas.

In light of the clash over the 1976 Agrarian Transformation, it is very significant that the most aggressive statements during the ARENA political campaign were signed by "the agricultural sector of ARENA" and especially by "ARENA members from the east." The style and vocabulary of these statements is similar to that of the statements by FARO in 1976, and the same arguments based on productive and nationalistic patriotism were set forth [see Ellacuría (1976); Chapter 4 *of this volume*]. The growers group within ARENA went so far as to say that "human history has not known a genocide comparable to what the Christian Democrats are doing to our people," as a result of "the credit regulations for cotton growing laid down by the Christian Democrat Party now in power" (ARENA, 1982).

ARENA's "STYLE"

Above and beyond its ideological propaganda and its public statements, the style ARENA employed during the political campaign expresses its values. It is especially remarkable that the symbolism employed by ARENA takes its cue from international movements, seemingly contradicting its particular vision of nationalism. For example, the party's name and its colors [red, white, and blue] suggest the current U.S. administration, headed by President Reagan, a conservative Republican (explicitly referred to in a paid ad on March 24). The slogan "today struggle, tomorrow peace, progress, and freedom," subtly hints at but also transforms the well-known trilogy of the French republic. Indeed, the ARENA emblem is almost an exact copy of that of the Guatemalan MLN [Movement of National Liberation], whose top leader defines his party as "the right of the right."

ARENA's behavioral style can be described with three terms: determination, clarity, and strength. ARENA's determination prompts it to do battle in the most conflictive and most dangerous places. With symbolic gestures that had a certain "macho" ring to them, ARENA launched its political campaign at the very place where the 1932 uprising broke out and where it was put down with the greatest violence. It also made a show of going to places where the guerrillas actually might be a threat. Such determination reflected a mixture of self-assurance and swagger vis-à-vis the guerrillas and the government and even the armed forces.

Along with its macho determination came "clear" speech. The language ARENA spoke was seemingly clear, a discourse based on slogans ("Homeland yes, communism no"), and simplistic statements about the cause of the present chaos ("Christian Democrat, dis-government"). Broad statements, catchy slogans, and Manichaean explanations (it's either black or white, good or bad) had the advantage of looking like irrefutable proof in the mass media. This style of ARENA, especially on the lips of its most well known leader, Major Roberto D'Aubuisson, gave people the impression that ARENA was "telling it like it is." That impression was reinforced by the personalizing and the continually accusatory things its spokespersons had to say. People's discontent and the social chaos they were experiencing found a ready explanation in the wholesale accusations ARENA directed against those in power.

The third feature of ARENA was its display of force. Public appearances by its representatives were always accompanied by visible armed protection and a more or less elaborate display of weapons. Most important, however, is the fact that ARENA never made efforts to deny, and even indirectly encouraged, the rumors to the effect that it was backed by a true "private army" and that it was connected to the paramilitary forces operating in the country. Whether true or not, these connections made ARENA look like a force that was not simply political, but political-military, and in this sense the equivalent on the right of what the FMLN represents on the left.

The Appeal of the Salvadoran Far Right

In the March 1982 election the far right showed that it could capture the votes of a considerable proportion of the Salvadoran electorate. Hence it is important to examine both ARENA's social base and how various sectors of the Salvadoran population were attracted by its positions and style.

ARENA'S INTERLOCUTORS

In order to determine who ARENA's supporters are, both now and potentially, we must find out to whom they direct their political discourse. ARENA's main interlocutors [those with whom they dialogue] seem to be the following: members of the armed forces, owners of land or medium-size businesses, and representatives of Mr. Reagan's administration in the United States.

It seems obvious that ARENA's first interlocutor is the Salvadoran armed forces (AF). All its public activities begin with the invocation "Colleagues, true people of El Salvador, Armed Forces" (or "companions in arms" when D'Aubuisson is speaking) and they contain some explicit allusion and even open appeals to the AF. Far from criticizing or censuring the AF, ARENA flatters and systematically courts its members, whom it calls the most genuine representatives of the Salvadoran nation, if not its saviors. ARENA sidesteps dealing openly with the manifesto of the young officers who carried out the October 1979 coup, but it attacks the reforms set in motion by that movement, attributing them entirely to the civilian side of the government junta. It is not the military who are responsible for the evils afflicting El Salvador, much less the armed forces as an institution, rather it is subversion by communists and by the Christian Democrat politicians in power that is responsible. ARENA lets the AF know that it supports unconditionally their struggle for national security against any kind of subversion, and hints that after taking office it will allow them a free hand to do what is necessary to "pacify" the country.

ARENA's second interlocutor consists of "medium" owners, whom it tries to convince that their problems and economic hardships are due to social and political reformism. Winning over these sectors is a crucial objective for ARENA, not only because of the impact they have on the economic life of the country, but because they provide a democratic face and serve as bridge to other sectors of the population. Medium owners are not directly affected by the reforms, and they may actually benefit from them, and hence may be tempted by reforms. Therefore, the representatives of big business regard it as very important that they win this sector over to their side and thus pull together a broad business front (the Producer's Alliance or Producer's Union) as a social base for their political options. ARENA's propaganda efforts to demonstrate the managerial inefficiency of the public sector and the disastrous results of the reforms in productivity and profit are a clear message to medium owners.

ARENA's third major interlocutor is the government of the United States, first and foremost the executive branch, but also the legislative branch. ARENA repeatedly tried to present itself as a valid option and even as the only realistic option for El Salvador, in contrast to the Christian Democrat card that the U.S. government has chosen to play. Hence the far right has established a lobbying office in Washington, tones down its ideological discourse in some ways, especially with regard to carrying out or continuing the reforms begun in the country, pressures U.S. diplomats publicly and privately, and even tries to gain the sympathy of some journalists so they will present a positive image of ARENA and D'Aubuisson to public opinion in the United States.

Nowhere in ARENA's propaganda discourse is there any effort to deal with the problems of the marginal sectors or the oppressed masses. Indirectly, however, through its display of determination and swagger, it sends a threatening message to those who might express disagreement with the country's social, political, and economic system. The assumption is that the traditional system is best for all individuals in the nation. The carte blanche given to military and paramilitary forces to achieve peace and national security is a message whose meaning is unmistakable for most of the Salvadoran population. By specifying that it addresses the "true Salvadoran people," ARENA is clearly stating that there is a "false Salvadoran people" whose identity can easily be deduced and which ARENA does not hesitate to point out.

ARENA's SOCIAL BASE

An examination of the interests that ARENA defends in its propaganda leaves no doubt about whose interests they are. Its defense of productivity and of private property regardless of distributive justice or the common good (Lindo, 1982), its radical opposition to any reform, whether "communist" or "communitarian," its support for the use of political repression to put down any popular dissidence or protest, all clearly prove that ARENA is defending the interests of Salvadoran big business. Hence it seems plausible to assume that representatives of this sector of society are present in ARENA's base. That assumption is confirmed in practice by the spokespersons and candidates ARENA presents, who are well known members of the major business organizations.

A social base, however, is not the same thing as votes cast. There is no certainty about the real number of votes cast on March 28, 1982. The Central Election Council declared that ARENA had received 402,304 votes out of a total of 1,551,687, that is, 25.93%. If, as is indicated by the only studies that have appeared thus far, it seems that the number of votes cast was inflated to twice the actual figure, ARENA would have received a total of approximately 200,000 votes (Elecciones, 1982; Las elecciones y la unidad, 1982; Leiken, 1982). However, not even all of these votes can be regarded as belonging to an ARENA social base. Those familiar with elections in El Salvador and who observed the process on March 28, witnessed a number of techniques used by ARENA to get votes: pressures from bosses, pressure by civilian and military people positioned near the ballot boxes, and assistance on "how" to vote given to the more ignorant as they approached the ballot box (Chitnis: 1982). Indeed even those who freely voted for ARENA could be motivated by a number of reasons, ranging from being aware of and in agreement with the interests the party upholds, to fear of losing a job, and to identifying emotionally with its leadership and the criticisms it was making.

In a survey taken a month and a half before the elections, of the 1,789 university students living in the greater San Salvador area, only 39.2% said they were going to vote, while 38.8% said they were undecided (Elecciones, 1982). Of that 39.2% who were going to vote, 39.7% said they were voting out of a fear of reprisals, 20.3% out of a desire for peace, and 10.9% because it was their civic duty and the rest for a variety of other reasons. Among the undecided group, 19.2% indicated that they did not know whether they would vote, precisely out of a fear of reprisals if they did not; another 12.2% pointed to the hardships of the objective situation, the next 10.7% mentioned the lack of alternative political parties, and 7.7% admitted they were confused. This all indicates at the very least that the electoral scene was not very clear, even to the most cultured and potentially best informed circles in the country, and that among the numerous reasons for voting, fear of reprisals played an important role.

When votes are counted, however, ballots look the same whether cast freely or out of fear, with a clear class consciousness or out of ignorance and alienation. The upshot is that the ARENA party unquestionably has a great deal of mobilizing ability. The fact that a "new" party could get 25.9% of the total votes cast means that it is an important social force in the country. In determining the social base of this party, however, the motives that led people to vote are important because only the votes of those who are free or who act out of conviction signify real support for the party's action.

One way of figuring out who these convinced party members are is to look at the various rallies and meetings organized by ARENA throughout the election campaign and to compare them with demonstrations held during the first government junta, which were promoted by various organizations under the ideological and social umbrella of ANEP. A necessarily superficial examination of who participated seems to indicate that the core of activists was the same in both cases and that this core was largely made up of a very aggressive group of women from the wealthiest and most powerful circles in the country. In December 1979 this group of women marched under the FAN [Broad National Front] banner to the headquarters of the armed forces. It surrounded the house of the United States Ambassador Robert White and staged a long sit-in protest in May 1980. FAN also gathered petitions and money to set up ARENA. It went along with various public forums around the country and was even present during the first sessions of the constituent assembly where it loudly supported the proposals of the ARENA representatives. If we are right in identifying ARENA's basic core activists as belonging to the wealthiest circles in the country, ARENA has generated a degree of political activism among the right which had previously been observed only in left-wing movements. For the first time in the modern history of El Salvador there is a systematic mobilization of its pro-oligarchical masses.

ARENA's APPEAL IN TERMS OF SOCIAL PSYCHOLOGY

The objective social interests of the core of ARENA coincide with the interests and values expressed in the party's key ideas. However, just as not all the bourgeoisie voted for ARENA, many of the votes freely cast for ARENA came from people in other sectors of society. Hence it is worth asking what appeal ARENA had for those whose objective social interests it clearly does not defend, and indeed combats. We have no studies that would enable us to come to a solid answer to this question. Given the lack of empirical data and in the light of similar processes, my hypothesis is that four factors can explain this attraction: opposition to the government, ARENA's macho style, the logic of power, and the image projected by its main leader.

During the last few years, social conditions in El Salvador have declined dramatically as a result of the interaction between the economic crisis and the political crisis which has turned into civil war. On top of massive unemployment, there is widespread terror caused by repressive violence; and on top of the daily anguish over whether there is something to eat, there is the suffering caused by the disappearance and murder of family members and friends. All of this is the basis for a deep discontent which could find some outlet in the demonstrations of the popular organizations until 1980. Since mid-1980, however, some people have seen no way out except by chosing to join the guerrillas. For large segments of the population, however, that option is neither realistic nor feasible. Because space for political dissent has been closed off and the opposition media have been muzzled or simply eliminated, and any protests or demands have been brutally crushed, the bulk of the Salvadoran people have stored up a huge amount of just resentment against those who control and administer the government.

It seems plausible to suggest that by gaining an image as a radical alternative to the Christian Democrat "dis-government," ARENA has been able to use some of this reservoir of frustration and suffering advantageously. Voting for the opposition in El Salvador has often expressed a rejection of established power rather than support for even well-known parties or movements of the moment, which, however, have profited from such a vote. Thus the ARENA party paradoxically may have benefitted from a rejection of established power in the March 1982 election. ARENA's violent criticisms directed towards the junta headed by Napoleon Duarte may have put into words a certain amount of the anger accumulated in large sectors of the population, who were powerless to find any other outlet for their discontent, and may have created an ideological impression that the social interests that ARENA upholds had nothing to do with El Salvador's social, political, and economic disaster.

Another possible fact attracting people to ARENA, one very connected to its posture of opposition to the government, is its style of action, which has already been mentioned. The determination of its ideological positions, the seeming clarity of its criticisms and its explanations of the country's problems, the haughty and defiant self-assurance with which it acts in public towards everyone, the blatant way it displays power, including the suspicion that it had paramilitary extensions, make ARENA something of a "political macho" with unquestionable appeal. Along with the content of its ideology, ARENA's way of behaving was through discourse that the pro-oligarchical sectors of Salvadoran society could identify with, since they were concerned over a reformist movement that has the support of military officers and Americans, are alarmed over the growing strength of popular movements and organizations, and worried about recovering all their traditional positions of power. Paradoxically, ARENA's swaggering self-assurance might also be attractive to people who have no economic, political, or social power and who merely see in ARENA an alternative more viable than that of the FDR/FMLN for ending the miseries of the present, including guerrilla war.

A further appeal of ARENA's ideological discourse as well as its behavioral style is the way it fits in with the traditional logic of power in the social organization of El Salvador. In this sense, ARENA is a "natural" product of the political system prevailing in the country, and its posture has the advantage that it can draw on the rationality that comes from being in accord with the established order. The viewpoints expressed by ARENA fit in with the very principles and values that have been preached traditionally in Salvadoran society. Its arguments can draw on the values of a moral pattern imposed for generations. Thus from this angle ARENA's assertiveness looks like a just defense of nationalism, and its appeal on behalf of the capitalist system is grounded in the logic and values that are normative in the social tradition of El Salvador. No doubt this connaturality of ARENA with the established power system and its moral patterns is attractive to certain people or sectors of the population who do not have the critical capacity to transcend the framework into which they have been socialized.

Finally, ARENA was able to make its case effectively by using the drawing power of its leader, Major Roberto D'Aubuisson. D'Aubuisson's charisma had already begun to emerge in political dealings with the armed forces and in the organizing and activities of the Broad Nationalist Front. D'Aubuisson was almost the prototypical incarnation of both ARENA's ideology and its style, and thus he provided a personalized model with which people could identify more easily than they could with a set of ideas or a political platform. D'Aubuisson was determined and clear, he was telling it "like it is." He did not mince words, he used street language, and he did not shrink from strong epithets or cutting expressions. Moreover he was a strongman, and because of his past had actual links to the military (in some circles where he was very popular), and his rumored present connected him to paramilitary bodies. All this gave D'Aubuisson a certain air of power and danger that ARENA's public relations people earnestly cultivated. The climax came when D'Aubuisson was only slightly injured in a serious attempt on his life.

Opposition stance, "macho" style, being in tune with the logic of the system, and being personalized in a leader: these seem to be the main elements that embody ARENA's appeal in terms of social psychology. For those within the ruling sectors who have a clear class consciousness, ARENA's most attractive feature is that it has proved to be a useful political instrument for defending and promoting their interests. The appeal that ARENA had among other sectors of the population, whose objective interests it does not defend but rather combats, can only be understood adequately in the light of other factors of social psychology, whether it be those here proposed hypothetically or others. It is almost impossible to quantify the size of the real vote ARENA received from social sectors whose objective interests are different. In any case, its success among the ranks of the dominant social classes as well as the way its public image apparently worked throughout the population cannot be ignored, whether or not this drawing power resulted in actual votes.

Conclusions: the Significance of ARENA

ARENA is a political party which has been used to articulate the social interests of big business in the Salvadoran social and political context of 1982. In terms of party organization it is still quite weak, and it is unlikely that it has stable enough bases to give it solidity and life outside of electoral periods or circumstances of social conflict. The fact that the core of its social base comes from bourgeois or pro-bourgeois circles probably means that its party activity will be limited and ad hoc, even on those occasions when ARENA has been obviously successful in organizing these sectors to adopt aggressive and active positions. Nevertheless, the very functional dependence that makes ARENA weak also makes it strong. Precisely because ARENA has proven to be an effective instrument for politically articulating and organizing the interests of Salvadoran big business, it is very likely that it will survive as a useful instrument and will become more established in the future, at least as long as this social sector has no better tool and the country's social and political structure do not change radically.

ARENA has emerged in the same manner as FARO, that is, as a political instrument necessary for setting in motion the pro-oligarchical response to the threat of significant social reforms. When the danger of the Agrarian Transformation vanished, so did FARO. We may assume that as long as there is the danger of the reforms proposed in the military's October 15 manifesto and demanded by the United States, ARENA or its equivalent will continue to exist. It also seems clear that the threat will remain as long as there is a popular movement like the one in El Salvador in recent years and a political-military coalition like the FMLN. ARENA is plainly big capital's political-military counterpart to the revolutionary organizations in El Salvador. Faced with demand for revolutionary change, various sectors, especially in the armed forces, seek to pursue such reforms as may satisfy some basic demands for distributive justice and stabilize the prevailing system within a modified social order. Hence it seems likely that ARENA will strengthen its party structure in the near future, especially if the recently announced process for presidential elections is carried out. It is quite possible, however, that ARENA's image would be tarnished if it held power, as is the case with the image of its leader, who heads the constituent assembly.

ARENA does not have to define its ideology with precision since it can reflect in its discourse the principles and values defended by the organizations that represent big business. ARENA's role is rather to be the political spearhead and the catalyst of support from other social sectors for the political and economic interests of big business in El Salvador. In this sense, ARENA has been and is still a useful mechanism for political organizing. It fits the demands of the formal democracy that the United States has currently imposed on the country. The success ARENA achieved in the recent election shows that its strength lies in the power of its social base. Hence it is not strictly speaking, a fascist movement, although we can note some ideological elements proper to that political tendency (its anti-communism, for example). Rather ARENA is a political body that is strongly related to business organizations, and it resembles movements started in other countries by what has been called the "new right," and which is promoted by a private sector determined to have a presence in the political arena.

ARENA has enabled the private sector to establish a new dialogue with the Armed Forces, whose reform faction is in contention with the faction that insists on playing the role they have played since 1932. ARENA has also served to prove how useful the "democratic way" and elections can be to the interests of big business. Under current conditions in El Salvador, the electoral system provides a suitable way in which the forces representing these business interests can reestablish themselves in their traditional positions of power, after some of those positions had been challenged by the events of recent years. Hence, we may conclude that the Salvadoran wealthy will continue to make use of this "democratic way," and that ARENA will be their main instrument in El Salvador's immediate future. [For later thinking on this issue, see UCA Editorial Board (1984); and Montes (1988b), Chapter 13, *this volume.*]

Ignacio Martín-Baró

17. From Dirty War
to Psychological War:
The Case of El Salvador*

TRANSLATION BY ADRIANNE ARON

War and Democracy in El Salvador

To fully understand the psycho-social problems of refugees,
essential that we understand the circumstances giving rise to their fl
(Kunz, 1981; Stein, 1981). The politician who goes into exile aft
government has been overthrown is not the same as the professi·
who leaves his or her country in search of a better life; nor is the
who flees because of a disgust with the violence of war the same as
who, pursued by death squads, must escape in order to stay alive.

According to the official image accepted by the international n
media, El Salvador since 1984 has been involved in a democratiza
process, begun with free presidential elections and characterized k
progressive opening of the political arena and a notable improvemer
respect for human rights. With these changes El Salvador seemec
have lost its status of "black sheep" of the Western world and becc
the example of how a small country, with the help of the United Sta
could fight to overcome underdevelopment while at the same t:
democratically fending off the attempts of international communisn
use it as a base for hegemonic control.

Unfortunately, this official image is a distortion of reality, peric
cally brought into question by what is actually happening inside
country. Without proceeding further, let us note a series of events t
occurred in El Salvador during the months of May and June, 1¢
producing a fear that the death squads and the worst forms of st
terrorism, such as existed in 1981-82, had returned. These eve

---

*Martín-Baró (1988a); see the Bibliography in the back of this book.

included the abduction, torture, and beheading of a campesino union leader, the kidnapping and disappearance of three other union leaders, and the capture and near slaughter of three campesinos who barely managed to escape alive—all by men identified as members of the AF—the destruction by dynamite of an office of COMADRES (the Committee of Mothers of Political Prisoners and the Disappeared); and the publication of a new blacklist* by the Secret Anticommunist Army. These events have obliged the government and the armed forces to issue immediate disclaimers of responsibility and reiterate in public their commitments to democracy and human rights.

The fear of a reappearance of state terrorism is, at the very least, [not] naive. In its objectives if not in its form, the dirty war has at no time stopped being an essential ingredient in the socio-political project that the United States is trying to achieve in El Salvador. Looking beyond ideological interpretations of all shades, the data leave no shadow of a doubt about the matter. The facts show that in El Salvador in 1986 there were no less than 122 assassinations attributed to the death squads—that is, ten assassinations a month, not counting other killings and violations of basic human rights attributable to governmental forces (IDHUCA, 1987).

The primary goal of the North American project is the elimination of the revolutionary movement; the restoration of democracy in the country is only secondary, or derivative. That is why, when the time was propitious, the project set out to get rid of all insurgent groups, rapidly and brutally, combining military action with a massive campaign of repression against the civilian population. When this campaign failed, the project entered into a new phase that sought to achieve the same objective through democratic forms that would justify the project itself. This produced a permanent contradiction between military necessities and political exigencies, between the objective of eliminating all significant opposition and protest, and the necessity of offering, or seeming to offer, an open political system. Essentially, the North American project for El Salvador had to find a form of dirty war that would allow it to realize its goals but spare it from having to pay the political costs. And the answer was thought to have been found in psychological warfare.

Our thesis is that the psychological war now being developed by the armed forces of El Salvador is a legacy of the dirty war that went on between 1980 and 1983. It is a parallel war that allows the same objectives to be attained, and that produces similar psycho-social consequences for the population, while safeguarding an image of formal democracy. This image of formal democracy enables the United States

---

*For an example, see narration on the campesino massacre in "Chalatenango" (1987) in the References cited in the back of this book.

to keep public opinion on its side and not lose the support of other democratic governments for its policies in the area. This is not to say that dirty war and psychological war are identical, but rather that the psychological war is the current expression of the old dirty war, at this stage of the Salvadoran conflict.

Parallel War

We will examine our thesis by contrasting three essential aspects of dirty war and psychological war: their objectives, their methods, and the psycho-social consequences they produce.

OBJECTIVES

Dirty war is not directed only, nor even perhaps primarily, at those who have openly risen in arms against an established régime. Dirty war is aimed at those sectors and individuals who make up the base of support—either material or intellectual, real or potential—of the insurgent forces. But since there exists no political or legal justification for a country to turn its whole army or its security forces against its own civilian population, the work is entrusted to clandestine groups, the famous "death squads." In this way the country can carry out a program for systematically eliminating enemies, both real and potential, without tarnishing the public image of the forces who do the work.

This is what occurred in El Salvador between 1980 and 1983: groups of "armed men in civilian dress" kidnapped, tortured, assassinated, and disappeared thousands of Salvadorans suspected of collaborating with the revolutionary movement or sympathizing with its cause. Conservative estimates suggest that there were no less than 27,000 victims of this dirty war between 1980 and 1983; that is to say, one out of every 200 Salvadorans (CUDI, 1980-1983). These groups always operated with total impunity, something which would not have been possible without the connivance, support, and protection of the country's military and political powers.

The dirty war achieved three important objectives:

1. A dismantling of the popular mass organizations. The very existence of organizations unsympathetic to the government became impossible, and those militants who were not exterminated had to flee to the countryside or go underground, or, choked with terror, abandon the struggle.

2. An elimination of many of the most significant opposition figures: for example, the leadership of the Democratic Revolutionary Front (a political organization comprised of the principal opposition organizations); the Rector of the University of El Salvador, Dr. Felix Ulloa; and the Archbishop of San Salvador, Monsignor Oscar Arnulfo Romero.

3. A weakening of the support bases of the revolutionary movement in all sectors of the population: professionals, students, workers, campesinos. In terms of these objectives, there is no doubt that the dirty war was successful—a macabre success to be sure, but successful none the less.

Still, the dirty war was very costly. Despite the anonymity with which the death squads operated, it was hard to convince world public opinion that such work could have been carried out without the collusion of the official forces. It became, then, an arduous task for the United States to justify its almost unconditional support of a régime that warranted condemnation for its systematic violation of fundamental human rights. Even harder was the task of getting new international support for the régime. The Reagan administration stood practically alone in defending the Salvadoran régime in international forums, accompanied only by governments like those of Pinochet or Stroessner.

For this reason, in 1984, in the face of unexpected military successes by the insurgents who were threatening to disarm the national army, it was understood that a new phase was needed for the Salvadoran war. To move ahead with the project for eliminating the revolutionary movement, the plan demanded an intensification of counterinsurgency, particularly by means of an air war. But it would be necessary to avoid the political costs of a massive repression that would impede the development of such a military war. Towards this end some process would have to be initiated to legitimize the war, and in the Western world there is nothing more seductive than the process of formal democracy. It was proposed, then, that there be a process of democratization which would parallel the process of pacification, in such a way that the military conquests would be transformed into political victories, while what transpired politically would insure a military win. The figure of Napoleon Duarte would play a crucial role in this new phase, as much for his image as a democratic man as for his connections with the International Christian Democrats who were so influential in Europe and in other Latin American countries.

If a restoration of democracy had really been sought, and if they had gone to the structural causes of the conflict, the new plan might have worked. But that would have involved a subordination of the war to democracy, rather than the other way around, and that in turn would have made the war a political instrument rather than making politics another instrument of war. A vision such as this would have gone completely astray from the North American government's diagnosis, which held that the Salvadoran war had to be fought against Soviet expansion because the danger to peace and democracy stemmed from "communist aggression," not from internal conditions of oppressive misery and structural injustice.

Driven by the anti-communist obsession of the Reagan Administration, the new phase of the Salvadoran war has tried to apply the "low intensity conflict" doctrine (Barry, 1986; Castro, 1986; Barry, Castro & Vergara, 1987), so as to produce a formalist democracy totally reduced to war plans; that is, one that serves as a political cover for a continued military war against revolutionary movements.

According to Barry (1986, pp. 23-35), low intensity war is set up on three fronts: on the battleground itself (using guerrilla-like tactics and trying to involve all social issues in the struggle); in the institutions of the United States (such as Congress); and in public opinion, national and international. As none of these three fronts attends adequately to the deep causes of the Salvadoran war, none of them gets to the roots of the discontent and rebellion. That explains why the new phase of the war required, as did the earlier one, a policy of systematic elimination of all bases of support for the insurgent movement. But there would have to be new forms for this elimination, forms that would respect the standards of low intensity war and, in the concrete case of El Salvador, the formal requirements of democracy. Out of this came the need for psychological war; for programs to annihilate the enemy, not by physically eliminating him, but by conquering him psychologically. The aim was to destroy the enemy as such, by winning "hearts and minds." With these methods it would no longer be necessary to hide the actors in anonymity; those responsible for the parallel war could be celebrated as patriots and national heroes.

The psychological war developing in El Salvador seeks, then, to be a democratic means for achieving the same ends as the dirty war. But does this really have to do with a democratic way of making war?

METHODS

To begin, it must be underscored that psychological war is, when all is said and done, a form of warfare. Like dirty war, and by definition, all war, it seeks to vanquish the enemy by the use of violence. To speak of "democratic war" can only be a contradiction in terms. According to some, psychological war pursues its conquest of the minds and hearts of the population in such a way as to obviate the need for any political alternative (Aguilera, 1986). According to others, psychological war intends to do no more than to "corrupt the social conscience of the adversary" (Volkogonov, 1986, see p. 39). But in the best of cases, psychological war does not seek cohesion in the population as an end in itself, as something that would follow from people's personal and social needs being met. Such cohesion is desired only for its instrumental value as a means of impeding support for the enemy. In other words, what is sought is the support of the people, not to satisfy their demands, but to win their minds and hearts without changing anything in their situation or living conditions, and without meeting any of their unfulfilled needs. What battlefield war and dirty war seek to achieve by physical destruction, psychological war hopes to achieve by destroying minds and rendering people useless. As in the case of torture, psychological methods come to be substituted for physical methods, but in both cases the effort is to crush the person, to destroy personal autonomy and the capacity to resist, not to broaden people's liberty or to expand their options.

It is important to clarify that psychological war is not confined to the realm of public opinion, as might be thought, and neither are its methods confined to the waging of propaganda campaigns. Psychological war attempts to influence the entire person, not just a person's beliefs and points of view. And for this to succeed, it must employ other methods in addition to propaganda campaigns.

From the psycho-social standpoint, what both dirty war and psychological war resort to, as their chief means of eliminating support to war enemies, is the sense of insecurity. There is nothing subjective about this [essential] insecurity. It corresponds faithfully to an objective social atmosphere, an atmosphere which requires people to disengage, and which is created intentionally by those who hold power unlawfully (Lira, Weinstein, and Salamovich, 1985-86).

To create this atmosphere of insecurity, dirty war uses terrorist repression; that is, it visibly carries out cruel acts that unleash uncontrollable fear in the population. While the repression itself physically eliminates those who are the direct targets of its actions, its terrorizing character tends to paralyze all those others who, in one or another way, might feel some identification with the victims. For this effect to be maximized, the terrorist state, and concretely, the dirty war, have to assure that the population is kept well informed about what is going on, even though publicity about such things is often self-defeating.

Psychological war, too, seeks to create a climate of uncertainty in order to achieve its ends. But instead of terrorist repression, it employs what we might call manipulative repression. It no longer tries to paralyze the civil population completely, but only to inhibit its potential for rebellion and at least prevent its effective support of the enemy. It is necessary, therefore, that the people have a continual dose of fear, and that is achieved by means of a systematic and unforeseeable dosage of threats and stimulants, of prizes and punishments, of acts of intimidation and examples of conditional protection. Thus, psychological war combines acts of "civic action" (a military version of public welfare) with operations of great war violence, comprehensive deals for people after imprisoning them for no reason, or generous offers to a variety of groups and social sectors following exhausting harassments. At any moment, the executors of psychological war might assume an overpowering position, to make it clear who is the boss, who gives or takes away, who defines and decides. The militarization of daily life and the main parts of the social world contributes to the omnipresence of overpowering control and repressive threats. Occasionally, an act of terrorist repression will revive a sharp sense of fear in the population.

This is how an atmosphere of insecurity is fostered, unpredictable in its consequences, and demanding of people a complete submission to the dictates of power.

One of the mechanisms of psychological pressure most commonly used in torture is making the person feel alone, abandoned by all relatives, friends, and companions, as if nobody cared any more (Watson, 1978; Corominas & Farré, 1978; Peters, 1985). In an analogous manner, one of the characteristic methods of psychological war is to produce a feeling of isolation in those groups and sectors that represent potential support for the revolutionary movement. In El Salvador there has been an attempt to isolate, through "sanitized corridors," all types of groupings and organizations suspected of being able to help, or of simply sympathizing with the insurgents. There are checkpoints and barriers to keep those who live in the zones of conflict from freely entering or leaving the areas where they live, and to stop anyone from carrying provisions or medicine into the area, or even in some cases from living or working there. Members of humanitarian organizations are systematically harassed, detained, interrogated, and searched; when they are not threatened, imprisoned, insulted, and beaten, they are publicly accused of serving as a cover and instrument of the revolutionary movements, and once such an accusation has been made it hangs over them permanently, threatening and endangering their lives. And when, as in the case of the mothers' committees, this permanent harassment is not enough to paralyze them, their offices are blown up as a clear warning that next time stronger measures might be taken.

In this context of insecurity, the official propaganda acquires more force with its insistent invitation to "join up with the democratic process," given that "now you are free to publicly express and publicly advertise any dissent." Through an ever-present campaign, the mass media inform people of continual desertions, real or presumed, of militant insurgents, together with information on guerrilla military operations that have failed and their "desperate" resort to the most abject terrorism. All this feeds a sense of insecurity, and a sense that sympathy for the guerrillas is pointless, because their struggle is futile. People are made to feel that to continue sympathizing with the struggle makes no sense because it is hopeless: they are impotent, the struggle cannot be won.

Dirty war, like psychological war, is a way of denying reality. In the case of dirty war, anonymity, clandestinity, and impunity convert the "death squads" into phantom movements too frightening even to talk about. Yet more frightening is the disappearance of many of their victims, an act that is systematically denied by the officials, who go so far as to insinuate that these people have left to join the guerrillas. This kind of behavior on the part of the authorities places their roles and purposes in some strange dimension, far removed from ordinary reality. In the case of psychological war, the reality of everyday life as such is negated and redefined by the official propaganda. Whatever is contained in the unending official dispatches becomes "reality," however obvious its distortion of the facts may be. This definition of reality as manufactured by established powers and widely broadcast by the mass media, preys upon and invades people's consciousness, so that they can no longer trust their own perceptions and interpretations of what is going on. It leaves them in a continual state of uncertainty, wondering whether they might not be mistaken (Martín-Baró, 1985e).

In this atmosphere of institutionalized lying, a true Orwellian inversion of words results. To kill becomes a praiseworthy act, while attending to life's necessities is converted into subversive behavior; destroying hospitals is exalted as a patriotic service, while providing medical care to war victims is condemned as a terrorist activity. To ignore the violence of the war or to brag about it is Christian virtue or a demonstration of nationalism, but to denounce the trampling of human rights or condemn human rights violations becomes "a communist instrumentalization of Christian faith" or the action of a "bad Salvadoran."

PSYCHOLOGICAL CONSEQUENCES

It is not possible to distinguish completely between the consequences of the military war and those of the parallel one, be it dirty or psychological. Basically they exist as two complementary dimensions of a single process. We shall limit ourselves here to discussing the impact of the war on the civil population, for the parallel war is oriented towards civilians, not towards people engaged in combat.

There is no doubt that the first consequence of the war is the physical elimination or annihilation of people. Assassination and imprisonment, disappearance, and torture continue to be relatively common practices in El Salvador, and the fact that they have diminished significantly compared to 1981–82 does not mean they have been reduced to quantitatively "tolerable" levels (Americas Watch, 1986).

Together with the physical wounds of war are the psychological scars—those caused by particular traumatic acts as well as those generated by the permanent atmosphere of harassment and insecurity. According to Guillermo Mártir (1986), the war has produced a significant change—an increase of up to 20%—in the incidence of psychosomatic illness among patients at the Salvadoran Social Security Institute. In a 1987 survey conducted by the IUDOP, 10% of the adult urban Salvadoran population indicated that the illnesses most prevalent among members of their families were nervous disorders (anxiety, tension, "nerves," etc.). In light of Mártir's findings it seems quite probable that this percentage would be even higher in rural areas, especially in those places most directly subjected to military actions and psychological warfare operations.

A very serious psychological consequence of the parallel war, in its dirty guise as well as its psychological form, is that it blocks the development of a type of personal identity. One who would choose either to become a political revolutionary or even simply choose to define the horizons of his or her life in such a way as to oppose the established political system, cannot follow such a course. Because these options are closed, those who would have selected them tend to see themselves as political defectives, unable to carry out the life project that would give meaning to their existence. To yield to the aggression gives rise to existential frustration and self-devaluation, while to resist is to put one's own life and that of one's family at risk. As Lira, Weinstein, and Salamovich point out, psychological war cultivates an intentional depoliticization of the population (1985-86). What we see, then, is not a political indifference on the part of the masses, nor some presumed passive Latin American character, but rather a forced inhibition of their political-social options.

The ethical-political conflict that people confront, especially with respect to the way their acts affect third parties (family and/or others) often ends in a flight from the country (Aron, 1987). In some cases this flight is set off by some apparently trivial or relatively minor event, objectively speaking—particularly when it is compared with other things the fleeing person has already gone through. But generally this "straw that breaks the camel's back" marks the limit of what a person can bear, indicating a caving in of his or her psychological resistance.

A very important collective consequence is the devaluation of the fight for justice and the moral discrediting of those who defend revolutionary causes. The institutionalized lie sullies revolutionary ideals and activities, linking them to sordid motives and immoral roles. The construction of a symbolic Orwellian world of necessity affects the collective conscience and the historical horizon of the people.

Figure 1 shows the analogy between dirty war and psychological war schematically, as two modalities of "parallel war."

Final Reflections

If our thesis is valid and this psychological war is just another modality of the same dirty civil war but adapted to the new phase of El Salvador's civil war, then some important conclusions follow for the understanding and treatment of mental health problems in Salvadoran refugees.

1. Although human rights violations by political repression might have quantitatively and qualitatively decreased in El Salvador, this does not mean there has been an end to the conditions that force people to seek refuge outside the country. In this sense we think it is just as much an error to claim that nothing has changed in El Salvador between 1981

Figure 1. The Two Modalities of "Parallel War"

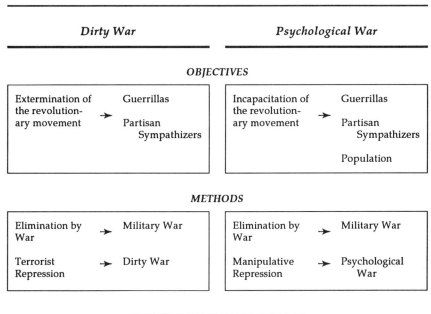

Dirty War	Psychological War

OBJECTIVES

Dirty War	Psychological War
Extermination of the revolutionary movement → Guerrillas / Partisan Sympathizers	Incapacitation of the revolutionary movement → Guerrillas / Partisan Sympathizers / Population

METHODS

Dirty War	Psychological War
Elimination by War → Military War	Elimination by War → Military War
Terrorist Repression → Dirty War	Manipulative Repression → Psychological War

PSYCHOLOGICAL CONSEQUENCES

Dirty War	Psychological War
· Physical Elimination · Psychic Traumas · Terror · Paralysis / Flight	· Physical Elimination · Psychic Traumas · Insecurity · Inhibition / Flight · Moral Discrediting

and the present as to say that today only economic circumstances justify a migration of Salvadorans to other lands. It becomes, then, essential to analyze the new forms of parallel war, and to determine the ways in which the psychological war might be producing results as deleterious as those of the dirty war, such that it, too, forces people to flee. Furthermore, the ideas presented here are as important for confronting the problems of those who flee as for those who, voluntarily or by force, return to the country.

2. It is crucial to emphasize the necessary collective—and therefore political—dimension of mental health (Martín-Baró, 1984c). As Eugenia Weinstein has so well put it, "a socially caused damage can only be socially repaired" (Weinstein, 1987, p. 38). One cannot think, then, that the problems of the refugees can be adequately solved through psychotherapy, whether it be individual or group therapy. The problems of the refugees require a true "socio-therapy," in the sense described by

Adrianne Aron for a social reconstruction of their lives and communities that were torn apart by repression and war (Aron, 1987, pp. 17-18).

3. A final reflection concerns the ethical responsibility of psychologists. It is known that some professionals cooperate, with greater or lesser degrees of consciousness, in the practice of psychological war. It is fitting to ask if the moment has not arrived, not only to clarify the ethical character of this co-operation, but to turn the psychological war around, with a massive campaign in favor of true peace (Departmento, 1986), and to do that as an essential part of the "socio-therapy" the country needs.

The Psychology of Liberation

Ignacio Martín-Baró

18. Towards A Liberation Psychology*

TRANSLATION BY ADRIANNE ARON

Psychology's Social Contribution in Latin America

Taken as a whole, psychology's contribution as science and as praxis to the history of the peoples of Latin America is extremely poor. To be sure, psychologists have not failed to concern themselves with the great problems of underdevelopment, dependency, and oppression that burden our peoples, but when it comes down to application, these concerns have often had to be channeled through a personal political commitment at the edges of the discipline, for the schemata of psychology break down when we try to use them to respond to the needs of the people.

I am not referring only to social psychology, whose crisis of meaning has been a much aired theme in the last decade. I'm referring to psychology as a whole: theoretical and applied, individual and social, clinical and educational. My thesis is that Latin American psychology, save for a few exceptions, has not only remained servilely dependent when it needed to lay out problems and seek solutions, but has stayed on the sidelines of the great movements and away from the distresses of the peoples of Latin America.

When one tries to name some Latin American contribution to the fund of universal psychology, the "social technology" of Jacobo Varela (1971) bears mentioning, as does the psychoanalytical thought of Enrique Pichon-Rivière of Argentina. Both deserve all our respect, and I would not want to minimize their contribution. Nevertheless, it is noteworthy that Varela's work was published originally in English and follows the line of North American attitude studies—as if a universal contribution by a Latin American required a surrender of the writer's origins and identity. And Pichon-Rivière's works, it is sad to note, are still scarcely known outside of Argentina.

Possibly, Latin American contributions with the most vigor and social impact can be found where psychology has given a hand to other

---

*Martín-Baró (1986d); see Bibliography in the back of this book.

areas of social science. What seems to me without doubt the most significant of such cases is Paulo Freire's conscienticized literacy method, growing out of the fertile mix of education with psychology, philosophy, and sociology (Freire, 1970, 1978). The now well accepted concept of the awakening of critical consciousness (*conscientización*), joins the psychological dimension of personal consciousness with its social and political dimension, and makes manifest the historical dialectic between knowing and doing, individual growth and community organization, personal liberation and social transformation. But, above all, the awakening of critical consciousness constitutes a historical response to Latin America's lack of the word—both the personal and the social word. It involves more than the possibility of people reading and writing the alphabet; it opens the possibility of their being able to read about themselves and write their own history. Sadly, despite the magnitude of Freire's contribution, little critical study is devoted to his work, especially when compared with the time and energy devoted to contributions as trivial as some of the so-called "learning theories" or some of the cognitive models so much in fashion today.

The paucity of the contribution of Latin American psychology is best appreciated when compared with other branches of intellectual endeavor. In sociology, for example, the theory of dependency has been an original force that explains underdevelopment without recourse to the "Protestant Ethic" that casts our Latin American cultures in a derogatory light. The rich contribution of our novelists is another example. It would not be an exaggeration to say that one learns considerably more about the psychology of the peoples of Latin America by reading a novel by García Márquez or Vargas Llosa, than by reading our technical works on character and personality. And, with a force much greater than our analyses and psychological prescriptions for modernization and social change, liberation theology has been able both to reflect and to stimulate the recent historical struggles of the marginalized masses.

In contrast to the Saxon culture, Latin culture tends to place great importance on personal characteristics and interpersonal relations. In a country like El Salvador, almost all problems, from the biggest to the smallest, get referred to the president of the republic, and he bears the responsibility for their resolution. He is called upon to deal with matters of war, as well as quarrels between neighbors, to stimulate economic recovery in the country as well as to shut down an indiscrete brothel located next to a school (Martín-Baró, 1973c). In this cultural context which tends to personalize and even psychologize all processes, psychology has a vast field for exerting its influence. Yet, instead of helping tear down the edifice of commonsense that in our cultures both obscures and justifies the interests of the powerful by representing their techniques of control as character traits, Latin American psychology subscribes to the reigning psychologism either by action or omission. It has even taken the principal categories of Freire's conscientized literacy and put them in the service of the system, by divesting them of their essential political dimension and turning them into purely psychological categories. Now, with the growing subjectification of its main foci, psychology continues feeding the cultural psychologism, offering it as a true "ideology of exchange" (Deleule, 1972). In our case, psychologizing has served, directly or indirectly, to strengthen the oppressive structures, by drawing attention away from them and towards individual and subjective factors.

Our effort here is not to establish a balance in Latin American psychology, in part because it still remains for it to develop beyond its partiality to quantitative data (Ardila, 1982, 1983; Díaz-Guerrero, 1984; Whitford, 1985). Given what psychology deals with, we must ask ourselves whether, with the tools at our disposal today, we can say, or more importantly, do, something that will make a significant contribution to solving the crucial problems of our communities. In our case more than anybody's, the principle holds that the concern of the social scientist should not be so much to explain the world as to transform it.

The Slavery of Latin American Psychology

One of the justifications that can be given for the poverty of Latin American psychology's historical contribution is its relative youth. As confirmation for this point of view, people point to the original proposals beginning to emerge from all over ("Psicología latinoamericana," 1985). The argument is valid, although insufficient, and it becomes dangerous if used as a shield against revising the deficiencies that have led us (and in many cases, continue leading us) to scientific marginalization and social breakdown.

In my opinion the roots of Latin American psychology's misery are sunk in a history of colonial dependence—not the history of Iberoamerican colonization, but rather the neo-colonialist "carrot and stick" imposed upon us a century ago. The "cultural stick" prodding our people on a daily basis finds in psychology yet another instrument, among others, to mold minds. It also finds in psychology a valuable ally for soothing consciences when explaining the indisputable advantages of the modern technological carrot.

The historical misery of Latin American psychology can be synthesized in three principal interrelated causes: its scientistic mimicry, its lack of an adequate epistemology, and its provincial dogmatism. We will examine each of these separately.

SCIENTIFIC MIMICRY

What has happened to Latin American psychology is similar to what happened to North American psychology at the beginning of the twentieth century, when it ran so fast after scientific recognition and social status that it stumbled. North American psychology looked to the natural sciences for a method and concepts that would legitimize it as a science. And in order to get social position and rank, it negotiated how it would contribute to the needs of the established power structure. What Latin American psychology did was to look to its already scientifically and socially respectable "Big Brother" and, by borrowing his methodological and practical conceptual tools, hoped to gain from the power structure in each country a social status equivalent to that attained by the North Americans.

It is debatable whether the profession of psychology has gained the social recognition it sought in Latin America. What is clear is that nearly all its theoretical and practical ideas have been imported from the United States. Hence, from the psychoanalytic and organicist focus that held sway from early on, owing to psychology's dependence on the schools of psychiatry, there arose a strong wave of orthodox behaviorism, with its heavy weight of extreme positivism and methodological individualism.

Today, many Latin American psychologists have discarded behaviorism and taken up one or other form of cognitive psychology, not so much because they were won over by the critics of the psychoanalytic or behavioral perspective, as because that is the new focus among academics in North America. The problem is not rooted so much in the virtues or defects of behaviorism or cognitive theories, but rather in the mimicry that leads us to accept successive models coming out of the United States, as if an apprentice were to become a doctor by hanging onto the stethoscope, or a child were to become an adult by putting on its father's clothes.

Uncritical acceptance of theories and models is precisely the negation of science's own fundamental principles. And the ahistorical importing of ideas leads to ideologizing thoughts whose meaning and validity, as the sociology of knowledge reminds us, excuse some social circumstances and foreclose inquiry into certain concrete questions.

LACK OF AN ADEQUATE EPISTEMOLOGY

The dominant models in psychology are founded on a series of assumptions that are rarely discussed, and even more rarely are alternatives to them proposed. I will mention five of these assumptions that, in my opinion, have held back the development of a Latin American psychology: positivism, individualism, hedonism, the homoestatic vision, and ahistoricism.

Positivism

Positivism, as its name indicates, is that scientific conception which holds that knowledge should be limited to positive facts, to events, and to their empirically verifiable relations. Discarding everything that could be characterized as metaphysical, positivism underlines the *how* of phenomena, but tends to put aside the *what*, the *because*, and the *why*. Dividing things up in this way, positivism becomes blind to the most important meanings of human existence. Not surprisingly, positivism is very much at home in the laboratory, where it can "control" all the variables, and where it winds up reduced to the examination of true trivialities that say little or nothing about everyday problems.

The most serious problem of positivism is rooted precisely in its essence; that is, in its blindness towards the negative from the beginning. Recognizing nothing beyond the given, it necessarily ignores everything prohibited by the existing reality; i.e., everything that does not exist but would, under other conditions, be historically possible. No doubt, a positivist analysis of the Salvadoran campesino would lead one to the conclusion that this is a *machista* and fatalistic person, similar to the way the study of the intelligence of Blacks in North America leads to the conclusion that the intelligence quotient of Blacks is on the average a standard deviation below that of Whites. To consider reality as no more than the given—that the Salvadoran campesino is just fatalistic, or the Black less intelligent—constitutes an ideologization of reality that winds up consecrating the existing order as natural. Obviously, from such a perspective the horizon drawn for Latin Americans is low, and the future that psychology can offer is poor.

Paradoxically, this positivism is combined in psychological research with a methodological idealism. It is an idealistic scheme that puts a theoretical framework first, ahead of its analysis of reality, and goes no further in its exploration of things than what is indicated by the hypotheses it has formulated. Considering that the theories were pulled out of very different positive situations from our own, this idealism can end up blinding us not only to the negativity of our human circumstances, but also to what is positive in them; that is, to what they in fact are.

Individualism

A second assumption of the prevailing psychology is contained in individualism, which proposes the individual as an entity with its own meaning as the final subject of psychology. The problem with individualism is rooted in its insistence in seeing as an individual characteristic that which oftentimes is not found except within the collectivity, or attributing to individuality the things produced only in the dialectic of interpersonal relations. Through this, individualism ends up reinforcing the existing structures, because it ignores the reality of social structures and reduces all structural problems to personal problems.

Hedonism

Much has been said of the reigning hedonism in psychology, although perhaps the degree to which it is embedded, even within the most divergent models, has not been sufficiently stressed—how psychoanalysis is as hedonistic as behaviorism, conditioning as much as Gestalt. I am led to wonder, though, whether hedonism can adequately explain the solidarity behavior of a group of Salvadoran refugees who no sooner learned about the earthquake that devastated the center of San Salvador, than they gathered up all their extra food and sent it to the victims of the hardest hit zone. The belief that behind all behavior there is always a quest for pleasure or satisfaction—does this not blind us to a different way of being human, or at least to a different, but equally real, facet of being human? To integrate hedonism into our theoretical framework as an assumption—is this not in fact a concession to the profit motive that underlies the capitalist system, and as such, an attribution to human nature of something that has to do with the functioning of a particular socio-economic system? (Martín-Baró, 1983a).

The Homeostatic Vision
The homeostatic vision leads us to distrust everything that is change and disequilibrium, to think badly of all that represents rupture, conflict, and crisis. From this perspective, it becomes hard, more or less implicitly, for the disequilibrium inherent in social struggle not to be interpreted as a form of personal disorder (Do we not speak of people who have "lost their balance?"), and for the conflicts generated by over-throwing the social order not to be considered as pathological.

Ahistoricism
The last assumption of the prevailing psychology that I want to mention is perhaps the most serious: its ahistoricism. The prevailing scientism leads us to consider human nature as universal, and to believe, therefore, that there are no fundamental differences between, say, a student at MIT and a Nicaraguan campesino, between John Smith from Peoria, Illinois and Leonor Gonzales from Cuisnahuat, El Salvador. Thus, we accept the Needs Scale of Maslow as a universal hierarchy, and we assume that with just a little adaptation and modification the Stanford-Binet will be able to measure the intelligence of our populations. [However] a conception of humanness that would see universality in a historical context, that is to say, in terms of natural history, would acknowledge that needs, as much as intelligence, are in good measure a social construction. Once that is granted, it is clear that models created in different circumstances from our own, and assumed to be cross-cultural and trans-historical, can lead to a serious distortion of what our peoples are really about.

What is needed is for our most basic assumptions in psychological thought to be revised from the bottom up. But this revision cannot be made from our offices; it has to come from a praxis that is committed to the people. Only through such a praxis of commitment will we be able to get a new perspective on the people of our communities, with a view not only of what they positively are, but of the negativity as well—of all they could be, but have been kept by historical conditions from becoming. This done, truth will not have to be a simple reflection of data, but can become a task at hand: not an account of what has been done, but of what *needs to be done*.

FALSE DILEMMAS

Latin American psychology's dependence has led it to debating false dilemmas, false not so much because they fail to [validly] represent theoretical dilemmas on paper, as because they do not respond to the questions of our reality. Three characteristic dilemmas still raising eyebrows in some quarters are, scientific psychology *versus* a psychology "with soul," humanistic psychology *versus* materialistic psychology, and reactionary psychology *versus* progressive psychology.

Psychology versus Christian Anthropology

The first dilemma, perhaps the one dealt with most successfully by academics, led to seeing an opposition between the thoughts of psychology and a Christian anthropology. "Rat psychology" was juxtaposed to a "psychology with soul," while psychologists and priests fought over the one role to be played out for the bourgeoisie or middle classes. Surely the dogmatism of many members of the clergy made them suspicious of psychology, whose theories they perceived as dangerous to religious faith and whose explanations they saw as a negation of the transcendent dimension of the human being. But neither did the Latin American psychologists, with their "Made in U.S.A." schemata know how to escape the dilemma, perhaps because they did not have a good enough understanding of their own ideas, let alone what they supposed the clergy were proposing.

Humanistic Psychology versus Materalistic Psychology

A second dilemma, more present today than the first, opposes a humanistic psychology to a materialistic or dehumanizing psychology. At the personal level this dilemma is disconcerting to me, because I think that a psychological theory or model is either valid or not, useful or not in practice, and in any case, able to work more or less, better or worse, as a psychological theory or model. But I fail to see how Carl R. Rogers might be more humanistic than Sigmund Freud, or how Abraham Maslow might be more humanistic than Henri Wallon. Rather, I think that if Freud has a better understanding of the person than Rogers has, or Wallon than Maslow, their theories make for a more adequate psychological enterprise and, in consequence, would make a better contribution towards humanization.

Reactionary Psychology versus Progressive Psychology

The third dilemma is that of a reactionary psychology versus a progressive psychology. The dilemma, again, is valid, although it gets set forth badly. A reactionary psychology is one whose application lends support to an unjust social order; a progressive psychology is one that helps people progress, to find the road to their personal and collective historical fulfillment. Thus, a psychological theory is no more reactionary for having come from the United States than one with origins in the Soviet Union is automatically progressive or revolutionary. What makes a theory reactionary or progressive is not so much its place of origin as its ability to explain or uncover reality and, above all, to strengthen or transform the social order. Regrettably, there is a great deal of confusion over this, and I know of academic centers and teachers who accept conditioning owing to Pavlov's nationality, and who are more attentive to political orthodoxy than to the historical verification of their ideas.

The above dilemma and the other two denote a lack of independence in setting forth the most glaring problems of the communities of Latin America. They indicate an inability to freely use those theories and models that praxis shows to be the most valid and useful, or the inability to devise new ones as needed. Behind the three dilemmas are hidden dogmatic postures, belonging more to a spirit of provincial dependency than to a scientific commitment to find, and more importantly, to do, what is true for our Latin American peoples.

Towards a Liberation Psychology

From the preceding reflections there clearly follows a conclusion: if we want psychology to make a significant contribution to the history our our peoples—if, as psychologists we wish to contribute to the social development of the countries of Latin America—we have to re-think our theoretical and practical equipment, but re-think it from the standpoint of the lives of our own people; from their sufferings, their aspirations, and their struggles. If I may be permitted to formulate this proposal in Latin American terms, we must affirm that any effort at developing a psychology that will contribute to the liberation of our people has to mean the creation of a liberation psychology; but to create a liberation psychology is not simply a theoretical task; first and fundamentally it is a practical task. Therefore, if Latin American psychology wants to get started on the road to liberation, it must break out of its own enslavement. In other words, to achieve a psychology of liberation demands first that psychology be liberated.

ELEMENTS FOR A LIBERATION PSYCHOLOGY

Recently I asked one of the most renowned liberation theologians what he would say are the three most important intuitive truths of that theology. Without much hesitation my good friend pointed to the following:

1. Affirmation that the object of Christian faith is a God of life and, therefore, that a Christian must accept the promotion of life as his or her primordial religious task. From this Christian perspective, what is opposed to faith in God is not atheism but rather idolatry; that is, the belief in false gods, gods which produce death. The Christian faith in a God of life must search, consequently, for all those historical conditions that give life to people, and in the concrete case of Latin America, this search for life demands a first step of liberating the structures—the social structures first, and next the personal ones—that maintain a situation of sin; that is, of the mortal oppression of the majority of the people.

2. True practice has primacy over true theory, orthopraxis over orthodoxy. Actions are more important than affirmations in liberation theology, and what one does is more expressive of faith than what one says. Therefore, the truth of faith must be shown in historical achievements that give evidence of and make credible the existence of a God of life. In this context, everything becomes meaningful that mediates the possibility of people's liberation from the structures that oppress and impede their life and human development.

3. Christian faith calls for a preferential option for the poor. The theology of liberation affirms that one has to look for God among the poor and marginalized, and with them and from them live the life of faith. There are multiple reasons for this option. In the first place, that was, concretely, the option of Jesus. Secondly, the poor constitute the majority of our peoples. But thirdly, it is only the poor who offer the objective and subjective conditions for opening up to the other, and above all, to the radically other. The option for the poor is not opposed to universal salvation, but it recognizes that the community of the poor is the theological place *par excellence* for achieving the task of salvation, the construction of the kingdom of God.

From the inspiration of liberation theology, we can propose three essential elements for the building of a liberation psychology for the peoples of Latin America: a new horizon, a new epistemology, and a new praxis.

A New Horizon

Latin American psychology must stop focussing attention on itself, stop worrying about its scientific and social status, and [instead] propose an effective service to the needs of the majority of the population. It is the real problems of our own peoples that ought to constitute the primordial object of our work, not the problems that concern people elsewhere. And at the present time the most important problem faced by the vast majority of Latin Americans is their situation of oppressive misery, their condition of marginalized dependency that is forcing upon them an inhuman existence and snatching away their ability to define their own lives. It stands to reason, then, that if the most incontrovertible objective need of the majority of the people of Latin America consists in their historical liberation from the social structures that continue to oppress them, it is towards that need that psychology must focus its concern and energy.

Psychology has always been clear about the necessity for personal liberation; that is, people's need to gain control over their own existence. Psychology has believed that, were it not for unconscious mechanisms or conscious experiences holding them back from their existential goals and personal happiness, people would turn their lives towards a pursuit of those objectives that they consider worthwhile. Nevertheless, psychology has for the most part not been very clear about the intimate relationship between an unalienated personal existence and an unalienated social existence, between individual control and collective power, between the liberation of each person and the liberation of a whole people. Moreover, psychology has often contributed to obscuring the relationship between personal estrangement and social oppression, presenting the pathology of persons as if it were something removed from history and society, and behavioral disorders as if playing themselves out entirely on the individual plane (Martín-Baró, 1984c).

Psychology must work for the liberation of the peoples of Latin America. As the conscientizing literacy of Paulo Freire has demonstrated, this involves breaking the chains of personal oppression as much as the chains of social oppression. The recent history of the Salvadoran people provides a case in point. Overcoming their existential fatalism (which some psychologists modestly or ideologically prefer to call "external control" or "learned helplessness," as if it were a purely intra-individual problem) entails for the Salvadoran people a direct confrontation with the structural forces that oppress them, deprive them of control over their own existence, and force them to learn submission and expect nothing from life.

A New Epistemology

If our objective is to serve the liberation needs of the people of Latin America, this requires a new form of seeking knowledge, for the truth of the Latin American peoples is not in their present oppression, but rather in the tomorrow of their liberty. The truth of the popular majority is not to be found, but made. That supposes at the very least, two aspects: a new perspective and a new praxis.

The new perspective has to be from below, from the same oppressed majorities whose truth is to be created. Have we ever seriously asked what psychosocial processes look like from the point of view of the dominated instead of from the viewpoint of the dominator? Have we thought of looking at educational psychology from where the illiterate stands, or industrial psychology from the place of the unemployed, or clinical psychology from the standpoint of the marginalized? What would mental health look like from the place of a tenant farmer on a hacienda, or personal maturity from someone who lives in the town dump, or motivation from a woman who sells goods in the market? Note that we say "from" the illiterate and the unemployed, from the tenant farmer and the woman in the market, not "for" them. This is not a matter of thinking for them or bringing them our ideas or solving their problems for them; it has to do with thinking and theorizing with them and from them. Here, too, the pioneering insight of Paulo Freire asserts itself. He put forth a pedagogy "of" the oppressed, and not "for" the oppressed; it was the very person, the very same community, which constituted the subject of its own conscientizing literacy, that in community dialogue with the educator had to learn to read its reality and write its historical word. And just as liberation theology has underlined the fact that only from the poor is it possible to find the God of life enunciated by Jesus, a psychology of liberation has to learn that only from the oppressed will it be possible to discover and build the existential truth of the Latin American peoples.

To take on a new perspective obviously does not mean throwing out all of our knowledge; what it supposes, rather, is that we will relativize that knowledge and critically revise it from the perspective of the popular majorities. Only then will the theories and models show their validity or deficiency, their utility or lack thereof, their universality or provincialism. Only then will the techniques we have learned display their liberating potential or their seeds of subjugation.

A New Praxis

All human knowledge is subject to limitations imposed by reality itself. In many respects that reality is opaque, and only by acting upon it, by transforming it, can a human being get information about it. What we see and how we see is of course determined by our perspective, by the place from which we begin our examination of history; but it is determined also by reality itself. Thus, to acquire new psychological knowledge it is not enough to place ourselves in the perspective of the people; it is necessary to involve ourselves in a new praxis, an activity of transforming reality that would let us know not only about what is, but also about what is not, and the measure by which we may try to orient ourselves towards what ought to be. As Fals Borda (1985) says, speaking of participatory research, only through participation do we get "the voluntary and living rupture of the asymmetrical relationship between submission and dependency, implicit in the binomial subject/object."

Generally, psychologists have tried to get inside the social process via the route of the powers that be. The attempt at scientific purity has meant in practice taking the perspective of those in power and acting from a position of dominance. As educational psychologists we have worked from the base of the school, not of the community; as industrial psychologists we have selected or trained personnel according to the demands of the owners and bosses, not according to those of the workers or their unions. And even as community psychologists we have often come into the community mounted on the carriage of our plans and projects, bringing our own know-how and money. It is not easy to figure out how to place ourselves within the process alongside the dominated rather than alongside the dominator; it is not easy even to leave our role of technocratic or professional superiority and to work hand in hand with community groups. But if we do not embark upon this new type of praxis, that transforms ourselves as well as trans-forming reality, it will be hard indeed to develop a Latin American psychology that will contribute to the liberation of our peoples.

The problem of a new praxis brings up the problem of power, and, therefore, the problem of the politicization of psychology. For many, this is a touchy subject, but no less important for that. To be sure, to adopt a perspective, to put oneself inside a popular praxis, is to take sides. There is an assumption that taking a stand represents an abdication of scientific objectivity, with bias confused with objectivity. The fact that something is biased, though, does not mean it is subjective; bias can be the consequence of interests, more or less conscious, but it can also be the result of an ethical choice. And while we are all affected by the class interests that bias our knowledge, not everybody makes conscious ethical choices consonant with those values. For example, although a position has to be taken with respect to torture or assassination, this does not mean that one cannot be objective in under-standing the criminal act or the actor, the torturer or the assassin. If we were not able to take an ethical stand while still maintaining objectivity, we might easily condemn as murder the death caused by a guerrilla, but condone and even exalt as an act of heroism, the death produced by a soldier or the police. Thus, I agree with Fals Borda (1985), who main-tains that practical knowledge acquired through participatory research should lead towards the people gaining power, a power that allows them to become the protagonists of their own history and to effect those changes that would make Latin American societies more just and humane.

THREE URGENT TASKS

The tasks, both theoretical and practical, that present themselves to a Latin American liberation psychology are many. I will present here three that seem to me of special and urgent importance: recovering historical memory, de-ideologizing common sense and everyday experience, and utilizing the popular virtues.

The Recovery of Historical Memory

The hard struggle for satisfying everyday basic needs forces the popular majorities to stay in a here and now without a before or after—in a permanent psychological present. Furthermore, the prevailing discourse puts forth an apparently natural and ahistorical reality, structuring it in such as way as to cause it to be accepted without question. This makes it impossible to derive lessons from experience and, what is more important, makes it impossible to find the roots of one's own identity, which is as much needed for interpreting one's sense of the present, as in glimpsing possible alternatives that might exist. The predominantly negative image that the average Latin American has of himself or herself when compared with other people (Montero, 1984) indicates the internalization of oppression, its incorporation into the spirit itself; fertile soil for conformist fatalism, and so very convenient for the established order.

To recover historical memory would mean "to discover selectively, through the collective memory, elements from the past that were effective for defending the interests of the exploited classes, and that become useful again for the objectives of struggle and *concientización*" (Fals Borda, 1985). It deals with recovering not only the sense of one's own identity, not only the pride of belonging to a people, but also of relying on a tradition and a culture, and above all, rescuing those aspects of identity that served yesterday, and will serve today, for liberation. Thus, the recovery of a historical memory supposes the reconstruction of some models of identification that, instead of chaining and caging the people, open up the horizon for them, towards their liberation and fulfillment.

De-ideologizing Everyday Experience

Secondly, a contribution to the de-ideologization of everyday experience is indispensable. We know that knowledge is a social construction. Our countries live burdened by the lie of a prevailing discourse that denies, ignores, or disguises essential aspects of reality. The same "cultural stranglehold" that day after day is handed out to the people of Latin America by the mass media, constitutes a reference point that has little bearing on the everyday experience of the majority of people, and even less on the poorer people. It goes along, deceptive and alienated, conforming to a fictional common sense that nurtures the structures of exploitation and conformist attitudes. To de-ideologize means to retrieve the original experience of groups and persons and return it to them as objective data. People can then use the data to formalize a consciousness of their own reality, and by so doing, verify the validity of acquired knowledge (Martín-Baró, 1985d, 1985e). This de-ideologization must be realized as much as possible in a process of critical participation in the life of the poorer people, which represents a certain departure from the predominant forms of research and analysis.

Utilizing the People's Virtues

Finally, we must work to utilize the virtues of our peoples. Going no further than my own people, the people of El Salvador, current history confirms, day after day, their uncompromising solidarity with the suffering, their ability to deliver and to sacrifice for the collective good, their tremendous faith in the human capacity to change the world, their hope for a tomorrow that keeps being denied to them violently. These virtues are alive in the popular traditions, in popular religious practices, in those social structures that have allowed the Salvadoran people to survive historically in conditions of inhuman oppression and repression—virtues that enable them today to keep alive faith in their destiny and hope in their future, in spite of a dreadful civil war that already [in 1986] has gone on more than six years.

Oscar Romero, the assassinated Archbishop of San Salvador, once said, referring to the virtues of the Salvadoran people, "With this people it is not hard to be a good pastor." How is it possible that we, Latin American psychologists, have not been able to discover all that rich potential in the virtues of our peoples and, consciously or unconsciously, have turned our eyes to other countries and other cultures when pressed to define objectives and ideals?

There is a big task ahead if we hope for Latin American psychology to make a significant contribution to universal psychology, and above all, to the history of our peoples. In light of the current situation of oppression and faith, of repression and solidarity, of fatalism and struggle that characterizes our peoples, that task must be one of a liberation psychology. But a psychology of liberation requires a prior liberation of psychology, and that liberation can only come from a praxis committed to the sufferings and hopes of the peoples of Latin America.

Ignacio Martín-Baró

19. Violence in Central America:
A Social Psychological Perspective*

TRANSLATION BY ANNE WALLACE

Central America: Crossroads of Violence

In less than a decade, Central America has become a true crossroads of violence. To some, the Central American conflicts are simply a version of the confrontation between the socialist East and the capitalist West; others see them as an expression of the conflict between the rich and powerful North and the poor and exploited South; still others consider them fundamentally the manifestation of an internal structural conflict between the élitist interests of exploitative social minorities and the basic necessities of the oppressed majority. Very possibly, these three types of conflict converge in Central America, although the influence of each differs in nature and magnitude. But, whichever explanation is closest to the truth, the undeniable fact is that today violence overwhelms the Central American people, who find themselves plunged daily into a costly bloodbath and thus unable to freely determine and give expression to their own history.

In El Salvador, it is estimated that the number of war dead now [1988] exceeds 65,000, the majority of them civilians, many of whom were brutally tortured or "disappeared." In Nicaragua, the Instituto de Formación Permanente (INSFOP) has put the number of civilians killed by the "contras" at 1,215 between 1981 and 1986 (CODEHUCA, 1986); and from August 6 to October 15, 1987 alone, Humberto Ortega, Nicaraguan Minister of Defense, acknowledged that there were 1,372 deaths in combat. These deaths included 783 "contras," 224 Sandinista soldiers and 365 civilians. And, in Guatemala, the Comité Pro-Justicia y Paz (1985) recorded 905 civilian assassinations carried out by the military or paramilitary forces in a single year (from November 1984 to October, 1985). It is not an exaggeration to estimate that, on average,

---

*Martín-Baró (1988d); see Bibliography in the back of this book.

someone dies every hour in Central America as a result of political violence. If we add the number of wounded to the number of dead, we must multiply the count and say that every twenty minutes a Central American suffers, bodily, the effect of socio-political violence. And if we add to this number all the people who, as a consequence of these same conflicts, either are threatened or imprisoned, or have to go into hiding or flee their homes, we come to the terrifying conclusion that every three minutes a Central American pays in flesh and blood the consequences of the violence of war that consumes the isthmus.

So far, we have only mentioned one type of social violence: that which is political-military in nature. If we add other forms of social violence, violence inside the home (men against women, parents against their children), as well as what happens in the various spheres of public life, we arrive at a picture both more complete and more distressing. Studies have shown that wars precipitate a rise in what is called common delinquency and criminality (Archer and Bartner, 1984). In the cases of El Salvador and Guatemala, we have witnessed a growing number of those who, under cover of war, or as a consequence of the war, use violence as the tool of their trade, and have turned assault and even kidnapping into their habitual occupation.

Faced with this avalanche of political and social violence, the Central American presidents signed "Esquipulas II" on August 7, 1988, in Guatemala. This accord is a notable effort to resolve at least the most critical aspects of the problem. However, we must not delude ourselves: from the moment the agreement was approved, the obstacles its application has encountered demonstrate how deeply rooted the Central American conflicts are, even in the most extreme form of war. They also reveal the power of the social forces and interests, notably the hegemonic and short-sighted interest of the present North American government, which have worked actively against the success of this peace plan.

But even if Esquipulas II were successful, one still could not reasonably hope for the scourge of generalized violence to disappear. It is true that the most massive forms of murder, such as military operations, would be reduced. But the problem of the "death squads," as well as all the repressive agencies which operate under the more or less guaranteed protection of the legal military structures, would still have to be resolved. In spite of the obvious differences, the case of Colombia is a telling one. After the accord reached between President Betancour and the guerrilla groups in 1984, a large group of the insurgents' political sympathizers formed a political party, the Unión Patriótica (UP), and embarked on their struggle within the established bounds of legality. From that moment in 1984 until October 11, 1987, a total of 471 leaders and sympathizers of the UP have been assassinated by the "death squads" who, in the main have clear ties to the armed forces. The last and most significant victim of these assassinations was the ex-presidential candidate of the UP, Jaime Pardo Leal. This act clearly exposes, once again, and conclusively, that this socio-political violence does not originate with those who try to change an unjust social order, but with those who, from their position of power and privilege, oppose any meaningful change, no matter what form it takes.

A social reconciliation permitting the establishment of a new framework for coexistence, where the use of both overt and covert violence is reduced to a minimum, is not only a political problem; it is also a psychological and cultural problem. It would serve little purpose to achieve peace between the opposing sides while maintaining the same structures of exploitation and domination, the same values of competition and power, the same ideal of a consumer lifestyle, which lead to unjust monopoly and social discrimination. This is where the role of psychology comes in and where the challenge lies for Central American psychologists. What, specifically, can we contribute, with our particular knowledge, towards addressing the problem of violence in our countries? To put it simply: what would each of us do if Central America's presidents asked us, in conjunction with other specialists, to formulate a working plan to eliminate the violence in the area? Confronted with such a proposal, we would probably understand how precarious our knowledge of violence is and how little we can do, in practical terms, to address this problem (Departamento, 1986). Nevertheless, at this point in history, I can see no problem more important for us as psychologists. Therefore, with the humility of those who know the limits of their own knowledge, but also with the persistence of those who know it is a vital issue in which their scientific and professional credibility are at stake, we must get to work and we must not evade our responsibility. Our people will judge the success or failure of our contribution.

Given the problem of generalized violence in Central America, two steps are necessary to examine the contribution that psychology can make: 1) to clarify the prevailing diagnostic analysis of the nature and causes of the overriding violence (beginning by reviewing several critical points of what could be called "the psycho-social history of Central American violence," (Martín-Baró, 1983a); 2) to examine all the resources psycho-social research offers us for constructive intervention in the arena of the violence (Zimmermann, 1983). Thus, we will propose a tentative plan for social psychological work, which may be discussed and criticized, but which will allow us to begin opening up new horizons for Central American psychology.

The Meaning of Violence

The first problem posed by the analysis of the violence in our countries is of a semantic order: violence is too generic a term and constitutes an umbrella which covers very different processes and behaviors. Bombing a village where it is suspected that there are guerrillas is certainly violence, but so is the beating with which a father punishes his son; the assassination of a union leader is violence, but an impassioned confrontation between two jealous lovers is no less violence; the torture inflicted on a political opponent in a clandestine jail is violence, but so is the assault on a citizen who is robbed of his possessions while waiting downtown for the bus in the capital. Now, if the term violence covers equally both physical aggression and moral attack, political repression and coercive education, large-scale military destruction and the impassioned encounter between lovers, its meaning becomes very abstract and vague. And, frequently, abstractions—which are not the same as theories—rather than revealing the truth, tend to obscure it.

In a recent analysis, Cueva maintains that we need to qualify the term "democracy" if we wish to understand the nature of the political processes which are being created in Latin America. "'Conservative democracies,' 'reformist democracies,' 'revolutionary democracies'": simply using these terms sounds almost like a provocation at a time when the dominant ideology is attempting to erase even the slightest vestige of discussion and analysis of the contents and orientations of the type of democracy that really exists" (Cueva, 1987). This pretense of a pure or unqualified democracy in Latin America's political reality serves to promote régimes whose democratic structures can disguise the renewal of traditional forms of domination and the effort to break up, in practice and in theory, all forms of popular struggle.

Something similar must be said about violence, although here it is not a matter of introducing qualifiers but of reifying the term. In fact, the dictionary defines the term "violence" as a "quality of being violent"; that is, the meaning of the noun derives from the adjective. The fact is that violence does not exist in the abstract; what does exist are violent acts—concrete ways of acting violently. So, in each case, the character of the violence must be judged by examining the actions described as violent, in order for us to discern its nature, scope, and roots so as to understand the violence in its material and historical actuality. Nothing conceals the nature of violence better than the statement which condemns, in the abstract, all violence "wherever it may come from," but which in practice, as Chomsky and Hermann (1979) unerringly point out, is only applied to the violent actions of those who oppose the [prevailing] social order (a typical example of this type of biased analysis can be found in Merari and Friedland, 1985).

THE VIOLENCE OF WAR, REPRESSION, AND CRIMINALITY

We need to look at the concrete forms of violence prevalent in our countries, instead of taking generic definitions, abstract theories, or presumptions of common sense as our point of departure. In earlier writings, I pointed to three predominant modes of violent action in Salvadoran life: the violence of criminal behavior, the violence of sociopolitical repression and the violence of the war (Martín-Baró, 1983a; 1983c). At that time, I emphasized the structural predominance of repressive violence, even as I indicated the quantitative and qualitative advance of the violence of the war. Today, the same analysis, applied not only to El Salvador but to Central America as a whole, must recognize that the violence of war has gained primacy. This change has not meant the disappearance of repressive violence; rather it has diminished in quantity, particularly when compared with the military escalation of the wars, and it has evolved qualitatively (Martín-Baró, 1988a; chapter 17, *of this volume*). Esquipulas II is the indirect acknowledgement of the magnitude of the violence of war, which has now reached such a point that it endangers the historical viability of the Central American states.

It is worth pointing out that the three forms of violence mentioned above—war, repression, and crime—converge in the actions of the "death squads," that hybrid product of oligarchs and military men, that illegitimate son of the compulsive drive of the United States for hegemony coupled with the national security requirements of Latin American régimes. The violence of war is directly linked to these "squads" which are normally drawn from military units or security forces, and which, frequently, are in charge of pursuing "the dirty war" expressly prohibited by legislation and by international accords. Repressive violence targets the civilian population, not the enemy army, and its objective is to acheive, by violent coercion, the political control not achieved through persuasion or social consensus. Criminal violence operates completely outside the law, and its repressive *modus operandi* often becomes a way of life based on an illegal business in the style of professional mafias.

These forms of violence in some cases reflect the personal characteristics of their perpetrators. Certainly, the cruelty to victims observed in certain assaults or the treatment of the civilian population in certain military operations often derive from the characteristics of their authors more than from any objective requirement of the actions themselves. However, what characterizes the predominant forms of violent actions at the present time in Central America is their depersonalization, and even their professionalization: assaults, bombings, kidnappings and torture are carried out with the same technocratic dispassion with which a watch is repaired or a chicken is cooked. This calls into question, from the outset, the mainstream psychological conceptions which look first to the individual for an explanation of acts of violence.

As is well known, aggressors must frequently resort to devaluing (Lerner and Simmons, 1966), dehumanizing, and even demonizing their victims—a recourse psychologically necessary in order to be able to carry out the violent acts against them (Samayoa, 1987). In this respect, I remember hearing the recording of a conversation between the pilot of a Salvadoran bomber and his commanding officer at the base. The pilot, who was flying over the town of Tenancingo, saw a group of people in a state of panic seeking cover in the local church and transmitted to the officer that they were civilians so he could not bomb them. But, from the command post, the officer insisted that "anything that moves is the enemy," that they were nothing but "subversives" and, therefore, that the pilot must bomb. Obviously, it is easier to shoot at a "terrorist" than at a young *campesino*, easier to torture a "communist beast" than a political dissident, easier to bomb a group of subversives than a group of families. Psychology has taught military strategists the advantage of separating the soldier from his victims with technical intermediaries. These turn a mass murder into the simple technical operation of pressing a button on an electronic screen. But, when technical shock absorbers are not possible, aggressors try to establish "psychological shock absorbers," like devaluing and even bestializing the victim (Fanon, 1963). This brings us to a second point essential for elucidating the problem of Central American violence: its ideologization.

Without fail, every act of violence is accompanied by a justification, which generally precedes and unleashes it; but in cases where it is accidental or unpremeditated it must immediately be justified. As in the case of Freudian "slips" which on becoming conscious are rationalized, the violent act tends almost mechanically to clothe its nakedness in justifications. But this is in no way a mechanical process; it is a logical consequence of the qualifying nature of violence. If every form of violence demands a justification, it is because violence does not justify itself. Thus, violence cannot be considered in the abstract as good or bad, contradicting one of the assumptions normally implicit in psychological conceptions. The goodness or evil of the violent form derives from the act that gives it substance, in other words from what a violent act signifies socially and produces historically. And this is where the ideological character of violence is clearly revealed.

THE IDEOLOGICAL CHARACTER OF VIOLENCE

What does it mean to say that violence has an ideological character? At least two things: 1) that it expresses or channels concrete social forces and interests within the framework of a conflict of classes; and 2) that it tends to hide the forces and interests which determine it. This signifies that the meaning of a violent act must be judged in the light of the forces and interests it advances in each specific case and, therefore, according to its effect on historical reality. To understand what an act of violence is, it is not enough to know which act it is; we need to know who is committing it, under what circumstances, and what its consequences are (Haber and Seidenberg, 1978). Only thus can one explain that a murder condemned when it is committed by a normal adult may be forgiven in the case of a mentally retarded person; and only this way can we comprehend that the same act considered murder when it is committed by a guerrilla is judged to be heroic when it is committed by a policeman. The action is the same; its social meaning is what varies. That meaning derives fundamentally from its relation to certain social interests, whether it favors the interests of some or those of others.

In El Salvador, the government as well as various para-governmental organizations have recently developed, with North American support and advice, an intensive campaign to combat the use of land mines, which they point out (rightly so) affect the civilian population and therefore constitute a violation of their human rights. The problem is that this campaign is directed exclusively against the FMLN, to whom they attribute the blame for casualties, whether they are victims of the FMLN or of others, real victims of the land mines as well as victims of other kinds of attacks. Where does the ideologization of the campaign lie? In the fact that the mines, as far as the dominant discourse is concerned, are always "terrorist mines," "subversive mines," or "FMLN mines," but never "the Armed Forces' mines," "government mines," or "North American mines." Yet, it is known that the army systematically uses land mines, as part of its military strategy, and that their mines also produce victims among the civilian population. Therefore, when the Armed Forces criticize the FMLN's mines, on the basis of respect for human rights, it is ideologizing the use of mines, which, in their own case they consider good and justifiable, but in the case of the FMLN, bad and reprehensible. Thus, the defense of human rights does not represent a real value governing the behavior of the AF, but rather it is simply one more tool for fighting the enemy. The goodness or evil of the particular violence of using mines is judged by whether they favor one's own or the rival's interests.

The ideological character of violent behavior allows us to understand two well known but insufficiently analyzed theses: 1) that always, and only, the violent behavior of the other is considered wrong and unjustifiable, never one's own behavior; and 2) that the social justification of violence generates the proliferation both of justifications and of violence itself (Hacker, 1973).

The creation of the figure of the enemy, whether it corresponds to a real person or not, is one of the basic ways in which to ideologize violence (Wahlström, 1987). According to the analysis by Finlay, et al., the enemy serves three types of functions: psychological, sociological, and political. Psychologically, "enemies help to identify the sources of frustration and justify actions which could otherwise be improper or illegal; they act as a focus for aggression and as a means of distracting attention away from other urgent and more intractable problems; and they provide a contrast by which to measure or inflate our own worth and values" (Finley, *et al.*, 1976). Sociologically, enemies serve to animate and strengthen repressive politics, to promote the internal solidarity and cohesion of a group, to justify carrying out various plans and to channel behavior and beliefs in the sanctioned direction. Finally, the enemy also serves political ends in the decision-making and socialization processes, helping to configure the ideal images of what a society should be and do, and thus differentiating between "us, the good guys" and "them, the bad guys" (Ascher, 1986).

In Central America, the image of the "enemy" is used as an object of fear, a deadly scarecrow, which serves to justify the very thing the governments of the area claim they want to combat. Clearly, the "great enemy" brandished by the Central American forces in power is "Soviet-style communism," which the Sandinista government of Nicaragua presumably embodies. Thus, Sandinismo has become the "great enemy" of the governments of the area, who feel themselves justified in attacking their own citizens in order to prevent the alleged Sandinista aggression, to repress all dissidence in order to prevent the alleged threat of communist totalitarianism and even to attack Nicaragua itself militarily by means of the "contras" in order to stop the alleged military exportation of the Sandinista revolution. The existence of the "enemy" justifies and promotes precisely what our governments say they wish to prevent: repression, intransigent totalitarianism, military aggression. Everything that is done, or claimed to be done, against that enemy is therefore justified, even though our governments make use of the same kinds of violent actions that they ascribe to and condemn in the enemy.

It would be blind to deny that the Nicaraguans or the Salvadoran insurgents also create an image of the enemy, which serves similar functions. As several studies have shown, the image of the enemy is one of the characteristic phenomena of socio-political polarization. The opposing sides see the same traits in each other, but invert them, so that from each side's perspective those in one's own group are "the good guys" while those in the enemy's group are "the bad guys" (Bronfen-brenner, 1961; White, 1966). Nevertheless, we must be very careful not to assume a total symmetry in the phenomenon of the "speculated image" of the enemy, since that would imply that it was a totally subjective phenomenon, with no correlation to objective reality. In every case a historical analysis of this speculated image should be made in order to ascertain its truth or falsehood and thus to determine whether it reveals reality validly or conceals its ideological character (Martín-Baró, 1983c). The fact that opposing groups find the same traits in each other does not preclude that the perception of one group more closely approximates objective reality than that of another group.

Central American violence is certainly not created by the image of the enemy, much less by those who at any particular moment are identified by one group or another as the historical embodiment of that enemy. Nevertheless, that image not only serves to justify already existing violence but also to foster greater violence.

STRUCTURAL VIOLENCE

The high level of violent coercion, required to maintain social hierarchies in the situation of structural injustice characterizing Central America means that the system requires a more stable justification than the circumstantial image of an enemy. During the 1970s, that justification was provided by the doctrine of "national security" which currently [in the 1980s] is being replaced by that of "low intensity conflict." Both doctrines agree that capitalist society faces a conflict of power between the social interests of the dominant classes and those of the dominated classes, and that all aspects of life are subject to this structural conflict, favoring some interests or others. Consequently, the counterinsurgency campaign must be a total war, incorporating all social sectors and all aspects of social life (Comblin, 1979).

The most significant difference between the doctrines of national security and low intensity conflict is probably the latter's insistence on the role of the so-called "psychological war" (Martín-Baró, 1988a; chapter 17, *of this volume*). The aim of the psychological war is to win people's "hearts and minds" so that they accept the requirements of the dominant order and, consequently, accept as good and even "natural" whatever violence may be necessary to maintain it. Ultimately, the psychological war seeks what we could call a militarization of the human mind. It is very difficult to comprehend the violence in Central America today without understanding the extent to which the dominant sectors' minds are militarized, and that they accept as good any form of violence which allows them to remain in power and to continue enjoying their privileges.

To summarize, the predominant forms of violence in Central America's current situation are, in this order: acts of war, acts of repression, and criminal acts. The most significant violent actions are justified by the threat of the powerful and omnipresent enemy, which is called communism and which adopts various guises depending on each particular case: Soviet expansionism, Sandinista totalitarianism, Marxist-Leninist subversion, guerrilla terrorism. The need to combat this enemy justifies the application of the very same violent measures that the governments of the area claim they are trying to prevent. Carrying out acts of violence to preserve the régime from the threat of the "enemy" clearly exposes the ideologization of the violence. In other words, the violence is an attempt to safeguard the social interests of the dominant classes and the formulizing of violence as negative therefore depends on who executes a violent act and who benefits from it.

By no means do I pretend to invoke a socio-political reductionism that reduces all forms of violent action to structural problems related to class struggle. I have maintained that one of the predominant types of violence in Central America is criminal. Much of the violent aggression punished by law is a direct consequence of personal problems or of strictly individual personality factors. Nevertheless, I also believe that even those kinds of violence cannot be understood unless they are placed in their social and political context. The violence of parents against their children, for instance, reflects not only internal family conflicts but also the characteristics of a culture which has placed the destiny of its children almost totally in the hands of their progenitors, who are frequently ill-prepared for this responsibility. But families are not autonomous islands, and culture does not emerge, nor is it transmitted, independently of the historical conditions of a society. For this reason, even the most unconscious forms of violent behavior must be understood in the here and now of circumstances which enable some ways of acting and not others, which offer some models and not others. To mention a specific case, during 1987, nearly one hundred people in El Salvador died from bombs thrown by soldiers into private homes, into public vehicles, or into parties and dances. In most cases, the perpetrators were drunk or got carried away by a sudden fit of rage. But we would understand very little about this new form of criminal violence if we kept it on the plane of individualist psychological explanation, even with the most recent cognitive neo-associationist theories (Berkowitz, 1984), and did not locate the behavior in the historical context of a structural conflict of classes, of a war which has dragged on for seven years now, and of an ideological apparatus that makes soldiers into "authorities" thereby legitimizing their violent behavior *a priori*.

Once we accept the irreducibility of the different forms of violence and reject any type of reductionist explanation, we must ask ourselves why violent behavior is resorted to so much in the present Central American situation. Why do the governments reserve for themselves alone the right to use violence to preserve the social order, rather than choose other, political forms of action? Why do fathers use the belt against their children so frequently? Why does the boss use the police or his bodyguards against the workers? Why does the group of demonstrators destroy the public buses?

THE EFFICACY OF VIOLENCE

We know perfectly well that many different things can cause violent behavior and that frequently a single behavior has several causes. There are also various factors which influence a given moment so that the chosen action is violent in character rather than otherwise. But, while it is true that violence can have various causes and can be unleashed by various circumstances, it seems that most of the time there is an overriding reason for using violence as a form of behavior: its instrumental usefulness (Sabini, 1978). Violence is chosen as a preferred form of behavior, so persistently, and at all levels, for a very simple reason: it is effective. In our society, one can obtain by violence what apparently cannot be obtained by other means. Therefore, although violence may not be very rational in many cases, it is certainly useful in almost all cases.

The primary reason for using violence in the countries of Central America is its usefulness and effectiveness; but this has a very distinct meaning and consequences, depending on the different forms of violence. That violence is the most effective way to maintain the established order means something very different from its being the most effective way to change that order. In the first instance, the problem is the unwillingness or the inability of those in power to solve social problems, which would allow them to maintain the social order on the basis of consensus rather than coercion, persuasion rather than terrorist repression. In the case of those who try to change the social order, it means that order does not offer them more effective, non-violent alternatives through which to achieve their objectives. The case of El Salvador is clear in this respect, since successive régimes have repeatedly blocked all efforts to bring about social change through peaceful, non-violent means even within the framework of the régime's own electoral rules. In the same way, the meaning of the usefulness of violence in the case of the father who punishes his children is different from its meaning in the case of the police officer who tortures the union leader; the meaning of its usefulness is different in the case of the attacker who kills his victim from its meaning in the case of the soldier who blows to bits the people attending a dance. In some instances, the most important aspect is the lack of behavioral alternatives, in yet others, it is group or cultural pressure, and in others, it is the ideological numbing at the service of certain social interests.

The instrumental usefulness of violence, being the most common reason for employing it so frequently, opens a window for psycho-social intervention. The goal is clear: make violent behavior less useful so that it becomes socially ineffective, especially the behavior which most damages the fundamental rights of persons and groups. How to achieve this goal is the specific challenge which we social scientists, including psychologists, have to address in Central America. With this goal in mind, I will synthesize briefly the resources which psycho-social research has to offer us and consider how to make use of those resources in a program which contributes to extricating our countries from the excruciating conjuncture of generalized violence in which they find themselves today.

3. A Psycho-social Plan to Counteract the Effectiveness of Violence

Note: Most of a section is omitted in which Martín-Baró reviews a body of research, mainly conducted in the United States, concerned both with individual and institutional violence, its psychological causes and consequences. Relating some of their conclusions to Central America, he writes (in part):

We have touched on a crucial point concerning the proliferation of violence in Central America: its impunity under the law. As long as the greatest acts of violence go unpunished, as long as the main proponents of massive aggression and state terrorism are protected by the cloak of institutional self-interest and(or) presumed "reasons of state," there is no hope for a meaningful reduction in the forms of or in the number of violent acts. On the contrary, it is very much to be feared that violence will continue to be the most adequate instrument for accomplishing any personal or group objective. In a recent study, Archer and Gartner (1984) examined data on violent actions in 110 nations and 44 big cities and came to the conclusion that most of their findings could be explained by a seemingly simple hypothesis: that when a country does violence to human beings through war or executions, it in effect incites its citizens to greater violence. What can we expect, then, of our countries, where institutionalized aggression reaches levels as horrendous as the campaigns of state terrorism waged in El Salvador and Guatemala? . . . .
. . . .

Zimbardo's studies (1970) have tried to show how the depersonalization or de-individualization of actions stimulates destructiveness and violence. We must therefore ask ourselves to what extent the violence which arises among us in the present circumstances is institutionalized in roles that are socially prescribed and adopted with their charge of impersonal violence and, therefore, without the agents' having to bear the weight of responsibility for what they do. Zimbardo's study . . . shows how the social system institutionally offers roles which require the exercise of violence in an impersonal form and without the burden of responsibility for the individual agent. In these conditions, how could violence fail to be effective and expedient? This is why it is up to the psychologist to encourage people to develop, once more, an indispensable critical consciousness to help them discover how intolerable and dehumanizing are the exigencies of the daily normality which is inculcated as natural, and to show them how to distinguish between exercising a critical consciousness and simply following the imposed norm, to distinguish the personal action from the social function. We know of many cases in which soldiers have fired their guns into the air, only to report later that they have caused enemy casualties. In this sense, the training for social deviation is a way of educating for peace in societies like ours which are structured and maintained with high levels of violence.

Conclusion

In Central America, we find ourselves in a situation of generalized violence, which is deeply rooted ultimately in conflicts arising from structural injustice and is fed by ideological justification, which in turn is propagated and multiplied because of its usefulness in acheiving objectives for which the social system offers no alternative provisions. Faced with this situation, psychology demands intervention at multiple levels, from the most personal to the most social. As Goldstein, et al. (1981) point out, "we can understand aggression better, control it more easily, and advance alternatives to it if we analyze it from an individual, group, community, and societal perspective simultaneously." We must reclaim the "social psychological history" of our violence all the way from its personal and social roots to its institutional elaboration in roles and laws, including all of the socializing instances and all the circumstantial mechanisms that facilitate and reinforce it.

According to the studies [reviewed in the omitted section], a program of psychological intervention should include, at least, four major objectives: **1)** To train people in personal control and in the development of skills and habits which allow them to channel their frustrations symbolically or constructively; **2)** To develop a critical consciousness in both school and home, of both the social models which are transmitted through the various socializing instances and the institutionalized exigencies of fixed social roles, unmasking the interests that they advance and the false justifications with which they disguise themselves. Among other things, this requires dismantling the ideology of the "enemy," situating problems where they really occur and not displacing them onto "scapegoats"; **3)** To promote an attitude of cooperation socially and, above all, of a lifestyle of austerity and solidarity consistent with the objective resources of the countries—a lifestyle which continuously strengthens sharing not monopolizing, and collective success not individualistic triumph; and **4)** To promote a new order of social relations which restores the whole meaning to each behavior and which obliges all actors (whether individuals or groups) to take on those areas of social responsibility which properly belong to them. In practice, this program means contributing to a process for the radical change of the alienating structures characteristic of the present social order.

Only in this new social context will violence cease to be the most economical and effective means at our disposal, whether for venting frustration, satisfying our needs, or achieving redress and social change. Ultimately, in a society affected by a conflict arising from oppression and structural injustice as serious as the one in our countries, the solution to the main problems of violence must necessarily involve the transformation of those structures, although that alone is not enough.

To return to my point of departure, the problem of generalized violence we are experiencing in Central America at present is neither primarily, nor fundamentally, a psychological problem, but rather an economic, political, and social problem. Nevertheless, for this very reason, it is also a psychological problem. Until now, the contribution of psychologists to the resolution of this extremely serious problem has been conspicuous by its absence, if not by the more or less implicit acceptance of the situation by those who, in the best of cases, have resigned themselves to alleviating some of the most visible individual consequences of that violence. Obviously, this has been and will continue to be necessary, but it is not enough and may not even be the most important thing.

The program outlined here represents an initial attempt at an alternative, which can and should be criticized, corrected, and extended but which, in any case, attempts to open windows onto a new horizon and to stimulate Central American psychologists to venture in that direction and thus to contribute to the construction of a new person in a new society. The problem is real; the challenge is real. And more real than all the rest is the suffering of the majority of our peoples, suffering which admits no further delays; all that is missing is our historic response.

Ignacio Martín-Baró

20. From Religion as Opium to Religion as Liberating Faith*

TRANSLATION BY MARIA INES LACEY

"Anyone inclined to cooperate with a pseudo-peace, a false order, imposed through repression and fear, must keep in mind that the only order and the only peace that God wants is that based in truth and justice. Faced with such an alternative our option is clear: we will comply with the order of God rather than the order of men."

Homily of July 1, 1979.   OSCAR ROMERO
                                                                   ARCHBISHOP

Religion in Latin America

. . . The societies that emerged from the Iberian conquests in America are deeply marked by religion, both by the power of the institutional church and the dynamism of popular religiosity. Most Latin Americans are Catholics, though recently there has been a rapid spread of pentecostal and fundamentalist groups throughout the continent, a fact of grave concern to the Catholic bishops (CELAM, 1982). In El Salvador, for example, reliable statistics tell us that between 60 and 70 percent of the population are Catholics; from 12 to 15 percent are Protestants of various denominations, and the rest are either non religious or belong to syncretic or non-Christian groups. Similar statistics apply with regard to most other Latin American countries. We will treat El Salvador as a kind of living laboratory, a small, intense representative of the conflicts and processes that are characteristic of all of Latin America, without suggesting that all of its details can be generalized to the other countries. . . .

Religion is a key element for understanding both the psychology of the people of Latin America and the whole gamut of political activities

---

*Martín-Baró (1987b); see the Bibliography in the back of this book.
    It should be noted that parts of the original article have been omitted.

and policies which are discussed and implemented there. Religious power has tremendous political significance, being all the more effective when it purports not to represent a political stance, but to be above partisan conflicts.

TWO SIDES OF LATIN AMERICAN RELIGION.

Analyzing religious life in Latin America brings to light two different political orientations derived from two distinct types of ecclesial being and acting. One type expresses a vertical, other worldly, and individualistic religion, which is allied with the dominant social sectors and sympathetic to conservative régimes. The other expresses a horizontal, this-worldly, communitarian religion, which is embodied among the oppressed social sectors and sympathetic to progressive régimes. The first will be called law-and-order religion and the second subversive religion.

Law-and-order religion corresponds to those religious forms which fulfill an alienating social function—those which Marx called "the opium of the people" (K. Marx, 1844; Maduro, 1979). Its most striking political characteristic rests on a view of God as principally responsible for judgment and for what is just in the social order, a view which detaches human beings from their historical roots in their quest for salvation. Paradoxically, political authority is seen both as sanctioned by God, whether or not it faithfully carries out its duties, and as subject to the final judgment of God also. However, only in the afterlife will there be reward or condemnation for what is done on earth. What really matters, then, is to prepare for the last judgment, so that earthly affairs are conceived merely as opportunities to gain favor before the divine tribunal so as to receive one's eternal reward.

This type of religion offers an illusory representation of reality; it couples a "divine" explanation of the order of things in this world, with a "way out" through God's intervention and through the last judgment in the next world. By putting destiny in God's hands, such a law-and-order religion offers fulfillment in the next life to socially alienated persons who, because they are deprived of the fruits of their labor, are denied any real sense of fulfillment in this life. And so the pious person's sights are placed on the afterlife, for which a concern to influence earthly politics is irrelevant. . . .

This generic characterization of law-and-order religion constitutes, of course, an "ideal type" (in Weber's sense), and in each concrete case it is manifest to a greater or lesser extent. However, it does capture a recognizable reality of Latin American countries where religion is a pillar of conservative régimes, including the most oppressive and exploitative. For example, in 1932 following the bloody repression of a peasants' uprising in El Salvador, the Catholic Church conducted a mission throughout the affected area (Anderson, 1976). Its central theme combined the necessity of submission to the order established by God with the threat of eternal damnation to all who rebelled against the authorities. Furthermore, the behavior and preaching of Argentina's Catholic hierarchy, during the recent military dictatorship's "dirty war" in that country, confirm that law-and-order religion is not just a thing of the past.

Subversive religion consists of those religious forms in which people are led, as an imperative of faith, to question and to attempt to transform any socio-political order based on the violation of human rights. Subversive religion offers to alienated persons, whose internalized oppression is reinforced by law-and-order religion, the opportunity to regain a sense of historical fulfillment. This orientation, which is also presented here as an "ideal type," has always been present in Latin American countries—from Bartolomé de las Casas to Oscar Romero—albeit as a minority tendency and as a dialectical counterweight to law-and-order religion. Although the adjective "subversive" is generally used pejoratively, because it is implicitly assumed that to destroy and overturn the prevailing social order (the meaning of "to subvert") is always a bad thing, in fact, to subvert an unjust political order may be, in principle, a citizen's moral obligation.

Subversive religion is not a passing fad of current times; nor is it an ideological appendage of Marxism or an instrument of "international communism," as it is often labeled by those in power. Rather, it is an authentic manifestation of Christianity that comes to the fore in a variety of historical circumstances. As Ernest Troeltsch noted years ago, a tendency within Christianity towards an idealistic anarchism promoting a community of love hostile to law and order coexists with a pull towards becoming a conservative institution utilizing secular organizations for its own benefit (Troeltsch, 1931, Vol. 1, pp. 80-82).

Since subversive religion and law-and-order religion represent "ideal types," actual individuals and groups may more or less manifest their characteristics, perhaps even in combination, but there are other religious groups that do not easily fit under either type. Although these latter groups have some political importance, it is less than that enjoyed by the more defined religious groupings in day to day social interactions, and even less in moments of crisis when conflict breaks out.

THE IDEOLOGICAL NATURE OF RELIGION

Whether religion supports an established régime or questions and subverts it, whether the Church legitimates the social order or condemns it, it is exercising an important political role. This very fact poses the question of how social interests are articulated with the various components of a particular religion. Because it can either be an alienating force or a liberating force, either subverting or serving the established order, religion by its very nature is not tied to any particular political position. So it offers a valuable ideological tool put to work when there is social conflict. Hence the need to examine what religious elements or practices are ideologically useful for promoting the interests of the various social sectors takes on added importance.

It is important to make a distinction between religion as social institution and religion as personal experience. The first one refers more to churches, the other to "religiosity." While both aspects are essential to understand religion's political role, this article will focus on religiosity, that is, on the religious experience of individuals and groups. The objective of the social psychological analysis presented here is to examine how different forms of religiosity, i.e. different religious beliefs, feelings, and practices, even within a single denomination or Church, reflect different social interests and consequently fulfill diverse political functions vis-à-vis the established social order.

Without entering here into a theoretical debate (Batson and Ventis, 1982 pp. 3-23), *religion* will be defined as the sum total of the beliefs, feelings, and behaviors which involve a supreme being, in relation to which individuals and groups explain the ultimate meaning of life and death (James, 1902). *Religiosity* will be defined as the diversity of forms by which individuals and groups live their religion. Religiosity may be characterized by three elements: **1)** religious representations; **2)** religious practices (and practices which derive from religion); and **3)** relationships and ties among members of a religious community.

Religious representations are the beliefs and symbols of a particular denomination or faith through which people interpret their life and reality. . . . They are modes of thought about God and God's relationship to the ultimate aspects of human life. They are rooted in the religious "common sensibility" of each community of believers, at the core of which two elements may be discerned: the salvation message offered to believers, and the symbols most used to grasp God's relationship with human beings.

Religious practices are those modes of conduct, whether of individuals or groups, which seek to rebind (Latin *re-ligare*) human beings with God, such as prayers, pilgrimages, religious readings, and liturgical acts. There are also modes of conduct which, while not religious in the sense defined, are, nonetheless, derived from religious convictions. For example, any religion normally includes values and ethical principles for defining the proper conduct of one's life. Hence we can speak of a "protestant" or a "catholic" ethic. In addition, religious beliefs frequently require that one behave in particular ways under certain conditions; as, for example, in the Catholic Church there is the well-known prohibition of the use of contraceptive means other than the rhythm method. These modes of conduct, while properly regarded as secular and non-religious, may also come to be regarded an essential part of the religious practice of the members of a church or denomination.

The *relationships* and *ties* among members of a denomination, church, or community may occur at different levels, ranging from immediate contact with the nearest occupant of a pew during a religious celebration, to national and international links among churches and communities. Some are intense, long lasting, and very important, while others are superficial, passing, and secondary.

Numerous psychological studies have sought to establish what the main dimensions of religious experience are (James, 1902; Allport, 1950; Batson and Ventis, 1982). For this analysis, it is assumed that religious typology appeals to two dimensions, corresponding to the two core elements of religious representations: 1) the vertical-horizontal dimension, referring to the relationships between humans and the divine; 2) the transcendental-historical dimension, referring to salvation.

The *vertical-horizontal* dimension alludes to the emphasis in each denomination's account of the relationship between God and human beings. At one extreme is the conception of God as a superior being, distant and inaccessible, with whom the only possible relationship is that of the creature to its creator, or that of subject to master; this implies hierarchical submission in a relationship that is totally vertical. At the other extreme are those to whom God is a being who is superior, yet close and accessible, with whom one can maintain a respectful friendship, more like a kind father than an austere monarch.

The *transcendental-historical* dimension deals with a conception of salvation either as something directly due to God's provenance and transcending this world, or as something that takes into account the tasks of this world (Neal, 1965). At one extreme are those for whom salvation is an act of God who intervenes directly in the world, independently of history's own dynamic, in order to establish the right order supernaturally and miraculously (apocalyptically). In the light of this conception, human beings need to be concerned only with praying and preparing for the advent of this total and definitive salvation. At the other extreme are those who hold that God acts only through human beings who must then assume the responsibility of transforming the world and society, which are to be brought to salvation from within their own historical dynamic, while recognizing that history is not solely of this world.

My basic hypothesis used here is that these two dimensions of religiosity are associated with very distinct religious representations, practices, and relationships, and that among the people of Latin America, they become vehicles of different social and political interests: the more vertical and transcendent the religiosity of people, the more they tend to support a conservative, law-and-order religion; whereas a religiosity which is more horizontal and historical tends to lead people to a subversive religion that favors progressive and even revolutionary social change. The fact that religion in Latin America has not been much studied by social psychologists is surprising considering its ideological importance and political impact. It is hardly even mentioned as a relevant issue in the most widely used psychology manuals and textbooks. Quite possibly this is a result of religion's ideological power which seeks to hide and deny its political impact and remain above objective studies.

Law-and-Order Religion

Currently a vast variety of religious groups and movements can be found in Latin American countries (CELAM, 1982; Dominquez and Huntington, 1984; Valderrey, 1985). The numbers of sects, especially Christian fundamentalist ones, keeps growing. Moreover, within the Catholic Church, marked traditionally by its almost monolithic unity, there are now clear divisions: 1) traditional groups; 2) traditionalist groups (such as, "God, Fatherland, and Family" which resemble neo-fascist movements right down to their para-military brigades); 3) groups linked to the Christian Base Communities; and 4) various charismatic groups.

THREE TYPES OF LAW-AND-ORDER RELIGION

The political impact of religiosity will serve as the fundamental criterion for establishing a typology of the principal forms of law-and-order religion in Latin American countries. We will examine how a social group's everyday life and its religious practices interact with the established political order; that is, how social power is channelled through the people's religiosity. Such an interaction need not be explicit. In order to have a politically significant impact, such interaction need not involve affiliation with a political party or activist engagement, since frequently it is the omissions or the withdrawal from action that bolster or undermine a régime most.

Using this criterion we can detect three main types of law-and-order religion in Latin America today: a) one which provides the expectation of a spiritual *compensation* in an afterlife for all the hardships and sufferings of this world; b) a second kind which promulgates a faith in God's direct intervention in socio-political affairs, thereby encouraging in the faithful the *evasion* of their historical responsibility insofar as it goes beyond purely personal change; and c) a third which offers individuals a *cathartic release*, a purely emotional sense of liberation from oppressive conditions.

Religion as Compensation in the Afterlife

This form of religiosity is most common among traditional Catholic groups for whom the stipulations of Vatican Council II and the meetings of the Latin American bishops at Medellín and Puebla have either had minimal impact or have been assimilated into traditional forms, once their rough edges were smoothed over. These groups can be found among the upper classes as well as the campesinos and the urban poor. They are not so prevalent within the middle sectors who, strongly influenced by liberal ideas, tend to reject an excessively other-worldly type of religion, which is often incompatible with the requirements of culture and science (e.g., in relation to sexual matters).

The *salvation message* of traditional Catholics conceives of life on earth as a testing ground, a pilgrimage towardss the true life which begins after death. Salvation presupposes that one gains favor with God through formally obeying his commandments as they are interpreted by the teaching authority (the magisterium) represented by the Church's hierarchy. Religion only speaks to the spiritual side of human life ("sacred history") and should not get into other aspects ("profane history"). The only influence of religion in "secular" life is realized through an ethic of intentions: a person's intentions are what distinguishes good and bad actions in the eyes of God; it is not so much what is done but how it is done that makes an act sinful or not. For this reason, a sin is always a personal or individual act; it makes no sense to speak of social or structural sins. It is only a person who sins, not a society or a social structure.

God's *image* among traditional Catholics is predominantly that of an omnipotent and omniscient creator, a supreme and perfect being, a being loving towards his creatures but also distant from them. To approach God one must enter a sacred realm through the mediation of consecrated individuals (priests) or ritual practices (liturgical rites). To the image of God the creator is added that of God the judge, thus completing his image as the infinite being, the "alpha and omega" of creation. Before him, as judge, one is ultimately accountable, and it is in his eyes that one must gain favor.

These religious representations, articulated as a religious "common sensibility," encourage formalistic *practices* in which the faithful are preoccupied with avoiding sinful acts, as defined by the commandments, and with complying with all the explicitly required activities: baptism of children, going to mass on Sundays and "days of obligation," confession and communion at least once a year, and marriage in the Church. One must be "well with God," seeking not to offend him (by committing sexual sins, for example), and periodically to be reconciled with him through confession and acts of "charity" towards the poor and the Church itself.

Traditional Catholic religiosity requires a minimum of *communitarian ties* and responsibilities. The fundamental relationship is directly between the individual and God, who is the only one who can judge one's intentions which are the root causes of sin. While in church services one may formally "offer peace" to fellow attenders in nearby pews, one need not know them, or consider that any further commitment towards them is required. Church members may join a confraternity to gain social prestige or a devotional group as a way to structure their desire to live a more fully religious life. But what really matters is their compliance with the commandments and the Church's teachings.

To summarize: this religiosity is 1) *formalistic*—almost contractual in nature: involving religious obligations to avoid sin, and so to gain favor in heaven; 2) *individualistic*—individuals are responsible to God for their actions, above all for the intentions behind them rather than their consequences; 3) *spiritualistic*—religion pertains only to one's spiritual life, one's personal and intimate relationship with God, and to formal religious practices.

The political implications of this type of religiosity are clear. Believers, as such, need only be concerned with their spiritual lives. Economic, social, and political matters are in the sphere of the profane which must be kept strictly separate from the religious. The emphasis both personally and socially is on what "not to do" (not to sin) rather than on what "to do." This promotes passivity vis-à-vis the political world, which is seen as particularly "corrupt." The passivity is only to be broken when there is an issue that threatens the Church or when legislation may encourage sinful practices such as abortion or divorce. Otherwise, a Catholic ought to maintain an attitude of respect and collaboration towards social and political authorities, being careful not to confuse the sacred with the profane, the religious with the secular. Catholics may enter the political arena, but only for purely personal reasons. When they do, they are expected to behave honestly, out of respect for the good name of their religion, and to take stands on causes which affect the Church.

In Latin America it is important to distinguish between those *traditional* Catholics whose traditionalism comes from their not having evolved and those (the *traditionalists*) whose traditionalism becomes a social and political banner that justifies combating any form of deviation with any means, including armed violence. While traditional Catholics are passive and conform to their established capitalist system, traditionalist Catholics turn this posture into an absolute requirement which is explicitly political. The latter are the ones who join movements such as "God, Fatherland, and Family" or organizations such as "Guerrillas for Christ the King." In the name of God they are ideologically combative against those they consider either hostile or simply opposed to their religious values and ideals, and they even resort to physical violence and assassinations. The Catholic organization "Opus Dei" (God's Work) is a model of traditional Catholicism which straddles traditional religiosity and religious traditionalism as a political posture.

Religion as a Millenarian Evasion

A second type of law-and-order religion is to be found among these "evangelical" Christians whose faith is millenarian and fundamentalist.

Fundamentalism originated in the United States around the turn of the century, aiming to defend the "fundamentals" of faith from the dangers of modern thought. Its basis is that "the Bible is the only source of authority on doctrinal and moral matters. . . . Fundamentalists consider the Bible to be free of errors. Such infallibility applies even to minor points since, if the Bible were wrong on those points, how could it be trusted on matters of life and death?" (Pixley, 1985 p. 33).

. . . .

Fundamentalism often evokes *millenarianism,* the conviction that Christ will reign over the world one thousand years before the final judgment, and that that moment is close at hand when Christ will come again, intervening directly in human affairs to initiate this reign.

Fundamentalism is most common in poor urban neighborhoods. As Pixley notes (1985, p. 34): "Fundamentalism is an attractive version of Christianity for those who have suffered the breakdown of their traditional communities where indisputable norms for what is right and true had prevailed. In an urban center, persons displaced from rural areas find a confusion of religious sects, scientific theories, and norms of conduct. Being oneself able to read a book of infallible revelation becomes a great source of security."

The fundamentalist *salvation message* is centered on strict compliance with everything that God prescribes in the Bible, interpreted by the "common sensibility" of the faithful. Biblical interpretation is thus framed by beliefs about life and society which each group takes to be the "natural" assumptions of life in its circumstances, so that the Bible ends up reaffirming precisely those patterns of socialization which each given social order presents as the principles of reality. In Latin American countries fundamentalism is profoundly anti-communist, not only because communism challenges the "natural" assumptions in which the common sensibility of the capitalist social order is rooted, but also because it is seen as a veritable "apocalyptic beast" offering a historical salvation, which it presents as an alternative to the only possible salvation. Fundamentalists do not fail to acknowledge the world's injustices, which they attribute to diabolical forces (following broadly disseminated preachings emanating from the United States) that corrupt human hearts, and that can be redeemed only with the final coming of Christ. "To the Christian fundamentalist political or union leaders are, at best, noble persons who don't know that the human decadence announced by God is impossible to arrest. At worst, they are diabolical agents sent to confuse humanity. In any case they must be rejected" (Pixley, 1985). For Christian fundamentalists, therefore, the road to salvation requires not only faithful compliance with all biblical prescriptions, interpreted through their own "good sense," but also a struggle against any other "salvation" apart from that of Jesus Christ. A marked preference is displayed by fundamentalists for apocalyptic *symbolism:* God as the supreme judge, the angel of the Lord overpowering the diabolical "beast," and Jesus Christ as the king who comes to reign over all of creation.

Fundamentalist groups are very demanding that the *practices* of the faithful agree with these principles. In their behavior, fundamentalists must demonstrate ostensibly their adherence to Christian principles: they must totally renounce all sinful activities (alcoholic consumption, gambling, extramarital sex, etc.), must comply faithfully with church requirements ranging from individual acts of piety (prayer, Bible reading) to ongoing participation in cult services and financial support of pastors, and they must also become fervent proselytizers. Thus the Church functions as the central point of reference in the life of a fundamentalist.

Fundamentalists develop strong *ties* to their church communities. Their conscious sense of being "the elect," their militant proselytism, and the ongoing activities of the cult forge strong networks. Sociologically this is typical of sects (Troeltsch, 1931). Often the community ties take on such intensity and importance that the Church ends up being everything to the faithful, becoming a true substitute for civil society.

From all of this it is obvious why fundamentalist religiosity has such clear political implications. On the one hand it rejects and condemns the injustice and immorality of the established social order as being contrary to the order prescribed in the Bible. On the other hand, however, it leads the faithful to eschew any responsibility to change the worldly order, since that responsibility is exclusively God's. Moreover, efforts to bring about social change are seen as pretentious, illusory, even diabolical, as they are attempts to assume Jesus' roles. So fundamentalists are resigned vis-à-vis the political order, and at the same time they reject and condemn anyone who is working for social change. Thus, they become convenient allies of established socio-political authorities, whose power they don't challenge even when they criticize their behavior as sinful.

It should be noted that groups such as the Mormons and Jehovah's Witnesses, which proselytize widely in Latin America, have similar socio-political characteristics even though they are not fundamentalist, since they recognize sources of revelation other than the Bible. . . .

Religion as Individualistic Catharsis

Pentecostalism is the third type of law-and-order religion. As the name implies, it emphasizes the receiving of the Holy Spirit by the faithful. . . . Pentecostalism occurs among not only Protestants, but also among those Catholics who are part of the "charismatic renewal movement" that has been strongly endorsed at the highest levels of the Church's hierarchy. Pentecostal Protestant groups have proliferated especially among poor Latin Americans, while the Catholic charismatic movement has penetrated into the middle- and upper-class sectors. Pentecostal churches expanded greatly between 1965 and 1980 and have now become the largest of the evangelical groups in Latin America (Valderrey, 1985).

In a nutshell, for Pentecostals the *salvation message* is the belief in a second coming of the Holy Spirit upon the faithful, who are thus sanctified and receive such gifts as the ability to speak in tongues, glossolalia. The coming of the Spirit must be preceded by an individual's conversion—by his or her being born again. Pentecostal symbolism conceives of God as a spirit or miraculous force, which transforms and sanctifies anyone who is possessed by it or whom it touches. Thus the visible miracle, principally the immediate cure, is the sign of the authenticity of a believer's faith.

Religious *practice* requires that pentecostals both exhibit a significant change in their personal lives indicating their sanctification by the Spirit and also participate frequently in the cult's services. Given that the Spirit descends upon each particular individual, an individualistic pietism is engendered, that is, a direct search for the inspiration and sanctification of the Spirit. A Pentecostalist cult characteristically involves its members' participation in prophecy (during which there are frequent shouts of approval, or praise, and the visible expression of feelings) and an emotionally charged atmosphere. It is the exact opposite of the Catholic solemn high mass: the Church is not a place in which to be respectfully silent, but rather a place for conversation, a place in which one expresses one's joys and sorrows, sings and dances, and liberates one's spirit.

Pentecostalism also emphasizes *community ties*, especially in the services of the cult. Within the Church all are equal, whether poor or rich, learned or illiterate, because the Spirit does not recognize worldly distinctions. Moreover, the intensity of the emotional experience generates a strong sense of bonding among "the brothers and sisters in the Spirit."

Pentecostalism has a complex political impact. On the one hand, the born-again person who has received the Spirit regains a sense of dignity and self value. In fact, Pentecostalism has served as a kind of historical refuge for some social groups who have been excluded from society's benefits; e.g., some Blacks of North America and many of the marginalized peoples of Latin America (Lalive, 1968). In this sense Pentecostalism has indeed supported the human and social aspirations of marginalized and excluded peoples. However, the Pentecostal impact tends to lead to the dead-end of purely individualistic change. The sense of equality in the Spirit pervading the cult, does not transfer to the outside world, and the recovery of dignity is hard to maintain outside of the Church's walls. Furthermore, by promoting a periodic emotional release the cult serves as a catharsis and a kind of escape-valve for day-to-day sorrows and frustrations. All the energy which could be channelled into social and political organizing is poured out and dissipated within the cult. It is not surprising then, as Valdeverrey (1985) points out, that the spread of Pentecostalism in Central America coincides with a convergence of interest between the higher echelons of power in the United States and powerful evangelical groups.

. . . .

See Table 1 in which the three types of law-and-order religion in Latin America are summarized.

Table 1. Three Types of Law-and-Order Religion in Latin America

	Traditional Catholics	*Fundamentalist Sects*	*Pentacostal & Charismatic Groups*
Salvation Message	God is creator and judge. Aim to go to heaven and avoid hell.	God has apocalyptic power. Await the final judgment.	God is the miracle-maker spirit. Receive the spirit.
Religious Practices	To comply with the commandments and obligatory sacraments.	Proselytism. To prepare for the coming of God.	Personal change. Participation in the cults.
Community Ties	Individualism. Occasional and superficial associations.	Awareness of being "the elect." Intense sense of unity with the "brothers and sisters."	Intense, emotional bonding in the celebrations.
Political Effects	The religious sphere is separate. Political passivity.	Resigned submission. "Only God can bring salvation."	Liberating; inward-turned individualism and catharsis.

THE POLITICAL IMPACT OF LAW-AND-ORDER RELIGION

Although the political implications of each of the principal types of law-and-order religion in Latin America have been noted, it is useful to present an overall view. From a social psychological perspective there are two main political effects of law-and-order religion: first, the detachment of the faithful from socio-political involvement; and second, the direct or indirect religious legitimation of conservative régimes.

Detachment from Politics

The three forms of law-and-order religion engender a religiosity which is both individualistic and personally introspective: the only thing that really matters is personal salvation, which is totally outside the political sphere (Falla, 1984). Sacred history is above profane history, and one must seek to enter the former. Life on earth is a time of testing, a time to become deserving of the other life and to prepare for the definitive coming of Christ.

Remaining detached from worldly politics is one of the believer's religious duties. The important thing is for an individual to change internally, to convert, to be sanctified, and to win favor with God. This does not mean one approves of the socio-political order. Indeed, the faithful are frequently aware that the world, where evil and sin prevail, is corrupt and so it should be condemned. However, only God's intervention can transform the world, whether through the conversion of people (including the authorities) or through his direct intervention. People who adopt this type of religion thus become part of "the silent majorities," which provide a *de facto* support for established régimes. Because "only God can solve the world's problems," there is no point in even discussing them let alone becoming a political activist. In a poll conducted in August and September 1986, to gather opinions about an announced dialogue for peace between the government and the insurgents of the FMLN, 21.9% of a representative sample of adult Salvadorans stated that "only God" could solve the war problem. This response was given predominantly by the poor, the uneducated, and the old women members of evangelical churches. While in some cases it appeared to reflect a sense of powerlessness in the face of an overwhelming problem, in other cases, the response was clearly the expression of a fundamentalist spirituality, putting in God's hands the gravest problem facing Salvadorans (Martín-Baró, 1986b).

It is important to note that the view of religion as separate from politics is also the traditional liberal conception, which bases the separation on the claim that religion is a private matter while politics is public. According to liberalism, the appeal to transcendental and absolute religious principles tends only to obfuscate the rationality so necessary in the political discourse that provides democratic legitimation of the exercise of power.

The Legitimation of Conservative Régimes

An important doctrinal aspect of law-and-order religion is the rejection of the injustice and sinfulness that it discerns in the socio-political order. How then can régimes which perpetrate evil, even using diabolical forces, be religiously legitimated by those who condemn them?

The answer is twofold. In the first place, *any* socio-political order is seen as bad. No concrete instances can be judged to be worse than others. Such a global condemnation tends indirectly to justify any régime in power, because some form of government is needed at least until the "reign of Jesus Christ is installed." Furthermore, by detaching themselves from the political arena, individuals express tacit acceptance of the established order.

In the second place, a strong anti-communism pervades all types of law-and-order religion. Communism is identified with the "anti-Christ," the "apocalyptic beast," and even the "devil." A communist is anyone who goes against the "common sensibility" appropriate to the established capitalist system; and in some cases this means any one who disagrees with the proposals made by U.S. political authorities, whose anti-communism sets the norms for evaluating truth. This is the only way to comprehend the pro-U.S. position of the Mormons and of what Valdeverrey calls the "religious multinationals" such as: World Vision International, the PTL T.V. network, the Campus Crusade, the Billy Graham Evangelical Association, the 700 Club and others. "Doctrinally these groups are fundamentalist; their goals, however, are more political than religious (Valdeverrey, 1985). (See also Dominquez & Huntington, 1984.) Significantly, they all supported the ultra-conservative Reagan Administration, pressuring it to break ranks with anyone seen as "soft" on communism (Ezcurra 1984).

The anti-communism of law-and-order religion confers legitimacy on any régime, which is guided by the doctrine of national security or which stands for the "defense of the values of Christian Western culture," by opposing any attempt to change social structures. Such governments can boast of having God on their side and of being God's instruments to combat atheistic communism. [In Chile] Pinochet represents a paradigmatic case. In El Salvador, law-and-order religious hierarchies—both Catholic and evangelical—more or less explicitly accept the Christian Democrats as the desirable Christian option, legitimating the Duarte government in its pursuit of war against sectors of the population that were identified as "communist" (Martín-Baró, 1985j).

Subversive Religion

POPULAR RELIGIOSITY

Ever since the Conquest there have been and are religious forms, which challenge the established socio-political order and seek to change it and which have existed in Latin America side by side with those that legitimate and give viability to it. These are forms of the subversive religion of the oppressed that confront the law-and-order religion of the oppressors. Although typically they have been minority movements, they have been socially significant. Bartolemé de las Casas [a sixteenth-century Dominican priest] may be one of the better known cases. Las

Casas opposed the social institutions which the Spanish Empire imposed in the American colonies [for the forced labor of Indians]. He saw these (*la encomienda, el repartimiento, la mita*) as unnatural and as forms of slavery contrary to the gospel. Thus, in the name of the same God that the Conquistadors invoked to justify an exploitative order, Las Casas proclaimed a social order more respectful of the human dignity of American native peoples.

In fact, although indigenous peoples were forcibly converted to Christianity, there was always some strong resistance, especially among those who preserved their ethnic background and never fully accepted those elements of religious control that would bind their spirits to the dominant order. *Popular religiosity* arises from this mixture of imposition and rejection. Frequently, the Catholic hierarchy (but not some of the evangelical churches) has devalued popular religiosity, treating it as backward, primitive, and simple-minded. It has persisted, nevertheless, representing a repository for Latin American peoples of the seeds of historical identity in the face of colonization, independence from the dominant culture, and rebellion against oppressive exploitation. If adopting a kind of fatalistic passivity allowed some oppressed sectors to survive historically, this popular religiosity enabled the oppressed to preserve important elements of their social identity.

From a social psychological perspective there are four notable characteristics of Latin American popular religiosity: 1) integration into popular culture; 2) primacy of accessible mediators; 3) the role of the body in rituals; and 4) assumption of collective responsibilities.

Abstract principles of Catholic doctrine have been *integrated* with other cultural elements so that they become meaningful in light of oppressed peoples' circumstances and responsive to the problems they face. Popular religiosity has tended to emphasize very concrete symbols, such as Mary's maternity and Jesus' passion.

As a reaction to the distance and unreachableness of the traditional God, popular religiosity has promoted an abundance of *accessible mediators*. Each people has had its own Virgin or has taken on the cult of the Virgin of Guadalupe, the dark lady of the Indian, Juan Diego. Many saints, whether recognized by the Church or not, have had more practical importance in popular devotion than Jesus Christ himself; e.g., Saint Jude, St. Christopher, and St. Martin de Porres.

People tend to live their religion more through their *bodies* than through cerebral forms, a tendency that fits well with their objective conditions. Processions and pilgrimages are more popular than the Mass; religious performances are more appreciated than homilies; singing and oral prayers are more common than meditation and solitary reflection.

In spite of the religious individualism pervading Catholic doctrine for centuries, Latin American religiosity has kept a clear consciousness of *collective responsibilities* (familiar and communitarian). Frequently a mother might blame herself for the sin of a child, and an entire family accept responsibility for an offense to God committed by one of its members.

These characteristics of popular religiosity are at the core of Latin American collective identity, containing the seeds for resisting domination which, in certain circumstances, germinate in organized rebellion and revolution. This is what has happened in different parts of the region since the sixties, as the 1969 Rockefeller Report noted.

Subversive religion was revitalized in Latin America in large part by changes brought about in the Catholic Church by Vatican Council II (1962–65). Looking at things from a social psychological point of view, we will highlight two of these changes: first, the Church ceases to define itself with reference to hierarchical authority and comes to conceive of itself primarily as a people, "the people of God" (Vatican II, 1975; Boff, 1984; Ribeiro de Oliveria, 1984); and second, the duality between the sacred and the profane is overcome; no longer is sacred history parallel to or above human history; there is only one history. The Church's role is to be a sacrament of salvation, not only announcing eternal life but also assisting in the building of a more just and fraternal society in the here and now.

The Catholic Church shifted simultaneously from a vertical (and hierarchical) concept to a horizontal (and communitarian) one, and from a transcendental to an historical concept [referring to the two dimensions of religiosity introduced in the first section of this chapter]. Such changes had an almost immediate impact among the Latin American faithful. With the new definition of the Church, the laity was invited to participate more actively and responsibly in ecclesial affairs. And the new vision of salvation history led to considering social realities as human products that require transformation in accordance with Christian principles. Thus, psycho-social space was opened for new religious practices, more communitarian than individualistic, in which working for social transformation became a sacrament of what is to be brought about, a credible image of the kingdom of justice, love, and peace announced by Jesus of Nazareth.

Vatican II had a greater impact in Latin America than in other parts of the world both because it is a continent with a vast majority of Catholics, and also because the socio-political circumstances of its peoples begged for an immediate theological reinterpretation (Dussel, 1979). That reinterpretation was provided by the Latin American bishops who met in Medellín in 1968 (CELAM, 1973). The bishops recognized that the inhuman conditions, in which the vast majority of Latin Americans live, expose the exploitative and oppressive nature of the prevailing social structures. In fact, they classified them sociologically as "institutionalized violence," and theologically as "structures of sin," since they cause the death of so many people. The bishops went on to conclude that Christians are obliged to oppose such structures and to struggle for a historical liberation that would enable the peoples to build a more just society in accordance with God's designs.

Since the Latin American poor were accustomed to interpret their harsh circumstances in religious terms, it was not difficult for them to comprehend that salvation should embrace their own history. As they had always encountered God through accessible, close-to-home mediators, it was readily understandable that Jesus and his followers opted for the poor, making them, preferentially, the locus where God is to be found and his salvation realized. Nor was it hard for them to accept that such an option requires a total commitment to combat structural sin and to transform society. Popular religiosity was thus fertilized and began to generate a diversity of religious practices, of which the Christian Base Communities are the most dynamic and have the greatest impact. Years later, after subversive religion had led the Catholic Church into serious confrontations with Latin American governments, and after reactionary forces had taken control of the Vatican, the Latin American bishops, meeting in Puebla (Mexico), reaffirmed that in view of the conditions prevailing in Latin America it was necessary to continue to emphasize that salvation embraces a historical process. They also confirmed the "preferential option for the poor" which, in a situation of grave social conflict, becomes a class option with serious political consequences.

Far from being merely ideological pronouncements, the messages of Vatican II, of Medellín, and of Puebla gave new life to popular religiosity. The theology of liberation, now considered a *bête noire* in Washington and the Vatican, consists of the variegated thematization of this new life flourishing among Latin American Christians.

CHRISTIAN BASE COMMUNITIES (CBCs)

The Christian Base Communities came into existence in the early 1960s, especially in poor urban sectors. They began as small groups of between eight and thirty people seeking to assume responsibility for those religious practices which do not require the presence of a priest; e.g., religious instruction, prayer and communal reflection about God's will for the lives of individual persons and of the community. Reinforced by Vatican II and Medellín, such initiatives proliferated rapidly throughout Latin America especially where they had the clear support of the Church's hierarchy. In Brazil alone some 200,000 CBCs were flourishing in the mid-1980s. Three major characteristics of CBCs, counterposed to those of law-and-order religion are: 1) a historical conception of salvation; 2) a commitment to transform the social order; and 3) a communitarian religious life.

Salvation as a Historical Process

Challenging the religious conception which places salvation on a plane parallel to that of human history, the CBCs affirm that the Christian salvation message reaches into peoples' lives and their concrete societies. Such a historical conception of salvation requires that conditions be addressed which impede the realization of the kingdom of God, understood not as something hoped for after death, but as an objective beginning to be realized in the here-and-now. Salvation in history must be a salvation of the one-and-only history.

CBC members see the historical realization of salvation as involving the dual tasks of denouncing and announcing. First and foremost, it is necessary to denounce all conditions of oppression and injustice, which are interpreted as structures of sin. So, alongside of the sins committed by individual persons, the CBCs discern social sin, the objective sinful condition of the structures that dehumanize and cause death among the majority of Latin Americans. This discernment leads them to the prophetic role of denouncing anything that they consider in religious institutions to be "idolatrous," which is how they label the connivance of such institutions with the structures of exploitation and injustice that legitimate "institutionalized violence." This denunciatory posture makes the CBCs unwelcome and the target of criticism of the economic powers as well as of the established law-and-order Church.

Coupled with prophetic denunciation is salvific annunciation. This is tied to the people's historical liberation and to the promotion of a "new exodus," that will enable a more just and more human society to be built in accordance with God's designs. It is, then, a requirement of faith to assume responsibility for changing sinful social structures, and this inevitably involves taking political positions. Personal change is not enough; it is necessary to work for a kind of structural change which favors, dialectically, personal change (Hewitt, 1986). Since their faith requires them to announce a new life in a new world, they attempt to identify concrete courses of action that might be steps in the building of this "utopia." But the CBCs don't fall into the trap of a new conception of Christendom, with millenarian overtones, in which religion would embrace all aspects of life. The task is to struggle for a new social order which is both responsive to the requirements of faith and justice, and respectful of the proper autonomy and specificity of each historical project, whether it be scientific, political, or cultural.

Commitment to Transform the Social Order

For the members of CBCs *orthodoxy*, or giving verbal assent to the truths of the faith, does not suffice for a Christian; *orthopraxis*, or the manifestation in behavior of what one believes to be true, is also necessary. The truth, to which the salvation message refers, is not only to be found but also to be made. It is not something just given to the Latin American popular majorities, rather they must strive for it. That is why Christians must commit themselves to work for justice and with popular movements that seek the historical liberation of the poor of Latin America.

Part of the distinctiveness of the Christians in the CBCs is their requirement of a socio-political commitment. As Christians in CBCs they cannot remain indifferent in the face of circumstances which exploit, marginalize, and oppress a people, preventing their development as human beings, as God's children. On the contrary, they must be committed to work unceasingly to eliminate the root causes of the dehumanization (which has both personal and collective aspects) present in their society. Only in this way will the announcement of salvation become visible and credible in the course of history. Just as Jesus' miracles were the sign of his salvation message, so too the miracle of social transformation, of a peoples' liberation from secular oppression will be the most credible sacrament of the kingdom of God that is announced in Latin America and throughout the Third World. For people to believe in and pray to a God of life, who is called the father of everyone, Christians must work for solidarity among human beings, and the Christian community itself must become a symbolic realization of what it announces.

Communitarian Faith

While a law-and-order religion harbors an inward-turned individualism, a subversive religion promotes communitarian responsibilities. Together the members of a community reflect upon the scriptures, pray, and organize themselves to work for justice. While it is persons who are saved, one finds God among those human beings who are at the service of others, especially the poorest and the oppressed. As the Gospel says: "How can you say you love God whom you don't see, if you don't love your neighbor whom you do see?" For the Christian in a CBC, the community is not a refuge, a place in which to vent one's frustrations, even though it does provide its members with security and understanding. Rather, the community is a reference point that facilitates consciousness raising, critical reflection upon one's life, the questioning of events from the perspective of faith, and commitment to the liberation struggles of the poor majority.

Clearly these three characteristics of the religiosity of the CBCs—salvation as a historical process, commitment to changing the social order, and a communitarian way of life—pertain to an "ideal" and are manifested in reality to a greater or lesser extent depending on each particular case. There are times when the dynamic life of a CBC leads its members to lapse into a form of millenarianism. For example, when civil war erupted in El Salvador in 1981, many Christians were carried away by expectations of an immediate triumph, which were based much more on their religious convictions than on a realistic socio-political analysis. Needless to say, such expectations made it harder to accept the fact that the war could not be won quickly but would be prolonged indefinitely. At other times, passing from religious to political consciousness results in ambiguities. Archbishop Romero repeatedly criticized both the efforts to turn religion into a political tool and the naiveté of certain CBC members who, almost mechanically, wanted to translate Christian beliefs into concrete political options (Martín-Baró, 1980a). Such exaggerations, nevertheless, confirm the descriptive validity of the three characteristics and also show that they play almost a normative role for the members of the CBCs. Table 2 summarizes the characteristics of subversive religion in Latin America.

Table 2. Subversive Religion in Latin America

Salvation Message	Structural sin; oppression	God as liberator
Religious Practices	Critical reflection about society	Preferential option for the poor and the oppressed
Community Ties	Communitarian faith	CBC Social solidarity
Political Effects	Critical consciousness	Organizing among poor people

THE POLITICAL IMPACT OF SUBVERSIVE RELIGION

The political repercussions of subversive religion are immediately evident from the characterization of the CBCs: not only do participants develop a critical consciousness of the established order which enables them to identify the structural root causes of oppression, but they also feel impelled by their faith to work actively to change social structures. Their three main aspects, which come clearly to light when studying El Salvador over the last fifteen years, can be identified as: 1) the awakening of a critical religious consciousness that allowed significant numbers to overcome their fatalism; 2) the organizing of CBCs that served as an impetus and a model for social and political organizing in the popular movements; and 3) the religious faith that gave meaning to the liberation struggles for many people and that provided hope in situations of incredible personal and collective suffering.

The Awakening of Critical Consciousness among the People

The most significant impact of Vatican II and Medellín was to break the fatalistic mentality of poor Salvadorans, especially peasants. Fatalism had long been an element of popular religiosity engendered by apparently immutable historical circumstances: the peasants' symbolic universe presumed the established order to be natural and ordained by God. Through religious reflections, discussions, and preaching they discovered that human beings, not God, are fully responsible for the injustice and oppression present in their country, whose established order is seen in the eyes of God as bad, sinful, and thoroughly revolting to a sound conscience.

It would be inaccurate to affirm that the critical religious consciousness is the main fomenter of the Salvadoran revolutionary movement. But peasants would not have joined it had they not overcome their religiously grounded fatalism which served to explain and justify their oppression (Cabarrús, 1983). The process of awakening critical consciousness was much aided by the method for teaching literacy developed by Paulo Freire (1970, 1978). This method builds upon "reading" history—becoming aware of the factors which determine the context of one's existence—and upon "writing" a new history—transforming, through organized collective action, these alienating factors, thus constructing a new social reality.

The critical religious consciousness promoted by Medellín led to the rapid and growing de-ligitimation of the Salvadoran régime. The rulers could no longer appeal to God as the ultimate guarantor of their authority, nor count on the unconditional support of the Catholic Church. They were forced to seek legitimacy through small-scale attempts at social reform; when these proved ineffective, the only way to stay in power was through brutal and massive repression.

A model for Organizing

The CBCs offered poor Salvadorans a new social experience: people, who had never participated in any type of organization, began to discover the benefits of unified action. The Salvadoran Constitution bars the formation of peasant unions, and since 1932 any form of association among peasants had met with persecution and repression in order to contain reformist demands that might limit the privileges of the landed oligarchy. Only the CBCs were open to the peasants as a practical model of social organization and collective action. Gradually, in the areas where the CBCs had been established, rural people began to organize themselves successfully, first in cooperatives and later in unions and political organizations (Montgomery, 1982).

Faith for the Struggle

The religious conception, which points to the need to eliminate oppressive structures (to eliminate sin), and to contribute to the popular movement for liberation which aims to construct a new, more human and just society (to build the kingdom of God), endows oppositional and even revolutionary political stances with a special meaning. For the Salvadoran poor, shedding their fatalistic outlook through the awakening of critical consciousness does not signify that they give up religious categories for interpreting their reality and existence. On the contrary, it is their faith that gives meaning to the changes that the Salvadoran poor are trying to bring about, and strength to endure and maintain solidarity in the most terrible living conditions, and hope to sustain courage throughout the long, drawn-out struggle.

Only in the light of this triple role of religion—awakening critical consciousness, providing a model, and inspiring—can we understand what Archbishop Romero represented in the revolutionary process of El Salvador. In few other cases is it possible to affirm so clearly that charismatic leadership was not based on personality characteristics (Martín-Baró, 1981b). Romero himself went through a process of conversion, in which his critical consciousness was awakened, opening his eyes to the nation's reality and to the use of religion as a smoke-screen to cover up intolerable injustices. Thus, the Archbishop's voice was then raised in denunciation, in questioning the legitimacy of the established order, and in the prophetic announcement of a new order demanded by God and whose realization should no longer be delayed to the hereafter (Martín-Baró, 1980a). He firmly supported the right of people to organize and even to use force to defend their historic right to life; however, he also felt free to denounce abuses on the part of the popular organizations and their turning of partisan interests into absolutes (Ellacuría, 1979c). Archbishop Romero's assassination was an action informed by the intelligent calculation that its symbolic value would be as significant as the actual loss that his death represented for the cause of the Salvadoran poor; it was intended not only to put an end to a life and a voice, but to annul, once and for all, the liberating role of religion in El Salvador.

The subversive potential of the religion emerging from Medellín provoked an immediate reaction in the centers of power. Already in 1969, a U.S. Presidential Mission [for the Western Hemisphere] warned of the dangerous subversive penetration of the Catholic Church [that was] impelling it towards revolution (Rockefeller Report, 1969). More recently the Santa Fe document was very explicit in one of its recommendations: "U.S. foreign policy must begin to counter (not react against) liberation theology as it is utilized in Latin America by the liberation theology clergy" (Council for Inter-American Security, 1980).

Such "countering" of liberation theology has been carried out in two ways: 1) through the systematic use of terror against disciples of subversive religion, a policy articulated in the "national security" doctrine (Comblin, 1979); and 2) an ideological attack worked out in such think-tanks as the Washington-based Institute for Religion and Democracy, and a massive campaign of fundamentalist missions throughout Latin America (Dominquez and Huntington, 1984; Ezcurra, 1984). Thus, repression was designed to nip in the bud any nascent signs of a popular church, while the fundamentalist penetration would provide a socially acceptable form of religious consolation.

Religious Conversion as a Political Process

Religious conversion . . . may represent a veritable primary re-socialization for a person (Berger & Luckman, 1968). It is not just a matter of changing values and religious practices; in many cases the convert is led to change his or her "world" significantly, that is, to change the categories fundamental to his or her interpretation and evaluation of reality, and is thus led to important changes in attitudes, habits, and forms of action.

A paradigm for religious conversion can be found in the biblical story of Saul, the persecutor of Christians, who became Paul, the apostle of the gentiles. The most common biblical interpretation characterizes this conversion as having been: a) sudden and dramatic, caused by a powerful external factor; b) psychological and personal in nature; and c) productive of radical change of the self (Richardson, 1985, p. 165). This interpretation is now considered questionable, largely because it is thought that the majority of conversions (whether religious or not) do not occur with those characteristics (Bromley and Richardson, 1983; Snow and Machalek, 1984). What is currently emphasized is that a conversion does not happen to a passive subject but is a change in which the person must be actively engaged. According to Richardson (1980, p. 50), it is part of a "conversion career" on which people embark and it cannot be understood without taking into account their plans, desires, and explicit motives.

A religious conversion can fulfill both a social and individual function. Socially, since the conversion can induce a person to assume certain attitudes or to behave in certain ways, it can be of service to particular groups or class interests which benefit from people having these attitudes and patterns of behavior, and so it is reinforced by them. From an individual viewpoint it may satisfy particular needs or respond to specific personal motivations, and for that reason it will be actively sought by the particular individual. In the light of these two functions, we can see the political character of a conversion; i.e., its consequences in the interplay of a country's social forces.

There is no other explanation for the fact that religious issues in Latin America are a concern for many governments, in particular that of the United States. Many studies indicate that this concern has been translated, on the part of official U.S. agencies, into tenacious efforts to promote religious proselytism throughout Latin America by those denominations and sects which foster conformism and political evasion (Dominquez and Huntington, 1984; Valderrey, 1985). The Iberian conquistadors saw the conversion of the native peoples to "the true faith" as an indispensable part of their task; they were aware, more or less explicitly, of the political role of religion. Today, once again, taking advantage of the need for security and consolation which most people cannot satisfy in any other way, religious conversion is being used as an instrument of political domination in Latin American countries.

While any conversion in Latin America today has a political character, its concrete content depends on whether it is to law-and-order or to subversive religion (Delgado *et al.*, 1987). Both the Rockefeller Report and the Santa Fe Document give evidence that the massive conversion of broad sectors of Latin Americans to subversive religion, following Vatican II and Medellín, has been troubling to the centers of power in the United States. The seeds of rebellion buried in popular religiosity began to sprout through the CBCs and have come to fruition in the popular organizations, unions, and political groups, which have challenged the dominant order. Given that significant sectors of the Catholic Church and of the main Protestant congregations (such as the Lutherans) have promoted a subversive religion, the ruling classes had to find an alternative religiosity which would further the reconversion of the populace to law-and-order religion in order to regain religious legitimation for their governments. The fundamentalist and pentecostal sects provide this alternative. For this reason, millions of dollars have been invested in recent years by the "transnational churches" in missionary campaigns throughout the region, aiming at converting the poor peoples to their beliefs.

In Latin America contradictory tendencies coexist side by side today. There are members of the Catholic hierarchy who, like Cardinal Arns [São Paulo, Brazil], back the liberation struggles of oppressed peoples, and others who, like Cardinal López Trujillo [Medellín, Colombia], organize missions in Nicaragua to sabotage the Sandinista revolution. There are base communities working from a faith perspective to build a more just society, and there are Christian groups who form anti-communist "squads." There are followers of law-and-order religion who see the hand of God behind Pinochet's boot and followers of subversive religion who see the "atheistic" policies of Fidel Castro as closer to their faith than the campaigns which Ronald Reagan promotes invoking the name of God. Religion in some cases lulls the historical frustration of the Latin American people like an opium of despair, and in other cases religion arouses their consciences and impels them to struggle for liberation. The option for one or the other form of religiosity is not purely a matter of individual values and subjective preferences; it is also a social and political decision with repercussions for the multiplicity of forces shaping the life of a people.

BIBLIOGRAPHY

The following chronological listings include the publications of Ignacio Ellacuría, Ignacio Martín-Baró, and Segundo Montes. They have been compiled by Hugh Lacey and Frances Cuneo, with the invaluable assistance of Adrianne Aron, Rodolfo Cardenal, S.J., and John Hassett.

The Publications of Ignacio Ellacuría

"Ortega y Gasset: hombre de nuestro ayer", *ECA 11* (1956a), No. 104, pp. 198-203.

"Ortega y Gasset: desde dentro", *ECA 11* (1956b), No. 105, pp. 278-83.

"Quién es Ortega y Gasset?", *ECA 11* (1956c), No. 110, pp. 595-601.

"El despertar de la filosofía", *Cultura* (San Salvador)(1956d), pp. 14-28.

"Marcelino, pan y vino", *ECA 12* (1957a), No. 122, pp. 665-69.

"Los valores y el derecho", *ECA 13* (1958a), No. 124, pp. 79-84.

"Bruselas, 1958, saldo negativo", *ECA 13* (1958b), No. 132, pp. 527-35.

"El Doctor Zivago como forma literaria", *Cultura* (1959a), No. 17, pp. 109-23.

"Santo Tomás, hombre de su siglo", *ECA 14* (1959b), No. 135, pp. 84-89.

"El comunismo soviético visto desde Rusia", *ECA 14* (1959c), No. 141, pp. 455-62.

"Religión y religiosidad en Bergson, I. La religión estática: su razón de ser", *ECA 15* (1960a), No. 145, pp. 6-11.

"Tomás de Aquino, intelectual católico", *ECA 15* (1960b), No. 146, pp. 79-84.

"El tomismo ¿es un humanismo?", *ECA 16* (1961a), No. 157, pp. 70-75.

"Religión y religiosidad en Bergson, II. La religión estática: sus formas", *ECA 16* (1961b), No. 159, pp. 205-12.

"El P. Aurelio Espinosa Pólit, S.J.", *ECA 18* (1963), No. 178, pp. 21-24.

"Antropología de Xavier Zubiri", *Revista de Psiquiatría y Psicología Médica (Barcelona)* (1964), No. 405-30, pp. 483-508.

La principialidad de la esencia en Xavier Zubiri. Doctoral dissertation, Universidad Complutense, Madrid (1965a).

Indices de "Sobre la esencia" de Xavier Zubiri. Madrid (1965b).

"Cinco lecciones de filosofía", *Crisis* (Madrid) 45 (1965c), pp. 109-25.

"La relegación, actitud radical del hombre", *Asclepio, Archivo Iberoamexicano de Historia de la Medicina* (Madrid) 16, (1966a), pp. 97-155.

"La historicidad del hombre en Xavier Zubiri", *Estudios de Deusto* (1966b), pp. 246-286; pp. 423-58.

"La juventud religiosa actual.", *Hechos y Dichos* (1967), pp. 124-34.

"Carta a un ordenado vacilante", *Hechos y Dichos* (1968a), pp. 355-62.

"El ateismo existencialista". *Dios-Ateismo.* I. Ellacuría, *et al.* Bilbao (1968b), pp. 191-212.

"Seguridad social y solidaridad humana", *ECA 24* (1969a), No. 253, pp. 357-65.

"Los derechos humanos fundamentales y su limitación legal y política.", *ECA 24* (1969b), No. 254-55, pp. 435-49. *Reprinted: 1970g; English translation is chapter 3 of this volume.*

"Violencia y cruz". *¿Qué aporta el Cristianismo al hombre de hoy? IV* Semana de Teología, Universidad de Deusto, Bilbao, 1969c.

"La idea de filosofía en Xavier Zubiri". *Homenaje a Zubiri*. A. Albarracín Teu-
lon, I. Ellacuría, *et al.*, 2 volumes. *Madrid:* Editorial Moneda Y Crédito,
1970a, pp. 477-85.
"Los laicos interpelan a su iglesia", *ECA 25* (1970b), No. 256-257, pp. 46-50.
"Progreso y revolución", *ECA 25* (1970c), No. 258, pp. 152-54.
"Los obispos centroamericanos aceleran el paso", *ECA 25* (1970d), No. 262, pp.
381-87.
"Teología de la revolución y evangelio", *ECA 25* (1970e), No. 265-66, pp. 581-84.
"Los centros privados docentes y sus problemas", *ECA 25* (1970f), No. 265-66,
pp. 585-86.
"Los derechos humanos fundamentales y su limitación legal y política", *ECA 25*
(1970g), No. 267, pp. 645-59. *Reprint of 1969b.*

"Liberación: misión y carisma de la iglesia latinoamericana", *ECA 26* (1971a),
No. 268, pp. 61-80.
"¿Teología política hace 400 años?", *ECA 26* (1971b), No. 278, pp. 747-49.
"Estudio ético-político del proceso conflictivo ANDES." *Análisis de una experi-
encia national*. I. Ellacuría, *et al*. San Salvador, 1971c, pp. 123-54.

"Filosofía y política", *ECA 27* (1972a), No. 284, pp. 373-85.
"Un excelente psicodiagnóstico sobre latinoamérica", *ECA 27* (1972b), No. 285,
pp. 499-505; Foreword to I. Martín-Baró, *Psicodiagnóstico de América
Latina*. San Salvador: UCA Editores, 1972c.
"La ley orgánica de la Universidad de El Salvador", *ECA 27* (1972d), No. 290,
pp. 747-61. *Reprinted: 1990q.*

"El seglar cristiano en el tercer mundo", *Búsqueda* (1973a), pp. 15-20.
"Un marco teórico-valorativo de la reforma agraria", *ECA 28* (1973b), No. 297-
98, pp. 443-57.
Teología política. San Salvador: Ediciones del Secretariado Social Interdioce-
sano, 1973c. *English translation:* 1976a.
"Imagen ideológica de los partidos políticos en las elecciones de 1972." *El Sal-
vador: año político 1971-72*. J. Hernández-Pico, I. Ellacuría, E. Baltodano
and R. Mayorga. San Salvador: UCA Editores, 1973d, pp. 321-62.
"Aspectos éticos del problema poblacional", *ECA 29* (1974a), No. 310-311, pp.
565-92.
"Carácter político de la misión de Jesús", *Miec-Jesí* (1974b), doc. 13-14, Lima.
English translation: 1984e.
"Presentación", *Realitas* (Madrid) (1974c), No. 1, pp. 5-9.
"La idea de estructura en la filosofía de Xavier Zubiri", *Realitas* (1974d), No. 1,
pp. 71-139.
"El espacio," *Realitas* (1974e), No. 1, pp. 479-514.

"La antropología filosófica de Xavier Zubiri." *Historia universal de la medicina*.
Pedro Laín Entralgo, ed. Vol. 8, Barcelona (1975a), pp. 109-12.
"Misión política de la Universidad", *ABRA* (El Salvador) (1975b), No. 8, pp. 2-7.

"Hacia una fundamentación filosófica del método teológico latinoamericano", *ECA 30* (1975c), No. 322-23, pp. 409-25.
"Diez años después: ¿es posible una universidad distinta?", *ECA 30* (1975d), No. 324-25, pp. 605-28. *Reprinted: 1990r; English translation is chapter 9 of this volume.*
"Tesis sobre posibilidad, necesidad y sentido de una teología latinoamericana". *Teología y mundo contemporáneo: homenaje a Karl Rahner*. A. Vargas Machuca, ed. Madrid: Ediciones Cristiandad, (1975e), pp. 325-50.

Freedom Made Flesh: The Mission of Christ and His Church. Maryknoll: Orbis Books, 1976a. *English translation of 1973c.*
"Filosofía ¿para qué?", *ABRA* (1976b), No. 11, pp. 42-48. Reprinted: 1987j.
"Iglesia y realidad histórica", *ECA 31* (1976c), No. 331, pp. 213-20.
"La historización del concepto de propiedad como principio de desideologización", *ECA 31* (1976d), No. 335-36, pp. 425-50. *English translation is chapter 4 of this volume.*
"La transformación de la ley del ISTA", *ECA 31* (1976e), No. 338, pp. 747-58.
"La 'cuestión fundamental' de la pastoral latinoamericana", *Sal Terrae* (1976f), pp. 563-572. *Reprinted 1978a.*
"Introducción crítica a la antropología de Xavier Zubiri", *Realitas* (1976g), No. 2, pp. 49-137.
"En busca de la cuestión fundamental de la teología pastoral", *Sal Terrae* (Aug.-Sep. 1976h).

"Teorías económicas y relación entre cristianismo y socialismo.", *Concilium* (1977a), No 125, pp. 282-90. *English translation: 1977b.*
"The Function of Economic Theories in Theological—Theoretical Discussion on the Relationship between Christianity and Socialism". *Christianity and Socialism*. J. Metz and J. Jossua, eds. New York: The Seabury Press, 1977b, pp. 125-31. *Translation of 1977a.*
"Fe y justicia", *Christus* (August, 1977c), pp. 26-33; (October, 1977d), pp. 19-34. *Reprinted: 1980a.*
"La contemplación en la acción de la justicia.", *Diakonía 1* (1977e), No. 2, pp. 7-14.
"La Iglesia de los pobres, sacramento histórico de la liberación", *ECA 32* (1977f), No. 348-49, pp. 707-22. *Reprinted: 1979f, 1980g, 1985a, 1991d.*
"Notas teológicas sobre religiosidad popular", *Fomento Social* (1977g), pp. 253-60.
"Por qué muere Jesús y por qué lo matan", *Misión Abierta* (1977h), No. 2, pp. 17-26. *Reprinted: 1978k, 1978l.*

"La 'cuestión fundamental' de la pastoral latinoamericana", *Diakonía 2* (1978a), No. 6, pp. 20-28. *Reprint of 1976f.*
"Historización del bien común y de los derechos humanos en una sociedad dividida". *Capitalismo: Violencia y anti-vida*. Elsa Tamez y Seul Trinidad, eds. Vol. 2. San José: EDUCA, 1978b, pp. 81-94. *English translation: 1982c.*

"El trasfondo económico-político de Puebla", *Boletín de Ciencias Económicas y Sociales* (1978c), No. 7, pp. 54-59.
"El pueblo crucificado, ensayo de soteriología histórica". *Cruz y Resurrección*. I. Ellacuría, et al. Mexico: CTR, (1978d), pp. 49-82. *Reprinted: 1980e, 1985a, 1989c, 1991e.*
"Entre Medellín y Puebla", *ECA 33* (1978e), No. 353, pp. 120-29.
"La teología como momento ideológico de la praxis eclesial", *Estudios Eclesiásticos* (1978f), No. 207, pp. 457-76.
"La iglesia que nace del pueblo por el espíritu", *Misión Abierta* (1978g), pp. 150-58. *Reprinted 1979n; 1985a.*
"La predicación ha de poner en contacto vivificante la palabra.", *Sal Terrae* (1978h), No. 778, pp. 167-76.
"Recuperar el Reino de Dios: des-mundanización e historización.", *Sal Terrae* (1978i), No. 780, pp. 335-44. *Reprint of 1979b.*
"Palabras de Dios y comunidad cristiana", *Servir* (1978j), No. 73, pp. 47-60.
"Por qué muere Jesús y por qué lo matan", *Diakonía 2* (1978k), No. 8, pp. 65-75; *Servir* (1978l), No. 75, pp. 383-98. *Reprint of 1977h.*
(**) "Zubiri en El Salvador", *ECA* (1978m), No. 361-362, pp. 949-50.

Iglesia de los pobres y organizaciones populares. O. Romero, A. Rivera y Damas, I. Ellacuría, J. Sobrino, and T.R. Campos. San Salvador: UCA Editores, 1979a.
"Recuperar el Reino de Dios: des-mundanización e historización de la Iglesia", *ibid* (1979b), pp. 79-85. *Reprinted: 1978i.*
"Las bienaventuranzas como carta fundamental de la Iglesia de los pobres", *ibid* (1979c), pp. 105-18. *Reprinted: 1981f; 1985a.*
(*) "La Iglesia y las organizaciones populares en El Salvador", *ibid* (1979d), pp. 147-161.
(*) "Comentarios a la Carta Pastoral", *ibid* (1979e), pp. 163-205.
"La Iglesia de los pobres, sacramento histórico de la liberacíon." *Selecciones de Teología* (1979f), No. 70, pp. 119-34. *Reprint of 1977f.*
(**) "La OEA y los derechos humanos en El Salvador", *ECA 34* (1979g), No. 363-64, pp. 53-54.
(**) "Recuperacíon de la universidad de El Salvador", *ECA 34* (1979h), No. 363-64. pp. 58-59.
(**) "El embajador divino exhorta a la tolerancia", *ECA 34* (1979i), No. 365, pp. 158-59.
"El concepto filosófico de tecnología apropiada", *ECA 34* (1979j), No. 366, pp. 213-23.
"Fundamentación biológica de la ética", *ECA 34* (1979k), No. 368, pp. 419-28.

Note: Several of Ellacuría's articles were written under the pseudonym, Tomás R. Campos; they are indicated by (*). Articles that were signed only with an author's initials are indicated by (**). THE EDITORS

"La seguridad nacional y la constitución salvadoreña", *ECA 34* (1979l), No. 369-
(*) 70, pp. 477-88.
"El papel de las organizaciones populares en la actual situación del país", *ECA*
(*) *34* (1979m), No. 372-73, pp. 923-46.
"La iglesia que nace del pueblo por el espiritú", *Servir* (1979n), pp. 551-64.
Reprint of 1978g.
"Biología e inteligencia", *Realitas* (Madrid) (1979o), No. 3-4, pp. 281-335.

"Fe y justicia". *Fe, justicia y opción por los oprimidos*. I. Ellacuría, A. Zenteno,
A. Arroyo. Bilbao: Editorial Desclée de Brouwer, 1980a. *Reprint of 1977c & d.*
"Universidad y política", *ECA 35* (1980b), No. 383, pp. 807-24. *Reprinted: 1990p.*
"El problema 'ecumenismo' y la promoción de la justicia", *Estudios Eclesiásti-*
cos (1980c), No. 213, pp. 153-55.
"Monseñor Romero, un enviado de Dios para salvar a su pueblo", *Sal Terrae*
(1980d), No. 811, pp. 825-32. *Reprinted: 1981b, 1990k, 1990l.*
"El pueblo crucificado, ensayo de soteriología histórica", *Selecciones de*
Teología (1980e), No. 76, pp. 325-41. *Reprint of 1978d.*
"Zubiri, filósofo teologal", *Vida Nueva* (Madrid) (1980f), No. 1249, p. 45.
"La Iglesia de los pobres, sacramento histórico de liberación", *Encuentro.*
Selecciones para Latinoamérica (1980g), No. 1, pp. 142-48. *Reprint of 1977f.*

"La iglesia en El Salvador: la salvación se realiza en la historia", *Aportes 1*
(1981a), pp. 34-35.
"Monseñor Romero un enviado de Dios para salvar a su pueblo", *Diakonía 5*
(1981b), No. 17, pp. 2-8. *Reprint of 1980d.*
"Discernir el signo de los tiempos", *Diakonía 5* (1981c), No. 17, pp. 57-59.
"El verdadero pueblo de Dios, según Monseñor Romero", *Diakonía 5* (1981d),
No. 18,pp. 27-57; ECA 36 (1981e), No. 392, pp. 529-54. *Reprinted: 1982o,*
1985a; English translation of extract: 1990e.
"Las bienaventuranzas como carta fundacional de la iglesia", *Diakonía 5*
(1981f), No. 19, pp. 56-59. *Reprint of 1979c.*
"El testamento de Sartre", *ECA 36* (1981g), No. 387-88, pp. 43-50.
(**) "Errores y sofismas de la Sra. Kirkpatrick", *ECA 36* (1981h), No. 389, pp. 192-93.
"¿Solución política o solución militar para El Salvador?", *ECA 36* (1981i), No.
390-91, pp. 295-324.
(**) "Un tal Jesús", *ECA 36* (1981j), No. 392, pp. 566-68.
"La declaración conjunta mexicano-francesa sobre El Salvador", *ECA 36*
(1981k), No. 395, pp. 845-66.
"El objeto de la filosofía", *ECA 36* (1981l), No. 396-97, pp. 963-80.
"La nueva política de la Administración Reagan en El Salvador", *ECA 36*
(*) (1981m), No. 390-91, pp. 383-414.
"La nueva obra de Zubiri," *Inteligencia sentiente" Razón y Fé* (1981n), pp. 126-39.
"Los pobres, lugar teológico en América Latina", *Misión Abierta* (1981o), pp.
225-40. *Reprinted: 1982d, 1985a.*

"El Reino de Dios y el paro en el tercer mundo", *Concilium* (1982a), No. 180, pp. 588-96. *English translation: 1982b.*

"The Kingdom of God and Unemployment in the Third World". *Unemployment and the Right to Work.* J. Pohier and D. Mieth, eds. New York: The Seabury Press, 1982b, pp. 91-96. *English translation of 1982a.*

"Human Rights in a Divided Society". *Human Rights in the Americas: The Struggle for Consensus.* A. Hennelly and J. Langan, eds. Washington: Georgetown University Press, 1982c, pp 52-65. *English translation of 1978b.*

"Los pobres, lugar teológico en América Latina", *Diakonía 6* (1982d), pp. 41-57. *Reprint of 1981o.*

"Una universidad para el pueblo", *Diakonía 6* (1982e), No. 23, pp. 81-88. *English translation: 1990f.*

"Conflicto entre trabajo y capital en la presente fase histórica: un punto clave de la 'Laborem Exercens'", *Diakonía 6* (1982f), No. 24, pp. 19-42; *ECA 37* (1982g), No. 409, pp. 1008-24.

(*) "Análisis coyuntural sobre la situación de El Salvador", *ECA 37* (1982h), No. 399-400, pp. 17-58.

"Universidad, derechos humanos y mayorías populares", *ECA 37* (1982i), No. 406, pp. 791-800. *Reprinted: 1990s; English translation is chapter 10, this volume.*

(*) "Interpretación global del proceso histórico, 15 de Octubre 1979—28 Marzo 1982", *ECA 37* (1982j), No. 403-4, pp. 599-622.

(*) "El Pacto de Apaneca: un proyecto político para la transición", *ECA 37* (1982k), No. 407-8, pp. 865-73.

"El auténtico lugar social de la Iglesia", *Misión Abierta* (1982l), pp. 98-106. *Reprinted: 1983a; English translation is chapter 15 of this volume.*

"Las elecciones en El Salvador", *Razón y Fe* (1982m), pp. 285-94.

"Las Iglesias latinoamericanas interpelan a la Iglesia de España", *Sal Terrae* (1982n), No. 826, pp. 219-30.

"El verdadero pueblo de Dios, según Monseñor Romero", *Selecciones de Teología* (1982o), No. 84, pp. 350-59. *Reprint of 1981d.*

"El auténtico lugar social de la Iglesia", *Diakonía 7* (1983a), No. 25, pp. 24-36. *Reprint of 1982l.*

"Luces y sombras de la Iglesia en Centroamérica", *Diakonía 7* (1983b), No. 26, pp. 111-21. *Reprinted: 1984i.*

"Mensaje ético-político de Juan Pablo II al pueblo de Centro América", *Diakonía 7* (1983c), No. 26, pp. 144-66; *ECA 38* (1983d), No. 413-14, pp. 255-72.

"La cooperación iberoamericana y la paz en Centroamérica", *ECA 38* (1983e), No. 417-18, pp. 629-40.

(**) "Zubiri sigue vivo", *ECA 38* (1983f), No. 419, pp. 895-96.

"Aproximación a la obra completa de Xavier Zubiri", *ECA 38* (1983g), No. 421-22, pp. 965-82. *Reprinted: 1984f.*

(*) "La estrategia del FMLN-FDR tras el proceso electoral de marzo de 1982", *ECA 38* (1983h), No. 415-16, pp. 479-92.

"La espiritualidad cristiana", *Diakonía 8* (1984a), No. 30, pp. 123-32.

"Visión de conjunto de las elecciones de 1984", *ECA 39* (1984b), No. 426-27, pp. 301-24.

"Historicidad de la salvación cristiana", *Revista Latinoamericana de Teología 1* (1984c), pp. 5-45. *Reprinted: 1987a, 1991b.*

"Estudio teológico de la 'instrucción sobre algunos aspectos de la teología de la liberación'", *Revista Latinoamericana de Teología 1* (1984d), pp. 145-78.

"The Political Nature of Jesus' Mission". *Faces of Jesus: Latin American Christologies.* J.M. Bonino, ed. Maryknoll: Orbis, (1984e), pp. 79-92. *English translation of 1974b.*

"Aproximación a la obra filosófica de Xavier Zubiri". *Zubiri 1898-1983.* I. Tellechea, ed. Victoria (1984f), pp. 37-64. *Reprint of 1983g.*

(*) "El FDR-FMLN ante las elecciones de 1984", *ECA 39* (1984g), No. 426-27, pp. 277-87.

(*) "Las primeras vicisitudes del diálogo entre el gobierno y el FMLN-FDR", *ECA 39* (1984h), No. 434, pp. 885-903.

"Luces y sombras de la Iglesia en Centroamérica", *Encuentro. Selecciones para Latinoamérica* (1984i), No. 31-32, pp. 317-320. *Reprint of 1983b.*

Conversión de la Iglesia al Reino de Dios: Para anunciarlo y realizarlo en la historia. San Salvador: UCA Editores, 1985a. (Also Santander: Sal Terrae Editorial, 1984.) *Includes reprints of 1977f, 1978d, 1978g, 1979c, 1981e, 1981o.*

"Función liberadora de la filosofía", *ECA 40* (1985b), No. 435, pp. 45-64.

"La UCA ante el doctorado concedido a Mons. Romero", *ECA 40* (1985c), No. 437, pp. 167-76. *English translation: 1990a.*

(*) "El diálogo del gobierno con el FMLN-FDR: un proceso paralizado", *ECA 40* (1985d), No. 439-40, pp. 489-500.

"Perspectiva política de la situación centroamericana", *ECA 40* (1985e), No. 443-44, pp. 625-37.

(*) "Lectura política de los secuestros", *ECA 40* (1958f), No. 443-44, pp. 684-700.

"FMLN, el límite insuperable", *ECA 40* (1985g), No. 446, pp. 890-97.

"La teología de la liberación es más necesaria que nunca", *Diakonía 10* (1986a), No. 38, pp. 186-89.

"Replanteamiento de soluciones para el problema de El Salvador", *ECA 41* (1986b), No. 447-48, pp. 54-75.

"Análisis ético-político del proceso de diálogo en El Salvador", *ECA 41* (1986c), No. 454-55, pp. 727-54.

"Factores endógenos del conflicto centroamericano: crisis económica y desequilibrios sociales", *ECA 41* (1986d), No. 456, pp. 856-78. *Reprinted: 1987k.*

"Voluntad de fundamentalidad y voluntad de verdad", *Revista Latinoamericana de Teología 3* (1986e), pp. 113-32.

"Beitrag Zum Dialog mit dem Marxisms.", *Orienterung* 15 Junio 1986, pp. 127-31, from *Theologie der Befreiung und Marxisms.* P. Rotländer, ed. Münster: Westf. 1986f.

"Pedro Arrupe, renovador de la vida religiosa". *Pedro Arrupe: Así lo vieron.* Alcala M., *et al.* Santander: Ed. Alem (1986g), pp. 141-71. *Reprinted: 1990o.*

"Historicidad de la salvación cristiana", *Selecciones de Teología* (1987a), No. 101, pp. 59-80. *Reprint of 1984c.*

"Caminos de solución para la actual crisis del país", *ECA 42* (1987b), No. 462, pp. 301-11; *Mensaje* (1987c), pp. 3-19.

"Nueva propuesta de diálogo del FMLN-FDR: los 18 puntos", *ECA 42* (1987d), No. 465, pp. 435-47.

"Análisis ético-político de Esquípulas II", *ECA 42* (1987e), No. 466-67, pp. 599-610.

"Propuestas de solución en el marco de Esquípulas II", *ECA 42* (1987f), No. 469-70, pp. 865-89.

"Aporte de la teología de la liberación a las religiones Abráhamicas en la superación del individualismo y del positivismo", *Revista Latinoamericana de Teología 4* (1987g), pp. 3-27.

"La teología de la liberación frente al cambio socio-histórico de América Latina", *Revista Latinoamericana de Teología 4* (1987h), pp. 241-63. *Reprinted: 1988f, 1989g; English translation is chapter 1 of this volume.*

"Lecciones del Irán-Contras para El Salvador", *ECA 42* (1987i), No. 465, pp. 289-99.

"Filosofía ¿para qué?". Pamphlet, UCA (1987j). *Reprint of 1976b.*

"Factores endógenos del conflicto centroamericano: crisis económica y desequilibrios sociales", *CINAS Cuadernos de Trabajo* (1987k), No. 9, 9-38. *Reprint of 1986d.*

"La superación del reduccionismo idealista en Zubiri". *In Congresso de filosofía, ética y religión*, vol. 4. San Sebastián, (1987l). *Reprinted: 1988c.*

"Trabajo no violento por la paz y violencia liberadora", *Concilium* (1988a), No. 215, pp. 85-94. *English translation: 1988b.*

"Violence and Non-violence in the Struggle for Peace and Liberation". *A Council for Peace.* H. Küng and J. Moltmann, eds. Edinburgh: T. & T. Clark (1988b). *English translation of 1988a.*

"La superación del reduccionismo idealista en Zubiri", *ECA 43* (1988c), No. 477, pp. 633-50. *Reprint of 1987l.*

"Los partidos políticos y la finalización de la guerra", *ECA 43* (1988d), No. 481-82, pp. 1037-51.

"Nuevo orden mundial propuesto por Gorbachev", *ECA 43* (1988e), No. 481-82, pp. 1099-101.

(**) "La teología de la liberacion frente al cambio socio-histórico de América Latina", *Diakonía 12* (1988f), pp. 129-66. Reprint of 1987h.

"El desafío de las mayorías pobres", *ECA 44* (1989a), No. 493-94, pp. 1075-80. *English translation is chapter 8 of this volume.*

"Utopía y profetismo desde América Latina: un ensayo concreto de soteriología historíca.", *Revista Latinoamericana de Teología 6* (1989b), pp. 141-84. *Reprinted: 1990t, 1991c; English translation is chapter 2 of this volume.*

"El pueblo crucificado, ensayo de soteriología histórica", *Revista Latinoamericana de Teología 6* (1989c), pp. 305-33. *Reprint of 1978d.*

"El diálogo en los primeros cien días de Cristiani", *ECA 44* (1989d), No. 490-91, pp. 683-94.

"Una nueva fase en el proceso salvadoreño", *ECA 44* (1989e), No. 485, pp. 167-97.

Implicaciones sociales y políticas de la teologia de la liberación. Ignacio Ellacuría, *et al.* Madrid: Escuela de Estudios Hispanoamericanos y Instituto de Filosofia, Consejo Superior de Investigaciones Científicas, 1989f.

"La teología de la liberación frente al cambio socio-histórico de América Latina", *ibid.* (1989g), pp. 69-90. *Reprint of 1987h.*

"En torno al concepto y la idea de liberación", *ibid.* (1989h), pp. 91-110.

"The UCA Regarding the Doctorate Given to Monseñor Romero", *Envío 9* (Jan. 1990a), pp. 15-18. *English translation of extract from 1985c.*

Filosofía de la realidad histórica. San Salvador: UCA Editores, 1990b.

"Teología de la liberación y marxismo", *Revista Latinoamericana de Teología 7* (1990c), pp. 109-36.

Companions of Jesus: The Jesuit Martyrs of El Salvador. Jon Sobrino, Ignacio Ellacuría, *et al.* Maryknoll: Orbis Books (1990d).

"Persecution for the Sake of the Reign of God", *ibid.* (1990e), pp. 64-75. *Translation of extract from 1981e.*

"The Task of a Christian University", *ibid.* (1990f), pp. 147-51. *Translation of 1982e.*

"The Writings of Ellacuría, Martín-Baró, and Segundo Montes." *The Jesuit Assassinations.* Instituto de Estudios Centroamericanos and El Rescate. Kansas City: Sheed and Ward, 1990g, pp. 1-26. *Very brief extracts from various writings.*

"Quinto centenario de América Latina ¿descubrimiento o encubrimento?" *Revista Latinoamericana de Teología 7* (1990h), pp. 271-82; *Diakonía 14* (1990i), pp. 15-32; *Christus 55* (1990j), No. 638, pp. 7-13.

"Monseñor Romero, un enviado de Dios para salvar a su pueblo", *ECA 45* (1990k), No. 497, pp. 141-46; *Revista Latinoamericana de Teología 7* (1990l), pp. 5-10. *Reprint of 1980d.*

"Historización de los derechos humanos desde los pueblos oprimidos y las mayorías populares", *ECA 45* (1990m), No. 502, pp. 589-96.

"La Iglesia y la UCA en el golpe del 15 de Octubre de 1979", *Presencia* (El Salvador), 2 (1990n), No. 7-8, pp. 132-38.

"Pedro Arrupe, renovador de la vida religiosa," *Revista Latinoamericana de Teología 7* (1990o), pp. 5-24. *Reprint of 1986g.*

"Universidad y política." *Modernizacíon educativa y universidad en América Latina.* H. Cerutto Guldberg, ed. Mexico: Magna Terra Editores, 1990p, pp. 35-71. *Reprint of 1980b.*

"La ley orgánica de la universidad de El Salvador". *Universidad y cambio social: los jesuitas en El Salvador.* H. Cerutti Guldberg, ed. Mexico: Magna Terra Editores, 1990q, pp. 45-62. *Reprint of 1972d.*

"Diez años después ¿es posible una universidad distinta?" *ibid.* (1990r), pp. 131-66. *Reprint of 1975d.*

"Universidad, derechos humanos y mayorías populares," *ibid.* (1990s), pp. 167-82. *Reprint of 1982i.*

"Utopía y profetismo", *Christus* 55 (1990t), No. 632, pp. 49-55. *Reprint of selections from 1989b.*

Mysterium Liberationis: conceptos fundamentales de la teología de la liberación. I. Ellacuría and J. Sobrino, eds. Two volumes. San Salvador: UCA Editores, 1991a. (Also Madrid: Editorial Trotta, 1990).

"Historicidad de la salvación cristiana", *ibid.*, vol. 1 (1991b), pp. 323-72. *Reprint of 1984c.*

"Utopía y profetismo", *ibid.*, vol. 1 (1991c), pp. 393-442. *Reprint of 1989b.*

"La Iglesia de los pobres, sacramento histórico de la liberación", *ibid.*, vol. 2 (1991d), pp. 127-54. *Reprint of 1977f.*

"El pueblo crucificado", *ibid.*, vol. 2 (1991e), pp. 189-216. *Reprint of 1978d.*

Veinte años de historia en El Salvador, 1969-1989. San Salvador: UCA Editores (forthcoming). *This volume reprints many of Ellacuría's writings on social and political anaylsis—including numerous unsigned editorals that he wrote in ECA, and articles with unidentified authorship in El Salvador: entre el terror y la esperanza (R.R. Campos, editor), San Salvador: UCA Editores, 1982.*

The Publications of Ignacio Martín-Baró

"La muerte como problema filosófico", *ECA 21* (1966a), No. 212, pp. 7-12.
"Miguel A. Sholojov, Premio Nobel de Literatura", *ECA 21* (1966b), No. 212, pp. 15-16.
"Un extraño remedio para la homosexualidad: su legalización", *ECA 21* (1966c), No. 213, p. 54.
"Pablo Antonio Cuadra, tierra y luz nicaragüense", *ECA 21* (1966d), No. 215, pp. 93-95.
"La forja de rebeldes", *ECA 21* (1966e), No. 221, pp. 287-88.

"La figura del año", *ECA 22* (1967a), No. 224, pp. 369-70.
"Rubén Darío entrevisto", *ECA 22* (1967b), No. 226, pp. 444-45.
"¿Quién le teme a James Bond?", *ECA 22* (1967c), No. 227, pp. 511-12.

"El pulso del tiempo; guerrilleros y hippies, blow up", *ECA 23* (1968a), No. 234, pp. 25-26.
"El complejo de macho, o el 'machismo'", *ECA 23* (1968b), No. 235, pp. 38-42. *Reprinted: 1970b.*
"Propaganda: deseducación social", *ECA 23* (1968c), No. 243, pp. 367-73.

"Psicología de la caricia", *ECA 25* (1970a), No. 264, pp. 496-98.
"El complejo de macho, o el 'machismo'", *ECA 25* (1970b), No. 267, pp. 677-83. *Reprint of 1968b.*

"Problemas actuales en psicopedagogía escolar", *ECA 26* (1971), No. 273, pp. 401-13.

"Una nueva pedagogía para una universidad nueva", *ECA 27* (1972a), No. 281-82, pp. 129-45.
"Del alcohol a la marihuana", *ECA 27* (1972b), No. 283, pp. 225-42.
"Peluqueros institucionales", *ECA 27* (1972c), No. 283, pp. 297-301.
"Munich 72; el ocaso de una mitología", *ECA 27* (1972d), No. 288-89, pp. 697-701.
"Presupuestos psicosociales de una caracterología para nuestros países", *ECA 27* (1972e), No. 290, pp. 763-86.
"Del futuro, la técnica y el planeta de los simios", *ECA 27* (1972f), No. 290, pp. 795-99.
"Hacia una docencia liberadora", *Universidades* (Mexico) (1972g), No. 50, pp. 9-26.
Psicodiagnóstico de América Latina. San Salvador: UCA Editores, 1972h.
"La desatención social del poder opresor", *ibid* (1972i), pp. 121-40. *Reprinted: 1976b.*

"Algunas repercusiones psico-sociales de la densidad demográfica en El Salvador", *ECA 28* (1973a), No. 293-94, pp. 123-32. *Reprinted: 1977c.*
"Antipsiquiatría y antipsicoanálisis", *ECA 28* (1973b), No. 293-94, pp. 203-6.
"Cartas al Presidente: reflexiones psicosociales sobre un caso del personalismo político en El Salvador", *ECA 28* (1973c), No. 296, pp. 345-57.
"Psicología del campesino salvadoreño", *ECA 28* (1973d), No. 297-98, pp. 476-95. *Reprinted: 1977b.*

"¿Quién es pueblo?: reflexiones para una definición del concepto de pueblo", *ECA 29* (1974a), No. 303-04, pp. 11-20.
"Elementos de conscientización socio-política en los currícula de las universidades", *ECA 29* (1974b), No. 313-14, pp. 765-83. *Reprinted: 1990x; English translation is chapter 11 of this volume.*
"De la evasión a la invasión", *ABRA (El Salvador)* (1974c), No. 0, pp. 19-24.

"Cinco tesis sobre la paternidad aplicadas a El Salvador", *ECA 30* (1975a), No. 319-20, pp. 265-82.
"El estudiantado y la estructura universitaria", *ECA 30* (1975b), No. 324-25, pp. 638-51. *Reprinted: 1990y.*
"El valor psicológico de la represión política mediante la violencia", *ECA 30* (1975c), No. 326, pp. 742-52. *Reprinted: 1976c.*
Elementos de conscientizacíon en los curricula universitarios. I. Martín-Baró, et al. Guatamala: FUPAC, 1975d.

Problemas de psicológia social en América Latina. Edited with introductory commentaries by I. Martín-Baró. San Salvador: UCA Editores, 1976a.
"La desatención social del poder opresor," *ibid.* (1976b), pp. 98-109. *Reprint of 1972i.*
"El valor psicológico de la represión política mediante la violencia," *ibid.* (1976c), pp. 310-27. *Reprint of 1975c.*

Psicología, ciencia y conciencia. Edited with introductory commentaries by I. Martín-Baró. San Salvador: UCA Editores, 1977a.
"Psicología del campesino salvadoreño," *ibid.* (1977b), pp. 479-506. *Reprint of 1973d.*
"Algunas repercusiones psico-sociales de la densidad demográfica en El Salvador," *ibid.* (1977c), pp. 429-42. *Reprint of 1973a.*
"Del cociente intelectual al cociente radical", *ECA 32* (1977d), No. 345, pp. 485-94.
Social Attitudes and Group Conflict in El Salvador. Master's Thesis, University of Chicago, 1977e.

"'Vivienda mínima': obra máxima", *ECA 33* (1978a), No. 359, pp. 732-33.
"Ley y orden en la vida del mesón". (Co-author, M. Herrera). *ECA 33* (1978b), No. 360, pp. 803-28.

(**) "Cien años de psicología", *ECA 34* (1979a), No. 368, pp. 432-33.
Household Density and Crowding in Lower Class Salvadorans. Ph.D. dissertation, University of Chicago, 1979b. *Abstract: 1980h.*
Haciendo la universidad. Guatemala: FUPAC, 1979c.

Note: Several of Martín-Baró's published articles were signed only with initials. They are indicated by (**). THE EDITORS

La voz de los sin voz: la palabra viva del Monseñor Oscar Arnulfo Romero. R. Cardenal, I. Martín-Baró, and J. Sobrino, eds. San Salvador: UCA Editores, 1980a.

"Monseñor: una voz para un pueblo pisoteado", *ibid.* (1980b). pp. 13-34. *Reprint 1990z; English translation: 1985i.*

"Fantasmas sobre un gobierno popular en El Salvador", *ECA 35* (1980c), No. 377-78, pp. 277-90.

"Ocupación juvenil: reflexiones psicosociales de un rehén por 24 horas", *ECA 35* (1980d), No. 379, pp. 463-74.

(**) "Desde Cuba y sin amor", *ECA 35* (1980e), No. 379, pp. 485-86.

"La imagen de la mujer en El Salvador", *ECA 35* (1980f), No. 380, pp. 557-68.

(**) "A la muerte de Piaget", *ECA 35* (1980g), No. 383, pp. 869-71.

"Household density and crowding in lower-class Salvadorans." *Dissertation Abstracts International 40* (1980h), No. 10-B, pp. 5077-78. *Abstract of 1979b.*

"La guerra civil en El Salvador", *ECA 36* (1981a), No. 387-88, pp. 17-32.

"El liderazgo del Monseñor Romero: un análisis psicosocial", *ECA 36* (1981b), No . 389, pp. 151-72.

"Actitudes en El Salvador ante una solución política a la guerra civil", *ECA 36* (1981c), No. 390-91, pp. 325-48.

"Aspiraciones del pequeño burgués salvadoreño", *ECA 36* (1981d), No. 394, pp. 773-88.

"Una juventud sin liderazgo político", *Boletín de Psicología 1* (1982a), No. 5, pp. 8-10.

"El llamado de la extrema derecha", *ECA 37* (1982b), No. 403-4, pp. 453-66. *English translation is chapter 16 of this volume.*

"Un psicólogo social ante la guerra civil en El Salvador", *Revista de la Asociación Latinoamericana de Psicología Social 2* (1982c), pp. 91-111.

"¿Escuela o prisión? La organización social de un centro de orientación en El Salvador." (Co-authors, V. Iraheta and A. Lemus de Vides). *ECA 37* (1982d), No. 401, pp. 179-92.

Acción e ideología: psicología social desde Centroamérica. San Salvador: UCA Editores, 1983a.

"Los rasgos femeninos según la cultura dominante en El Salvador", *Boletín de psicología 2* (1983b), No. 8, pp. 3-7.

"Polarización social en El Salvador", *ECA 38* (1983c), No. 412, pp. 129-42.

"Los sectores medios ante el plan Reagan: una perspectiva sombría", *ECA 38* (1983d), No. 415-16, pp. 517-22.

(**) "Estacazo imperial: abuso y mentira en Grenada", *ECA 38* (1983e), No. 421-22, pp. 1018-21.

"La necesidad de votar: actitudes del pueblo salvadoreño ante el proceso electoral de 1984". Co-author: V. A. Orellana. *ECA 39* (1984a), No. 426-27, pp. 253-64.

(**) "El ultimo discurso de Alvaro Magaña", *ECA 39* (1984b), No. 428, pp. 425-27.

"Guerra y salud mental", *ECA 39* (1984c), No. 429-30, pp. 503-14. *Reprinted: 1990d, 1990n.*

(**) "El terrorismo del estado norteamericano", *ECA 39* (1984d), No. 433, pp. 813-16.

"La sumisión a la autoridad como valor social en El Salvador", *Boletín de Psicología 3* (1984e), No. 11, pp. 19-26.

"La desideologización como aporte de la psicología social al desarrollo de la democracia en Latinoamérica", *Boletín de la AVESPO* (Asociation Venezolana de Psicología Social) 8 (1985a), No. 3, pp. 3-9.

"Valores del universitario salvadoreño de primer ingreso", *Boletín de Psicología 4* (1985b), No. 15, pp. 5-12.

"De la conciencia religiosa a la conciencia política", *Boletín de Psicología 4* (1985c), No. 16, pp. 72-82.

"El papel del psicólogo en el contexto centroamericano", *Boletín de Psicología 4* (1985d), No. 17, pp. 99-112. *Reprinted: 1990c.*

"La encuesta de opinión pública como instrumento desideologizador", *Cuadernos de Psicología* (Universidad del Valle, Cali) 7 (1985e), No. 1-2, pp. 93-108. *Reprinted: 1990a.*

"El trabajador social salvadoreño: situación y actitudes", *ECA 40* (1985f), No. 438, pp. 229-40.

"La oferta política de Duarte", *ECA 40* (1985g), No.439-40, pp. 345-56.

"La hacinamiento residencial: ideologización y verdad de un problema real," *Revista de Psicología Social* (Mexico), (1985h), pp. 31-50. *Reprinted: 1990b.*

"Oscar Romero: Voice of the Downtrodden". *Voice of the Voiceless.* O. Romero. Maryknoll: Orbis (1985i). *English translation of 1980b.*

"La ideología familiar en El Salvador", *ECA 41* (1986a), No. 450, pp. 291-304.

"El pueblo salvadoreño ante el diálogo", *ECA 41* (1986b), No. 454-55, pp. 755-68.

"Socialización política: dos temas críticos", *Boletín de Psicología 5* (1986c), No. 19, pp. 5-20.

"Hacia una psicología de la liberación", *Boletín de Psicología 5* (1986d), No. 22, pp. 219-31. *English translation is chapter 18 of this volume.*

"La ideología de los sectores medios salvadoreños", *Revista Mexicana de Psicología 3* (1986e), No. 1, pp. 59-65.

Así piensan los salvadoreños urbanos (1986-1987). San Salvador: UCA Editores, 1987a.

"Del opio religioso a la fe liberadora". *Psicología Política Latinoamericana.* Martiza Montero, ed. Caracas: Panapo (1987b), pp. 229-68. *English translation is chapter 20 of this volume.*

"El latino indolente: carácter ideológico del fatalismo latinoamericano", *ibid.* (1987c), pp. 135-62.

"Votar en El Salvador: psicología social del desorden político", *Boletín de la AVEPSO 10* (1987d), No. 2, pp. 28-36.

"¿Es machista el salvadoreño?" *Boletín de Psicología* 6 (1987e), No. 24, pp. 101-22.

"El reto popular a la psicología social en América Latina", *Boletín de Psicología* 6 (1987f), No. 26, pp. 251-70.

"Psicología social desde Centroamérica: retos y perspectivas". Interview. *Revista Costarricense de Psicología* 5 (1987g), pp. 71-76.

"From Dirty War to Psychological War: The Case of El Salvador." *Flight, Exile, and Return: Mental Health and the Refugee.* A. Aron, ed. San Francisco: CHRICA, (1988a) pp. 2-22. *Reprinted as chapter 17 of this volume; Spanish translation: 1990f, 1990p.*

"La violencia política y la guerra como causas del trauma psicosocial en El Salvador", *Revista de Psicología de El Salvador* (formerly *Boletín de Psicología*) 7 (1988b) No. 28, pp. 123-41. *Reprinted: 1990e, 1990o. English translation: 1989d, 1989e, 1990j, 1990k.*

"La mujer salvadoreña y los medios de comunicación masiva", *Revista de Psicología de El Salvador* 7 (1988c) No. 29, pp. 253-66.

"La violencia en Centroamérica: una visión psicosocial", *Revista Costarricense de Psicología* 12 (1988d), No. 13, pp. 21-34. *Reprinted: 1990g; English translation is chapter 19 of this volume.*

"El Salvador 1987", *ECA* 43 (1988e), No. 471-72, pp. 21-45.

"Opinión preelectoral y sentido del voto en El Salvador", *ECA* 43 (1988f), No. 473-74, pp. 213-23.

"Los grupos con historia: un modelo psicosocial", *Boletín de AVESPO* 11 (1988g), No. 1, pp. 3-18.

La opinión pública salvadoreña, (1987-1988). San Salvador: UCA Editores, 1989a.

"La opinión pública ante los primeros cien días del gobierno de Cristiani", *ECA* 44 (1989b), No. 490-91, pp. 715-26.

"Psicología política del trabajo en América Latina", *Revista de Psicología de El Salvador 8* (1989c), No. 31, pp. 5-25.

"Political Violence and War as Causes of Psychosocial Trauma in El Salvador", *International Journal of Mental Health* 18 (1989d), No. 1, pp. 3-20; *Journal of La Raza Studies* (San Francisco State University) 2 (1989e), No. 1, pp. 5-13. *English translation of 1988b; Reprinted: 1990j; 1990k.*

"Los medios de comunicación masiva y la opinión pública en El Salvador de 1979 a 1989", *ECA* 44 (1989f), No. 493-94, pp. 1081-93.

Review of F.J. Hinkelammert, *La fe de Abrahm y el edipo occidental. Revista Latinoamericana de Teología* 6 (1989g), No. 17, 241-43.

Sistema, groupo y poder: Psicología social desde Centroamérica II. San Salvador: UCA Editores (1989h).

"Asking Questions in El Salvador: As Dangerous as Expressing Them". Interview. *Links* 6 (1989i), No. 2, p. 10.

"Encuestas pre-electorales en El Salvador", *ECA 44* (1989j), No. 485, pp. 229-32.

Introduction to *Todo es según el dolor con que se mire*. E. Lira, ed. Santiago: ILAS (1989k). *English translation: 1990i.*

"La institutionalización de la guerra", *Revista de Psicología de El Salvador 8* (1989l), No. 33, pp. 223-45.

"La encuesta de opinión pública como instrumento de desideologización", *Revista de Psicología de El Salvador 9* (1990a), No. 35, pp. 9-22. *Reprint of 1985e.*

"El hacinamiento residencial: ideologización y verdad de un problema real", *Revista de Psicología de El Salvador 9* (1990b), No. 35, pp. 23-51. *Reprint of 1985h.*

"El papel del psicólogo en el contexto centroamericano", *Revista de Psicología de El Salvador 9* (1990c), No. 35, pp. 53-70. *Reprint of 1985d.*

"Guerra y salud mental", *Revista de Psicología de El Salvador 9* (1990d), No. 35, pp. 71-88. *Reprint of 1984c.*

"La violencia política y la guerra como causas del trauma psicosocial en El Salvador", *Revista de Psicología de El Salvador 9* (1990e), No. 35, pp. 89-107. *Reprint of 1988b.*

"De la guerra sucia a la guerra psicológica: el caso del El Salvador", *Revista de Psicología de El Salvador 9* (1990f), No. 35, pp. 109-22. *Spanish translation of 1988a. Reprinted: 1990p.*

"La violencia en Centroamérica: una visión psicosocial", *Revista de Psicología de El Salvador 9* (1990g), No. 35, pp. 123-46. *Reprint of 1988d.*

"¿Trabajador alegre o trabajador explotado? La identidad nacional del salvadoreño", *Revista de Psicología de El Salvador 9* (1990h), No. 35, pp. 147-72.

"Reparations: Attention Must be Paid", (1990i) *Commonweal,* March 23, 1990. *English translation of 1989k; Reprinted as chapter 5 of this volume.*

"Political Violence and War as Causes of Psychosocial Trauma in El Salvador", *Manchester Guardian Weekly* (1990j), Jan. 14, 1990; in J. Sobrino, *et al., Companions of Jesus.* Maryknoll: Orbis (1990k), pp. 79-97. *Reprint of 1989d.*

Psicología Social de la Guerra: trauma y terapia. I. Martín-Baró, ed. San Salvador: UCA Editores, 1990l.

"Introducción", *ibid.* (1990m), pp. 13-19.

"Guerra y salud mental", *ibid.* (1990n), pp. 23-40. *Reprint of 1984c.*

"La violencia política y la guerra como causas del trauma psicosocial en El Salvador", *ibid.* (1990o), pp. 65-84. *Reprint of 1988b.*

"De la guerra sucia a la guerra psicológica: el caso de El Salvador", *ibid.* (1990p), pp. 159-173. *Reprint of 1990f.*

"Guerra y trauma psicosocial del niño salvadoreño", *ibid.* (1990q), pp. 233-49.

"The Writings of Ellacuría, Martín-Baró, and Segundo Montes". *The Jesuit Assassinations.* Instituto de Estudios Centroamericanos and El Rescate. Kansas City: Sheed and Ward, 1990r, pp. 1-26. *Very brief extracts from various writings.*

"Religion as an Instrument of Psychological Warfare", *Journal of Social Issues 46* (1990s), pp. 93-107.

"Interview with Fr. Ignacio Martín-Baró." Interview by William Cadbury. *Northwest Review* 28 (1990t), pp. 9-13.

"La familia, puerta y cárcel para la mujer salvadoreña", *Revista de Psicología de El Salvador 9* (1990u), No. 37, pp. 265-77.

"Una entrevista con Ignacio Martín-Baró." Interview by Erick Cabrera. *Revista de Psicología de El Salvador 9* (1990v), No. 37, pp. 299-308.

"A Psychologist in El Salvador: An Interview with Ignacio Martín-Baró Two Years Before His Murder." Interview by Alison Harris. *The Psychologist 3* (1990w), pp. 264-66.

"Elementos de conscientización socio-política en los curricula de las universidades". *Universidad y cambio social: los jesuitas en El Salvador*. H. Cerutti Guldberg, ed. Mexico: Magna Terra Editores (1990x), pp. 83-108. *Reprint of 1974b.*

"El estudiantado y la estructura universitaria", *ibid.* (1990y), pp. 109-30. *Reprint of 1975b.*

"Monseñor: una voz para un pueblo pisoteado", *Christus 55* (1990z), No. 632, pp. 28-38. *Reprint of 1980b.*

The Publications of Segundo Montes

"¿Retrocede la ciencia?", *ECA 18* (1963), No. 183, pp. 207-9.

"Situación moral de la juventud centroamericana y sus causas", *ECA 24* (1969a), No. 245, pp. 33-41.
"Hacia un sana pedagogía", *ECA 24* (1969b), No. 247, pp. 113-21.
"Los medios de comunicación social y su repercusión en la pedagogía", *ECA 24* (1969c), No. 251, pp. 261-64.

Sexo y juventud: encuesta a jóvenes de El Salvador y Panamá. San Salvador: UCA Editores, 1970a.
"Primer curso latinoamericano de educación sexual y planificación familiar", *ECA 25* (1970b), No. 256-57, pp. 42-45.
"¿Hay alguna solución al problema demográfico en El Salvador?", *ECA 25* (1970c), No. 258, pp. 131-35.
"El matrimonio a la luz de la fe", *ECA 25* (1970d), No. 263, pp. 409-14.
"Encuesta sobre iniciación sexual", *ECA 25* (1970e), No. 265-66, pp. 565-72.

Tercer Mundo: Education. San Salvador: UCA Editores, 1971a.
"La estética en la publicidad", *ECA 26* (1971b), No. 270, pp. 205-6.
"Visión sociológica de la realidad educativa salvadoreña", *ECA 26* (1971c), No. 271, pp. 250-63.
"Situación actual del campesinado salvadoreño", *ECA 26* (1971d), No. 273, pp. 421-34.

"Velasco Ibarra", *ECA 27* (1972a), No. 283, pp. 281-84.
"El viaje de Nixon a China", *ECA 27* (1972b), No. 283, pp. 291-95.
"El factor demográfico en la problemática salvadoreña", *ECA 27* (1972c), No. 285, pp. 457-64.

"Situación del agro salvadoreño y sus implicaciones sociales", *ECA 28* (1973a), No. 297-98, pp. 458-75.
"El acuerdo de París", *ECA 28* (1973b), No. 295, pp. 289-90.

"Familia y paternidad responsable", *ECA 29* (1974a), No. 303-4. pp. 21-30. *Reprinted: 1975a.*
"Políticas de planificación de la tecnología familiar en El Salvador", *ECA 29* (1974b), No. 310-11, pp. 494-542.

"Familia y paternidad responsable", *ABRA (El Salvador)* (1975a), No. 3, pp. 15-22. *Reprint of 1974a.*
"En busca de una imagen para América Latina" *ABRA* (1975b), No. 4, pp. 15-20.
"La liberación femenina", *ECA 30* (1975c), No. 316-17, pp. 115-28.

"La mujer salvadoreña en el Año Internacional de la Mujer", *ECA 31* (1976), No. 327-28, pp. 39-52.

"Análisis sociológico de nuestra cultura", *ABRA* (1977), No. 19, pp. 29-33.

"La penetración de la tecnología en El Salvador a través de la educación", *Boletín de Ciencias Económicas y Sociales 1* (1978a), pp. 58-59. *Reprinted: 1979c.*

"El financiamiento de la educación en El Salvador", *ECA 33* (1978b), No. 358, pp. 596-608.

Estudio sobre estratificación social en El Salvador. San Salvador: UCA Editores, 1979a.

El Compadrazgo: una estructura de poder en El Salvador. San Salvador: UCA Editores, 1979b. *Parts are reprinted in 1982b; 2nd edition, 1987b.*

"La penetración de la tecnología en El Salvador a través de la educación", *ECA 34* (1979c), No. 366, pp. 250-63. *Reprint of 1978a.*

(**) "Las universidades católicas en América Latina", *ECA 34* (1979d), No. 371, pp. 815-16.

"¿Es posible la democracia en un país subdesarrollado?" *ECA 34* (1979e), No. 372-73, pp. 971-84. *Reprinted: 1980a, 1980b; English translation is chapter 6 of this volume.*

"¿Es posible la democracia en un país subdesarrollado?" In *Democracia y lucha de clases en América Latina.* Centro de Informacion y Documentación de Bolivia, 1980a, pp. 7-36; *Ciencias Sociales* (1980b), No. 7, pp. 111-31. *Reprint of 1979e.*

El agro salvadoreño (1973-1980). San Salvador: UCA Editores, 1980c. *A section,* "La tenencia de la tierra en El Salvador," *is reprinted in 1982b.*

"Reflexiones sobre 'las clases medias'", *Boletín de Ciencias Económicas y Sociales 3* (1980d), p. 171.

"La supuesta neutralidad de la ciencia", *Boletín de Ciencias Económicas y Sociales 3* (1980e), pp. 203-5.

"La estratificación social ¿'funcional' para qué tipo de sociedad?", *ECA 35* (1980f), No. 375-76, pp. 55-72.

(**) "Los juegos olímpicos de Moscú", *ECA 35* (1980g), No. 379, pp. 487-88.

(**) "El 14 de mayo em el Río Sumpul", *ECA 35* (1980h), No. 380, pp. 597-98.

"2 de noviembre: unidad y dispersión", *Boletín de Ciencias Económicas y Sociales 4* (1981a), p. 279.

(**) "Fallido golpe de estado en España", *ECA 36* (1981b), No. 389, pp. 194-97.

"Los sectores medios en El Salvador: historia y perspectivas", *ECA 36* (1981c), No. 394, pp. 753-72.

"En torno a la estructura social salvadoreña", *ECA 36* (1981d), No. 398, pp. 1123-30. *Reprinted in 1982b.*

Sociología general. San Salvador: UCA Editores (1982a).

Sociología latinoamericana. S. Montes, *et al.*, eds. San Salvador: UCA Editores, 1982b. *Includes reprinted parts of 1979b, 1980c, 1981d.*

"A propósito de las revoluciones", *Boletín de Ciencias Económicas y Sociales 5* (1982c), pp. 374-75.

Note: *Several of the articles published by Montes were signed only with initials. They are indicated by* **(**)**. THE EDITORS

"Max Weber no se sentiría satisfecho", *Boletín de Ciencias Económicas y Sociales 5* (1982d), pp. 400-402.

"Las elecciones y el poder en El Salvador", *ECA 37* (1982e), No. 399-400, pp. 59-66.

"¿Cuál es el modo de producción dominante en El Salvador?", *Boletín de Ciencias Económicas y Sociales 6* (1983a), pp. 30-37. *English translation is chapter 12 of this volume.*

"Crítica a una crítica: sobre el modo de producción dominate en El Salvador", *Boletín de Ciencias Económicas y Sociales 6,* (1983b), pp. 231-35.

(**)   "Opiniones sobre la visita del Papa", *ECA 38* (1983c)No. 413-14, pp 330-31.

"El pueblo no organizado ante la situación del país", *ECA 38* (1983d), No. 415-16, pp. 523-28.

El Salvador: las fuerzas sociales en la presente coyuntura. San Salvador: UCA Editores (1984a).

"Una neutralidad activa de Costa Rica para la paz en Centroamérica", *ECA 39* (1984b), No. 423-24, pp. 31-42.

"Condicionamientos sociopolíticos del processo electoral", *ECA 39* (1984c), No. 426-27, pp. 187-96.

"Hambre a causa del armamentismo", *ECA 39* (1984d), No. 429-30, pp. 491-502.

"La situación de los salvadoreños desplazados y refugiados", *ECA 39* (1984e), No. 434, pp. 904-20.

"La UPD (Unidad Popular Democrática) y el pacto social", *ECA 39* (1984f), No.
(**)   434, pp. 924-27.

"El papel de la religión en la planificación familiar", *Boletín de Ciencias Económicas y Sociales 8* (1985a), pp. 30-42.

"Las responsabilidades de los estudiantes universitarios dentro de la sociedad", *Boletín de Ciencias Económicas y Sociales 8* (1985b), pp. 302-8.

"Las elecciones del 31 de marzo", *ECA 40* (1985c), No. 438, pp. 215-28.

"Las fuerzas sociales ante el proyecto democristiano", *ECA 40* (1985d), No. 439-40, pp. 380-88.

"Los desplazados y refugiados salvadoreños", *Relaciones Internacionales* (1985e), No. 13, pp. 9-21. *Reprinted: 1986j.*

"Las fuerzas sociales y el diálogo," *Boletín de Ciencias Economicas y Sociales 8* (1985f), pp. 404-16.

El Salvador 1985: Desplazados y refugiados. San Salvador: IDHUCA (1985g).

El Salvador 1986: En busca de soluciones para los desplazados. San Salvador: IDHUCA (1986a).

El Agro Salvadoreño (1973-1980). San Salvador: UCA Editores (1986b).

"El Salvador: la tierra, epicentro de la crisis", *Boletín de Ciencias Económicas y Sociales 9* (1986c), pp. 240-56. *English translation is chapter 14 of this volume.*

"El proceso de democratización en El Salvador", *Boletín de Ciencias Económicas y Sociales 9* (1986d), pp. 293-303; in *Sistemas electorales y representación política en Latinoamérica*, Madrid: Instituto de Cooperación Iberoamericana, 1986e, pp. 283-94.

"El problema de los desplazados y refugiados salvadoreños", *ECA 41* (1986g), No. 447-48, pp. 37-53.

"La familia en la sociedad salvadoreña", *ECA 41* (1986g), No. 450, pp. 305-19.

"A la búsqueda de soluciones para los desplazados salvadoreños" *Relaciones Internacionales* (1986h), No. 17, pp. 25-43.

"Los indígenas en El Salvador", *Boletín de Ciencias Económicas y Sociales 9* (1986i), pp. 147-55.

"Los deplazados y refugiados salvadoreños", *Revista Mexicana de Psicología 3* (1986j), pp. 66-76. *Reprint of 1985e.*

El Salvador 1987: Salvadoreños refugiados en los Estados Unidos. San Salvador: IDHUCA, 1987a.

El compadrazgo, una estructura de poder en El Salvador. 2nd edition. San Salvador: UCA Editores, 1987b. *First edition: 1979b.*

"La crisis salvadoreña y las consecuencias de una repatriación masiva de refugiados en los Estados Unidos", *Boletín de Ciencias Económicas y Sociales 10* (1987c), pp. 5-15.

"Los salvadoreños en Estados Unidos y la nueva ley de migración", *ECA 42* (**) (1987d), No. 459-60, pp. 99-101.

"Los límites y posibilidades que enfrentan la participación política en el campo salvadoreño", *ECA 42* (1987e), No. 463-64, pp. 305-21.

"La crisis social agudizada por la crisis política salvadoreña: la migración a Estados Unidos, un indicador de la crisis", *ECA 42* (1987f), No. 468, pp. 675-86. *Reprinted: 1988i.*

Salvadoran Migration to the United States: an Exploratory Study. Co-author: J.J. García. Washington: Center for Immigration Policy and Refugee Assistance, Georgetown University, 1988a.

Los derechos económicos, sociales y culturales en El Salvador. Co-authors: Florenín Meléndez and Edgar Palacios. San Salvador: IDHUCA, 1988b. *English translation of selections makes up chapter 7 of this volume.*

El Salvador 1988: estructura de clases y comportamiento de las fuerzas sociales. San Salvador: IDHUCA, 1988c.

"Las elecciones del 20 de marzo de 1988", *ECA 43* (1988d), No. 473-74, pp. 175-89.

"Los derechos económicos, sociales y culturales en El Salvador", *ECA 43* (1988e), No. 476, pp. 515-38.

"Los derechos humanos en las plataformas de los partidos políticos", *ECA 43* (1988f), No. 481-82, pp. 1079-88.

"Levantamientos campesinos en El Salvador", *Realidad Económico Social* (formerly *Boletín de Ciencias Económicas y Sociales*) 1 (1988g), pp. 79-100.

"Clases y movimientos sociales en El Salvador: caracterización, desarrollo e intervención" *Realidad Económico Social 1* (1988h), pp. 305-31. *English translation is chapter 13 of this volume.*

"La crisis social agudizada por la crisis política salvadoreña", *Relaciones Internacionales* (1988i), No. 24-25, pp. 7-19. *Reprint of 1987f.*

La resistencia no violenta ante los regímenes salvadoreños que han utilizado el terror institucionalizado en el período 1972-1987. Segundo Montes, coordinator. San Salvador: IDHUCA, 1988j.

"Migration to the United States as an Index of the Intensifying Social and Political Crisis of El Salvador", *Journal of Refugee Studies 1* (1988k), pp. 107-126.

Refugiados y Repatriados, El Salvador y Honduras. San Salvador: IDHUCA, 1989a. *English translation of extract: 1991a.*

"Las elecciones presidenciales del 19 de marzo de 1989", *ECA 44* (1989b), No. 485, pp. 199-209.

(**) "La nueva propuesta del FMLN", *ECA 44* (1989c), No. 486-87, pp. 353-56.

(**) "A propósito del informe de la delegación europea sobre el asesinato de Jürg Weis", *ECA 44* (1989d), No. 486-87, pp. 365-67.

(**) "Otra propuesta más del FMLN", *ECA 44* (1989e), No. 488, pp. 481-84.

"El problema de los derechos humanos en El Salvador," *ECA 44* (1989f), No. 493-94, pp. 1095-1102.

"Impacto de la migración de salvadoreños a los Estados Unidos, el envío de remesas y consecuencias en la estructura familiar y el papel de la mujer", *Realidad Económico Social 2* (1989g), pp. 5-33.

"Estado, crisis y nuevos actores sociales en Centroamérica: el caso de El Salvador", *Realidad Económico Social 2* (1989h), pp. 377-95.

"God's Grace Does Not Leave." Interview. *Companions of Jesus*. J. Sobrino, *et al.* Maryknoll: Orbis Books, 1990a, pp. 134-37.

"The Writings of Ellacuría, Martín-Baró, and Segundo Montes." *The Jesuit Assassinations*. Instituto de Estudios Centroamericanos and El Rescate. Kansas City: Sheed and Ward (1990b), pp. 1-26. *Very brief extracts from various writings.*

El Salvador 1989: Las remesas que envían los salvadoreños de Estados Unidos. San Salvador: UCA Editores, 1990c.

"Salvadoran Refugees in Honduras". Foreword to B. and S. Cagan, *This Promised Land, El Salvador*. New Brunswick: Rutgers University Press, 1991a. *English translation of extract from 1989a.*

"La gracia de dios nunca se va", *Carta a las Iglesias 11* (1991b), No. 233, p.1.

REFERENCES CITED IN THE TEXT*

Aguilera, G. "La contrainsurgencia rural en Guatemala." *Centroamérica: la guerra de baja intensidad ¿Hacia la prolongación del conflicto o preparación para la invasión?* Cuadernos de Pensamiento Propio. Managua: CRIES, 1986.

Allport, G. W. *The Individual and His Religion.* New York: Macmillan, 1950.

Americas Watch. *Settling into Routine: Human Rights in Duarte's Second Year.* New York: Americas Watch, 1986.

Anderson, T.P. *El Salvador 1932: los sucesos políticos.* Costa Rica: EDUCA, 1976.

Andino Martínez, C. "El estamento militar en El Salvador," *ECA* (1979), pp. 614-30.

Antoncich, R. "Hermenéutica del magisterio de la Iglesia, especialmente respecto a propiedad privada," *Servir* (1976), pp. 25-50.

Archer, D. and R. Garther. *Violence and Crime in Cross-national Perspective.* New Haven: Yale University Press, 1984.

Ardila, R. "International Psychology," *American Psychologist 37* (1982), pp. 323-29.

Ardila, R. *La psicología en América Latina: pasado, presente y futuro.* México: Trillas, 1983.

ARENA "Principios ideológicos y objetivos," *El Diario de Hoy* (Oct. 22, 1981).

Arias Gómez, J. "Anastasio Aquino: recuerdo, valoración y presencia," *La Universidad* (Universidad de El Salvador) (1964), pp. 61-112.

Aron, A. "Problemas psicológicos de los refugiados salvadoreños en California," *Boletín de Psicología 6* (1987), No. 23, pp. 7-20.

Aron, A. "Martín-Baró on Psychology and Politics." Paper presented at a conference, "The Moral and Social Responsibility of the University: The Thought of El Salvador's Murdered Jesuits," Swarthmore College, November 17, 1990.

Ascher, W. "The Moralism of Attitudes Supporting Intergroup Violence," *Political Psychology 7* (1986), pp. 403-425.

Avila, C. *Ownership: Early Christian Teaching.* Maryknoll: Orbis Books, 1983.

Barry, D. "Los conflictos de baja intensidad: reto para los Estados Unidos en el Tercer Mundo (El caso de Centroamérica)," *Centroamérica: la guerra de baja intensidad. ¿Hacia la prolongación del conflicto o preparación para la invasion?* Cuadernos de Pensamiento Propio. Managua: CRIES, 1986.

Barry, D., R. Castro, and R. Vergara. *La guerra total: la nueva ideología contrainsurgente en Centroamérica.* Cuadernos de Pensamiento Propio. Managua: CRIES, 1987.

Bartra, R. *Diccionario de sociologia marxista.* Mexico: Grijalbo, 1973.

Batson, C. and L. Ventis, *The Religious Experience: A Social-psychological Perspective.* New York: Oxford University Press, 1982.

*Whenever possible, we have replaced an author's references to a Spanish translation with references to English language sources. THE EDITORS

Belo, F. *Lecture matérialiste de L'evangile du Marc*. Paris: Editions du Cerf, 1975.

Benoit, P. & M. Boismard. *Synopse des quatre évangiles*. Paris: Editions du Cerf, 1972.

Berger, P.L. and T. Luckmann. *The Social Construction of Reality: a Treatise in the Sociology of Knowledge*. Garden City: Doubleday, 1966.

Berkowitz, L. "Some Effects of Thoughts on Anti and Prosocial Influence of Media Events: A Cognitive-neo-associationist Analysis," *Psychological Bulletin 95* (1984), pp. 410-27.

Berryman, P. "Ignacio Ellacuría: An Appreciation," *America*, July 7, 1990.

Boff, L. "Significado teológico del pueblo de Dios e Iglesia popular," *Concilium* (1984), No. 196, pp. 441-54.

Brandon, S.G.F. *Jesus and the Zealots*. New York: Scribner's, 1967.

Bromley, D. and J.T. Richardson, eds. *The Brainwashing/Deprogramming Controversy*. Toronto: Edwin Mellen Press, 1983.

Bronfenbrenner, U. "The Mirror Image in Soviet-American Relations: A Social Psychologist's Report," *Journal of Social Issues 17* (1961), pp. 45-56.

Browning, D. *El Salvador: Landscape and Society*. London: Oxford University Press, 1971.

Burdeau, G. *La Democracia*. Barcelona: Ariel, 1970.

Cabarrús, C.R. *Génesis de una revolución*. México: Ediciones de la Casa Chata, 1983.

Cabarrús, C.R. "El Salvador: de movimiento campesino a revolución popular." *Historia Política de los campesinos latinoamericanos*. P.G. Casanova, eds. México: Siglo XXI, 1985.

Campos, T.R. "La seguridad nacional y la constitución Salvadoreña," *ECA* (1979), pp. 477-88. (See Ellacuría, 1979k.)

Cardenal, R. *Historia de una esperanza: vida de Rutilio Grande*. San Salvador: UCA, 1985.

Casín, I. *La hacienda colonial*. San Salvador: Ministerio de Educación, 1972.

Castro, O. and R. José. "El plan de contrainsurgencia norteamericano para El Salvador y los cambios en las fuerzas armadas gubernamentales," *Centroamérica: la guerra de baja intensidad. ¿Hacia la prolongación del conflicto o preparación para la invasión?* Cuadernos de Pensamiento Propio. Managua: CRIES, 1986.

CELAM. Texts from the Second General Conference of Latin American Bishops in Medellín, Colombia. Washington, D.C.: U.S. Catholic Conference, 1973.

CELAM. *Sectas en América Latina*. Guatemala: CELAM, 1982.

"Chalatenango: degollados en operativos contrainsurgentes," *Cartas a las Iglesias*, No. 142, June 16-30, 1987, pp. 13-16.

Chitnis, L. "The Elections in El Salvador in March, 1982." Report for a Human Rights Group of the British Parliament. London, 1982.

Chomsky, N. and E. S. Hermann. *The Political Economy of Human Rights*. Vol 1: *The Washington Connection and Third World Fascism*. Boston: South End Press, 1979.

CODEHUCA. *Informe sobre la situación de los derechos humanos en Centroamérica*. Nos. 8-9, 1986.

Colindres, E. "La tenencia de la tierra en El Salvador," *ECA 31* (1976), pp. 463-472.

Colindres, E. *Fundamentos económicos de la burguesía salvadoreña.* San Salvador: UCA, 1977.

Comblin, J. *The Church and the National Security State.* Maryknoll: Orbis Books, 1979.

Comité Pro-justicia y paz de Guatemala. *Situación de los derechos humanos en Guatemala: Noviembre 1984-Octubre 1985.* Guatemala, 1985.

Compher, V., L.Jackson, and B.Morgan, *Going Home. Building Peace in El Salvador: The Story of Repatriation.* New York: The Apex Press, 1991.

Congregation for the Doctrine of the Faith, *Instruction on Certain Aspects of the "Theology of Liberation."* Boston: St. Paul Editions, 1984.

Corominas, J. and J. M. Farré, eds. *Contra la tortura.* Barcelona: Fontanella, 1978.

Cortés y Larraz, P. *Descripción geográfico-moral de la diócesis de Goathemala* (2 vols.). Guatemala: Biblioteca "Goathemala" de la Sociedad de Geografía e Historia de Guatemala, 1958.

Council for Inter-American Security (Committee of Santa Fe). *A New Inter-American Policy for the Eighties,* 1980.

CUDI Proceso (1980-1983). *Passim.*

CUDI *La economía salvadoreña, 1981-82.* San Salvador: UCA, 1982.

Cueva, A. "Los límites de la democracia en América Latina," *Polémica* (San José) *16* (1987), No. 2, pp. 60-67.

Dada Hirezi, H. *La economía de El Salvador y la integración centroamericana 1945-1960.* San Salvador: UCA, 1978.

Deleule, D. *La psicología, mito científico.* Barcelona: Anagrama, 1972.

Delgado, E.M., *et al. El fenómeno de la conversión religiosa en las comunidades eclesiales de base y un grupo evangélico pentecostal de la zona metropolitana de San Salvador.* Thesis: UCA, 1978.

Departamento de Psicología y Educación, UCA. "Psicología, diálogo y paz en El Salvador," *ECA* (1986), No. 454-55, pp, 711-19.

De Sebastián, L. "El presupuesto nacional de 1979," *ECA* (1979), pp. 153-57.

De Sebastián, L. *La deuda externa de América Latina y la banca internacional.* San Salvador: UCA, 1987.

Diario Latino. Daily newspaper in El Salvador.

Díaz-Guerrero, R. "Contemporary Psychology in Mexico," *Annual Review of Psychology 35* (1984), pp. 83-112.

Discurso del BID. "América Latina ante su liberación." *ECA* (1971), pp. 108 -12.

Domínguez, E. and D. Huntington. "The Salvation Brokers: Conservative Evangelicals in Central America," *NACLA Report on the Americas 18* (1984), pp. 2-36.

Durkheim, E. *The Division of Labor in Society.* Glencoe, Ill., 1952.

Dussel, E. *De Medellín a Puebla: una década de sangre y esperanza (1968-1978).* México: Edicol, 1979.

Eagleson, J. and P. Scharper. (eds.). *Puebla and Beyond: Documentation and Commentary.* Maryknoll: Orbis Books, 1979.

ECA. "Reforma agraria en El Salvador," *ECA* (1973), July-August, whole issue.

ECA. "Transformación agraria," *ECA* (1976a), Sept.-Oct., whole issue.

ECA. "A sus órdenes, mi capital," Editorial, *ECA* (1976b), pp. 637-43.

ECA. "Hacia donde va la educación en El Salvador," *ECA* (1978), August, whole issue.

ELLACURÍA, I. See Publications of Ignacio Ellacuría in this volume.

"Elecciones". *Proceso*, Nos. 63-67.

El Mundo. Daily newspaper in El Salvador.

Ezcurra, A.M. "La lucha ideológica, el papel de las iglesias en USA y la política de la Administración Reagan hacia El Salvador." In CINAS. *América Central y la estrategia de la nueva derecha norteamericana*. Cuaderno de Trabajo, No. 2. México: Centro de Investigación y Acción social, 1984.

Falla, R. *Esa muerte que nos hace vivir: un estudio de la religión popular de escuintle (Guatemala)*. San Salvador: UCA, 1984.

Fals Borda, O. *Conocimiento y poder popular: lecciones con campesinos de Nicaragua, México y Colombia*. Bogotá: Siglo XXI, 1985.

Fanon, F. *The Wretched of the Earth*. New York: Grove Press, 1963.

Finlay, D.J., *et al. Enemies in Politics*. Chicago: Rand McNally, 1967.

Freire, P. *Pedagogy of the Oppressed*. New York: Herder and Herder, 1970.

Freire, P. *Education for Critical Consciousness*. New York: Seabury Press, 1978.

Friedman, M. *Essays in Positive Economics*, 5th ed. Chicago: University of Chicago Press, 1966.

Friedman, M. "Capitalismo y libertad," *Facetas 12* (1979), pp. 10-13.

García, A. "Las clases medias y el sistema de poder." *América Latina: Dependencia y subdesarrollo*. San José: EDUCA, 1973.

García Roca, J. "Idolos de muerte en la sociedad actual," *Misión Abierta* (1985), No. 52-53, pp. 42-58.

Goldstein, A.P., *et al. In Response to Aggression*. New York: Pergamon Press, 1981.

Gonzáles, G.A., "Democracia aparente, democracia de participación limitada o simplemente democracia," *ECA* 34 (1979), pp. 527-32.

Gurvitch, G. *Teoría de las clases sociales*. México: EDICUSA, 1971.

Gutiérrez, G. *A Theology of Liberation*. Maryknoll: Orbis Books, 1973.

Haber, S. and B. Seidenberg. "Society's Recognition and Control of Violence." *Violence: Perspectives on Murder and Aggression*. I.L. Kutash, *et al*. San Francisco: Jossey-Bass, 1978.

Hacker, F. *Agresión*. Barcelona: Grijalbo, 1973.

Hedges, C. "Religion and Revolution," *The Dallas Morning News*, March 2, 1986.

Hegel, G.W. *Hegel's Philosophy of Right*. Oxford: Oxford University Press, 1952.

Hengel, M. *Eigentum und Reichtum in der fruhen Kirche?* Stuttgart: Calwer, 1973.

Hernández-Pico, J., *et al. El Salvador: Año político 1971-72*. San Salvador: UCA, 1973. (See Ellacuría, 1973d.)

Hewett, W.E. "Strategies for Social Theory Employed by Communidades Eclesiais de Base in the Archdiocese of Sao Paulo," *Journal for the Scientific Study of Religion 25* (1986), pp. 16-30.

Ibisate, F.J. "¿Es capitalista el 'capitalismo salvadoreño'?" *ECA* (1979), pp. 535-44.

IDHUCA. *El Salvador 1985: desplazados y refugiados.* San Salvador: UCA, 1985. (See Montes, 1985g.)

IDHUCA. *El Salvador 1986: En busca de soluciones para los desplazados.* San Salvador: UCA, 1986. (See Montes,1986a.)

IDHUCA. *Los derechos humanos en El Salvador en 1986.* San Salvador: IDHUCA, 1987.

Innocenti, Z. *Evolución del empleo en la industria (1970-81).* Thesis, UCA, 1983.

IUDOP. *Informes varios sobre diversos sondeos de opinión.* San Salvador: UCA, 1986-88 (mimeo).

IUDOP. *Informe preliminar sobre las opiniones de la población urbana acerca de la situación del sistema de salud en El Salvador.* San Salvador: IUDOP, 1987.

James, W. *The Varieties of Religious Experience.* New York: Longman, 1902.

Jaspers, K. *Philosophy.* 3 volumes. Chicago: University of Chicago Press, 1969-71.

Jeremias, J. *Jerusalem zur Zeiz Jesu.* Gottingen: Wandenhoech & Ruprecht, 1969.

John XXIII *Mater et Magistra,* 1961. (*Christianity and Social Progress.* Boston: St. Paul Editors).

John XXIII *Pacem in Terris,* 1963. (*Peace on Earth.* Boston: St. Paul Editions).

John Paul II *Laborem Exercens,* 1981. (*On Human Work.* Boston: St. Paul Editions).

John Paul II *Sollicitudo Rei Socialis,* 1987. (*On Social Concern.* Boston: St. Paul Editions).

Kunz, E.F. "Exile and Resettlement: Refugee Theory," *International Migration Review* (1981), No. 53-54, pp. 42-51.

La Prensa Gráfica. Daily newspaper in El Salvador.

Lalive D'Espinay, C. *El refugio de las masas: estudio sociológico del protestantismo chileno.* Santiago: Editorial del Pacífico, 1968.

"Las elecciones y la unidad nacional: diez teses críticas." Editorial, *ECA* (1982), pp. 233-58.

Leiken, R. Testimony before the Foreign Affairs Committee of the U.S. Senate, April 1, 1982.

Lenin, V.I. *The Lenin Anthology.* R.C. Tucker, ed. New York: Norton, 1975.

Lenin, V.I. State and Revolution (1917), in Lenin (1975).

Lerner, M. J. and C.H. Simmons, "Observer's Reaction to the 'Innocent Victim': Compassion or Rejection?" *Journal of Personality and Social Psychology 4* (1966), pp. 203-10.

Lindo, H. F. "La economia en época de guerra," *ECA* (1982), pp. 493-506.

Lira, E., E. Weinstein, and S. Salamovich. "El miedo: un enfoque psicosocial." *Revista Chilena de Psicología 8* (1985-86), pp. 51-56.

Lopez Vallecillos, I. "Fuerzas sociales y cambio social en El Salvador," *ECA* (1979), pp, 557-590.

Maduro, O. *Religión y lucha de clases*. Caracas: Ateneo de Caracas, 1979.

MAG. "Políticas y decisiones del gobierno del Presidente José Napoleón Duarte sobre la deuda agraria," *La Prensa Gráfica*, May 5, 1986, p. 64.

MARTÍN-BARÓ, I. See Publications of Ignacio Martín-Baró in this volume.

Martí de Vases Puig, C. "Normas internacionales relativas a los derechos económicos, sociales y culturales." *Anuario de Derechos Humanos*. Madrid: Universidad Complutense, 1983.

Mártir, J.G. "Guerra civil e incremento de enfermedades psicosomáticas en El Salvador en los años 1981-1984 tomando como muestra a los asegurados del Instituto Salvadoreño del Seguro Social," *Boletín de Psicología 5* (1986) No. 21, pp. 151-60.

Marx, K. *The Marx-Engels Reader*. R.C. Tucker, ed. New York: Norton, 1972.

Marx, K. "Towards a Critique of Hegel's *Philosophy of Right*" (1844), in Marx (1972).

Marx, K. "The Civil War in France" (1870), in Marx (1972).

Marx, K. "Letter to Joseph Weydemeyer" (1852), in Marx (1972).

Masferrer, A. *Obras escogidas*. San Salvador: Editorial Universitaria, 1971.

Menjívar, R. *Formación y lucha del proletariado industrial salvadoreño*. San Salvador: UCA, 1979.

Merari, A. and N. Friedland. "Social Psychological Aspects of Political Terrorism." *Applied Social Psychology Annual*, No. 6: *International Conflict and National Public Policy*. O. Ostuart, ed. Beverly Hills: Sage, 1985.

Milliband, R. "El estado y la revolución," *Revista Mensual 1* (1977-78), No. 8-9, pp. 79-91.

Miranda, J.P. *Marx and the Bible*. Maryknoll: Orbis Books, 1974.

Montero, M. *Ideología, alienación e identidad nacional: una aproximación psico-social al ser venezolano*. Venezuela: Ediciones de la Biblioteca. Universidad Central de Venezuela, 1984.

MONTES, S. See Publications of Segundo Montes in this volume.

Montgomery, T.S. *Revolution in El Salvador. Origins and Evolution*. Boulder: Westview Press, 1982.

Montoya, A. *La concentración de la actividad comercial*. San Salvador: UCA, 1982.

El Mundo. Daily newspaper in El Salvador.

Neal, M.A. *Values and Interests in Social Change*. Englewood Cliffs: Prentice-Hall, 1965.

Olano, G. and M. Orellana, "Consideraciones sobre la situación financiera de las cooperativas de la Fase I de la reforma agraria," *Boletín de Ciencias Económicas y Sociales* (1985), pp. 77-94.

Paul VI *Populorum Progressio*, 1967. (*On the Development of Peoples*. Boston: St. Paul Editions).

Paul VI *Octogesima Adveniens*, 1971. (*The Coming Eightieth*. Boston: St. Paul Editions).

Peña, F. *Análisis comparativo de la pequeña empresa capitalista y no capitalista*. San Salvador: UCA, 1982.

PERA. *V Evaluación del proceso de la reforma agraria*. San Salvador, Dec. 1985.

Pérez, R.G., *et al*. *La reforma agraria como mecanismo de redistribución en El Salvador (1980-1984)*. Thesis: UCA, 1986.

Peters, E. *Torture*. New York: Basil Blackwell, 1985.

Pius XI *Quadragesimo Ano*, 1931. (*On Social Reconstruction*. Boston: St. Paul Editions).

Pixley, J. "El fundamentalismo," *Estudios Ecuménicos* (México) 3 (1985), pp. 32-35.

Pleitez, W. "Elementos para evaluar los efectos de la reforma agraria sobre el nivel de empleo del sector agropecuario salvadoreño," *Boletín de Ciencias Economicás y Sociales* (1983), pp. 174-92.

Portelli, H. *Gramsci y el bloque histórico*. México, 1978.

La Prensa Gráfica. Daily newspaper in El Salvador.

Proceso. Weekly magazine of news and analysis, UCA.

"Psicología latinoamericana." Editorial, *Boletín de Psicología* 4 (1985), pp. 39-41.

Ribeiro De Oliveira, P. "¿Qué significa analíticamente 'pueblo'?" *Concilium* (1984), No. 196, pp. 427-40.

Richardson, J. T. "Conversion Careers," *Society 17* (1980), pp. 47-50.

Rockefeller Report. "Quality of Life in the Americas—Report of a Presidential Mission for the Western Hemisphere," *Department of State Bulletin*, December 8, 1969.

Roszak, T. *The Making of a Counterculture*. Garden City: Anchor Books, 1969.

Rubianas, E. *El dominio privado de los bienes según la doctrina de la Iglesia*. Quito: Ediciones de la Universidad Católica, 1975.

Sabini, J. "Aggression in the Laboratory." *Violence: Perspectives on Murder and Aggression*. I.L. Kutash, *et al*. San Francisco: Jossey-Bass, 1978.

Samayoa, J. "Guerra y deshumanización: una perspectiva psicosocial," *ECA* (1987), pp. 123-225.

Samayoa, S. and G. Galván. "El movimiento obrero en El Salvador: ¿resurgimiento o agitación?" *ECA* (1979a), pp. 591-600.

Samayoa, S. and G. Galván. "El cierre patronal de las empresas: prueba de fuego para el sindicalismo revolucionario en El Salvador," *ECA* (1979b), pp. 793-800.

Segundo, J.L. *The Liberation of Theology*. Maryknoll: Orbis Books, 1976.

Seminario Permanente sobre la Economía Nacional del Departamento de Economía. "La Fase III de la reforma agraria y las condiciones de vida de sus beneficiarios," *Boletín de Ciencias Económicas y Sociales* (1983), pp. 365-82.

Sermeño, L. "Comportamiento reproductivo de la juventud: el caso de El Salvador," *ECA* (1988).

Sevilla, M. "Visión global sobre la concentración económica en El Salvador," *Boletín de Ciencias Económicas y Sociales* (1984), pp. 155-90.

Sierra Bravo, R. *Doctrina social y económica de los Padres de la Iglesia*. Madrid: COMPI, 1967.

Snow, D.A. and R. Machalek. "The Sociology of Conversion," *Annual Review of Sociology 10* (1984), pp. 167-90.

Sobrino, J. *Christology at the Crossroads*. Maryknoll: Orbis Books, 1978.

Sobrino, J. *Spirituality of Liberation*. Maryknoll: Orbis Books, 1988.

Sobrino, J., I. Ellacuría, *et al*. *Companions of Jesus: The Jesuit Martyrs of El Salvador*. Maryknoll: Orbis Books, 1990.

Solórzano, J.J. "Análisis e interpretación de la deuda agraria y el crédito al sector reformado," *Boletín de Ciencias Económicas y Sociales* (1986), pp. 51-8.

Stein, B.N. "The Refugee Experience: Defining the Parameters of a Field of Study," *International Migration Review* (1981), No. 53-54, pp. 320-30.

Stein, E. "Comunicación colectiva y transformación agraria," *ECA 31* (1976) pp. 535-56.

Stein, E. "Los medios de comunicación colectiva en El Salvador ante las exigencias de un Diálogo Nacional," *ECA* (1979), pp. 647-72.

Strasma, J., *et al*. *Agrarian Reform in El Salvador* (mimeo). Washington: Checchi and Company, 1983.

The Encyclopedia of Philosophy. 8 volumes. New York: Macmillan, 1967.

Thielicke, H. *Theological Ethics*. 2 volumes. Grand Rapids: Eerdmans, 1979.

Thome, J.R. "Reforma Agrária en El Salvador," *Boletín de Ciencias Económicas y Sociales* (1984), pp. 235-53.

Troeltsch, E. *The Social Teaching of the Christian Churches*. 2 volumes. London: Allen & Unwin, 1931.

UCA. *Análisis de una experiencia nacional*. San Salvador: UCA, 1971.

UCA. *Manual de organización y consideraciones justificiativas*. San Salvador: UCA, 1972.

UCA. *El Salvador: entre el terror y la esperanza: los sucesos de 1979 y su impacto en el drama salvadoreño de los años siguientes*. San Salvador: UCA, 1982.

UCA Editorial Board, "El Salvador, 1984." *NACLA Report on the Americas 18* (1984), No. 2, pp. 13-47.

Ungo, G.M. "Los derechos humanos: condición necesaria para la paz y convivencia social en El Salvador," *ECA* (1979), pp. 489-526.

Valderrey, J. "Las sectas en Centroamérica," *Boletín Pro Mundi Vita* (1985), No. 100, whole issue.

Varela, J. *Psychological Solutions to Social Problems: An Introduction to Social Technology*. New York: Academic Press, 1971.

Vatican Council II, *The Conciliar and Post Conciliar Documents*. Boston: St. Paul's Editions, 1975. (Originally published in 1965.)

Volkogonov, D. *Guerra Psicológica*. Moscow: Progreso, 1986.

Wahlstrom, R. "Enemy Image as a Psychological Antecedent of Warfare." *Essays on Violence*. J. M. Ramírez, *et al*., eds. Sevilla: Publicaciones de la Universidad de Sevilla, 1987.

Watson, P. *War on the Mind: The Military Uses and Abuses of Psychology*. New York: Basic Books, 1978.

Weinstein, E. "Problemática psicológica del retorno del exilio en Chile: algunas orientaciones psicoterapéuticas," *Boletín de Psicología 6* (1987), No. 23, pp. 21-38.

White, R. K. "Misperception and the Vietnam War," *Journal of Social Issues 22* (1966), pp. 1-156.

Whitford, J. *Apuntes de algunos aspectos de la historia de la psicología en Nicaragua*. Managua: Universidad Centroamericana, 1985.

Wundt, G. *Etica*. Madrid: Jarro, 1917.

Zimbardo, P. J. "The Human Choice: Individuation, Reason, and Order Versus De-individuation, Impulse, and Chaos." *Nebraska Symposium on Motivation*. W.J. Arnold and D. Levine, eds. Lincoln: University of Nebraska Press, 1970.

Zimmermann, E. *Political Violence: Crises and Revolutions*. Cambridge, Mass.: Shenkman, 1983.

Key to Abbrieviations & Acronyms

AF	Armed Forces of El Salvador
AIFLD	American Institute for Free Labor Development
ANDES	National Association of Educators of El Salvador
ANEP	National Association of Private Enterprise (El Salvador)
ARENA	Republican Nationalist Alliance (El Salvador)
CBC	Christian Base Community (*the English for CEB*)
CEB	Comunidad Eclesial de Base (*the Spanish for CBC*)
CELAM	Latin American Bishops Conference
CINAS	Center for Investigation and Social Action (Mexico)
CN	National Coordinating Body (El Salvador)
CODEHUCA	Commission for the Defense of Human Rights in Central America
COMADRES	Committee of Mothers of Political Prisoners and the Disappeared
CP rights	Civil and Political rights
CRIES	Regional Coordinator of Economic and Social Investigation (Nicaragua)
CRM	Revolutionary Coordinating Body of Mass Organizations (El Salvador)
CUDI	Documentation and Information Center of the UCA
EAP	Economically Active Population
ECA	*Estudios Centroamericanos*. Monthly publication of the UCA
EDUCA	Department of Education of the UCA
ESC rights	Economic, Social and Cultural rights
FAN	Broad National Front (El Salvador)
FARO	Agricultural Front of the Eastern Region (El Salvador)
FDR	Democratic Revolutionary Front (El Salvador)
FENAPES	National Association of Small Enterprise (El Salvador)
FMLN	Farabundo Martí National Liberation Front (El Salvador)
IDHUCA	Human Rights Institute of the UCA
INSFOP	Institute for Permanent Formation (Nicaragua)
IRA	Agrarian Reform Institute (El Salvador)
ISSS	Salvadoran Institute for Social Security
ISTA	Salvadoran Institute for Agrarian Transformation
IUDOP	Institute for Public Opinion of the UCA
MAG	Ministry of Agriculture and Granaries
NACLA	North American Congress on Latin America

OAS	Organization of American States
ORDEN	Democratic Nationalist Organization (a paramilitary organization)
PCN	Party of National Conciliation (El Salvador)
UCA	University of Central America (Universidad Centroamericana José Simeón Cañas)
UES	University of El Salvador
UNDC	National Worker-Peasant Union
UNTS	National Union of Salvadoran Workers
UP	Patriotic Union (Columbia)
UPD	Popular Democratic Unity (El Salvador)